THE MILLENNIAL SOVEREIGN

SOUTH ASIA ACROSS THE DISCIPLINES

SOUTH ASIA ACROSS THE DISCIPLINES

❖❖❖

EDITED BY DIPESH CHAKRABARTY, SHELDON POLLOCK,
AND SANJAY SUBRAHMANYAM

Funded by a grant from the Andrew W. Mellon Foundation, and jointly published by the University of California Press, the University of Chicago Press, and Columbia University Press.

Extreme Poetry: The South Asian Movement of Simultaneous Narration by Yigal Bronner. (Columbia)

The Social Space of Language: Vernacular Culture in British Colonial Punjab by Farina Mir. (California)

Unifying Hinduism: Philosophy and Identity in Indian Intellectual History by Andrew J. Nicholson. (Columbia)

Everyday Healing: Hindus and Others in an Ambiguously Islamic Place by Carla Bellamy. (California)

South Asia Across the Disciplines is a series devoted to publishing first books across a wide range of South Asian studies, including art, history, philology or textual studies, philosophy, religion, and the interpretive social sciences. Series authors all share the goal of opening up new archives and suggesting new methods and approaches, while demonstrating that South Asian scholarship can be at once deep in expertise and broad in appeal.

THE MILLENNIAL SOVEREIGN

SACRED KINGSHIP AND

SAINTHOOD IN ISLAM

A. Azfar Moin

COLUMBIA UNIVERSITY PRESS   NEW YORK

Columbia University Press
Publishers Since 1893
New York   Chichester, West Sussex
cup.columbia.edu
Copyright © 2012 Columbia University Press
Paperback edition, 2014
All rights reserved

Library of Congress Cataloging-in-Publication Data
Moin, A. Azfar.
The millennial sovereign : sacred kingship and sainthood in Islam / A. Azfar Moin.
    p.   cm. — (South Asia across the disciplines)
Includes bibliographical references and index.
ISBN 978-0-231-16036-0 (cloth)—ISBN 978-0-231-16037-7 (pbk.)—
ISBN 978-0-231-50471-3 (e-book)
1. Kings and rulers—Religious aspects—Islam. 2. Sovereignty—Religious aspects—Islam. 3. Muslim saints. I. Title.

JC375.M65 2012
297.2'72—dc23
                                                                              2012001237

Cover design: Shaina Andrews
Cover image: Freer Gallery of Art

*For my teachers
and my family*

CONTENTS

List of Illustrations   ix
List of Tables   xi
Acknowledgments   xiii
Note on Transliteration   xvii

1. Introduction: Islam and the Millennium   1

2. The Lord of Conjunction:
Sacrality and Sovereignty in the Age of Timur   23

3. The Crown of Dreams:
Sufis and Princes in Sixteenth-Century Iran   56

4. The Alchemical Court:
The Beginnings of the Mughal Imperial Cult   94

5. The Millennial Sovereign:
The Troubled Unveiling of the Savior Monarch   130

6. The Throne of Time:
The Painted Miracles of the Saint Emperor   170

7. Conclusion: The Graffiti Under the Throne   211

Notes   241
Bibliography   309
Index   331

ILLUSTRATIONS

MAP

1. The Mughal and Safavid empires (c. 1600) xx

FIGURES

1.1. Mughal and Safavid rulers of the sixteenth and seventeenth centuries 2
6.1. Shaykh Muʿin al-Din Chishti holding a globe (detail from folio) 190
6.2. Jahangir holding a globe (detail from folio) 191
6.3. Jahangir shoots Malik ʿAmbar (detail from folio); painted by Abuʾl Hasan, c. 1620 194
6.4. Emperor Jahangir triumphing over poverty (detail from folio); attributed to Abuʾl Hassan (Nadir al-Zaman), c. 1620 199
6.5. The St. Petersburg Album: allegorical representation of Emperor Jahangir and Shah ʿAbbas of Persia (detail from folio); painted by Abuʾl Hasan, c. 1618 205
6.6. Jahangir preferring a Sufi shaikh to kings (detail from folio); painted by Bichitr (act. 1615–1650) 207
7.1. Jahangir presents Prince Khurram with a turban ornament; painted by Payag, c. 1640 228
7.2. Jahangir receives Prince Khurram from his return from the Deccan; painted by Murar, c. 1640 230
7.3. Jahangir receives Prince Khurram from his return from the Deccan (detail from folio) 231

7.4. Shah Jahan with Asaf Khan from the late Shah Jahan Album (detail from folio); painted by Bichitr, c. 1650.   232
7.5. Isfahan. "Shah Tahmasb and Humayun"   236
7.6. Isfahan. "Shah ʿAbbas the Great and the Uzbek Vali Mohammad Khan"   238

TABLES

4.1. The social hierarchy under Humayun as God's caliph and Lord of Conjunction   113
4.2. Imperial administration arranged according to Humayun's augury   115
4.3. The schedule of Humayun's court arranged according to the planets   116
4.4. The twelve "Golden Arrows" or alchemical ranks of Humayun's entourage   119
4.5. Humayun's imperial services organized according to the four elements   120
4.6. The color of Humayun's clothes selected according to the planets   121

ACKNOWLEDGMENTS

THIS BOOK has been in the making for nearly a decade. The central idea was born in Austin, where I spent three most intellectually invigorating years from 2002 to 2005. Because of the extraordinary generosity and guidance of Denise Spellberg, Gail Minault, Kamran Ali, Mohammad Ghanoonparvar, and Akbar Hyder, the fields of Islamic history, South Asian history, cultural anthropology, Persian language and literature, and Sufism opened up for me while I was there. The project evolved further in Ann Arbor as a doctoral dissertation supervised by Barbara Metcalf. I will remain deeply in her debt for many things but most of all for her perspectives on the history of Islam in South Asia, which became foundational for me. I am also grateful to my other mentors at Michigan: Thomas Trautmann, whose insights on India and time have shaped my thinking; Kathryn Babayan, who helped me navigate the cultural landscapes of early modern Iran; Juan Cole, whose erudition and fondness for debate inspired and focused my arguments; and Paul Johnson, who gave me the confidence to pursue an anthropological approach to the study of religion. In addition, special thanks to Sumathi Ramaswamy and Sussan Babaie for opening up the world of Mughal and Safavid visual culture.

The writing process began in earnest when I participated in a workshop at the Institute of Historical Studies at the University of Texas at Austin in 2009. Thanks to Julie Hardwick, the director of the institute, for giving me the chance to interact with the wonderful community of scholars there, and to Denise Spellberg for her discussion of my paper, which later became the chapter on Timur. I completed the book in 2011 while teaching at Southern Methodist University. There, I am grateful to the Dedman College of Arts and Sciences, the dean's office, the Clements Department of History, and the Central University Libraries for providing the professional, administrative, and research resources that were crucial in finalizing this project. My colleagues in the History Department were especially kind and supportive. Also, it was the expertise and professionalism of Wendy Lochner at Columbia University Press and the efficiency of the editorial staff there that made this publication possible. Thanks also to the anonymous reviewers and the SAAD series editorial board, whose insightful questions and perceptive comments enriched the argument.

Several scholars read and discussed substantial portions of the final draft. I especially appreciate the comments I received from Kamran Ali, Kathryn Babayan, Lisa Balabanlilar, Shahzad Bashir, Johan Elverskog, Barbara Metcalf, Eva Orthmann, Jyotsna Singh, Denise Spellberg, and Thomas Trautmann. Over the years, I benefited from presenting my work in academic settings and more informally over a cup of tea or in an e-mail exchange. Some of the more ambitious ideas in the book materialized because of all the scholars, colleagues, and friends who were willing to listen, question, share, and argue. They include Can Aciksoz, Behrad Aghaei, Muzaffar Alam, Aun Ali, Noman Baig, Christine Baker, Nile Green, Raza Ali Hasan, Hasan Ali Khan, Rajeev Kinra, Mathangi Krishnamurthy, Derek Mancini-Lander, Farina Mir, Siyar Ozsoy, Mohamad Khan Pasha, Frances Pritchett, Sholeh Quinn, Yael Rice, Mubbashir Rizvi, Francis Robinson, Ruken Sengul, Halide Velioglu, Ebru Turan, Taymiya Zaman, and many others.

The generosity of the following institutions made possible the research required for this book: the Foreign Language and Area Studies (FLAS) fellowship program for the study of Persian at UT Austin, a number of research grants from the Rackham School of Graduate Studies and the History Department at the University of Michigan, a fellowship for extended archival research in the United Kingdom from the American Institute of Pakistan Studies, and an affiliation as a visiting research scholar with the Institute of Historical Studies and the South Asia Institute at UT Austin. In London, I would like to thank the staff of the British Library, the Royal Collection at the Windsor Castle, and the Victoria and Albert Museum. Susan Stronge at the V&A was especially generous with her time and knowledge of Mughal art. In Islamabad, I benefited from the rich archives of the Iran Pakistan Institute of Persian Studies. I am also grateful to Zafar Ishaq Ansari at the Islamic Research Institute of the International Islamic University for introducing me to scholars at the institute and making available its resources.

Finally, heartfelt thanks to my parents in Pakistan, Fazil and Shaheen Moin, and my aunt and uncle in London, Kishwer and Aslam Aziz, for putting up with me and my books on extended research trips. This book owes the most to Faiza Moin, who stood by me when I left a corporate career to pursue a life of teaching and scholarship. To her and my two children, Imaan and Kamran, I owe the greatest appreciation for patiently bearing the seemingly unending days and nights of printing, reading, and typing. In the hope of even better days ahead with them, I end this acknowledgment.

NOTE ON TRANSLITERATION

I HAVE USED a minimalist transliteration scheme in an attempt to contain the confusion arising from the array of overlapping source languages—Persian, Arabic, Turkish, Urdu, Hindi, and Sanskrit—and from the many conflicting disciplinary conventions for rendering them. This means that there are no diacritical marks, although the letters *ayn* and *hamza* are indicated. Preference is given to "Indo-Persian" pronunciation and spelling: Akbarnama instead of Akbarname, Shahnama-i Shah Ismaʿil instead of Shahnameh-yi Shah Ismaʿil, and *qazi* instead of *qadi*. Frequently anglicized names and expressions appear as such—Ali instead of ʿAli and ulama instead of ʿulamaʾ—unless they occur in transliterated phrases. Less common words and names, such as Zulfiqar (Dhu al-Fiqar), are generally transliterated only upon first occurrence. The Persian letter *vav* is rendered using *v* for Persian origin words, such as *javan*, but the letter *w* is used in the case of Arabic origin words, even when they appear in Persian sources: *amwal* instead of *amval*. Transliterated words and spelling conventions from secondary works and published translations are reproduced without modification, except that diacritical marks are dropped. So if a cited work has ḳiran (an alternative spelling of *qiran*), it is rendered as ḳiran. Similarly, the name Badaʾuni also appears as Badayuni and Badauni according the secondary source being cited. One hopes that most of these variations and other irregularities should be obvious to specialists and, since they do not affect meaning, should not get in the way of the general reader.

THE MILLENNIAL SOVEREIGN

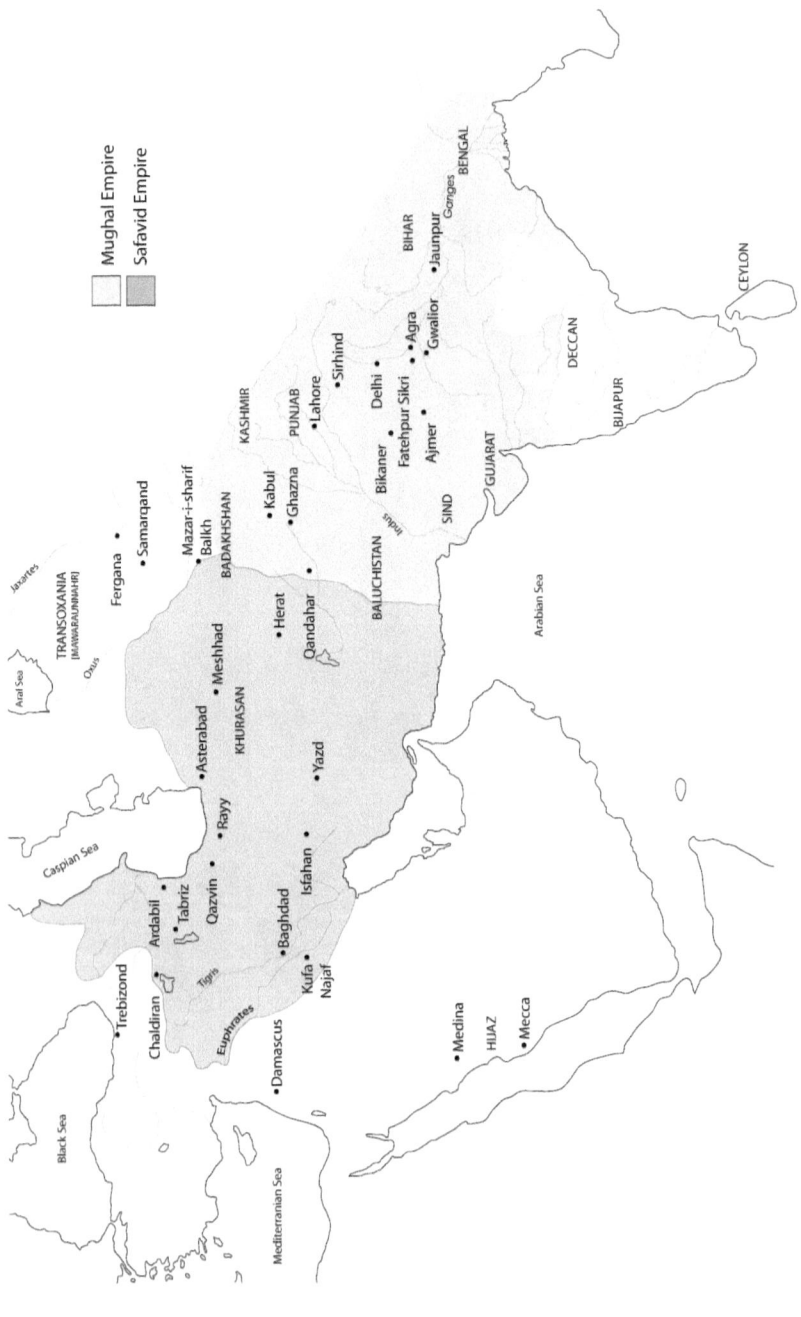

MAP 1 The Mughal and the Safavid empires (c. 1600) with surrounding areas, major cities, and regions mentioned in the book.

{1} INTRODUCTION

ISLAM AND THE MILLENNIUM

THIS BOOK brings into dialogue two major fields of scholarship that are rarely studied together: sacred kingship and sainthood in Islam. In doing so, it offers an original perspective on both. In historical terms, the focus here is on the Mughal empire in sixteenth-century India and its antecedents and parallels in Timurid Central Asia and Safavid Iran.[1] These interconnected milieus offer an ideal window to explore and rethink the relationship between Muslim kingship and sainthood. For it was here that Muslim rulers came to express their sovereignty and embody their sacrality in the manner of Sufi saints and holy saviors.

The Mughal dynasty of India (1526–1857) and the Safavid one of Iran (1501–1722) exemplified this mode of sacred kingship. The early and foundational monarchs of these two lineages modeled their courts on the pattern of Sufi orders and fashioned themselves as the promised messiah. In their classical phases, both the Mughals and the Safavids embraced a style of sovereignty that was "saintly" and "messianic." Neither a coincidence nor a passing curiosity, this similarity resulted from a common pattern of monarchy based upon Sufi and millennial motifs. There developed in this period an ensemble of rituals and knowledges to make the body of the king sacred and to cast it in the mold of a prophesied savior, a figure who would set right the unbearable order of things and inaugurate a new era of peace and justice—the new millennium. Undergirded by messianic conceptions and rationalized by political astrology, this style of sovereignty attempted to bind courtiers and soldiers to the monarch as both spiritual guide and material lord.

The most famous case of such an attempt is that of the powerful Mughal emperor Akbar (r. 1556–1605). As the epitome of this mode of sacred

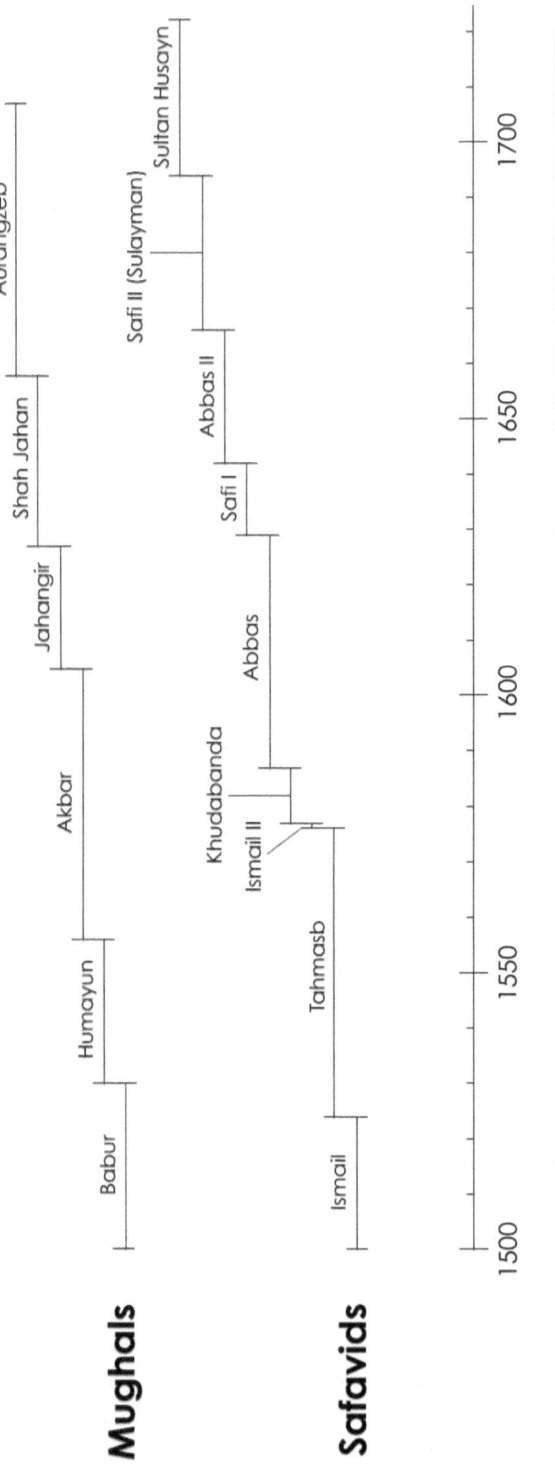

FIGURE 1.1 Mughal and Safavid rulers of the sixteenth and seventeenth centuries.

kingship, he not only established a lasting empire in South Asia of unrivaled grandeur but also fashioned himself as the spiritual guide of all his subjects regardless of caste or creed. At the height of his reign, Akbar was accused of declaring the end of Islam and the beginning of his own sacred dispensation. There was some substance behind these accusations. Akbar had unveiled a devotional order in which his nobles and officers of all religious and ethnic stripes were encouraged to enroll as disciples. Although not given an official name, this institution of imperial discipleship (*muridi*) became known as the Divine Religion (Din-i Ilahi). It generated an immense controversy—a controversy, it can be said, of global proportions. Reports and rumors of how a great Muslim emperor had turned against Islam were followed with interest in Shiʿi Iran, Sunni Transoxania, and Catholic Portugal and Spain. Akbar was accused of heresy, schism, and apostasy from Islam. He was charged with claiming to be a new prophet and even a divinity descended to earth. Despite the outcry and criticism, however, Akbar's rule flourished in India, and his circle of devotees thrived. Discipleship became a Mughal imperial institution under Akbar and evolved after him.

Unsurprisingly, Akbar's spiritual pursuits became the focus of numerous studies in modern times. All manner of explanations—political, psychological, and spiritual—were used to make sense of the Mughal emperor's religious experiments. Although these studies differed in method and conclusion, they had one trait in common: they utilized a framework of analysis that was limited to Akbar's India. Whether these studies treated this episode as an eccentricity of the emperor's personality or saw it as a Muslim ruler's radically liberal and precociously secular attempt at a tolerant religious policy, they generally agreed that it was a phenomenon particular to Akbar's reign and dominion. In other words, the manner in which the emperor's sacrality was enunciated and institutionalized was assumed to have neither history nor comparison.

This assumption becomes untenable, however, when we examine the forms and timing of the Mughal emperor's sacred assertions. Akbar had claimed to be the world's greatest sovereign and spiritual guide at the turn of the Islamic millennium. He had fashioned his imperial self, in effect, in the mold of the awaited messiah. In doing so, he had embraced a powerful and pervasive myth of sovereignty. It was widely expected that the millennial moment heralded a grand change in the religious and political affairs of the world. A holy savior would manifest himself, it was thought, to usher in a new earthly order and cycle of time—perhaps the last historical era before the end of the world. In his pursuit of sacred sovereignty, Akbar was neither the first nor the only one to pour his sovereign self into such a messianic mold. He had competed for the millennial prize with many others. Indeed, the emperor's critics considered his spiritual pretensions to be far from original. On the contrary, they accused him of trying to mimic the messianic success of the founder of the Safavid empire in Iran, Shah Ismaʿil (r. 1501–1524).

When not yet in his teens, Shah Ismaʿil had become the hereditary leader of the Safavid Sufi order in northwestern Iran. With the aid of armed and fanatically loyal Turkmen devotees, he had conquered and reunited Iran after more than a century of fragmentary politics. Shah Ismaʿil's soldier-disciples charged into battle, it was said, without armor, because they expected their saint-king's presence to provide sufficient protection. The young shah was for them the promised messiah—the *mahdi* of Islamic traditions. That Akbar's millennial project in India evoked comparisons with Shah Ismaʿil's militant messianism in Iran is indicative of a strong similarity between the two enduring Muslim empires of sixteenth-century Iran and India. It brings into focus the startling fact that both Islamic polities, in their formative phases, had seriously engaged with messianic and saintly forms of sovereignty. This similarity, importantly, was not a coincidence but the result of a shared history.

The imperial projects of the Mughals and the Safavids in the first half of the sixteenth century had competed for the same set of material resources, patronage and kinship networks, and cultural symbols. Akbar's Timurid father and grandfather, Humayun and Babur, had both sought refuge and military assistance from the Safavids at low points in their royal careers and had witnessed the workings of the Safavid court and Sufi organization up close. The Safavids, in turn, had adopted the highly stylized forms and fashions of the latter-era Timurid courts as they evolved from a Sufi order into an imperial dynasty. The two nascent sixteenth-century empires had drawn upon a shared cultural context and learned from the other's modes and methods. It was no accident that in both these polities a similar style of monarchy developed, in which claims of political power became inseparable from claims of saintly status.

More generally, this conjuncture of kingship and sainthood was a product of recent historical development. It first took root in and spread from the geographical territories of Iran and Central Asia that had been ravaged by the Mongol invasions of the thirteenth century. These invasions had severely disrupted established urban centers, political cultures, and religious associations across much of Muslim Asia. In their wake, a new sociopolitical order took shape, in which the growing networks of Sufi orders and Sufi shrines played a significant and constitutive role. There was hardly an aspect of public or private life in the eastern Islamic lands that remained untouched by these institutions of "mysticism" and networks of "devotion." The lives of kings were no exception. Thus, in the post-Mongol centuries, the institution of kingship became locked in a mimetic embrace with the institution of sainthood.

Unsurprisingly, then, the greatest of Muslim sovereigns of the time began to enjoy the miraculous reputations of the greatest of saints. Some, like the famous conqueror Timur (or Tamerlane, d. 1405), from whom the Mughals traced their descent, may not have made such claims openly, but they were, nevertheless, venerated as spiritual guides by their followers and given miraculous genealogies by their descendants. Others, like the Safavid Shah Ismaʿil, already belonged to acclaimed Sufi families. Indeed, Shah Ismaʿil had been born a saint in the sense that he had inherited the devotion of his father's large circle of disciples. It would be wrong to suggest, however, that these Muslim sovereigns assumed the trappings of saintly piety and renounced the world and its sinful ways. More accurately, they adopted the trappings of saintly power and embraced the world as heaven-sent saviors. The "messianic" and "saintly" nature of their sovereignty was adduced by astrological calculations and mystical lore, embodied in court rituals and dress, visualized in painting, enshrined in architecture, and institutionalized in cults of devotion and bodily submission to the monarch as both saint and king.

Why then, one may ask, has modern scholarship had difficulty seeing the coherency and durability of this pattern of sacred kingship in Islam? The answer in simplest terms is that Sufism and Muslim kingship have been studied mostly in a bifurcated fashion, the former in religious studies and the latter in political history. The differences in approach and method between the two disciplines have led to Sufis and kings being conceived and portrayed in opposing spheres of culture, the one sacred and the other profane. It has also led to a model of religion and politics within Muslim societies that is too formal and textual, giving too much weight to doctrine and not enough to practice. Approaches adhering to this model are bound to dismiss a Muslim king's spiritual assertions as besotted and idiosyncratic. Similarly, they are constrained to see a Sufi mystic's claim to material power as unrelated to his saintly endeavors. Such constraints must be overcome, however, to make sense of a milieu in which mystics and monarchs were collaborators and competitors. Indeed, in early modern India and Iran, royal and saintly families intermarried and patronized one another. Sufi tutors educated princes, and scions of saints served as imperial generals. Queens were sent to the homes of mystics to give birth, and saintly shrines were constructed inside palace walls. Hereditary cults and dynastic lines became, in effect, physically intertwined and materially blurred as the courts and shrines in Iran and India came to adopt the same repertoire of sacrality and style of sovereignty.

Admittedly, from the pious and well-worn perspectives of Islamic law and political theory, the phenomenon of Muslim kings transmuting into saints and messiahs venerated by courtiers and worshipped by soldiers seems markedly heretical and transgressive, not to mention paradoxical. Conventional views of Islam would have Muslim sovereigns always looking to the ulama and using doctrinal notions of the caliphate to legitimize their rule. This book challenges such conventional wisdom by emphasizing, instead, the performative aspect of Muslim kingship. Rather than turn to abstract legal, philosophical, and ethical writings, it constructs the cultural logic of sacred kingship from the concrete acts of rulers, which were often performed publicly in a competition for popular admiration and awe.

While the texts and traditions of doctrinal Islam continued to be patronized in this milieu in a routine enough manner, they did not serve as the fount of charismatic inspiration. Inspiration came from a source that was surprisingly different and, on the face of it, paradoxical: "heretical" conceptions of sacred authority attracted a Muslim sovereign more than "orthodox" notions of Islam. A substantial part of this study is dedicated to resolving this paradox. It does so by giving ritual practice and performance an interpretive priority over religious doctrine and law. For what may appear as "heresy" from a doctrinal point of view was, in many cases, a ritual engagement with popular forms of saintliness and embodied forms of sacrality that were broadly and intuitively accepted by much of the populace as morally valid and spiritually potent. To make way for this perspective, however, we must set aside many conventional assumptions and timeless truths about Islam. Instead, we must examine from first principles the social processes that transmuted kings into saints and saints into kings. To appreciate how such phenomena could occur in "Islam," we must first grasp the significance of the "millennium."

ISLAM AND THE MILLENNIUM

In most studies of Muslim milieus, group identities of sect, doctrine, and devotional loyalty are assumed to be more fixed and hegemonic than they historically were. For example, the Mughals of India are treated as Sunni Muslims, as are their Central Asian Timurid ancestors.[2] When the Safavids are compared with the Mughals, the former are assumed to be Shi'i Muslims.[3] If an element of commonality is assumed between these two dynasties, it is ascribed to the "mystical" practices of Sufism. This intellectualist view of Islam neatly divided into Sunnism and Shi'ism, with Sufism overlapping, treats Muslim cultures as rigid wholes to be understood on the basis of scriptural sources, great scholars, and their respectable writings. This view, although easy to grasp and convenient to work with, is innocent of the actual workings of culture and historical change.

The early modern period of Iran and India was a time of immense historical change and cultural innovation for Islam. A new type of massbased Sufism centered on popular cults of the saints and hereditary forms of spiritual leadership had taken shape only a century or so before the rise of the Mughals and Safavids in India and Iran.[4] The practices and symbols of this emergent form of religiosity were far more significant in shaping Muslim worldviews than the texts and traditions of doctrinal Islam. Take, for example, the case of Shi'ism in early modern Iran. Although Iran is thought to have been converted to Shi'ism by imperial edict under the Safavids beginning in the sixteenth century, this process was gradual—even desultory—and took more than a century to gather momentum. Further, while the population of Iran eventually had to accept Shi'i doctrinal tenets, this "conversion" also necessitated juridical Shi'ism to modify and re-create itself institutionally according to the dictates of local Sufi practices and popular saintly lore.[5] At the end of this process, Shi'ism itself had undergone substantial cultural transformation. A thirteenth-century Shi'i jurist, for example, would have been unable to recognize many of the Shi'i rituals, narratives, and public ceremonies of eighteenth-century Iran.[6] This is because in the intervening four centuries, much of the social and religious life of Iran—and, indeed, of most Muslim communities in Asia—had been shaped by the rise of highly institutionalized, networked, and hereditary cults of Sufi saints.

A result of this historical development was that Islam came to be experienced by most people in early modern Iran and India—Muslims and non-Muslims alike—through the mediation of holy men and their bodies. In phenomenological terms, Islam existed in society primarily in the form of sacred and saintly presences, whether alive in physical form, active in enshrined graves, apparent in dreams, or resurrected in blood descendants and anointed successors. The dominant experience of sacred authority for most people—elite or common—was concrete and embodied rather than abstract and textual. The language for making sense of and articulating this experience, moreover, came from the Sufi traditions of "mysticism" and "sainthood." This is a point worth emphasizing, because modern scholarship tends to resolve questions of sovereign authority in Islam in favor of enduring scriptural texts and legalistic doctrine. Such models, however, based on abstract concepts and theoretical debates, need to be adjusted in order to study a milieu in which sacred authority was primarily conceived in corporeal forms and engaged via tactile means.

Hence, the theoretical position taken in this study is that the nature of sacred authority must be understood by paying close attention to its social dimension. It gives priority, in other words, to the assumption that styles of sacrality are shaped by their social environments. Such a socially inflected perspective complements existing approaches to the study of sovereignty in Islam that emphasize, instead, the role of scriptural traditions or the intellectual efforts of religious leaders. It also enables a more context-sensitive model of sacred authority embodied by Muslim sovereigns, one rooted not in classical texts of Islamic law and doctrine but in inhabitable cosmologies and performative narratives of sovereignty. It necessitates an ethnographic approach, which reveals how Muslim rulers frequently drew inspiration less from scriptural Islam than from broader processes of social memory, devotional practice, and popular myth and which explains why Muslim kingship became intertwined with the symbols and narratives of a shrine-centered Sufism organized around the hereditary cult of the saint. This form of sainthood regulated the religious and social life of the period, in cities and towns, villages and pastoral communities, and courts and military encampments. As this saintly style of sacrality fused with kingship, it led to a new synthesis of practical politics and spiritual practices.

Such a perspective brings into relief a pervasive cosmology and narrative of sovereignty in early modern Iran and India: that of the millennium and the messiah. The religious history of this era is marked by Sufi movements led by men who claimed to be heaven-ordained saviors and earthly embodiments of divinity. These saints and holy men often made a bid for both political power and spiritual supremacy. Indeed, Timurid Iran and Central Asia has been called a "messianic age," full of activist Sufis.[7] While these movements will be mentioned in later chapters, here it will suffice to discuss two foundational aspects of the millennium-messiah myth, namely, its corporeal and temporal dimensions.

In a fundamental sense, the discourse of messianism was about embodied forms of sacred authority. It prophesied the coming of a savior who would end an era of injustice and chaos and usher in a new one of peace and righteousness. This correction was expected to take place, moreover, not primarily by doctrinal intervention or revival of religious law—although this was often claimed in messianic apologia—but rather by the sheer physical presence, the thaumaturgical body, of the messianic being. The efficacy of this myth was not confined to the sphere of "religion," but rather it was sustained by a number of popular and elite knowledges about authority, power, and historical change. To put it another way, in a literal and "thin" sense the messianic myth was a prophecy about the coming of the savior or the millennial being, but in a descriptive and "thick" sense, it simultaneously invoked a series of interrelated cultural meanings about embodied forms of sovereignty.

For instance, the scriptural notions of the messiah (*mahdi*) and the renewer (*mujaddid*), the mystical concepts of the pole or *axis mundi* (*qutb*) and the perfect individual (*insan-i kamil*), and the kingly notions of divine effulgence (*farr-i izadi*) and the Lord of Conjunction (Sahib Qiran) all referred to human agents who could usher in and maintain the just religiopolitical order of a particular historical era. As this study will argue, these linkages and connections were both felt and acknowledged at the time, explicitly in elite philosophical metaphysics that sought to explain the role of human actors in maintaining the rhythm and balance of the cosmos and implicitly in popular tales and stories about prophets, saints, kings, and other heroic saviors. In other words, many concepts of embodied sovereignty that may at first glance appear to be discretely contained in separate spheres of literary writings and oral traditions were in fact practically intertwined and symbolically condensed in the myth of the holy savior. Accordingly, seen from inside the cultural world of early modern India and Iran, metaphysical traditions about the nature of the soul, cosmological ideas about time, historical eras and the age of the world, and astrological techniques for predicting changes of religions and dynasties appear knitted together in a complex science of the millennium.

The inner workings and principles of classification of this science, however, are barely within our mental grasp. This form of knowledge belongs, in other words, to a forgotten episteme. The burden of this study is to recover this millennial epistemology and to show how it constituted both elite and popular worldviews in early modern Iran and India. Accordingly, it evaluates afresh beliefs and practices that were widespread at the time but are ignored in modern scholarship as marginal and heretical. For example, an idea central to explaining the reincarnation of the messianic being from one era of time to another was the transmigration of the soul (*tanasukh*) from body to body. This concept is usually thought to be part of Indic religious traditions and anathema to Islam. Nevertheless, many early modern Muslims thought that it was through transmigration that the messianic soul appeared as an embodiment of a past savior in the present or the future.[8] Transmigration of the soul was certainly a controversial idea in Islamic learned circles, and it could draw condemnation from religious authorities. It was explicated in writing only with extensive apologia and qualifications. Yet it still persisted in elite texts with different degrees of explicitness and, more importantly, held wide sway in the broader imagination of this period. Not only deviant Sufi groups espoused this idea but also respectable Muslim scholars and philosophers.

Rather than follow Muslim heresiographers in dismissing transmigration as against the tenets of Islam, we must pursue the conundrum of its continued significance in early modern Muslim milieus. The answer will lead us to the discovery that transmigration was an important component of millennial theories of kingship and widely made and widely believed messianic claims of Sufi saints. Indeed, the recycling of the soul was much more than just an idea. Rather, it was a social fact experienced by far too many people simply to vanish under the onslaught of a few critical texts. Much like claims of divination, magic, and prophecy, this concept, too, enjoyed a social reality among elite and commoner alike. To understand why this was so, we have to examine learned metaphysical explanations of how saints could physically embody the divine soul side by side with miraculous stories of Sufis being able to be project themselves to many places at once. This means, in terms of method, grounding intellectual history firmly in social reality and paying close attention to the relationship between social structure and the persistence of particular types of cosmologies.[9]

This brings us to the second key aspect of the messianic myth: its temporal component, which was also sustained by the social practices of the milieu. Put simply, the messianic myth was related to the concept of the millennium by the notion that the savior was expected to appear at the end of a thousand-year cycle or the beginning of another one. This new cycle of time could be, moreover, the last one before the end of the world, giving the millennial scheme an eschatological coloring. Nevertheless, the primary view of time undergirding the idea of the millennium was cyclical.[10] This cyclical view of time was based on the regular rotation of the heavenly bodies and, accordingly, was informed by the sciences of astronomy and astrology. These sciences, which structured the everyday lives and routines of all classes of people, also allowed for a malleable interpretation of the temporal span of the millennium.

Even though the thousand-year era was of prime importance, its beginning and end could be suitably adjusted. Many auspicious subsets and fortunate fractions of the important "thousand" were readily available to fine-tune the myth as needed. The millennium, thus, could be used to put the messianic myth into practice with differing degrees of temporal intensity. The messiah could appear imminently or in the distant future. He could have been a figure in the past or one manifest in the present. Also, there were many ways to invoke the power of this myth, using an array of divinatory knowledge such as scriptural interpretation, apocalyptic lore, dream visions, and numerological and astrological predictions. Such flexible techniques were not the result of mere superstition, however. Rather, their coherency and salience was related to contemporary knowledges and practices of "time."

To understand the salience of the millennium for Timurid, Mughal, and Safavid sovereigns, we must first grasp the fact that for the people of that era the future was as important as the past, divination as important as genealogy, and astrology as valuable as history. Indeed, as far as practices of sacred kingship were concerned, history and astrology were sister disciplines. Astrologers worked as annalists, and historians served as oracles. The intermeshed practices of courtly record keeping and time keeping were a testament to this linkage. Moreover, astrology was as "political" a science as history. Kings and their enemies used astrology to ascertain the health of the realm and the lifespan of the present dispensation. It is no accident that sovereigns often issued new calendars coinciding with their ascension. Besides being a public announcement of sovereignty, much like issuing new coins, such an act was also an attempt to reset the cosmic clock. Similarly, Sufis and their mystical competitors also made recourse to astrology to prove their sanctity and mark their place in the spiritual hierarchy of the cosmos. In short, as a powerful form of knowledge concerned with the time of spiritual and dynastic dispensations and the health of the body politic, astrology sustained temporal myths like the coming of the millennium, presided over by a righteous sovereign in the form of a savior, a saint, or a conqueror.

An astrological-cyclical view of time, then, is critical for understanding the institution of sacred kingship in this milieu. It brings to light a "millennial" sovereignty that was not bound by a single religious tradition but universally extended to all the communal constituencies of early modern Islamic empires, whether Muslims, Christians, Jews, Mongols, Hindus, Buddhists, or others. Moreover, it points to an important continuity with cosmological knowledge from the pre-Islamic traditions of India, Iran, and Greece and the even more ancient ones of Sumeria and Akkadia. Modern historians of science have pointed out these continuities, but these studies, though invaluable, are mainly of a technical nature.[11] They focus on the development in mathematical techniques and diffusion of precise cosmological theories among elite practitioners rather than on the place and function of the "science" of astrology in different social settings. Nevertheless, it is evident from the vast number of "Islamic" astrological and astronomical manuscripts from Iran and India that the effect of these knowledges was broad, substantial, and enduring. Indeed, astrology was practiced with greater consistency and sophistication in Muslim courts and societies than in those of early medieval Christians. In Christendom, astrological knowledge was crude, and court astrologers were comparatively rare until the twelfth century, when translations of Arabic treatises and astronomical tables became more widely available.[12] It is ironic, then, that there are many more comprehensive and sophisticated studies of "Christian" astrology than there are of the "Islamic" variety.[13]

One reason for the general neglect of astrology, moreover, is the less than respectable status it enjoys today. If the subject of astrology and politics is brought up in polite conversation, it inevitably leads to anecdotes about Nancy Reagan's fondness for the divinatory arts. When this research was presented at academic conferences, many well-intentioned scholars cautioned that a strong emphasis on astrology might end up presenting premodern Muslims in an "irrational" light and revive many Orientalist stereotypes of the overly "mystical" East.[14] This, needless to say, is far from the intended goal. Most Orientalist stereotypes about Islam or India were the product of post-Enlightenment thought, in which "Asiatic" civilizations were generally considered to have been left behind by the

West and in need of scientific and social progress. In fifteenth- and sixteenth-century Europe, however, few such "enlightened" concerns were expressed about the Orient. By contrast, the idiom of saintliness and messianism was itself quite predominant in Western Christendom.[15] In early modern Europe, for example, millennial and apocalyptic narratives were often used to describe developments in Muslim empires, such as those of the Ottomans, which threatened Christianity. As Sanjay Subrahmanyam suggests, there may even have been a "global" conjuncture of millenarian discourses in the sixteenth century.[16] In short, by underscoring the salience of astrology as popular practice and elite science, the goal of this study is not to pass judgment on the irrationality of past Muslim societies but rather to highlight the way their rationality was constructed differently than that of "moderns," whether Eastern or Western.

Accordingly, this book makes an effort to not impose present-day standards of respectability and taste in evaluating the knowledges, norms, and practices of a very different past. Such an approach is necessary in order to recover and reinstate a large number of sources that have otherwise been neglected as being of marginal value. For example, in two book-length studies of the religious developments at the court of the Mughal emperor Akbar, there is rarely a reference to the use of astrology of either Persian or Indian varieties.[17] In comparison, the chronicles of Akbar dedicate a substantial amount of space to the technical discussion of the emperor's horoscope, running to about fifty pages in the printed English translation even after leaving out many charts found in the original Persian manuscript.[18]

Overall, *The Millennial Sovereign* recovers this cultural world of early modern Islam by being sensitive to the categories, symbols, and narratives that shaped the public discourse of the time. By cutting across disciplinary boundaries and regional historiographies, it avoids the paths followed by previous scholarship. Accordingly, it reaches well beyond the Persian and Arabic chronicle tradition to incorporate genres such as miniature painting, illustrated epics and histories, and Sufi hagiographies. Moreover, it explores the cultural imagination of this milieu via sources that are often classified—and marginalized—as related to oral and popular culture, such as popular stories, apocalyptic treatises, astrological histories, and manuals of magic. In doing so, it underlines the social significance of intellectual traditions such as astrology and alchemy that enthralled elites and commoners alike. Importantly, it also recovers the quotidian practices and popular mores that shaped the culture of kingship.

The monarch, sacred though he may have been, enacted his sovereignty in the world of everyday life. Muslim sovereigns lived very mobile lives, performing their sacrality in public and participating in the same carnivals and parades that enchanted and entertained the populace. These sites of culture sustained a number of "bizarre" bodily practices, magical techniques, votive rituals, and entertaining spectacles involving humans and animals. Accordingly, popular imagination left a strong stamp on sacred kingship.

THE EVERYDAY WORLD OF SACRED KINGSHIP

While there are numerous descriptive histories of premodern Muslim sovereigns—caliphs, sultans, khans, shahs, and padishahs—the institution of Muslim kingship itself has received little analytical attention.[19] There exists an extensive and useful literature on Islamic political thought, but it mainly treats the topic of kingship in the mold of intellectual history.[20] This mode of scholarship is concerned more with continuities in elite textual articulations than with developments in actual social institutions and practices. How—or indeed if—prescriptive and philosophical texts animated Muslim rulers is a question that remains unsettled. Given the highly itinerant nature of kingship in this period, few Muslim princes were groomed in isolated palaces, poring over books under the gaze of wise ministers. Rather, the social personality of kings developed via constant circulation through the realm in an ongoing dialectic with the social ideals and popular myths of their diverse subject populations. Premodern kingship, in other words, had a strong performative element to it that cannot be recovered just from prescriptive texts.

Interpretive studies of kingship in other premodern settings have underlined its performative aspects and cultural embeddedness.[21] This scholarship, in which cultural anthropology has played a strong role, shows that it was the ability of monarchs to perform a script—sometimes multiple, conflicting ones—that drew toward their person the collective desires of the various groups in their dominion.[22] Such approaches serve as a model for this study. Accordingly, it begins with the assumption that kingship and sovereignty cannot be understood from abstract arguments preserved in elite texts but must be explored through the concrete practices of those in power and the symbols they sought to manipulate. These symbols and practices, moreover, were sustained and made coherent more by everyday actions and transactions than by canonical texts of doctrine or philosophy. In other words, the primary site where the "sacred" resided was in everyday life and popular imagination, not elite genres of writing. What we need, then, is an ethnography of sacred kingship that recovers the social processes by which the charisma of the sovereign was produced, institutionalized, and transmitted to posterity.

Elite texts, however, constitute most of our sources. To recover everyday life and cultural practice from these works is an uphill task. These sources must be read against the grain. Texts from different genres must be read alongside and against one another. Rumors, slurs, and innuendo must be given due weight while confessional statements treated with caution. It is only with close reading—and a good deal of speculation—that we can get behind the conventions of genre and styles of rhetoric to uncover the collective attitudes and internalized biases of cultural actors. To lend some structure to these speculations, however, this study turns to a tradition of sociology and anthropology that has long theorized about the collective nature of the sacred. This strand of social science draws upon Émile Durkheim's notion that the sacred is nurtured in an ensemble of social practices, which, invisible to social actors, does its work of shaping their collective imagination and providing them with shared classifications of thought.[23]

Take, for example, Michael Taussig's insight that the way to discover the sacred is to uncover the public secret, "that which is generally known but cannot be articulated."[24] In a similar discussion on the ineffable nature of the sacred, Maurice Godelier states,

> the sacred is a certain type of relationship that humans entertain with the origin of things, such that, in this relationship, the real humans disappear and in their stead appear duplicates of themselves, imaginary humans ... accompanied by an alteration, by an occultation of reality and an inversion of the relationship between cause and effect.[25]

According to these social theorists, the workings of the "sacred" in society are neither rules driven nor obvious to individuals. Rather, the sacred is embedded in a complex social process that shapes worldviews and ethos, informs concepts of time and space, provides categories of thought, defines taboos, channels desires, and reproduces social and economic structures in a way that cannot be encapsulated by or derived from a set of normative texts and institutions. This view is opposed to the more commonly used approach of trying to find the sacred center of a civilization in its formal religious institutions. Specifically, in terms of Muslim milieus, it is not sufficient to locate the "sacred" in the Quran, the sayings of the Prophet, and the traditions of Islamic law derived from these sources.

Indeed, the way early modern Muslim sovereigns transgressed the norms of doctrinal Islam reveals that their engagement with the sacred lay in some other sphere of culture. Their antics, shocking as they may seem from a modern "reformed" Muslim perspective, were much more than ignoble heresy or popular superstition. Even if these rulers had little regard for the juristic norms of Islam, it does not follow that they had complete disregard for the sacred, as if they did not feel the force of its threat or the pull of its desire. Their "magical" actions, such as consulting astrologers and soothsayers or visiting shrines of holy men, cannot be explained away as political ploys or discarded as rank superstition. If these actions had been socially marginal or transparently political in the eyes of the people, then the "charade" of kingship would not have worked; that is to say, the sacrality of kings would not have appeared to be part of the natural order of things.

In asserting the primacy of collective practices and public symbols for understanding the nature of sacred sovereignty in Islam, this book enters into a larger debate on the history of Islamicate societies on the place and function of popular culture. It takes a position with a small but growing number of studies on premodern Muslim milieus that do not take for granted either the rigidity or the all-encompassing nature of Islamic law. This scholarship has underlined, instead, the frequent presence and sometimes predominance of deviancy in premodern Muslim settings.[26] Such evidence raises the question: which phenomenon is the more historically significant one, the preservation of received tradition by the elite or the process of adapting it and making it one's own by the populace?[27] Indeed, one may ask, what actually constitutes the anthropology of Islam, the universal "discursive tradition" preserved and transmitted by learned men[28] or the more malleable and differentiated meanings created by local and popular traditions?[29] For the period under study, a focus on the continuity of a set of literary traditions closely adhering to the conventions of genre draws attention away from the way most people—literate or not—made sense of their experience of heterogeneity, change, suffering, and the marvelous that could not be explained by recourse to a scholastic tradition. In short, to privilege certain textual traditions as socially significant and treat the content of genre-bound texts as history erases the lived experience of the time.

Accordingly, the goal here is to focus less on textual traditions and more on social processes. In concrete terms, it is to examine the ritual process by which ordinary humans became sacred sovereigns. This means paying close attention to how kings and saints socially produced their sacrality through specific symbolic techniques and by undergoing stages of ritual development. As theorists of ritual have argued, becoming sacred—that is, dramatically changing one's social position—requires engaging with a potentially "dangerous" sphere of culture. It is dangerous because it transgresses the institutionalized relationships of social structure. Moreover, the process does not guarantee an advance in social status but, in fact, carries a strong possibility of social condemnation and ridicule.[30] Major attempts to access temporal or spiritual power, however, have to pass through these ritual stages and court their dangers. This is a crucial insight because it suggests, for our purposes, that accusations of "heresy" and "deviance" may profitably be read as reports of ritual engagement with the sacred. Indeed, in following this insight, this book shows the ritual role that millennial heresies played in the making of kings and saints in fifteenth- and sixteenth-century India and Iran.

RETHINKING SIXTEENTH-CENTURY INDIA AND IRAN

Over the sixteenth century, the nascent Timurid conquest state in northern India evolved into the administratively complex and institutionally enduring Mughal empire of South Asia. At the end of this era, India lay transformed, economically, politically, and culturally—and so did the Mughals. If the first Mughal ruler, Babur (d. 1530), had come to India speaking and writing in Turkish and hunting wild ass on horseback, his great-grandson, Jahangir (d. 1627), was most comfortable speaking in "Hindi" and shooting tigers while perched on an elephant. Indeed, if Jahangir had met Babur, the only language the two men could have easily conversed in would have been Persian. Persian became the language of administration and culture in the Mughal empire and remained so until the early nineteenth century.[31] By one estimate, under the Mughals there were more Persian-literate people in India than there were in Iran.[32] A great number of Iranian soldiers, administrators, merchants, and men of religion and learning came to Mughal India to seek their fortune, leaving an indelible print on the languages, cities, buildings, and religions of India.[33]

Accordingly, this study breaks from traditional approaches to the study of Mughal India by integrating a substantial amount of primary sources from and scholarly literature on Safavid Iran and Timurid Central Asia. This is necessary if we are to overcome the national boundaries and "area studies" groupings that have partitioned the histories of this milieu according to present-minded concerns. For example, in the case of South Asia, major themes of historical research are often driven by the region's modern encounter with Western colonialism and imperialism and the ensuing rise of communal "Hindu" and "Muslim" nationalisms.[34] In this context, the late medieval and early modern eras are often studied to determine the degree to which seeds of religious violence that plague modern South Asia were sown in the era before colonialism, that is, the era of Islamic rule. In studies of Iranian history, on the other hand, it is the distinctive Shiʿi religiopolitical identity of modern Iran, brought into sharp relief with the Islamic revolution of 1979, that provides the dominant framework for inquiry. In this case, the sixteenth-century process by which the Sunni-Sufi population of Iran was converted to Shiʿi-Jurist Islam gains primary importance for understanding the roots of Iran's distinctive religious nationalism.[35]

These national and regional concerns are valid ones. However, they posit collective subjects of history in pairs of opposites that betray our categories of thought more than they help uncover a past in which these dichotomies had yet to take definite shape or become the central concern of public life and political praxis. A consequence of this compartmentalization of historical thought is that Mughal India and Safavid Iran seem to belong not just to two different historical narratives but, as it were, to two clashing phenomenological worlds:

MUGHAL EMPIRE	SAFAVID EMPIRE
South Asia	Middle East
India	Iran
Hinduism	Islam
Sunnis	Shiʿis
Sufis	Jurists

To break out of the grooves carved out by these present-day categories, it needs to be emphasized that the histories of the Mughals and the Safavids were intertwined, deeply so in their first century. Beginning in the early sixteenth century, the two empires developed in close interaction and competition with each other. The two polities were also equal participants in the global transformations that were reshaping the political geography of the early modern world. A vast quantity of New World metal, for example, ended up in the Mughal empire, in payment for the cotton textiles and spices that the region exported to Europe. Similarly, the Safavids created an imperial monopoly in Iranian silk in order to take advantage of the growing trade with the West. Portuguese missionaries and English ambassadors tried to gain influence at both these courts, and European merchants competed for trading monopolies on the coasts of India and Iran.

Despite these regional interconnections, Mughal India is rarely studied with reference to Safavid Iran. The conventional approach is to pay more attention to the Mughals' rivalry with the Indo-Afghan rulers they replaced in northern India. While this convention is essential for recounting the political history of the Mughal empire, it can be a distraction for understanding the culture of Mughal sacred kingship. From the perspective of the Mughals, the Indo-Afghan courts and kingdoms possessed neither the high-status lineages nor the ritual grandeur enjoyed by the Chinggisids, Timurids, and Safavids of Central Asia and Iran. More important for the new dynasty were the entrenched Indian Sufi lineages, such as the Shattaris, Chishtis, and others, with whose help the early Mughal rulers began to insert themselves into local patronage networks. But even this mode of establishing sovereignty, in which political webs were interwoven with spiritual ones, was already a core part of the Mughals' Central Asian and Iranian experience.

Mughal kingship, far from arriving in India in a pristine "Islamic" form and then becoming muddled with local "un-Islamic" practices, was already a complex and flexible mélange at its advent. The cultural institutions that the Mughals used in South Asia to deal with a diversity of religious practice and belief were not invented wholesale in the "syncretistic" religious environment of India but largely brought over from the heterogeneous conditions of Timurid and Safavid Iran. Upon arrival in India, the Mughals were not shocked by the widespread belief there in the transmigration of the soul. They had already witnessed the social import of this "heretical" phenomenon in Safavid Iran. The Mughal practice of establishing close connections with networks of devotional brotherhood and "deviant" mendicant orders was based on similar traditions of rule in Timurid Iran and Central Asia. The Mughal devotional cult for imperial officers and courtiers had an immediate and living precedent in Safavid practice. The Mughal dependence on Indian astrologers did not reduce their dependence on Iranian ones. On a negative note, the Mughals did not learn to tear down the holy sites of their enemies only on arriving in "Hindu" India. They and the Safavids were already well versed in the destruction and desecration of sacred buildings—often Sufi shrines—to punish foes and rebels. These strategies of warfare and domination were common across India and Iran, Hinduism and Islam.

The shared history of sacred kingship in Iran and India enables a rethinking of the "coming of Islam to India" narrative. It has been noted that Islam plays a role in the recounting of South Asian history that is at the same time "too much and too little."[36] Too much, because it provides a facile view of history where a thousand years of "foreign" Muslim rule in India is notable only for its religious violence. Too little, because India is seen as being distant from the center of Islam—the Middle East and its Semitic civilization—to be of much use in understanding Islam in its historical forms. This contradiction of an overstated Islam in South Asian history and an understated India in Islamic history can be overcome by exposing the common roots of Safavid and Mughal sacred kingship and the competition for messianic and saintly status between the two dynasties. To put it another way, the Mughals of India were as much a part of "Islam" as the Safavids of Iran, because they were just as interested in the "millennium." At the same time, India suffered much less "Islam" under the Mughals, who did not impose it upon the local population, than Iran did under the Safavids, who, over the long term, enacted a policy of forced conversion to Twelver Shi'ism.

Ultimately, there is little value in using a "clash of civilizations" model to make sense of the Mughal empire, that is, by treating it as a case of a "Muslim" dynasty ruling over a "Hindu" population. This is because Mughal sacred kingship styled the monarch to be above religious and sectarian divisions. Moreover, this development had as much to do with the history of sacred kingship in Iran and Central Asia as it did with the Mughals' need to adapt to their Indian and largely non-Muslim environment. Even when well established in Hindustan, the Mughals were attuned to contemporary developments in Safavid Iran and devised and advertised their policies accordingly. In the late sixteenth century, when the Safavids began to abandon their millennial heritage, extirpate messianic cults in

Iran, and forcibly convert their subjects to doctrinal Shiʿism, the Mughals welcomed the persecuted and exiled Iranian "heretics" with open arms. These Iranians came because, as an embittered critic of the emperor Akbar noted, India "is a wide place, where there is an open field for all licentiousness, and no one interferes with another's business."[37]

ORGANIZATION

If the story of the Mughals ends in India, it begins in Central Asia and Iran. The Mughals of India were proud descendants of two famous Mongol world conquerors, the pagan Chinggis Khan (or Genghis Khan, d. 1227) and the Muslim Timur (or Tamerlane, d. 1405), under whom the Muslim societies of Iran and Central Asia had experienced immense upheaval and transformation. Even as they became an inseparable part of the Indian cultural landscape, the Mughals continued to trace their dynastic origins from Timur and practice the norms of comportment of Chinggis Khan.[38] Accordingly, chapter 2 focuses on the Perso-Mongol heritage of the Mughals. Specifically, it explores the process by which Timur became a master symbol of sacred kingship that endured for centuries in social memory across Iran and India. That this memory was preserved and transmitted in a millennial mode is evident from Timur's famous but little-understood title, Lord of Conjunction (Sahib Qiran). Chapter 3 shows how Timur's legacy lived on in Iran and Central Asia in the early sixteenth century. It traces the intersecting careers of Shah Ismaʿil and Babur and outlines the ritual processes and cosmological constraints that forged the social personality of these two sovereigns, a Sufi and a prince.

Babur died soon after conquering northern India, leaving his successor Humayun to elaborate the symbolic and ritual schemes for the new Timurid court. Chapter 4 shows how the new symbolic representations of Humayun's kingship were deeply informed both by popular religious formations in India and by the messianic style of kingship in Safavid Iran. Chapter 5 examines the way in which Akbar, son of Humayun, enacted a grand performance of saintly and messianic kingship. As such, the millennial scheme of Akbar was the culmination of a two-century-long evolution of sacred kingship, one rooted in the memory of Timur and shaped by widespread notions of sainthood in early modern Iran and India. Akbar's heir, Jahangir (d. 1627), was the first Mughal sovereign to inherit a stable and fully functioning institution of messianic kingship adapted to the Indian environment. Jahangir's innovations to this institution, however, were in the form of sacred art, which is explored in chapter 6. The last chapter concludes with a fresh look at key developments and continuities over the seventeenth century, in the reign of Shah Jahan and later, when, it is usually thought, this mode of sacred kingship began to wane.

{2} THE LORD OF CONJUNCTION

SACRALITY AND SOVEREIGNTY IN THE AGE OF TIMUR

THE STYLE of Muslim kingship that evolved in the fifteenth and sixteenth centuries was deeply rooted in the memory of Timur (r. 1370–1405). A Barlas Turk of common birth, he rose from Central Asia to conquer territories in Anatolia, Syria, Iraq, Iran, India, and Russia, and he was on his way to subjugate China when he died. The awe that Timur inspired at the time is difficult to imagine today. Thus modern scholarship tends to treat Timur as his enemies did: Timur the Lame (Timur-i Lang), or Tamerlane, an unspeakably cruel conqueror who wrought destruction on a continent not yet recovered from the ravages of the Mongol invasion led by Chinggis Khan.[1] However, this image ignores an important strand of social memory that revered Timur as the charismatic "Lord of Conjunction" (Sahib Qiran) and made him a central object of admiration and imitation for later Muslim sovereigns.

The way Timur was idolized more than two centuries later can be seen vividly in the actions of his descendant, the Mughal emperor Shah Jahan (r. 1628–1658), of Taj Mahal fame. In a direct reference to Timur, Shah Jahan called himself the Second Lord of Conjunction (Sahib Qiran-i Thani).[2] But this was more than a mere reference. It was an attempt at mimesis. We can see this in the exquisitely illustrated chronicles of Shah Jahan's reign: the opening folios show the two Lords of Conjunction, sitting on thrones facing each other, as if one is signifying the other.[3] In a massive work on astronomy commissioned by Shah Jahan and entitled "The Grand Accomplishment of the Second Lord of Conjunction" (*Karnama-i Sahib Qiran-i Thani*), the preface also suggests a deep ontological equivalence between the two men.[4] The mimetic medium here was not visual but "literal," that is, involving the hidden properties of letters.

Using a table that broke down the numerological value of the Persian letters of the words "Lord of Conjunction" (Sahib Qiran), "Timur," and "Shah Jahan," the Mughal astronomer showed how these names were intimately linked in a series of resemblances with one another and with the number 365, the number of days in the annual cycle of the sun, the "King of the Heavenly Spheres" and the planet of kings.[5]

Shah Jahan and Timur were fused together alchemically by the artist's brush, the letters of the Persian alphabet, and the cycles of the sun. This fusion was not just metaphorical, a matter of image and text. It was also metonymical, a matter of ritual and mythical enactment. In 1646, Shah Jahan launched from India an audacious campaign to regain the Central Asian territories of Timur, an endeavor without any visible economic reward.[6] This campaign is better understood, perhaps, as a pursuit of sacred memory. Indeed, a few years earlier, an artifact of Timur had come to light. A man presented himself at Shah Jahan's court claiming to have the Persian translation of the original Turkish memoirs of Timur, which he had "discovered" in the library of the governor of Yemen.[7] Despite the fantastic narrative of the newly found memoir and its discrepancies with the official fifteenth-century Timurid chronicle, Shah Jahan accepted the text as the sacred words of Timur. It was preserved and passed down the Mughal dynastic line in India, beautifully copied out and illustrated, into the nineteenth century.[8]

Not just the Mughals of India but also the Safavids of Iran and the Ottomans further west were in awe of the memory of Timur.[9] He was more than a memory in the common sense of the word. His exploits and achievements sparked royal imaginations and spurred kings into action. He was, in other words, a mythical figure of kingship and a dominant symbol of sovereignty. To appreciate the historical development and inner workings of the institution of sacred kingship that Timur engendered, we must first understand the manner in which he came to have such a grip on the cultural imagination of the time. Specifically, we must ask how the myth of Timurid sovereignty—the myth of being a Lord of Conjunction—developed in the first place, and how it was elaborated and passed on as a model of sacred kingship.[10]

These questions require an approach that goes beyond the existing scholarship on Timur's reign, the organization of his army, the alliances he made, the battles he fought, and the cities he built. What is needed, instead, is a serious investigation into the lore surrounding the conqueror and into the social conditions that gave these legends the force of truth. The guiding issue, in other words, is not a finer understanding of Timur as an individual but an appreciation of his social persona as a charismatic monarch. The charisma of a public figure, however, has a transient, ephemeral quality to it and survives only if it manages to congeal in social memory.[11] Thus, tracing the process by which Timur's sacred persona developed and became institutionalized means paying close attention both to Timur's actions and intentions as well as to broader processes of narrative and memory making that gave his image shape. In short, it requires an ethnographic study of how Timur performed his sovereignty, both as a person and as a memory. It is only then that we can make sense of a man who enacted such a multilayered drama of sovereignty that it led a modern scholar to describe him as "one of the most complex, puzzling, and unattractive figures in the history of Persia and Central Asia."[12]

TIMUR'S MONGOL LEGACY

What makes Timur so puzzling is that even when he had become the undisputed master of much of Asia, he refused to publicly call himself a king. Instead, he continued to rule in the name of the descendants of Chinggis Khan, the undefeated Mongol conqueror of humble origins whose sudden rise to power in Asia in the thirteenth century could only be described as miraculous.[13] The miracle of Chinggis was not in Islam's favor, however. He was not Muslim, and for almost a century most of his Mongol descendants did not adopt Islam. Thus, in the thirteenth and early fourteenth century a large number of Muslim societies in Asia were ruled by non-Muslims. At this time, Islam lost its position as the foremost public idiom of justice and legitimacy. The Chinggisid code *yasa* gained supremacy, and shamanism, Buddhism, and Christianity competed with Islam at the Mongol courts.[14] Nevertheless, by the turn of the fourteenth century, the Mongol aristocracy in Iran and Central Asia had begun to adopt a pattern of seminomadic, Persian, and Muslim life. This process was not free from tension, however. In Timur's time, for example, the sophisticated Persianized Mongols were called half-breeds (*qaraʾunas*) by their more nomadic cousins from the steppe. The latter were in turn labeled as robbers or raiders (*jete*) for their rough and ready demeanor and disdain for urban life.[15]

Timur rose to power in this cultural ferment and became the emblem of this new style of aristocratic existence, of building grand cities but living in luxurious tents pitched in suburban pleasure gardens, and of patronizing classical traditions of Islam but practicing norms of comportment that drew sustenance from other semiotic realms, namely the traditions of ancient Iran and the norms (*tuzuk*) of Chinggis Khan. Accordingly, his sacred persona drew less upon scriptural sources of Islam and more upon collective processes of memory and meaning making. This is not to say that the intellectual traditions of Islam had lost their vitality but to argue that such scholastic writings did not structure the symbolic terrain on which the competition for sovereignty took place. Indeed, Timur's famous title, Lord of Conjunction, has no basis in Islamic scriptural traditions. Rather, it derives from the science of astrology. Yet, as will be argued below, it was a deeply sacred category of sovereignty for Muslims and non-Muslims alike.

Why Timur adopted this title or why was he remembered for centuries by it are questions that remain unanswered.[16] Despite its fame in Timur's time, Lord of Conjunction is an expression that has lost its meaning in ours. No scholarly study of the Timurid period treats it in detail. Even simple definitions of the term are often misinformed and inconsistent. The way Timur's title has slipped through the epistemic cracks of modern historiography is indicative of a larger gap in our knowledge central to understanding this formative moment in Islamic history. This lost fragment of the Timurid cultural system consisted of a web of symbols, narratives, and practices through which sovereignty came to be imagined, negotiated, and competed over. The invocation of being a Lord of Conjunction was an extremely potent move, and many religious figures and leaders of social movements competed with Timur for this title. It is in this competition for sacrality and sovereignty that we begin to see a new style of sacred kingship emerging, a style that became enshrined in the memory of Timur. That is to say, it was Timur who became uniquely identified with the label Lord of Conjunction. So began the age of Timur, the age of being a Lord of Conjunction. To view this process, it is necessary to unlock the meaning this expression held for its aspirants in Timur's time and later. This requires not only a literal definition but also a thick description of the term Lord of Conjunction, as it came to be used in different contexts for varying ends by Timur, his followers, and his rivals.[17]

IBN KHALDUN'S PROPHECY CONCERNING THE RISE OF TIMUR

The earliest mention we have of Timur as Lord of Conjunction in a non-Timurid source is in a report of the eminent Arab historian, judge, and intellectual Ibn Khaldun, who spent a month at Timur's courtly encampment in Syria. Ibn Khaldun was in Damascus when Timur arrived with his army in the year 1401, having conquered and brutally ravaged Delhi and northern India two years earlier. During the siege of the city, Ibn Khaldun learned that the conqueror had enquired after him. Seeing that the city was about to fall now that the defending Mamluk army had retreated to Egypt, and in fear of a plot against his life for supporting a negotiated surrender of the city, the seventy-year-old scholar had himself lowered from the city walls and brought to Timur's courtly encampment. When given the chance to speak, Ibn Khaldun told Timur that he had been waiting for this moment for thirty or forty years. Ibn Khaldun explained:

> Before this, when I was in the Maghrib, I had heard many predictions (*hidthan*) concerning [Timur's] appearance. Astrologers who used to discuss the conjunction (*qiran*) of the two superior planets were awaiting the tenth conjunction in the trigon, which was expected to occur in the year 766 AH (1364). One day . . . I met in Fez in the Mosque of al-Qarawiyin the preacher of Constantine . . . who was an expert in this art (*kana mahiran fi hadha alfann*). I asked him about this conjunction which was to occur, and its implications. He answered me, "It points to a powerful one who would arise in the northeast region of a desert people, tent dwellers, who will triumph over kingdoms, overturn governments, and become the masters of most of the inhabited world." I asked, "When is it due?" He said, "In the year 784 AH (1382 AD); accounts of it will be widespread." Ibn Zarzar, the Jewish physician and astrologer of Ibn Alfonso [son of Alfonso of Castile, known as Pedro the Cruel, d. 1369], king of the Franks, wrote to me similarly; also my teacher, the authority on metaphysics Muhammad ibn Ibrahim al-Abili . . . said to me whenever I conversed with him or questioned him about it, "This event is approaching, and if you live, you will surely witness it." We used to hear that the Sufis in the Maghrib also were expecting this occurrence. They believed, however, that the instrument (*qaʾim*) of this event would be the Fatimid [a descendant of Ali and his wife Fatima, the Prophet's daughter] to whom the prophetic traditions of the Shiʿa and others refer. Yahya ibn ʿAbd Allah, grandson of Sheikh Abu Yaʿqub al-Badisi, foremost among the saints of the Maghrib, told me that the Sheikh had said to them one day as he came from morning prayer, "Today the Fatimid Savior (*al-qaʾim al-fatimi*) was born." That was in the fourth decade of the eighth century. Because of all this I, too, had been watching for the event; so now, on account of my fears, it occurred to me to tell him something of it by which he would be diverted and might become kindly disposed toward me.[18]

Ibn Khaldun had done his research, interviewing merchants from Iran ahead of Timur's arrival in Syria.[19] Accordingly, he chose a form of flattery to match the lore surrounding Timur. In so many words, he called Timur a Lord of Conjunction whose rise to the mastery of the world was signaled by a "conjunction of the two superior planets"; a leader awaited by the most learned men of the age, by Sufis, astrologers, and physicians, by preachers and metaphysicians, by Muslims and Jews,[20] in Muslim North Africa and in Christian Spain; a man who would inaugurate a new era, possibly the last one before the end of time; a man who was potentially the awaited messiah descended from the prophetic line (al-qaʾim al-fatimi).

Lord of Conjunction was, as Ibn Khaldun knew, a messianic category derived from the science of conjunction astrology. It is not surprising that this messianic label had become part of Timur's lore, because, at the time, messianism—the millenarian belief in the arrival of a savior[21]—was a prevalent social phenomenon. To follow an eminent scholar of Timurid Iran, this expectation of the rise of an ideal sovereign, a true caliph, a *mahdi* (messiah), was on the "concrete plane" perhaps the only coherent theme of religious life.[22] There exists no in-depth historical explanation of why this period became the "messianic age" of Islam.[23] In its absence, the generally accepted argument remains the one given for most instances of millenarianism: social and economic deprivation.[24] In other words, the dismal state of affairs after the Mongol conquests, which destroyed the political order and flattened social structures across the eastern Islamic world, provided a space for a number of religious movements that expressed themselves in a messianic idiom, promising a sudden turn for the better. There are excellent studies of some of these movements.[25] However, when it comes to the study of political culture or institutions of kingship, few have explored the nexus of "popular" millenarianism and sovereign messianism, especially in the case of Timur.[26] This is surprising, given that the widespread messianic myth was clearly a "political" one; that is to say, it was integrally connected to notions of sovereignty and authority. This much is evident from Ibn Khaldun's own famous writings on the philosophy of history.

CONJUNCTION ASTROLOGY AND THE MESSIANIC WORLDVIEW

It is intriguing that Ibn Khaldun called Timur the messiah, because elsewhere he derided "the common people, the stupid mass," who believed in such things as the imminent arrival of the savior.[27] Which Ibn Khaldun should we take more seriously, the historian's historian who despised the superstitions of the masses (*khurafat al ʿamma*)[28] or the self-professed collector of apocalyptic predictions and messianic prophecies? This issue is resolved once we realize that Ibn Khaldun's disdain for the gullibility of the masses did not apply to the discipline of astrology, on which his own ideas of the millennium were based. Today, Ibn Khaldun is renowned for his sociological approach to history but not for his knowledge of astrology and divination. This bias in modern scholarship is understandable, since astrology today is thought of derogatorily as "magic." Although now considered to be outside the respectable categories of either religion or science, astrology used to be an integral part of both.[29]

There are few detailed studies of the place and function of astrology in Muslim societies.[30] However, it is to our advantage that astrology was at the time a "global" science, with texts, methods, and results shared across the Christian and Islamic worlds.[31] Hence, the insights offered by Keith Thomas in his landmark work on early modern England hold true, in broad terms, for Timur's milieu as well. Thomas showed that before the scientific revolution of the seventeenth century, astrology was not only a popular practice but also an intellectually demanding science. Its basic assumptions were not esoteric but part of the educated person's knowledge of the world and the cosmos. Indeed, as a systematic and comprehensive explanation of human and social affairs, astrology had few contemporary rivals.[32] In short, astrology was an important intellectual tradition that contributed to elite theories on the interrelatedness of temporality, sovereignty, and the body politic.

What concerns us here is conjunction astrology, which used the cyclical motion of the celestial spheres and the periodic alignment or "conjunction" of the planets to divide historical time into meaningful eras. A mixture of ancient Iranian, Indian, and Greek traditions, it was first propounded in Islamic times by Mashaʾallah (d. c. 815),[33] an Iranian Jewish scholar, and spread through the works of Abu Maʿshar (d. 886, known as Albumazar in Europe), who became the most famous astrologer of medieval times.[34] To put it schematically, these astrologers used the conjunction of the two "superior planets," Saturn and Jupiter, as a way of ordering historical events and predicting the future. Saturn and Jupiter were called the superior planets because they were the two most distant bodies among the seven "planets" visible to the naked eye, namely, the moon, Mercury, Mars, the sun, Venus, Jupiter, and Saturn. Jupiter-Saturn conjunctions recurred every twenty, 240, or 960 years, depending upon how they were calculated, and were called "small," "medium," and "great," respectively.[35] Ibn Khaldun explained the basics of conjunction astrology in his famous treatise on the philosophy of history, the *Muqaddima*:

> The great conjunction indicates great events, such as a change in royal authority (*mulk*) or dynasties (*dawla*), or a transfer of royal authority from one people to another. The medium conjunction (indicates) the appearance of persons in search of superiority and royal authority; the small conjunction indicates the appearance of rebels or propagandists, and the ruin of towns or of their civilization.[36]

Conjunction astrologers were in great demand, as Ibn Khaldun himself noted. "Rulers and *amirs* [leaders] who want to know the duration of their own dynasties show the greatest concern for these things."[37] He quoted many astrologers on conjunctions.[38] According to one such authority, Prophet Muhammad's birth in the seventh century had occurred under a conjunction of Saturn and Jupiter in the sign of Cancer. The Prophet of Islam, in other words, was a Lord of Conjunction. Another astrologer related that Sassanian astrologers had foretold the advent of Islam to the Persian king who was about to lose his throne to the Arabs. This conjunction signaled the end of the Persian-Zoroastrian dispensation and the beginning of the Arab-Islamic one. This obviously raised the question of when the era of Muslim and Arab supremacy would end. Apparently, scriptural traditions did not provide the last word on Islamic eschatology. Astrologers also had a range of opinions to offer.

One eminent astrologer, for example, calculated that Islam would wane in precisely 960 years, that is to say, upon the millennial anniversary of the conjunction that had signified the birth of Islam. Such predictions were also available, Ibn Khaldun reported, with other sacred lore and calculations in books of Shi'i apocalyptic literature called *jafr*.[39] In sum, conjunction astrology was an elite intellectual tradition embraced by kings and rebels, court astrologers and "schismatic" groups, Muslims and non-Muslims. Inspired by the revolution of the heavens, it sustained the truly ancient doctrine of the millennium: that prophetic and imperial dispensations last no longer than a thousand years and that they are destined to be overthrown or renewed at some regular interval of time—a predictable fraction or multiple of the millennium.[40] This doctrine made eminent sense in an age when the world was thought to last no longer than seven or eight thousand years from the birth of Adam.[41]

Lord of Conjunction, then, was in its most energetic form a millennial title, which signified change in religiopolitical order on a global scale and, potentially, the end of the world. But, more generally, the science of astrology allowed a conjunction to have a range of meanings. A condensed symbol, it could expand and change color to match the social situation and audience. A conjunction could signify a lucky general, a fortunate king, a world conqueror with a lasting dispensation, a prophet with a law, a messiah, or all of the above rolled into one. It spanned the domain of religion and politics, encapsulating the ancient Iranian adage that kings and prophets are twins. Most importantly, however, Lord of Conjunction was distinct from other titles of kings and prophets in that it contained within it a unique conception of temporality. It made explicit a worldview based on cycles of time. In this conception, historical time seemed to fold back upon itself: new events occurred and new figures appeared, but they were the fulfillment of earlier ones that had prefigured them.[42] This polyvalence and cyclical temporality ensconced in the term Lord of Conjunction was of great use to Timur and, even more so, to his successors.

THE DEVELOPMENT OF TIMUR'S SACRED PERSONA

Let us return to the moment when Ibn Khaldun, in his long-winded way, called Timur the Lord of Conjunction. Instead of acknowledging Ibn Khaldun's flattery, Timur replied that he was merely a general (*amir*). He asked for the "real" king, a teenaged descendant of Chinggis Khan, to be produced for the benefit of the historian. The lad, Timur was informed, had slipped away from the line of courtiers and out of the tent.[43] The conqueror responded with similar modesty when Ibn Khaldun compared him to the great emperors of the past—Khusraw, Caesar, Alexander, and Nebuchadnezzar—insisting that he was only akin to, and indeed shared a genealogy with, Nebuchadnezzar, who had not been a sovereign but a mere general of the Persians. We are faced here with a conundrum. Timur publicly refused to accept the messianic title of Lord of Conjunction or even be acknowledged as an independent sovereign.[44] Solving this riddle is the key to understanding how the Timurid myth of sacred kingship developed.

Ibn Khaldun's report, written after 1401, suggests that Timur's formal, public portrayal as Lord of Conjunction probably occurred at the very end of his reign and, even more likely, after his death in 1405. What we know about Timurid historiography supports this conjecture. All the extant chronicles of Timur's reign, with one exception, were composed and completed more than two decades after Timur's death. The exception is the chronicle written by Nizam al-Din Shami, which Timur had commissioned himself, but even that was begun in 1401, the year Ibn Khaldun met Timur, and finished in 1404, one year before Timur died.[45] In Shami's chronicle, it was a Chinggisid who was crowned King of the World (Padishah-i Jahan); Timur was not "given" any formal title. The later chronicle of Sharaf al-Din Yazdi revised Shami's account of the accession ceremony, depicting it as the moment of Timur's ascension to the throne, calling him shah, while promoting the Chinggisid puppet ruler to the position of "khan."[46] Although both of these chronicles called Timur "Lord of Conjunction," neither of them pointed to the precise moment when he adopted the title but simply used it to refer to him from the beginning.[47] To make sense of the games Timur and his successors played with his image, there is no choice but to wade through the murky period toward the end of his reign and the two decades after his death. The process of Timurid mythmaking can only be guessed at, but its broad outlines are reasonably clear.

As was mentioned earlier, Timur upheld the "legal fiction" of Chinggisid supremacy until late into his reign.[48] But this was not merely a matter of law. As one historian has astutely observed, there also seems to have been something propitious about it.[49] In other words, Timur's public deference to Chinggisid supremacy was a ritual act meant to preserve the right cosmological balance. Timur was not the first and only person to participate in this bit of magic. Mongols, both Muslims and non-Muslims, made up a significant part of the army, and descent from Chinggis Khan was a sacred marker of sovereign status. Even the Mamluk rulers of Egypt, often sworn enemies of the Chinggisids, in diplomatic negotiations asked for a Chinggisid princess bride, Tulunbay Khatun who arrived in Egypt in 1320.[50] The Mamluks' desire for a Chinggisid princess is understandable. They were a "slave" dynasty without noble blood. Faced with similar inadequacy early on in his career, Timur incorporated himself into the Chinggisid legacy by becoming a Chinggisid son-in-law, upholding Chinggisid law, and maintaining Chinggisid puppets on the throne.

We should not lose sight of the ritual domain in which Timur performed these acts. As his stature grew with his conquests, he attempted to surpass Chinggis Khan in other performative, not to mention gruesome, ways: the wholesale destruction of cities; the rape, enslavement, and slaughter of their inhabitants; and the building of towers of skulls on a scale that outdid the Mongol conqueror.[51] His reputation for public displays of cruelty seems to have exceeded even that of Chinggis Khan.[52] Although unpalatable today, these actions etched a reverent awe for Timur in the social memory of the time. Indeed, early to mid-sixteenth-century copies of Timur's chronicles include miniature paintings that depicted the conqueror's military victories—complete with towers of skulls—with the same verve as they illustrated the wedding celebrations of Timurid princes in which an eminent Islamic scholar of Samarqand inducted them into the Hanafi school of Sunni Islam (*bar nahaj-i qawa'id-i millat-i hanafi*).⁵³

In effect, Timur's charisma at the height of his reign began to rival his Mongol icon. Yet its cultural expression took on a very different form from that of Chinggis Khan. Let us briefly examine this process. The two conquerors' legendary status was based on a similar sense of wonder about the secret of their world-conquering success. After all, both men had been little more than sheep raiders and horse thieves in their youth. What could explain this sudden rise to greatness? As Ibn Khaldun observed in the case of Timur:

> This king Timur is one of the greatest and mightiest of kings. Some attribute to him knowledge (*al-ʿilm*), others attribute to him heresy (*iʿtiqad al-rafd*) because they note his preference for the "members of the House" [of Ali]; still others attribute to him the employment of magic and sorcery (*ʿala intihal al-sihr*), but in all this there is nothing; it is simply that he is highly intelligent and very perspicacious, addicted to debate and argumentation about what he knows and also about what he does not know.⁵⁴

Ibn Khaldun's healthy skepticism notwithstanding, Timur's rise to power was, as many suspected, attributable to a wide range of possibilities: "knowledge" (of the occult?), devotion to the Prophet's family, or magic and sorcery. It can be argued that Timur's sacred aura was a result of this collective need for a cosmological explanation to render meaningful his meteoric and cataclysmic rise to power. Moreover, the conception and articulation of this sacredness was shaped by established social institutions and cultural forms. In the case of Timur, these institutions and forms belonged to a historically specific style of Sufism that had begun to regulate the religious and social life of the region in the aftermath of the devastating Mongol conquests.

Around the fourteenth century, in the politically fragmented aftermath of the Mongol invasions and wars, mystical brotherhoods in Iran and Central Asia began breaking out of their monastic shells and reaching out to the masses.⁵⁵ Sufi orders absorbed local saint cults, Sufi shrines became important centers of pilgrimages and social life, and Sufi leadership became hereditary. The result was a tremendous increase in the material, cultural, and martial resources commanded by Sufi leaders, their kin, and their devotees. Thus began an era of competition and interdependence between mystics and kings, of Sufi politics and royal saintliness, in which religion shaped, and was shaped by, royal tastes and rituals.[56] We must turn to these recently minted institutions and intellectual traditions and practices of Sufism in order to appreciate how Timurid charisma was constructed and imagined. For the processes of cultural production that transmuted kings into saints were spawned not in the domain of kingship but in the realm of sainthood.

If the Damascene historian Ibn Arabshah[57] (d. 1450), a well-known detractor of Timur, is to be believed, the conqueror already enjoyed a cultlike following among a group of his soldiers who treated him as their spiritual guide. These men

> took him as their guide and protector independent of God, glorying in this and being outrageously insolent [about it]. Indeed, their denial of Islam (*kufr*) and their love for him were so great that had he claimed the rank of prophet or even divinity, they would have believed him in his claim. Each and every one of them sought to gain God Almighty's favor through devotion to him, making a vow to him when they fell into dire straits and [then] fulfilling it. They persisted in their false belief and their denial of Islam throughout his lifetime, and after his death they brought offerings to his tomb and made [ritual] sacrifice there. So strong was their [psychological] attachment (*musahaba*) to him that they attained the [spiritual] stage (*maqam*) where they [were able to] visualize [him] contemplatively (*muraqaba*).[58]

These soldiers had a bond with Timur much like that of a Sufi devotee's to his *pir* or master. In their eyes, he was already a *qutb* (*axis mundi*) around whom the world revolved and a *qibla* (focus) upon whose image they would meditate. The devotion of these men toward Timur was tinged with *ghuluww* (exaggeration), that is, a tendency to treat the spiritual guide as divine.[59] We cannot dismiss this phenomenon as the belief of illiterate men or as shamanistic practices prevalent in the Mongol milieu.[60] In fact, this saintly process of sacralizing was very much at work in the way Timur's "hagiography" developed in elite circles after his death.

It was mainly upon the death of a Sufi leader that he was proclaimed a saint, his burial place revered, and his miracles described publicly by his inner circle, that is to say, by those who had been privy to the true extent of his spirituality but had been forbidden by the master to openly proclaim his greatness. Much the same happened in the case of Timur and his fame as Lord of Conjunction. It was upon his death that Timur's charisma was given official, coherent, and ornate shape by his successors. Although already a legend in his lifetime, it was only as a memory that Timur could openly become a Lord of Conjunction, complete with a holy genealogy, a shrine worthy of veneration, and miraculous powers such as the ability to predict the future and read men's minds. As a Safavid astrologer-historian would note more than two centuries later, Timur had been so clairvoyant that he had no need for an astrologer.[61]

The formal posthumous sanctification of Timur was part of the same dynamic that reduced the importance of Chinggis Khan as the principal source of Timurid sovereignty. Even before Timur's rise to power in the fourteenth century, the pendulum of sacred sovereignty was swinging away from Chinggis Khan and toward Islam. While it would not be correct to assume a clean and sudden break from the Chinggisid past, it seems that such a trend had existed in Timur's time and gathered strength after his death among his successors. Timur's son Shahrukh was first to dismantle publicly the Chinggisid façade. Shahrukh declared the supremacy of the Islamic *shari'a* over the Mongol *yasa*, abandoned the practice of taking Chinggisid brides for his sons, and together with his sons patronized the production of official histories that elided many references to Mongol practices in Timur's time.

As discussed above, in the revised chronicles Timur alone appears as the absolute sovereign; the Chinggisid puppets on the throne are no longer called the King of Islam (Padishah-i Islam).[62] In addition, Timur is given stronger Islamic credentials; he makes more visits to Muslim holy men and their shrines than he did in the earlier chronicles. Sharaf al-Din Yazdi, composer of the most admired "revised" Timurid chronicle, also provided one of the earliest elaborations of Timur's cosmological position as Lord of Conjunction:

Two individuals have come who by the strength of their arms, bravery and courage ... have strengthened the religion of Islam ... and brought the entire world under their dominion. The first one is Sikandar Zulqarnayn [Alexander, the Two Horned One], who is mentioned thus in the holy book: "they ask you about Zulqarnayn; say, I will tell you his story; we established his power on earth" [Quran, 18:83–84]. His manifestation (*zuhur*) and campaigns (*khuruj*) occurred in the cycle of the Greater Luminary (Nayyir-i ʿAzam) [the sun]. The second is Hazrat Sahib Qiran ... Amir Timur Guregan.... His manifestation and campaigns occurred in the time of the Lesser Luminary (Nayyir-i Asghar), that is to say the cycle of the moon. Both these men are from the progeny of Japheth son of Noah.[63]

Timur here is equated and made to share a common biblical genealogy with Alexander of Macedonia. The latter is represented as a prophet mentioned in the Quran and as, of course, a Lord of Conjunction. The words used to describe Timur's and Alexander's reigns, *zuhur* and *khuruj*, meaning "manifestation" and "holy campaign," respectively, have messianic connotations. And we see again the notion of cycles of time associating the reign of each conqueror with the sun and the moon.

Yazdi did not give the astrological meaning of the "cycles" of the sun and the moon. However, he was most likely drawing upon the Iranian astrological tradition, through which many Zoroastrian notions had lived on in Islam and in which these two heavenly bodies were considered to be the "Good Luminaries," created but immortal beings who were "commanders over the stars."[64] Such Zoroastrian traditions regarding the sun and moon had entered Islam in various philosophical and occult forms, most importantly via the Illuminationist (Ishraqi) metaphysics of the famous twelfth-century thinker Suhrawardi (d. 1191), who had even composed prayers in Arabic to ask the sun for knowledge and salvation.[65] Furthermore, the famous *Shahnama* (Book of Kings) of Firdawsi, which had also kept alive many pre-Islamic Iranian cosmological concepts such as those of returning cycles of time, refers to the "Sun of Iran" and the "Moon of Turan (land of the Turks)."[66] In addition, solar symbolism was used on royal flags and standards at the time, most famously in the image of the sun on the back of a lion, which was a royal emblem seen in the region from at least the twelfth century.[67] While the sun and lion were ancient symbols of kingship common across many cultures, the sun on a lion's back was also used at this time for the zodiacal sign of Leo. In short, these astrological symbols were part of a thriving cosmology of sovereignty that sustained a cyclical conception of time and the rebirth of the Lord of Conjunction.

Yazdi did not limit the use of this cyclical, messianic conception of time to Timur and Alexander, the Lords of Conjunction of yore. He also applied it in a more muted Islamized form to describe his living patrons. He called Timur's heir, Shahrukh, the centennial *mujaddid* or renewer of religion, expected to rise in the eighth-century Hijri, according to the Prophet's words (*al-mawʿud bi lisan al-nabuwwat*).[68] Chinggis Khan, on the other hand, was discussed neither as the source of Timurid sovereignty nor as a Lord of Conjunction, although he appeared as part of the noble Mongol genealogical tree.

FROM CHINGGIS KHAN TO ALI

But if Timur's successors moved away from his long-held claim to be the protector and servant of the Chinggisids, what replaced this claim? Is it correct to assume, as it has been until now, that the order of Chinggis Khan gave way to the order of scriptural Islam? Can a man be replaced with a textual tradition? It is difficult to imagine how this could be the case in a milieu where notions of authority were embodied rather than abstract— where physical descent, actual and fictive kinship, and practices of bodily incorporation were the most "natural" ways of making alliances and establishing sovereign claims.[69] Although Chinggis Khan was losing some of his primacy as a symbol of kingship, it would be hasty to assume that an entire way of being dissolved with him. Rather, what seems to have happened is that Chinggis Khan coexisted for a time with and was eventually superseded by another symbol of power—a man from whom a uniquely Islamic sovereignty could be traced by descent. This was Ali ibn Abi Talib (d. 661), the son-in-law of the Prophet and the only male progenitor of his descendants, from whose line the savior was expected to appear.[70]

As Ibn Khaldun observed, Timur already had a reputation for conferring favor upon the descendants of the Prophet, the Sayyids or Alids.[71] After his death, Timur's successors emphasized their closeness to Ali much more explicitly. The most important and, indeed, the most intriguing evidence of this shift away from Chinggis Khan toward Ali as a source of sovereignty is the engraving on Timur's tomb, in the Grave of Amir (Gur-i Amir) complex in Samarqand.[72] It was his grandson, Ulugh Beg (d. 1449), famous as a philosopher-king for his pursuits in mathematics and astronomy, who had a massive block of nephrite jade carried from the borders of China for Timur's tombstone.[73] The inscription on this stone dates from around 1425, some twenty years after Timur's death, when the revised chronicles of Timur's reign were being finalized under the watch of Shahrukh and his son Ibrahim Sultan. It traces Timur's genealogy all the way to Buzunchar, son of the princess Alanquva, the "being of light" of Mongol mythology, who was also an ancestor of Chinggis Khan. Using this device, the Timurids claimed kinship with the Chinggisids on equal terms via a common ancestor in "mythical" time. In this aspect, however, the stone inscription is no different than what is found in the revised Timurid chronicles. What is unique in the inscription is the added assertion—in Arabic—about the miraculous birth of Timur and Chinggis Khan's common ancestor:

> And no father was known to this glorious ancestor, but his mother [was] Alanquva. It is said that her character was righteous and chaste, and that "she was not an adulteress" [Quran 19:20]. She conceived her son through a light which came into her from the upper part of a door and "it assumed for her the likeness of a perfect man" [Quran 19:17]. And [the light] said that it was one of the sons of the Commander of the Faithful, Ali son of Abu Talib.[74]

The inscription uses fragments of Quranic verses from the chapter on Mary, which relates the story of the birth of Jesus, to describe Alanquva's chaste condition and the miraculous birth of her progeny.[75] However, unlike in the Quranic narrative, where an angel appears in human form to give Mary the gift of a son conceived without a human father, here it is a descendant of Ali who helps Alanquva conceive Timur's ancestor. The implications are clear: Timur was a descendant of Ali, but only through an Alid's miraculous appearance in luminous form to a chaste Mongol princess who then gave birth to a Jesus-like being, the ancestor of future Mongol kings. This claim may seem fantastical, absurd, and heretical to us, but it is important to note that it did not come from the minds of illiterate soldiers or shamanistic Mongols. The use of Arabic rather than Persian, Turkish, or Mongolian—the spoken languages of the masses—and the cryptic references to the Quran not only enhanced the mystique of the message but also indicate that the producers and primary consumers of the inscription were those trained in the Islamic religious sciences.

We do not know who among Ulugh Beg's scholarly entourage composed the Gur-i Amir inscription. Undoubtedly, however, it was a scholar with advanced religious learning; plausibly, it was someone with a background and training like that of the historian Sharaf al-Din Yazdi, who crafted the cosmological connection between Timur and Alexander. Yazdi was not a mere chronicler. He was also a master of the ʿulum-i ghariba (occult sciences) and enjoyed close links with Naqshbandi and Niʿmatullahi mystical orders.⁷⁶ This meant, of course, that he was good with numbers, a master of working their manifest mathematical properties as well as their hidden metaphysical ones. Unsurprisingly, he was an accomplished astronomer and astrologer. Two decades after Yazdi finished writing the revised Timurid chronicle *Zafarnama* (Book of Victory), he was employed by Ulugh Beg to work with his team of mathematicians in his astronomical observatory in Samarqand. In short, in the episteme of the time, science, mathematics, scriptural knowledge, and occult lore were united in an intellectual quest to decipher the patterns of time and cosmos.

To summarize, before Timur could become a Lord of Conjunction in his own right, his charisma had depended on how he ritually and symbolically engaged with the memory of Chinggis Khan and Ali. On the plane of Islamic history, as we understand it, it is difficult to see the equivalence between these two men. Indeed, they could not be farther apart. Chinggis was a cruel "pagan" conqueror who uprooted Islam and imposed his own law in its place. Ali, on the other hand, was a foundational figure of Islam—first cousin and son-in-law of the Prophet, the fourth caliph of Islam, revered by his partisans (*shiʿa*) as the first leader (*imam*) of the Muslims after the Prophet. Indeed, Timur's juggling of these two symbols behind the modest façade of being an *amir* upholding Sunni Islam while slaughtering and plundering on an unimaginable scale is what makes him so difficult to characterize today. However, the differences between Ali and Chinggis Khan fade away when we realize that both figures were Lords of Conjunction of the highest order, men destined to inaugurate new epochs and dispensations.⁷⁷ After Timur's death, the Timurids began to shift away from Chinggis Khan as the dominant symbol from which to derive their sovereignty. There were two aspects to this dynamic. First, Timur was publicly proclaimed a Lord of Conjunction comparable to the Alexander of the Quran, a sanctified figure of kingship greater than Chinggis Khan. Second, in an important gesture toward Islam, the Timurids became partisans and, indeed, "fictive" kin of Ali.

ALI AS A SOVEREIGN IN POPULAR IMAGINATION

The Timurids are generally held to be Sunni Muslims. Yet in their devotion to Ali and their pilgrimage to Shiʿi holy sites they were so constant that in the words of one historian, "an 'officially' Shiʿi dynasty could hardly have been more obsequious."⁷⁸ The most astounding phenomenon was the "discovery" of Ali's grave in Balkh during the reign of the Timurid Husayn Bayqara (r. 1469–1506), a find that led to a substantial shrine and a town around it now called Mazar-i Sharif (Noble Shrine).[79] The site received such massive Timurid patronage that pilgrimage to it was officially promoted as an alternative to the *hajj* to Mecca. This Timurid preference for Ali has been explained as part of the group religiosity of the times, in which Sufi and Shi'i elements came together in the light of a "reachieved Islamic unity."[80] This was a time when allegedly Sunni and Sufi figures were producing texts that would later become canonical Shi'i works, when popular stories and oral legends were being integrated with formal doctrine to shape new devotional narratives centered on the memory of Ali.[81] Thus the explanation for why Timur and his successors held such a fascination for Ali does not lie in Islamic textual traditions but in the devotional loyalty to Ali that animated the religious imagination of the time.

There are few detailed explanations of the phenomenon of Alid loyalty.[82] It implied a preference for Ali, an extra reverence reserved for him and his descendants over other iconic figures of Islamic history. It is plausible that the rise of the popular Sufi orders in post-Mongol Iran and Transoxania and their absorption of Isma'ili ideas of the spiritual primacy of Ali had something to do with it.[83] Indeed, nearly all the Sufi families in this period traced their descent from Ali and, through him, to the Prophet. Ali was revered in this period as the first saint (*wali*) of Islam. His descendants, the Sayyids, were akin to a caste-like status group that carried within its blood a permanent charisma. Sayyids were the preferred choice for religious office and Sufi rituals. Timur lavished special attention on them. For example, he enjoyed playing chess with an eminent Sayyid, who, despite being a Sunni jurist, boasted that he had been taught the game in a dream by Ali himself.[84] All this, however, is only part of the story.

Ali also enjoyed a reputation as the greatest warrior of Islam, a champion of the battlefield. Similar to the vast poems of war and conquest about pre-Islamic Iranian kings and heroes in the famous *Shahnama* (Book of Kings) of Firdawsi (d. 1020), there existed as early as 1089 a versified epic relating the exploits of Ali called the *Alinama* (Book of Ali).[85] Another popular epic by a Timurid-era poet, Ibn Husam (d. 1470), who styled himself the "Second Firdawsi," is the *Khawarnama* (Book of Khawar), featuring Ali as the chief protagonist.[86] These tales in their oral form not only provided entertainment and "enthusiasm" (*hamasa*)[87] but also supplied much of the symbolism with which people, especially warriors, imagined themselves and identified with Islam and its heroes. Even in their stylized courtly forms, these works were a mixture of Islamic historical material and recycled stories of pre-Islamic Iranian heroes. For example, in the *Khawarnama*, Ali goes on a series of fantastic adventures fighting dragons and monsters much like Rustam of the *Shahnama*, but Ali begins his journey in the Hijaz and returns at the end to Medina, where his father-in-law, the Prophet, and his two sons, Hasan and Husayn, await him with open arms.[88] Overall, we have to be careful in making too sharp and general a distinction between "history" and "myth," between popular and elite culture, or between religion and entertainment. This was a bias of only a small minority from this period. Indeed, the early seventeenth-century Deccani Urdu *Khawarnama*, which is replete with paintings of gory battle scenes, was not dedicated to a warring king but to the Adil Shahi princess Khadija Sultan Shehrbano,[89] a devout Shiʿi lady who patronized this work as a devotee of Ali.[90]

Ali was not the only hero of these epics. Many of his partisans and followers were also extremely popular as protagonists of these stories.[91] These were figures like Mukhtar (d. 687) in the *Mukhtarnama* and Abu Muslim (d. 755) in the *Abu Muslim-nama*, who had led messianic revolts against the Umayyads in the name of Ali in the seventh and eighth centuries, respectively.[92] Ali and his supporters faced competition, however, from other popular heroes. There was Hamza, an uncle of the Prophet and a great warrior. And there were of course the ever-popular ancient Iranian heroes like Rustam and Darab of the Firdawsian tradition. The question, however, is whether these obviously legendary tales had any transcendental significance—whether these stories could be used to move people, shape their imagination, and bond them together. To find an answer, we must enter the localities where these stories were told: aristocratic tents nestled in grand symmetrical gardens, inner-city neighborhoods controlled by artisanal groups, and, most importantly, the military camps (*ordu*) of the marches.

Timur's army was a diverse, complex, and semipermanent organization built up of various tribal entities, armies of regional kingdoms, conscripted men, and volunteers. Besides the Chagatay Mongols, who formed the original kin-based core, the army included people who were nomad and settled, Muslims and Christians, Turks, Tajiks, Arabs, Georgians, and Indians.[93] The chronicler Ibn Arabshah, always inimical to Timur, described the religious composition as follows:

He had in the army Turks that worshipped idols and men who worshipped fire, Persian Magi, soothsayers and wicked enchanters and unbelievers. The idolaters carried their idols; the soothsayers spoke in verses and devoured that which had died and distinguished not between the strangled and the beasts slain with a knife. Diviners and augurs, who observe times and seasons, examined the entrails of sheep and from what they saw therein judged concerning the fortune of every place and what would befall in every region of the seven climes, whether security or fear, justice or injustice, abundance of crops or want, sickness or health and every other event, nor did they easily err.[94]

From Ibn Arabshah, we get a sense not only of the diversity of practice and belief in Timur's army but also of the awe for the power of his diviners. Other travelers to the region also commented on the multitudes of nations and religious communities gathered together by Timur. For example, when Ruy González de Clavijo (d. 1412), the Castilian ambassador, was being taken across Iran and Transoxania to meet Timur, he observed the tents and herds of nomads near major cities wherever there were grassy plains and plentiful water. When he reached Samarqand, he reported that Timur lived in grand tents in beautiful royal gardens built on the outskirts of the city, not far from the tents pitched for the army. The city itself was overflowing with people, "both men and women ... of many nations, Turks, Arabs, and Moors, Christian Armenians, Greek Catholics, and Jacobites, and those who baptize with fire in the face, who are Christians with peculiar opinions [most likely Hindus]," brought there from distant lands conquered by Timur.[95] Clavijo saw many of these people living under trees and in caves outside the city, for there was no place for them inside the city walls.[96] We have little ethnographic information on what went on in these vast tent encampments or in the cities filled with displaced people, forced migrants, slaves, refugees, traders, and fortune seekers. The few sources that break out of the stylized political narrative of the Persian chronicles are European travel accounts.[97] A particularly interesting but much ignored one is the memoir of the Bavarian soldier Johann Schiltberger (d. c. 1440).[98]

Schiltberger was captured by the Ottomans in a battle against the Hungarians. When the Ottomans were defeated by Timur's army, he passed into their hands as a prisoner of war and slave. He spent nearly three decades in the Arab Middle East, Iran, and Central Asia. As a runner and in other capacities, he traveled extensively with the Timurid army, even going far north into Russia. Eventually he escaped and made his way back via Constantinople to Germany, where he wrote and published his travel memoir. This is how Schiltberger described the religion of the "Infidels":

> It is to be noted that the Infidels have five religions. First, some believe in a giant called Aly [Ali], who was a great persecutor of Christians. Others believe in one who was called Molwa who was an Infidel priest. The third believe, as the three kings believed, before they were baptised. The fourth believe in fire, because they say that Abel, the son of Adam, brought his offering to Almighty God, and the flames of the fire were the offering; therefore they believe in this offering. Among the fifth, some believe, and the largest number among the Infidels believe, in one who is called Machmet.[99]

The first impulse of the historian is to dismiss Schiltberger's observation as the garbled account of an ignorant and biased Western Christian who, most likely, dictated his adventures in the exotic East to a scribe with a colorful pen. There is no denying Schiltberger's use of biblical categories to make sense of what he saw. But Schiltberger was correct in observing that most Muslims followed "Machmet" (that is, Prophet Muhammad), and he also narrated a few pages later a surprisingly well-informed account of the main religious obligations of Islam and the etiquette Muslims followed in mosque worship. And the diversity of religious belief he reported is supported by Ibn Arabshah's account quoted above. So it is worth taking Schiltberger seriously.

What are we to make of the "giant called Aly" whom Schiltberger mentions first? This seems to be a reference to the Ali of epic traditions. After all, it was only with the strength of a giant that Ali was able to single-handedly unhinge and lift the heavy gate of the castle of Khyber, an incident much celebrated and illustrated in the written versions of the legends surrounding Ali.[100] Schiltberger brought up Ali again when describing the history of early Islam. He reported that "Machmet" had been adopted by the king of Babylon. When the king died, "Machmet" married the king's wife and became a "Calpha" (a corruption of the word *khalifa*). Then he appointed four subordinates (the first four caliphs of Islam). The "fourth was named Aly," whom "Machmet" made "chief over all his people." Earlier, Schiltberger had mentioned Ali while describing the religion of the Iranian city of Ray. There, he observed, people "do not believe in Machmet as do other Infidels. They believe in a certain Aly." In sum, Ali appeared to Schiltberger as someone who was believed to be the true successor of the Prophet as the leader of the Muslims, a great warrior of superhuman strength, and someone who was revered even more than the Prophet in some cities. "Machmet," moreover, appears in this account as a king incorporated by marriage into the line of Persian (Babylonian) kings.

At first glance, Schiltberger's descriptions of Islamic history and Muslim beliefs appear ill informed, as they diverge widely from the well-known textual versions. But perhaps we need to read this work not as a historical document that would aid us in arriving at a better chronology or a finer understanding of events but analyze it in anthropological terms. There is little indication that Schiltberger ever learned to read or write the languages of the Islamic lands or that he pursued a serious intellectual inquiry into its learned traditions. His information was gathered from listening and speaking to ordinary people in the military camp and the cities he visited with the army. By this argument, we get in Schiltberger's jumbled description not just a view of an outsider puzzled by strange symbols and narratives but also a report of the bricolage of the "natives."[101] That is to say, the organic connections wrought between the Prophet of Islam and the king of Persia, between Ali the Giant and Ali the chief of all Muslims, while not historically accurate, were attempts to make sense of the present with signs that were, nevertheless, the detritus of history.[102] These signs, moreover, were communicated in malleable form in the oral epic traditions that sustained the religious and popular life of the camp and the city squares. The assertions above would have been arbitrary and unsubstantiated if it were not for the "heresiographical" writings of eminent Muslim scholars who condemned such "popular thought." One such scholar of the Mongol period, famous even today as a puritanical critic of popular religion, was Ibn Taymiyya (d. 1328).

An expert in the Hanbali school of jurisprudence, Ibn Taymiyya had lived in Damascus under Mamluk rule. He is renowned for his trenchant critique of what he saw as widespread deviancy among Muslims.[103] Ibn Taymiyya was not a reclusive scholar, however. Active in organizing resistance against Mongol attacks, he was also familiar with the culture of the military camp. In his writing against the Shi'a, Ibn Taymiyya was so exasperated by what he perceived as their historically unsound arguments that he compared them to the misconceptions (zann) of the common people, who routinely muddled their concepts of time and space.[104] According to Ibn Taymiyya, even learned Shi'i assertions were

> like the mistaken belief prevalent among the common people who imagine that the Prophet [d. 632] . . . was a follower of one of the four schools

of jurisprudence and that Abu Hanifa [d. 767, founder of the Hanafi school] and the other [founders like him] lived before the Prophet; and like the group of Turkmen who imagine that Hamza [d. 625] was responsible for great victories and they relate these stories among themselves while the learned know well that he only saw the battles of Badr and Uhud and was killed on the day of Uhud [in the year 625]; and like the large number of people who imagine that among the graves in Damascus are those of the wives of the Prophet . . . Umm-i Salma and others . . . while the scholars know that none of the Prophet's wives ever came to Damascus . . . ; and like those ignorant ones who imagine that the grave of Ali is in Najaf while the learned know it is in Kufa . . . [105]

As Ibn Taymiyya's frustration against the warped imagination of the common people shows, historical time mattered little when it came to sacred symbols that shaped popular imagination.[106] For many, the place of these symbols in classificatory schemes based on local practice mattered more than their place in the dialectic of universal history. Not only time was tamed according to local practice; so was space. Shrines of holy figures, often heroes of oral traditions, served as the sacred centers of local religious practice. Entertaining stories of biblical prophets had existed since the earliest Islamic times, and their graves appear scattered across medieval Muslim geography.[107] In the Timurid period, the same process occurred with the miracle tales and shrines of Sufi saints. Timur, for example, made more than one stop to ask for divine help (*istimdad*) at the shrine of Abu Muslim, whose fame as a proselytizer and campaigner (*sahib al-daʿwa*) for the sovereignty of the Alids was kept alive by the orally recited tales of the *Abu Muslim-nama*.[108] It was not as if the intelligentsia did not try to assert proper historical consciousness, but woe betide the scholar who tried to tell the crowd that their storyteller had gotten his names and dates mixed up.[109] In general, boundaries between religion, oral culture, and public entertainment are hard to draw in this period. Further, we cannot necessarily assume that the learned elite were somehow above these concerns and did not make recourse to "mythical thought."[110] This was certainly true in the case of Hamza of the Turkmen tradition, against which Ibn Taymiyya fulminated so vehemently.

Hamza was indeed a popular hero of oral traditions of the marches.[111] Nevertheless, literary versions of the story abound in manuscript collections, and we know of its popularity among the most learned of men.[112] The tales of Hamza belonged to pre-Islamic Iranian lore that survived in oral culture as Iranians converted to Islam.¹¹³ In the process, an Iranian hero became conflated with the historical figure of Hamza, the warrior uncle of the Prophet. In life, Hamza was a childhood playmate and foster brother of the Prophet who died during the latter's life in the battle of Uhud in 625. In the epic, however, Hamza is born with the horoscope of a great sovereign and becomes, in effect, the Prophet's earthly and cosmological twin: while the latter receives the revelation of Islam, it is Hamza who rides out of Arabia, fighting the forces of evil and spreading the order of Islam all the way from Greece to Ceylon. The legendary stories of Hamza are structured by a plot that can only be described as millennial. Should it surprise us, then, that in the epic our hero is called Amir Hamza Lord of Conjunction?

OTHER LORDS OF CONJUNCTION: THE AVATARS OF ALI

The tales of Hamza, Lord of Conjunction, were a cause of concern to partisans of Ali. The famous Timurid-era Sufi master Sayyid Muhammad Nurbakhsh (d. 1464), for example, bitterly complained that the popularity of Hamza detracted from the heroism of Ali. Nurbakhsh, however, had a unique reason for upholding Ali as the warrior-king of early Islam. He claimed that he was Ali's embodiment, the *mahdi* (messiah), and the true sovereign of the age. He had made his messianic claim during the reign of Timur's son Shahrukh, who had him arrested several times. After Timurid authorities imprisoned Nurbakhsh in a deep well for more than fifty days, he publicly recanted his messiah-hood. It is important to note that Nurbakhsh was not a crazy dervish, an antinomian mendicant living on the margins of society.¹¹⁴ He was a Sayyid from an eminent family and highly trained in the religious sciences. As someone who articulated a coherent synthesis of Sufism and Shiʿism, he is counted among the most important religious figures of the period.¹¹⁵ The order he founded flourished in Iran and Kashmir for centuries.

Nurbakhsh has fortunately left us with a work that can be called his messianic manifesto. Written in Arabic, it provides a detailed proof and explanation of his claim to be the *mahdi*, along with the religious and political implications of that claim. Given his popularity and his entanglements with the Timurid authorities, this manifesto is worth examining closely. Nurbakhsh maintained that it was the Abbasids—a dynasty that had risen to power in the eighth century with the support of Alids but ended up persecuting them—who had invented legends (*asatir*) like that of Hamza to undermine the reputation of Ali:

> The greatest of [the Abbasid] fabrications are two: one is the story of Hamza (*qissat hamza*) which relates to the past; and the other, the story of the messiah (*qissat al-mahdi*), which pertains to the future. Both of these are lies and false accusations against the claims of the Alids. The first is meant to distract people from commemorating Ali's bravery; and the other, to prevent them from accepting an Alid as an Imam after the twelve Imams. Limiting the number of Imams to twelve is also one of [the Abbasids'] tricks.[116]

The Abbasids, charged Nurbakhsh, had distorted both the past and the future, deliberately spreading corrupt history and false prophecy. This is not surprising, because astrology was a key factor among the proofs he gave for his messianic claim and in his claim to earthly sovereignty. He quoted, among others, the Greek astronomer Ptolemy and the Zoroastrian sage and seer Jamasp.[117] But what is the connection between Nurbakhsh's two seemingly unrelated complaints about the legends of Hamza and the messiah? The answer becomes clear in the context of Nurbakhsh's messianic claim. He had claimed to be the rightful imam (leader), and thus he was against the quietist Twelver Shiʿi doctrine that the imamate had been limited to the first twelve holders of that office. He also believed himself to be the reincarnation or embodiment of Ali, the first and greatest of the imams. Ali, he asserted, was the only one among the Shiʿi imams who had possessed kingship. None of the successive imams ever enjoyed earthly sovereignty. With the cycle of imamate completed in Nurbakhsh, he believed that as the embodiment of Ali he was the true sovereign and king. By promoting Hamza as the hero of early Islamic history, he complained, the Abbasids meant to take away from the bravery (*shujaʿat*) of Ali and, by association, of his avatar, Nurbakhsh.

But how did Nurbakhsh become the embodiment of Ali? His explanation of the spiritual mechanism by which someone like him could become a messiah is intriguing. Instead of using the extremist or "exaggerated" (*ghulat*) explanation of transmigration of the soul or metempsychosis (*tanasukh*),[118] in which the soul leaves the body upon death to be reborn in another, he offered a version deemed more acceptable to mainstream Islamic traditions. He called this *buruz* (projection), a phenomenon in which "a complete soul pours into a perfect being (*kamil*) in the same way that epiphanies pour into him and he becomes their locus of manifestation."[119] In *buruz*, the projecting body did not die, and the receiving one did not have to be in the womb, as was the case with transmigration. The notion of *buruz* had been used by other Sufi theorists to explain how saints were able to be in more than one place at the same time, but it was Nurbakhsh who used it to explain messianism. In his case, the phenomenon of *buruz*—the descent of the messianic soul into Nurbakhsh's body—was witnessed by one of his followers, who saw

> in Irbil in the year 827 [1423–1424], that one day people gathered together to wait for Jesus to descend from the sky. He saw that he descended in the form of light rather than body, and flowed toward me [i.e., Nurbakhsh] and held me. The same night I saw that I was present in the sky and in a human body on earth in the same instant.[120]

Have we strayed hopelessly afar from the discussion of how Timur became a Lord of Conjunction? Or have we circled back to the inscription carved on Timur's tombstone in Samarqand around this time, in which Alanquva was impregnated by a ray of light that took on the form of a descendant of Ali? The "bizarre" Timurid claim of being descended from Ali was based on a concept of the returning messianic soul, the same "exaggerated" concept that Nurbakhsh propagated with considerable success in a sanitized neoplatonic version.[121] This may explain why even though Nurbakhsh hardly presented a significant military threat, he was pursued by the Timurids and lived in constant fear of his life and freedom. His followers went into a trance and danced in ecstatic joy when the news of Shahrukh's death was brought to their master, because for them the Timurid ruler was the Antichrist.[122] Conversely, from the Timurid perspective, Nurbakhsh's claim was transgressive not only because it deviated from accepted doctrine but because there could only be one legitimate sovereign, one true successor of Ali, and one Lord of Conjunction of the age.

Nurbakhsh was not alone in his spiritual challenge to Timurid sovereignty. His metaphysics was a variation on a well-worn theme. Take, for example, the case of the three famous and well-studied messiahs of Timurid Iran. Nurbakhsh, whose name meant "giver of light," has already been discussed. His more militant contemporary, Mushaʿshaʿ (d. 1461), based in southern Iraq, had a similarly inspired name.[123] The word *mushaʿshaʿ* was derived from the Arabic verb *shaʿshaʿa*, which "connotes dispersion, as light shining or liquid becoming diluted in water," an effect he felt at two moments of defeat in battle.[124] A believer in transmigration of the soul (*tanasukh*), Mushaʿshaʿ had taught the mysteries of the name of Ali. A similar case of divine infection occurred with the founder of the influential and widespread Hurufi (letterist) mystical movement, Fazlallah Astarabadi (d. 1394).[125] Fazlallah saw a bright star in a dream, which poured forth all its light into his right eye. He declared himself the inaugurator of the third and final cycle of time—the cycle of divinity, which had followed the earlier cycles of prophethood and sainthood.[126] Fazlallah was executed by one of Timur's sons on Timur's orders, but not before he tried to make the prince a devotee. In an assassination attempt, one of Fazlallah's followers nearly succeeded in killing Shahrukh as he was leaving a mosque. Before his death, the Hurufi master, himself a Lord of Conjunction, had left behind poetry warning the Timurids of the consequences of not following him:

> If the Khan of Khans, lord of the hosts, does not become my kin,
> I am the Lord of Conjunction of the world; I will destroy his kin and army.[127]

It is in this environment—one of messianic claims reverberating through the empire and graves of potential messiahs dotting the landscape—that Nurbakhsh's theories begin to make more sense. His explanation of the "projection of the soul" (*buruz*) was uniquely suited to this cultural landscape in that it allowed for multiple messiahs to reappear through history and even coexist at the same time. There was no reason why the complete soul could not descend into multiple perfect beings, a fact pointed out by later expounders of Nurbakhsh's idea.[128] Its philosophical niceties aside, the theory was an attempt to make sense of a lived reality in which every region had its own sacred presence of a divinely inspired savior[129]—most often dead but quite often alive—and in which much of the religious and entertaining lore in the public squares and military encampments was about saints who could multiply at will and Lords of Conjunction whose destiny it was to conquer the world.

This is an important point, because too frequently it is assumed that the efforts of great thinkers moved society rather than the other way around. For example, the Illuminationist (Ishraqi) philosophy of the famous thinker Suhrawardi (d. 1191) is said to have enjoyed a great revival in early modern India and Iran, informing not only metaphysical writings but courtly literature.[130] Why did this philosophical school, which was already centuries old, regain its charm during this period? We have no answers, unless we are willing to turn metaphysical speculation right side up and root it in the earth of social reality. The attraction of Illuminationist thought may have had something to do with its comprehensive cosmology and angelology based on ancient Iranian traditions that not only gave primacy to the sun and its illuminating powers but also looked favorably on the transmigration of the soul.[131] To put it baldly, Suhrawardi's philosophy appeared custom made to fit the social fact of millenarianism. But should this surprise us? It was, after all, the age of Lords of Conjunction.

A MESSIANIC SCRIPT OF KINGSHIP: THE ASTROLOGICAL HISTORY OF JAMASP

One could criticize the above account on the grounds that it has been constructed arbitrarily from fragmentary sources—an inscription here, a chronicle there—and mistakenly represented as a coherent view from within the culture. How can we be sure that a cultural actor from the Timurid period would have been able to make sense of the argument above, in which Chinggis Khan, Alexander, and Ali appear as figures of the same type or signs in the same series? To allay these concerns and obtain a more "emic" view into the Timurid cultural episteme, it is worth examining a fifteenth-century Persian work on astrological history entitled *Kitab Jamasp fi Tawaliʿ al-Anbiyaʾ* (the Book of Jamasp Concerning Horoscopes of the Prophets).[132]

This work is a challenge to interpret. It is anonymous, and its place of production and extent of circulation is unknown. Upon first examination, its contents appear to be a confusing mixture of ancient myths, historical knowledge, and prophecies about the end of time. Moreover, it does not even mention Timur or his descendants. All we know is that it was produced roughly somewhere in fifteenth-century Iran and has survived in remarkably good condition. Despite all these difficulties, however, it is a revealing source for our purposes, for it neatly encapsulates the worldview of a milieu that gave rise to a Lord of Conjunction. Even its anonymity does not pose a problem once we realize that it was meant to be "anonymous." The purported author is a legendary Zoroastrian sage named Jamasp, who lived in the time of Zoroaster and became a renowned source of Iranian apocalyptic traditions.[133]

The text consists of the horoscopes of major figures of world history taken from biblical, Islamic, and Iranian traditions. The time period covered is from the very beginning (the birth of Adam) to the very end (the destruction of the world). Since Jamasp supposedly lived in the time of the pre-Islamic Iranian king Gushtasp (Vishtasp), the text gives us the "history" of the world from the birth of Adam until this king's reign and thereafter assumes the form of prophecy. In short, it is a condensed history-prophecy of the world, one based on a cyclical concept of time in which conjunctions mark the coming and going of religiopolitical figures and changes in world affairs. It even uses the conjunction (*qiran*) as a measure of time equal to twenty years, stating the "prediction," for instance, that the Prophet's age will be three and one-sixth of a conjunction, that is, sixty-three years.

Its attribution to Jamasp notwithstanding, this Persian work is written from a Muslim perspective and is in fact an Alid polemic. Writing in an arcane-seeming Persian script, our pseudo-Jamasp tries to use the form, feel, and fame of the ancient Zoroastrian *Jamaspnama* to get across a new messianic message in old millenarian garb.[134] Its "philo-Alidism" is clearly enunciated in the way Ali and his descendants are given a prime role in the future of the world. While the Prophet is called Lord of Conjunction, Ali's horoscope is made much more elaborate and praiseworthy. Ali is said to be a relative of the Prophet, who is:

> Tall, ruddy (*ba surat ashqar*), brave and agile. Every enemy who sees him will run away and his sword will dominate the entire world. He will always be victorious and from east to west all the kings of the earth will fear him. Despite all this he will remain a dervish and will never have wealth or treasure. He will be killed by his slave. They will call him a lion and his ascendant will be a conjunction in Cancer, with the Moon and Venus in the ascendant. [The conjunction of] Mars and Saturn [indicating misfortune] in the house of sons will be the cause of his sons' death. . . . [The planets indicate that] he will certainly be a dervish, and will be one with that prophet (*ba an payghambar yaki bashad*). He will take kingship away from the kings of old and will conquer fourteen realms. . . . Instead of a cap (*kulah*) he will tie a long turban. It would take too long to detail all his ways and customs. He will turn fire-temples into ruins and kill the Zoroastrian priests and put an end to our kingship and our customs. None of the prophesied ones will do to us what he will do. . . . All fortune and success will be his. He will be a man broad of face and forehead, fierce-eyed (*surkh chashm*), with a pleasing demeanor and a smiling face, kind to friend and stranger alike. Although a master of the sword (*sahib-i shamshir*), whatever he does, he will do with sound judgment (*ba hujjat*).[135]

Pseudo-Jamasp presents Ali as a world conqueror. It does not mention any of the other caliphs of early Islam. Instead, it discusses the villains and heroes of Shiʿi history, for example, the Umayyads, who usurped Alid sovereignty in the seventh century, and Abu Muslim, who organized the messianic revolution in the eighth century to overthrow them. Alexander is another figure whose horoscope is as elaborate and fortunate as that of Ali. The world conqueror who receives one of the worst reviews, however, is Chinggis Khan. In the words of the "Zoroastrian" oracle, Chinggis Khan is an infidel Turk (*munkir-i turki*) who will come forth from the East:

> Red-skinned (*surkh rang*), cat-eyed, short and eunuch-faced (*khadim shakal*), he will lead a great campaign (*daʿwa*) and take the world. He will be called Chinggis Khan and he will subjugate all. He will conquer mostly by trickery and deviousness. No one will see his face. All will flee him. Four climes of the earth will be ruined at his hand and the world will become a desert. Twenty days of supply should be carried from city to city . . . otherwise all will die of hunger and people will eat human flesh. Our noble religion [Zoroastrianism] will suffer and mosques and towers all will be ruined. . . . And the wrath of God will be such that our places of worship will be burned and women will be stripped naked and paraded around the military camp (*ordu*) and the marketplace. May God Almighty protect the women and children of Muslims and unbelievers from such humiliation.[136]

The contrast between Chinggis Khan and Ali could not be more striking. If the Mongol is depicted as a mean, unsavory character, Ali appears as a tall, robust, and athletic youth. If Chinggis Khan uses trickery to win battles so that he is never seen, Ali is a true warrior, a lion, who defeats his enemies openly. But Ali is more than a warrior. One with the Prophet, he is the agent through which the new Islamic order spreads through the world. He is the Lord of Conjunction who brings the Iranian-Zoroastrian dispensation to an end, a fate that pseudo-Jamasp seems serenely resigned to accept. Last but not least, Ali is a dervish, a Sufi who shuns all wealth and treasure even when he becomes the master of the world. He changes the ways and customs of the world. Instead of a cap (worn by the Mongols), he ties a long turban (worn by Sufi warriors). The historically minded will be critical of this worldview, in which Ali becomes a world conqueror and even, anachronistically, a turban-wearing Sufi. But this is precisely the outlook that shaped the Timurid cultural imagination. In the official chronicle composed at the end of Timur's reign, Ali is praised not as a caliph but as the youthful model of chivalry (*fata*), as well as Lord of Zulfiqar (Sahib-i Dhu al-Fiqar) and Lord of Duldul (Sahib-i Duldul), labels that invoke, respectively, Ali's fabled two-pointed sword and trusty ride.[137] This was the Ali not of Sunni or Shi'i doctrine but of the popular preaching and oral epic tradition—an imaginative and imaginary realm inhabited, as we have seen, by Lords of Conjunction.

Chinggis Khan is also the last "historical" figure in the text; after this point, the cast of characters that appear before the end of the world is borrowed from a mixture of Islamic apocalyptic traditions. The important ones included the Alid ('Alawi), the Antichrist (Dajjal), the one who has the characteristics of Jesus (*sift-i 'isa' darad*), and the successor of Jesus (*wali 'ahd-i 'isa'*). That is to say, pseudo-Jamasp asserted that the descendants of Ali and Jesus-like figures will be pivotal in bringing about a just political order after the Mongol depredations and before the end of the world. Based on this internal evidence, it appears that the work was composed sometime after the Mongol invasion of the thirteenth century and was of value to those expecting an Alid savior to rise and put an end to the Mongol order in Iran. Overall, this is an outlook that fits well with the ethos behind the Timurid claim to be descended from Ali in a Jesus-like manner. Accordingly, it provides a neat script for the drama Timur's successors enacted in their move away from Chinggis Khan toward Ali as the ultimate symbol of sovereignty.

CONCLUSION

It is generally recognized by scholars that details of the religious history of Timurid Iran are particularly difficult to pin down.[138] It is not possible, for example, to declare with certainty whether a particular region or city followed Sunni Islam or the main sect of Shi'ism. In general, the import of juridical Islam itself is difficult to assess for large parts of the population and, surprisingly, even for monarchs. Timur presents a classic case of this problem. He kept most people guessing about his religious loyalties, not to mention his sacred powers.[139] When arguing with Sunni divines, he used Shi'i arguments. When attacking Shi'i enemies, he charged them with religious deviance. Some believed that he was above the sectarian fray, that he communicated with an angel, and that he had even ascended to heaven on a forty-step ladder. The way Timur and his successors transgressed the norms of classical Islamic traditions does not mean, however, that they had no regard for the "sacred." Timur's actions, such as upholding Chinggisid sovereignty, providing for the descendants of the Prophet, consulting astrologers and soothsayers, and visiting shrines of holy men, cannot simply be reduced to political ploys. If these actions had been so transparently propagandist at the time as they appear to us, then they would not have possessed any efficacy. But they did not only in Timur's time but for centuries after him, as Timurid forms of sacrality became institutionalized and shaped the formation of imperial polities in fifteenth- and sixteenth-century India and Iran.

Timurid notions of sovereignty were shaped by the messianic myth of the Lord of Conjunction. This was a time of transition. The existing Mongol order was receding. Its symbol was Chinggis Khan. Another Islamic order was arising. Its symbol was Ali. The sacred myth that could explain this grand change in world affairs was the rise of a messianic figure who would inaugurate the new era. Timur inhabited this myth and performed it with relish. What everyone knew but could not say was that he was the Lord of Conjunction. Ibn Khaldun, an outsider, let it slip in court and recorded for posterity Timur's public denial that he was the Lord of Conjunction. Other sources tell us that a group of Timur's own soldiers had worshipped him, as a saint, messiah, or divinity, much as the followers of Nurbakhsh, Mushaʿshaʿ, and Fazlallah Astarabadi had venerated these men. The milieu of the military camp, with its oral epic traditions and heroic ideals, encouraged enthusiastic and concrete modes of sacrality over textual religious doctrines. In such a setting, the fact of charismatic sovereignty was mostly what mattered, an embodied sovereignty that could be transmitted through blood or milk. Timur's successors openly proclaimed this fact upon Timur's death. The machinery of imperial tradition making began its work, and sages of the realm used esoteric lore to express what had popularly been known—Timur was the Lord of Conjunction, the descendant of Ali, the awaited messiah.

In sum, Timurid claims to power were based on an engagement with the particular embodied forms of sacrality dominant at the time. Reports of this ritual theater reach us either as heresies or as grandiose claims of being the Lord of Conjunction. There is, however, more than just religious deviance or bombastic language in these reports. There is instead a ritual process at work, in which sovereign legitimacy was being forged. The way to win was not, as is normally assumed, to impose one's "ideology" on the masses but rather the other way around: to pour oneself into the mythic molds of the hero, the saint, and the messiah—molds shaped by collective imagination and social memory. Reputations of kings and saints were made or ruined depending on how their engagement with the sacred was enacted, publicized, and collectively remembered. Successful ones became saints, world conquerors, and messiahs. Unsuccessful ones were labeled as heretics, corrupt tyrants, and the Antichrist. The next chapter traces this dynamic for the formative period of the two large polities, the Mughal and the Safavid empires, that took shape almost a century after Timur and built upon the patterns and institutions bequeathed to them by the Timurid imperial project.

{3} THE CROWN OF DREAMS

SUFIS AND PRINCES IN SIXTEENTH-CENTURY IRAN

IN IRAN, the century after Timur was one of short-lived empires and unstable confederations. Timur's successors had been reduced within a few generations to a set of petty kingdoms scattered across what is today Central Asia, eastern Iran, and Afghanistan. Here, the Timurids competed with noble lineages claiming descent from other "mythical" sources of sacred sovereignty, namely Chinggis Khan, Ali, and Alexander.[1] In the jostling for sovereignty and the right to plunder and tax that came with it, none seemed able to claim more than a temporary allegiance of his commanders and soldiers. Even bonds of kinship seemed to hinder more than help in a Turkic social setting where generations of intermarriage, polygyny, and the high value of maternal kin ties created a complex web of relationships, producing competing demands of loyalty and an abundance of potential kings.[2]

Yet in this chaotic milieu, the style of kingship remained dominated by the memory of Timur. The heirs of Timur, despite their loss of political power, had come to command great prestige as purveyors of royal behavior and aristocratic refinement. Indeed, one can argue that in the fifteenth century, Timurid courts and princely retinues, concentrated in eastern Iran and present-day Afghanistan, were the main centers of the long-acting "civilizing process"—the cultivated manners, habits, and tastes—that shaped elite Persianate "social personality" across large swaths of Asia.[3]

The formation of the Safavid and Mughal empires must be understood within this historical and cultural context.[4] The two Turkish-speaking founders of these dynasties, the Safavid Shah Isma'il I (1487–1524) and the Timurid Mirza Babur (1483–1530), grew up under the shadow of

Timur. Their careers, however, have drawn little comparative interest from historians. This is understandable, given that both men did little more than conquer. Their efforts at imperial consolidation and administration were rudimentary at best, as were their attempts at cultural production. But if we focus our attention less on the functioning of stable empires and more on the question of how these imperial systems took shape and became stable in the first place, this moment in history regains its significance. Further, such a change in perspective enables us to view these two struggling dynasts as belonging not to two different strands of the past—Safavid Iran and Mughal India—but to the same historical milieu. Despite their diverse backgrounds and diverging careers, the two men began their sovereign careers with common goals and experienced the same set of cosmological constraints and ritual processes that shaped their social personality as sovereigns.

BABUR AND SHAH ISMAʿIL: SOVEREIGNS IN A SHARED REALM

Even though the lives of Babur and Shah Ismaʿil intersected at several key moments, the historical image of these two men has been rendered in two very different historiographical veins. Babur, we are told, was a Sunni Muslim of the sober and orthodox variety. Born to a minor Timurid ruler of Transoxania and his Chinggisid wife, he became a refined prince who wrote a thoughtful and reflective autobiography and, considering the temperament of the time, was a tolerant ruler who kept his religion to himself and did not impose it upon his subjects in India.[5] By contrast, the historical picture of Shah Ismaʿil is that of a Shiʿi Muslim of a particularly extreme heterodox strain. The son of an Alid Sufi master and a Turkmen-Greek princess of the Aqqoyunlu dynasty of northwestern Iran, he became an ecstatic demagogue who whipped his followers into revolutionary frenzy with apocalyptic verse and messianic propaganda and imposed his religious creed on the conquered population of Iran on pain of torture and death.[6] The question, however, is: if these two men had such ostensibly different social personalities, what compelled and enabled them to collaborate with each other, fight common enemies, exchange gifts and favors, patronize the same courtiers and artists, and even transact sacred oaths? Whatever the differences may have been between Babur and Shah Ismaʿil, these have clearly been magnified and reified by the bifurcated historical narratives of later times.

If we chip away at the teleological crust of Mughal and Safavid historiography, however, the period of Babur and Shah Ismaʿil appears in a very different light. We get a glimpse of the formative phase of kingship, when the political outlook and imperial style of the two dynasties had not as yet taken mature shape. Instead of separate and fully formed Timurid-Sunni and Safavid-Shiʿi "ideologies," we witness an era of imperial pubescence, with its rites of passage, exhilarating moments, and desperate acts. The mood of the time had a subjunctive and expectant quality to it: omens and portents were everywhere, new cosmologies were experimented with and novel rituals tried out, and grand claims were made and painful compromises struck without thought to the dynastic angst it would cause later generations. The Safavids, for one, had to come to terms with Shah Ismaʿil's charismatic reputation of being a divinity descended to earth as an embodiment of Ali.[7] The Mughals, in turn, had to contend with the embarrassment of Babur's submission to the Safavid messiah at a desperate moment in his life. To judge the import of these acts we must set aside the received categories of history, which locate Babur and Shah Ismaʿil at the opposite ends of a cultural spectrum. Instead, we must see these men as actors with a common subjectivity operating in a shared discursive realm, one in which competition for sovereignty occurred in a ritual fashion that still bore the stamp of Timur, Lord of Conjunction.[8] After all, Shah Ismaʿil and Babur were fighting for the same territorial prize: the former dominions of Timur.

To see the two men's sovereign ambitions in similar cultural terms, however, requires a double shift in perspective. On the one hand, Shah Ismaʿil, whose image as a mystagogue and messiah appears strange to us, needs to be made more familiar. On the other hand, Babur, who seems familiar as a rational and pragmatic ruler, needs to be shown operating in a stranger realm. Given the messianic controversy surrounding Shah Ismaʿil, it is easier to see him participating in a symbolic domain of sacred sovereignty similar to the one Timur had inhabited. However, Babur's sober image as the wielder of rational forms of authority makes matters more complex. The main source for this no-nonsense image is Babur's memoir, a rare first-person account written in Chagatay Turkish, which Stephen Dale in his wide-ranging study described as "preternaturally modern."[9] Indeed, reading Babur's book at times feels as if one has stumbled upon early modernity in the guise of a well-read and well-mannered Turkish prince who possessed an ethos close to our own. Had the age of messianic kingship passed Babur by?

At first glance, this appears to be the case. For one, Babur did not call Timur a Lord of Conjunction in his memoir.[10] Moreover, he made no such claim for himself. His miracles were modest ones, consisting mainly of dreams—discussed further below—in which his patron Sufi saints delivered him victory or from harm. Babur, in an important sense, adhered to the social norm that discouraged the self-narration of one's spiritual achievement or written publicity of one's sacrality while alive—an etiquette that even Timur seemed to have followed.[11] Thus, one of Babur's major spiritual achievements was narrated not during his lifetime but almost half a century later by his daughter, Gulbadan Banu.[12] She related how her father had miraculously saved her brother Humayun's life. As the young prince lay deathly ill, Babur circumambulated him, asking for Ali's intercession and offering to take the place of his dying heir. Babur's prayers were answered and his offer accepted. As the prince recovered, the king fell ill and passed away. The way Babur's miracle was "remembered" after his death is reminiscent of how Timur openly became Sahib Qiran after he passed away. This is not to say that Babur was sanctified at the same level as his famous world-conquering ancestor. Nevertheless, in Mughal dynastic memory, Babur possessed a spark of saintliness, a sacred link with the divine, which gave him the ability to perform miracles with succor from Ali.

Even though Babur never achieved a sovereign stature equivalent to that of Timur, he and his memory experienced the same processes that had rendered Timur as the Lord of Conjunction. However, this worldview is only made visible in his writing if we read it in harmony with the sign-laden *mentalité* of his time and the social institutions that shaped it.[13] This means paying close attention to a number of acts, observations, and anecdotes in Babur's account that modern readers skip over because they seem strange and trivial. Babur also called these phenomena "strange" (*gharib*), but he accorded them a seriousness that today would be considered eccentric. In doing so, however, he was not alone. At the time, occurrences with a touch of the wondrous, the bizarre, the inexplicable, and the marvelous—the descent of the messianic soul into a human body, for example—were not treated as cultural marginalia and consigned to intellectual oblivion.[14] Instead, such phenomena were investigated, classified, and verified by religious and political authorities.[15] To grasp this as an important aspect of public life is a first step in appreciating that a considerable part of the social role of kingship involved being able and willing to confront and deal with "strangeness."

THE STRANGENESS OF BABUR'S WORLD

In 1494, a "strange event" (*waqiʿa ghariba*) occurred in the bucolic valley of Fergana, situated about three hundred miles from Samarqand. It involved a great-great-grandson of Timur, Umar Shaykh Mirza, who had ruled this region from a fortress perched on the edge of a deep ravine. Suddenly, along with his doves (*kabutar*) and dovecote, he toppled off his fortress and "gave up the ghost."[16] This event would have gone unnoticed if it had not been for the keen diary-keeping habit of his son, Babur.[17] This was an important moment for Babur, who began his memoirs with it: "In the month of Ramadan in the year 899 [June 1494], in the province of Fergana, in my twelfth year I became king." He did so, one could say, because this was the day he came into his own. But why did he call his father's death strange? Let us examine a suggestion. Battle, poison, disease, and old age were all expected or "natural" reasons for the death of a sovereign, but falling off the castle wall while feeding one's birds was not. Since there was no obvious cause, the unexpected event itself became a cause.[18] That is to say, its inexplicability transformed the event into an omen—a sign whose signified lay not in the past or the present but in the future. We know that this omen was not immediately fulfilled. Upon his father's death, Babur did not in fact become king. It was Babur's uncle who snatched away the reins of power. Ten years would pass before the young prince proclaimed himself king (*padishah*) in Kabul,[19] and it would take more than three decades to make him famous as the conqueror of Hindustan. Thus, it was at the end of his life that Babur's fame solved the temporal puzzle of his father's strange demise and fulfilled the omen that had launched his sovereign career. For Babur, who polished his diary and gave it a narrative frame late in life in India, this must have seemed like the appropriate moment to begin the story of his kingship.

Babur's memoir, like other literary and historical works from the period, is littered with such "coincidences." It is patterned by a causality that is no longer to our taste. To our modern sensibility, this interpretation would only be acceptable—if at all—as a literary-critical one. We would hesitate, in other words, to see it as a product of experiential reality. Herein lies the difference between our mode of thought and the one that held together the late Timurid cultural world. We, for example, shrug off inexplicable coincidences and sudden events, finding it odd if anyone ponders too long and in too public a manner over them. Conversely, in Babur's milieu it would have been considered unwise to leave strange coincidences and patterned occurrences unexamined. An aspect of this difference is located in how "time" was experienced and made cosmologically relevant.[20]

For example, take these two "strange" anecdotes. In relating a battle involving his famous uncle, Husayn Bayqara (r. 1469–1506), the last Timurid ruler of Herat, Babur recorded the role a particularly perilous Wednesday had to play: "It is a strange coincidence (*gharaʾib-i waqiʿa*) that on the very Wednesday on which Sultan-Husayn Mirza defeated Badiʿuzzaman Mirza, Muzaffar-Husayn Mirza defeated Muhammad-Muʾmin Mirza in Astarabad. It is even stranger that a man named Charshamba [Wednesday] un-horsed Muhammad-Muʾmin Mirza and brought him in."[21] Similarly, in another place, Babur commented on how a certain battle had proved to be a fated one for men named Ibrahim: "Some very great begs and superb warriors, such as Ibrahim Tarkhan, Ibrahim Saru, and Ibrahim Jani, were lost in this battle. It is strange (*gharib*) that in one battle three great begs named Ibrahim were lost."[22]

Babur's notes on such patterns of correlated words, names, numbers and dates—which he termed "strange" (*gharib*)—are a reflection of the fact that he was trained and attuned to seek out such resemblances. Importantly, this was not a private pastime but a public one. Indeed, there was a widespread cultural traffic in these signs, which occurred at all levels of society. At the highest stratum, the discovery of hidden patterns was a pleasurable aesthetic and intellectual pursuit of the elite. At the fashionable court of the last Timurid king of Herat, Husayn Bayqara (d. 1506), for example, the most desirable form of verse was the "enigma" (*muʿamma*), in which the listener had to guess the hidden pattern in a poet's couplet.[23] Late in his life, when he could afford to, Babur also patronized a famous "enigmatist" who had previously served Shah Ismaʿil.[24] But there was more to this pursuit than mere aestheticism. The discovery or production of such a pattern—such as a clever verse chronogram to indicate the birth of a prince—was also a political act, useful for offering praise and demonstrating allegiance. Conversely, such metaphorical devices could be used negatively, for delivering curses and insults. But these practices were not simply rhetorical. Rather, they were undergirded by a strong cosmological framework. According to the learned traditions of the time, patterns of letters, words, numbers, and even colors had an association with rhythms of the cosmos. Mastery of a system of knowledge that could encode, decode, and manipulate such patterns was considered to be critical for rulers. Princes were tutored and kings served by those who possessed such knowledge, while Lords of Conjunction like Timur were considered masters of such affairs in their own right.[25]

It is important, then, to view the discovery, production, and consumption of such meaningful patterns as more than an aesthetic activity or literary exercise underwritten by a frivolous court culture. Rather, it should be seen as a widely sanctioned "practical" activity operating in realm of the concrete, that is, not only via words but also through actions and objects. Observe, for example, how one of Babur's Mongol soldiers offered him a gift at the beginning of a war campaign: "Alone Tufan Arghun faced [a man named Ishqullah who was coming toward him], they exchanged sword blows, and Tufan unhorsed his opponent, cut off his head, and brought it while I was passing Sang-i Lakhshak. We took it as a good omen (*shugun*)."[26] Compare this with Timur's encounter with an antinomian dervish, Baba Sangu, on his way to conquer Khurasan in 1385.[27] The holy man, "absorbed" in God (*az ashab-i jazaba bud*), threw a piece of meat at Timur. Timur took the act as a blessing and omen of victory and marched on. Similar accounts of physical or dream appearances of Sufi saints just before battle are common in Timurid chronicles.[28]

Rather than judge these events as true or false or treat them as literary devices, the analytical challenge is to grasp the social process that turned such disparate cultural products—refined verses, dream visions, disembodied heads, pieces of meat—into common operators in a ritual domain. This perspective brings into focus a busy traffic in omens that structured quotidian life as well as crucial moments of war and politics. Illiterate soldiers participated in this exchange with as much enthusiasm as the most learned of courtiers. In effect, this exchange in signs and omen was a "total social fact" that, because of its widespread and compulsory nature, created obligations and provided a type of social glue.[29] Such a system also gave a great deal of power to the brokers of these "strange" cultural products and the masters of this ritual domain. These were the experts in the "sciences of strangeness" (*'ulum-i ghariba*): wise men, philosophers, astrologers, physicians, and dream interpreters who promised to leave no sign unexamined, no dream unexplained, and no event meaningless. No king could ignore their presence or fail to acknowledge them if he was to conquer and rule, for these were the people who kept a finger on the pulse of the body politic and an eye on its health and stability. This will become clear as we examine how rulers such as Babur imagined the characteristics of the land and the qualities of the people they ruled.

THE SACRED KNOWLEDGE OF KINGSHIP

In Babur's description of the valley of Fergana, his father's pastoral dominion, we discover a land of simple pleasures.[30] The fruits—melons, grapes, pears, apricots, pomegranates, and almonds—were excellent and abundant. Running water and pleasant gardens graced a country full of game and sporting birds. The people were feisty, ready with their fists. Not all of Fergana's qualities were so rustic, however. A village near the town of Margilan (also called Marghinan in Arabic) was famous for producing the author of the *Hidaya*, a famous work of Islamic jurisprudence used across Transoxania.[31] But Margilan also supplied Transoxania with its most renowned exorcists, people who could overpower *jinns*.[32] Their service was in great demand in a region where "the custom of exorcism is widespread." High-spirited folk and wayward demons were not the only things to watch out for when visiting Babur's valley. Even parts of the landscape were mischievous. The mountains north of the town of Khodzent made the air unwholesome, causing an inflammation of the eye that did not spare even the sparrows. A similar eye disease in Andizhan, a town known both for a famous musician and its unhealthy air, was called Cancer (*aqrab*) by the physicians. And near the town of Osh, on the lower slopes of the Bara Koh, was a mosque named Gemini (*masjid-i jawza*). In the mountains surrounding Fergana was found the prized red-barked *spiraea* tree. Excellent for making staffs, whip handles, bird cages, and arrows, people also carried it to "faraway places for good luck." If one looked for it, these mountain forests also yielded a plant that Babur thought to be the mandrake—a favorite ingredient of alchemists and sorcerers.

Babur's description of his birthplace is notably free of the discriminations we would make today. Good fruit existed with unwholesome air. Experts in jurisprudence were a source of pride, as were masters of exorcism. Wood that was good for making arrows also brought good luck. Mountains that yielded forest produce also gave magical plants. Diseases were linked to mansions of the zodiac (Cancer), and so were mosques (Gemini). The people, the land, and the cosmos were knitted together into a whole, unmarred by boundaries of taste or relevance that we would erect, such as between the visible and the invisible world, between practical technology and magical technique, and between religious law and supernatural trait. Rather, in giving such detail, Babur seemed to "show off" his deep knowledge of the country. Such knowledge was indispensable for a king to have over any country he acquired.

It was in Kabul, a mercantile entrepôt on the "silk road" to South Asia situated about four hundred miles south of Fergana, that Babur first styled himself king (*padishah*).[33] Kabul was a new territory for Babur. The excitement he betrayed at seeing Canopus (Suhayl), "a brilliant star low on the southern horizon,"[34] indicated that this may have been the first time he had come down this far south. Canopus is a navigational star visible only below a certain latitude in the northern hemisphere. But it was also a sign of fortune (*nishan-i dawlat*) that lifted Babur's spirits, as one of his noblemen recited the following verse:

Canopus, how far do you shine and when do you rise?
You are a sign of fortune to all upon whom your eye lights.

Babur certainly needed the encouragement, having been chased out of his ancestral lands by the Chinggisid Uzbeks. In Kabul, safe from Uzbek depredation, he settled down to rule his new territories and set about "knowing" this country in the same way as he had known Fergana.[35]

In Babur's description of his new territory we get—besides an appreciation of its good fruits, excellent wine, and wholesome air—a picture of a trading crossroads teeming with people from all over Asia. "Every year seven, eight, or ten thousand horses come to Kabul. From Hindustan, caravans of ten, fifteen, twenty thousand pack animals bring slaves, textiles, rock sugar, refined sugar, and spices.... Goods from Khurasan, Iraq, Anatolia, and China can be found in Kabul, which is the principal depot of Hindustan."[36]

With trade came a great diversity in people and languages: "Eleven or twelve dialects are spoken in Kabul Province: Arabic, Persian, Turkish, Mongolian, Hindi, Afghani, Pashai, Parachi, Gabari, Baraki, and Lamghani."[37] Babur enumerated in detail the tribes who lived in his dominion, the places where highwaymen lurked, the passes through the mountains, and sites to ford rivers, and he displayed an impressive knowledge of numerous other useful facts. However, interspersed with this knowledge of the land and its peoples, Babur demonstrated a keen awareness of its sacred places and a curiosity about its miracles.

Near Kabul was a footprint of Khwaja Khizr, an immortal Quranic figure who had once guided Moses and was believed to be still walking the earth to guide saints and emperors.[38] In the district of Alishang, one could visit the tomb of Noah's father, Mehter Lam.[39] In the district of Kunar, Babur circumambulated a shrine where a famous mystic, Mir Sayyid-Ali Hamadani (d. 1384), had died while traveling through this region. These local sites representing globally famous people were not mere curiosities for Babur. Rather, it seems to have been his "policy" to investigate the sacred topography of his new kingdom.

For example, in the year he came to Kabul, Babur was informed about a village shrine where the tomb moved when prayers were offered. Upon arriving at the shrine, Babur saw the miracle with his own eyes. Then he discovered that it was a trick: "They had put a screen over the tomb, which, when they made it move, made it seem as though the tomb was moving, just as it seems to people riding in a boat for the first time that the shore is moving."[40] Although Babur chastised the attendants and had the false screen destroyed, he did not condemn the "spurious" shrine. Instead, he had a proper dome built over it.

The exposure of trickery did not take away from the holiness of a place or the possibility of its sacred nature. Miraculous sites had to be taken seriously, verified, and protected from abuse. Moreover, such places were not merely mentioned in oral lore but also in respectable literary sources. Babur had read in a history book about how Sabuktekin, a tenth-century Turkish ruler of Ghazni, a city not far from Kabul, had defended himself against an attack by an Indian raja by throwing filth in a certain spring. It was written that if this stream was polluted it gave rise to a violent hailstorm. Babur wrote regretfully, "No matter how much I searched for the spring in Ghazni, no sign of it could be found."[41]

Mastery over weather was a crucial weapon of war and rule. No Turkish ruler was without a servant skilled in working the "rain stone" (*yada* or *yat*), useful for bringing down a storm on the enemy or putting out a raging fire.[42] Babur named three of his officers who possessed this skill.[43] One of them worked up a thunderstorm on the Ganges as an impressive display for some visiting Mongol princes. Babur wrote, "I invited the princes on to my boat. Tokhta Buqa Sultan worked the rain stone. A violent wind arose and it began to rain. It was terrible! The weather was so bad that some of us had *ma'jun* [an opiate] even though we had had some the day before."[44] To have such men in imperial service was of strategic significance, just as it was important to find out if the enemy possessed such skills. Babur cited a spy report in which his ally, the Safavid ruler Shah Tahmasb, had gathered a 105,000-man army to attack the despised Uzbeks in Herat. The Uzbeks were reportedly unperturbed, because they planned to deploy expert rainmakers to trap the superior Safavid forces:

The Uzbeks learned of this and, taking no notice of their foe, decided in council as follows: "Let all of us khans and sultans sit in Mashhad. We will assign twenty thousand men to a few princes to encircle the area of the Qizilbash's [the Safavid soldiers] camp and not allow them to stick their heads out. When the Sun enters Scorpio we will order the rainmakers to cause rain, and thus reducing them to inability, we will take them."[45]

What are we to make of Babur's interest in miracle graves, magic springs, saintly footprints, and rain-making stones, which he pursued with as much intellectual vigor as other more "rational" types of knowledge about the peoples and regions he ruled? Were such phenomena little more than sideshows to the "real" political and religious spectacle of court intrigues and transgressions of law that was supposed to concern rulers? Babur, an eminently learned prince, made no such distinctions.[46] These "strange" matters attracted his interest and were brought to his attention in intelligence reports in much the same way as other more mundane affairs. Certainly, one can say that these phenomena enjoyed a reality at the time that is no longer substantial for us. But what is more difficult to grasp is that this reality was given substance not just by false science or blind faith—what we would term magic and superstition—but also by social institutions that shaped thought and channeled curiosity. In other words, pursuit of such knowledge was part of the institution of kingship and indispensable for wielding political authority.

To illustrate this point, let us examine Babur's confrontation with a famous Persian astrologer, Muhammad Sharif. Babur's knowledge and interest in astronomy and astrology is well attested from his writings.[47] This particular astrologer had first come to see Babur and offer his services (*mulazimat*) when the latter had been suffering from a serious illness, unable to leave his tent.[48] Although Babur did not say, it would be safe to assume that Sharif played a role in treating the king. Astrology at the time deeply informed medical knowledge.[49] Babur, for example, once attributed a recurring earache to the cycles of the moon.[50] But astral knowledge was not only a science of the human body; it was also a science of the social body. Just as astrologers could explain choleric irruptions as celestially induced imbalances of humors in the physical body, they could predict rebellion and heresy as cosmically driven disorders in the body politic and suggest the appropriate time for countermeasures. Thus, it was in moments of uncertainty and danger—disease and disturbance—that the "ecumenical" knowledge of physicians and astrologers became critically important.[51] From Babur's own account, we know that battle formations and time of attack were often planned according to the configuration of the planets and their physical location vis-à-vis the army.[52] We can imagine Babur's consternation when on the eve of a momentous battle in India his Iranian astrologer issued the direst of predictions.

In 1527, Babur's hold on his newly conquered Indian territories was fragile. He faced the experienced Rajput warrior Rana Sangha, who possessed an army that had struck fear into the heart of Babur's officers.[53] The morale of Babur's men, unused to Indian conditions and facing a large and disciplined force, had begun to flag. His Hindustani allies had begun to leave him. His own diagnosis of the problem involved the "ill-omened" (*shum nafs*) astrologer:

> At such a time, when there was such hesitation and fear among the soldiers over past events and loose talk, as has been mentioned, Muhammad Sharif the doom-and-gloom astrologer, although he did not dare speak to me personally, with great exaggeration told everyone he met that Mars was presently in the west and anyone who fought from that direction would suffer defeat. The more these disheartened people consulted the prophet of doom, the more disheartened they became.[54]

The way Babur dealt with this challenging situation is revealing. Instead of punishing the difficult astrologer, Babur set about negating his gloomy predictions with a set of propitious measures. First, he publicly declared his intention to renounce wine. Three hundred of his commanders and soldiers joined him in enacting this pledge of temperance. The offensive beverage, many jars of which had been recently brought from Kabul for royal consumption, was either turned into vinegar or poured onto the ground. Babur ordered a step-well to be dug—a particularly Indic act of expiation—in the place where the earth had swallowed up the wine. He also ordered a charitable building built next to the well. He further announced that if the battle was won, Muslims would no longer suffer the infamous *tamgha* tax on trade, a Mongol practice. These two "momentous events"- renunciation of the un-Islamic drink and repeal of the un-Islamic tax—were written up in imperial decrees and "copied and dispatched to the entire realm."[55] Finally, Babur gathered his commanders and made them swear on the Quran that they would hold their ground in battle. Despite these efforts, desertions grew and important Indian commanders abandoned Babur. Some plundered the countryside on their own. Others joined the "infidel" enemy's camp. Nevertheless, with the planets propitiated, somehow Babur's remaining soldiers took heart. The battle was fought and the enemy defeated. At this juncture, one would have expected Muhammad Sharif to make his escape and for Babur to hunt him down. But surprisingly, the astrologer turned up to congratulate the victorious king and received a substantial reward. Babur wrote: "I cursed him roundly and made myself feel much better. Although he was heathenish (*kafirvash*) and pessimistic (*shumnafs*), terribly conceited, and very cold, he had a long service record, so I gave him a lac [hundred thousand] with the proviso that he not remain in my realm."[56]

The fact that Babur offered a large bribe to the troublesome astrologer to leave his kingdom shows the latter's high status and the importance of his ecumenical knowledge. Moreover, the way Babur acted "Islamically," forsaking wine, demonstrates how astrology and Islam were linked together in practice. It was astrological knowledge of possible defeat and loss of sovereignty—not the confrontation with an "infidel" enemy—that led to the invocation of an Islamic ritual of atonement, the giving up of wine. This was no frivolous pledge. Babur swore that he never touched wine again. He simply made do with opium.

To summarize, Babur's actions as a king were structured and constrained by more than just a Mongol code of conduct, Persian ideal of justice, or Islamic tradition of law. In practice, he had to navigate a political landscape enveloped in a web of signs—omens, cosmic patterns, and invisible forces—which were in an important sense more "universal" and "real" than any code, ideal, or legal tradition. Much of the news Babur received and the knowledge he acquired of his enemies, subjects, territories, and army was filtered and colored by this semiotic prism. His astuteness and sagacity, then, is to be measured not by whether he scoffed at such phenomena but by how sensitively he read these signs and acted accordingly, deflecting the foul and incorporating the efficacious ones into his imperial program. But it would not do to reduce such practices too simply to superstition, faith, or political calculation of an individual. Rather, these should be viewed as constituting a domain sustained by social institutions and widespread social practices.[57] The rituals Babur engaged in were not the empty gestures and silent words of a private rite or individual prayer. By reacting ritually, Babur was in fact responding to social situations. By manipulating symbols publicly he was engaging with social institutions and, in the process, mobilizing men and material.[58] He was, in other words, exercising his sovereign agency.

Such public acts absorbed a substantial portion of the king's time and energy. One reason for this was that rulers like Babur had to establish their dominion without a centralizing bureaucratic order and an enumerating, naming, and documenting state. This had to be done, moreover, on a population that was both highly mobile and diverse in terms of ethnicity, religion, and language. An absence of institutions that produced social classifications and fixed social identities should have, on the face of it, led to an unstable polity and incoherent social discourse. The reason this did not occur was because such social institutions did exist, but in forms that were decentralized and distributed across the ecumene.[59] An astute ruler had to locate these cultural sites and demonstrate an ability to engage with them. In a sense, the role of the king and the script of kingship were inscribed in social institutions that were largely outside the control of courtly circles. In the absence of a strong state apparatus, kings engaged with these institutions through a circulating sovereign presence and a mastery of local knowledge.[60] Indeed, reading Babur's memoir one is constantly surprised by how few barriers existed between him and the locals. For example, when he was ruling Kabul, Babur went out on a tour of the autumn harvest and decided to throw a "private" party in his tent. To this, he invited a woman because he had "never seen a woman drink before," a wandering dervish, and a couple of local "men who played the *rubab*."[61] Constant movement of the ruler for military campaigns, hunts, pilgrimage to holy sites, or seasonal migration from summer to winter quarters thus served to bring the body politic under sovereign surveillance and authority. Moreover, this circulation allowed the king both to contribute toward and tap into a network of news and opinion managed by various "knowledge communities."[62] These were communities whose social position was a function not primarily of wealth but of their specialized knowledge of ecumene and society.

Such a perspective on kingship brings into focus the power and privilege of intermediary groups—holy men, Sufis, storytellers, astrologers, and physicians—which are often neglected in scholarship. Such groups controlled key nodes of social knowledge and opinion formation. They also provided access to "affective" knowledge, a window into local idioms of thought and opinion.[63] Their control over local knowledge created spheres of autonomy within the polity and as such provided a check on the ruler's authority. Although the "strange" forms of knowledge these groups dealt in—divination, dream interpretation, astrology, apocalyptic verse, morality tales, miracle stories, and edifying epics—today do not fit into "respectable" categories of religion or politics, at the time they played an important role in the dissemination of political messages and news as well as in the formation of social memory.[64] In other words, the cultural logic of the discourse of "strangeness" becomes more apparent and less strange once we take into account the collective practices and social institutions that sustained it. Armed with these insights, we are ready to take a closer look at Babur's ritual development as a king.

BABUR'S DREAMS OF SAMARQAND

Although Babur is famous today for conquering Hindustan, it was really his early and sustained quest to become the master of Samarqand that forged him as a king. For about twenty years, from the year of his father's death in 1494 until 1513, Babur strove to acquire and rule from Samarqand, a city that, he wrote, had been founded by Alexander, conquered by Arabs in the reign of the third caliph Usman, and made into his capital by Timur. It is difficult to overstate the attraction Samarqand held for Babur, who gave a loving and detailed description of it in his memoir. However, he was only able to realize his dream for short periods of time in 1496, 1500, and 1511.[65]

The first time Babur took Samarqand was two years after his father's death. Being barely fourteen at the time, he only had nominal control over his affairs. Rather, the conquest of Timur's city was a joint project in which the young Timurid was a partner—possibly, a junior one—by dint of his lineage. Babur admitted that victory would not have been possible without the help of Khwaja Qazi, a prominent notable of the region. Khwaja Qazi was the scion of a rich and educated family that had produced many judges (qazi) and high religious authorities, including Shaykh al-Islam. Descended from famous Sufi masters, he had also been a disciple of Khwaja ʿUbaydullah Ahrar (d. 1490), the most famous Naqshbandi saint of the Timurid period, whose leading role in matters of economy, welfare, politics, and war was legendary.[66] Not only were Khwaja Qazi's spiritual credentials impeccable, but he was also a man of considerable means. As a significant show of support for young Babur—who had little to offer his soldiers besides an opportunity to plunder—Khwaja Qazi[67] had distributed eighteen thousand head of sheep among those fighting on Babur's side. However, upon conquest, Babur's men and allies found that the besieged and ravaged city had little left in it to loot, and they began to desert and mutiny. Again, it was Khwaja Qazi who negotiated with the unruly commanders. The negotiations failed, and Babur had to abandon Samarqand, having ruled the city for only a hundred days. In the ensuing skirmishes, Khwaja Qazi was captured by the opposing camp and executed. The news of his death deeply aggrieved Babur, who considered him to be a true saint. He wrote: "What better proves his sainthood (*wilayat*) than that within a short time there was no trace left of those who had him killed? ... His bravery too indicates his sainthood."[68]

The case of the wealthy and saintly Khwaja Qazi shows that Samarqand, like most cities of the region, could not be taken or ruled without support from urban notables who, in this milieu, drew their status from an association with regional Sufi orders. These patrician Sufis did not fit the image of the proverbial world-renouncing mystic. Rather, men like Khwaja Qazi were authority figures who controlled the city with their wealth, prestige, and charitable organizations. From Babur's account and other sources, we know that Naqshbandi leaders could help raise armies, control the city rabble, offer political refuge, intercede in princely disputes, act as ambassadors, and negotiate with conquerors on the city's behalf. They enjoyed a close relationship with royal and aristocratic families, often acting as teachers, tutors, and mentors to youths of noble birth.[69] In short, with their aristocratic connections and local, urban ties, these Sufis—sometimes literally—held the keys to the city and could act as kingmakers.

Unsurprisingly, then, in planning his next attempt on Samarqand in 1500, Babur once again turned to a Naqshbandi leader. This time it was Khwaja Yahya, a son of the renowned Khwaja ʿUbaydullah Ahrar. Babur had high hopes of receiving saintly assistance, because he wrote "if the Khwaja agrees, Samarqand can easily be taken without fighting or battle."[70] Although disappointed when he only received a lukewarm response from the Sufi leader, Babur did not give up. As he sat one day in counsel with his nobles, the discussion turned to how long it would take to conquer the city. All manner of estimates were put forth, some based on pragmatic calculations and others on auspicious ones: "Some said by summer (it was then late autumn), some said a month, some said forty days, some said twenty days. Noyan Kukaldash said 'We'll take it in fourteen days.'"[71] It was to be as the last man had said. The city would be taken—as if by a miracle—in less than a fortnight. The miracle occurred in the shape of a "strange dream" that Babur saw just days before the conquest:

> I dreamed that Khwaja ʿUbaydullah [Ahrar] had arrived and I had gone out to greet him. He came and sat down. The tablecloth must have been laid somewhat unceremoniously before him, for it seemed that he was

offended. Mullah Baba looked at me and motioned. I motioned back as if to say, "it's not my fault. The steward is to blame." The Khwaja understood and accepted this apology. Then he rose, and I rose to escort him. In the entry way he took me by the arm, the right or the left, I don't remember which, and lifted me so that one of my feet was off the ground. In Turkish he said, "Shaykh Maslahat berdi" [Shaykh Maslahat has bestowed (the city)]. A few days later I took Samarqand.[72]

Khwaja ʿUbaydullah Ahrar was, as mentioned earlier, the famous but deceased father of the equivocating Khwaja Yahya. Even though the son—a living saint—did not offer a firm commitment, his father came posthumously in a dream to Babur's aid. The second figure mentioned in the dream, Shaykh Maslahat, was an even more ancient saint whose tomb in Khujand (Khodzent) was a famous pilgrimage site venerated by Timur himself. It was at Shaykh Maslahat's shrine that Babur had found refuge in 1497 after having lost Samarqand the first time.[73] So with the blessing of these two buried but still active saints, Samarqand fell in two weeks, miraculously, without even a fight.

This time around, Babur's control over Samarqand lasted for almost a year. Then the Uzbeks arrived under the command of the dreaded Shaybani Khan. Besieged, with supplies running out, Babur had no choice but to abandon the city once again. The year 1501 was a particularly ignominious one for him. Not only did he lose his prized city, but to secure his freedom he also had to part with his older sister and only sibling, Khanzada Begim, whom Shaybani Khan captured and took as his wife. The nineteen-year-old Babur, defeated and without an army, was pursued by his enemies. After a skirmish, Babur escaped with a few men and hid in a country garden. He sent for help, but his companions betrayed him and sent a message instead to the enemy. Babur sensed that treachery was afoot but resigned himself to fate. As he bowed down in prayer, preparing for death, he fell asleep:

> I dreamed that Khwaja Yaʿqub, son of Khwaja Yahya and grandson of Khwaja Ubaydullah [Ahrar], was coming toward me on a dappled horse, surrounded by a group also mounted on dappled horses. "Grieve not," he said. "Khwaja Ahrar has sent me to you. He has said that we were to assist you and seat you on the royal throne. Whenever you are in difficult straits, think of us and speak. We will be there. Now victory and triumph are coming to you. Raise your head and awake!"[74]

Soon after Babur awoke, a band of riders entered the garden. The men turned out to be Babur's trusted retainers. When asked how they had known where to find Babur, one of them replied that Khwaja Ahrar had informed him in a dream where to find Babur: "When we fled from Akhsi and got separated, I came to Andizhan because the khans had gone there. In a dream I saw Khwaja Ubaydullah [Ahrar] saying, 'Babur Padishah is in a village called Karnon. Go, get him and come, for the royal throne belongs to him.'"[75]

How should we treat the interconnected and patterned dreams of Babur and his men? Reading them in a text, we tend to view dreams as metaphors—as a more poetic way of describing reality. Or we dismiss them as propaganda meant to provide legitimacy and uphold ideology. To take dreams as fact feels like a deeply misplaced empiricism. Our uneasiness toward dreams may be explained by the fact that we, unlike our premodern Muslim counterparts, are neither reared from childhood to retain and recount our dreams nor trained as scholars in the science of dream interpretation. Conversely, in Babur's time, dreams served as emotive metaphors and powerful propaganda tools precisely because dreaming was a social fact: dreaming was a widespread social practice that operated within the cultural logic of "strangeness" described earlier.[76]

Dreams implied a prophetic connection with the invisible world and were considered a highly regarded source of truth.[77] Oneirocriticism, dream interpretation, was both akin to and competitive with astrology as a divinatory science against which even the Islamic legal tradition had few arguments.[78] By the time of the influential scholar Al-Ghazzali (d. 1111), the prophetic power of dreams was generally explained by Plato's theory of the intellect: only when the physical senses were at rest during sleep and could not interfere with the perceptive power of the intellect could it perceive the noblest truths of the world of being. Supported by high philosophy, dreaming was also grounded in everyday discourse. Dreams were a serious topic of public discussion and frequently referenced in religious, political, and military affairs. Not all dreamers were of equal ability and not all dreams of equal value, however. Clear dreams, which required no interpretation, and especially those in which prophetic, saintly, or royal figures appeared, contained the highest truth content.

In sum, the ability to see clear, unambiguous dreams indicated a refined intellect and a pure soul. This gave dreaming a powerful ontological property. By bringing saintly and prophetic figures from the past into the present, dreams could bend time and transmute it, turning profane moments into sacred ones. When seen, dreams could sacralize social relations and, when narrated, they could operationalize political alliances. For example, we saw in the case of Babur and the Naqshbandis how dreams transformed mundane political pacts into spiritual bonds and routine events of war into fulfillments of saintly prophecy. In terms of efficacy, dreams worked in two directions. On the one hand, a dream could touch and change the self of the seer and, on the other hand, it could articulate the self with networks of community. In the latter sense, dreaming was, oddly, a public ritual much like Babur's declarative forsaking of wine. But in the former sense, dreaming could function as a lifecycle ritual that marked the crossing of socially prescribed thresholds in the development of the self. Babur fought countless battles in his life, but he narrated his dreams only during his early and desperate struggle for Samarqand. These dreams, then, must be viewed as marking the rite of passage of a budding Timurid sovereign. It is no accident that these visions occurred at a moment in Babur's life when he was a dispossessed prince in search of dominion—a liminal condition that was an accepted part and expected phase of a Timurid prince's political development.[79]

If Babur's dreams were indeed rituals of sovereignty, then the role of Naqshbandis in them takes on a deeper significance. They reveal how deeply Naqshbandi Sufi families were embedded in the moral and political economy of Transoxania. Sovereignty over the region was theirs to grant. Samarqand could only be acquired through the spiritual intercession of past Naqshbandi saints and the material assistance of living ones. This makes it truly remarkable that in his third and final attempt on Samarqand in 1511, Babur abandoned the Naqshbandis and instead embraced their archnemesis. This was the Sufi brotherhood of the Safavids, which, under its youthful leader Shah Isma'il, had moved beyond the role of kingmaker to claim sovereignty for itself. Between 1501, when he had taken the Aqqoyunlu capital of Tabriz in the west, and 1510, when he defeated the Uzbeks and conquered Herat in the east, Shah Isma'il became the sole sovereign of Iran. But he was no ordinary king. He was also the perfect guide (*murshid-i kamil*) and the messiah. All the prominent Sufi and aristocratic families now faced the same stark choice. They could submit to the new order and accept the political and spiritual overlordship of the Safavid shah and shaykh. Or they could resist and be annihilated.

THE RISE OF SHAH ISMA'IL

The rise of Shah Isma'il was a cataclysm of a magnitude not felt in the region since the conquests of Timur. A twelve-year-old boy had achieved over roughly ten years what no one else had been able to for over a century. Shah Ismaʿil had brought eastern and western Iran under one rule and launched an aggressive assault on Transoxania. His soldiers had accomplished this, moreover, with a ferocity and ruthlessness reminiscent of Timur's methods. It is not surprising that the founder of the Safavid dynasty became, like the earlier Lord of Conjunction, a mythical figure in his lifetime.[80] This is in sharp contrast to Babur, who remained an "ordinary" figure and about whom contemporary sources other than his own memoir have very little to say. To understand the nature of Babur's relationship with Shah Ismaʿil, it is important to develop an appreciation for the popular image and political stature of the latter. For, in the first decade of the sixteenth century, when Babur was scraping together a living by raiding Afghan villages and keeping his sovereign ambitions alive by writing down his dreams in a diary, Shah Ismaʿil was enacting the myth of being a Lord of Conjunction, and news of his invincibility and miraculous victories was echoing across Asia and Europe.

The earliest and richest accounts we have of Shah Ismaʿil are from Italian and Venetian sources that refer to him as the "Sofi."[81] The Europeans had been keenly following the politics of northwestern Iran, because they sought an ally there against the powerful Ottomans, with whom they competed for trade routes. They knew that Shah Ismaʿil's maternal grandmother, the Aqqoyunlu queen Despina Khatun, was a Christian princess from the small Greek kingdom of Trebizond on the Black Sea coast.[82] Consequently, their accounts were full of reports about the rise of a new child-king, son of Martha, who may in fact be a secret Christian. It was believed, erroneously, that in the internecine violence that broke out after the death of Uzun Hasan, the Aqqoyunlu king, Shah Ismaʿil had been given refuge and taught the scriptures by a Christian Armenian priest on an island on Lake Van.[83] This "good priest, who professed to be an astrologer and to know the course of events from the aspect of the heavens, cast his [Ismaʿil's] horoscope and foresaw that he would yet become lord of all Asia."[84] The author of this account knew, however, that Shah Ismaʿil's conquering career came to an abrupt end with his defeat by Ottomans at Chaldiran in 1514. But even then, he observed that "if the [Ottoman] Turk had been beaten, the power of Ismaʿil would have become greater than that of Tamerlane, as by the fame alone of such a victory he would have made himself absolute lord of the East."[85]

Despite the mythical stature of the two conquerors, Shah Ismaʿil's rise to power as Lord of the East is a very different story from how Timur the

Lame had become the Lord of Conjunction. When Shah Isma'il appeared on the political stage, he already had a gilded lineage connecting him to Ali and to the Aqqoyunlu ruler of western Iran.[86] But what made Shah Isma'il different from any other general or prince was his position as the head of the Safavid Sufi order. This gave him a substantial advantage over other claimants to kingship—an ability to recruit and inspire devoted and loyal fighting men. The Safavid Sufi order had become militarized under Shah Isma'il's grandfather, Junayd, who had gathered a number of devotees among nomadic Turkmen tribes. Shah Isma'il inherited this spiritual position from his own father, Haydar. In other words, he did not become a messiah but rather was born as one. In the eyes of his Sufi followers, Shah Isma'il was Ali reborn and divine. It was said that his soldiers prayed in camp facing his tent and trusted him to protect their lives by his miraculous abilities. They were willing to sacrifice their lives for their adolescent perfect spiritual guide (*murshid-i kamil*). An European observer noted:

> This monarch is almost, so to speak, worshipped, more especially by his soldiers, many of whom fight without armour, being willing to die for their master. They go into battle with naked breasts, crying out "Schiac, Schiac," which, in the Persian language, signifies "God, God." Others consider him a prophet; but it is certain that all are of opinion that he will never die.[87]

The devotion of Shah Isma'il's soldiers toward him was something few princes could hope to possess. By contrast, Babur faced great difficulty throughout his life in raising an army of men loyal to him for an extended period of time. What Babur did not have was the elaborate recruitment and indoctrination apparatus of the Safavid Sufi mission (*da'wa*).

Two generations before Shah Isma'il, the Safavids had developed an extensive network of preachers and proselytizers targeting the Turkmen tribes of Anatolia, the southern Caucasus, and Azerbaijan. This network of dervish agents was managed by a hierarchical organization of deputies (*khalifa*) and head deputies (*khalifat al-khulafa*).[88] The message transmitted through this network was that the messiah had arrived and was rallying men of true faith to him. It was a message, moreover, that was designed to resonate with the Alid beliefs and practices already widespread in the region. The gist of these beliefs and practices was the spiritual primacy and divinity of Ali, who, it was expected, would periodically return to earth to end tyranny and establish justice. As mentioned earlier, heresiographical literature of the period termed such groups extremists or exaggerators (*ghulat*), in that they exaggerated the significance of Ali to the point of divinity.[89] However, it is important to realize that for the population that was the target of Safavid agents (*daʿi*), these notions were not heretical in the sense of being a deviation from majority belief but, rather, a significant part of the norm. The "exaggerated" forms of Alid loyalty were prevalent not only in the nomadic Turkmen milieu but also in urban chivalrous organizations and brotherhoods of craft guildsmen across the region.[90] The messianic movements of the previous century—Nurbakhshi, Hurufi, Mushaʿshaʿ, and others—had also paved the way for many of these "strange" ideas and practices to be systematized and made compatible with elite Sufi metaphysics and philosophy, which, it is critical to note, overlapped with the "sciences of strangeness" and the rituals they sustained. In sum, the Safavids did not arise suddenly out of a vacuum but rather evolved gradually—and in keeping with the times—from a sedate, urban, and largely Sunni spiritual brotherhood in Ardabil into a militant, aggressive, and undeniably ghulat mystical order that came to dominate Iran and nearly overtake Ottoman Anatolia.

As a child of about twelve in 1501, it is unlikely that Shah Ismaʿil was directly in charge of the organization. Rather, control in the early years seems to have been in the hands of one of his brother-in-laws, who was also a chief of the Safavid mission (*khalifat al-khulafa*). But Shah Ismaʿil was a crucial symbol for the project as the spiritual guide and messiah. This we can judge from poetry attributed to him, written in a simple Azeri dialect of Turkish, which was used in Safavid missionary propaganda.[91] This poetry is all we have from Shah Ismaʿil, who, unlike Babur, did not leave behind a detailed narrative of his life. In these poems, Shah Ismaʿil claimed to be the embodiment of divine truth (*haqq*), Ali, Jesus, the twelve Shiʿi Imams, and, importantly, great warriors and emperors of the pre-Islamic Iranian past. It is significant that Shah Ismaʿil's verse, written under the pen name Khataʾi (Sinner), became widely adopted as devotional poetry and scripture in different Turkish-speaking Sufi communities and Alid sects in the region.

SUFI MOVEMENTS AND MESSIANIC EXPECTATIONS

One group that preserved the poetry of Khataʾi was the Bektashi Sufi order of Anatolia.[92] The Bektashis were popular among Ottoman soldiers at least since the late fourteenth century and later became recognized as the spiritual order that ministered to the crack slave infantry units known as the Janissaries. The fact that among the soldiers of the "Sunni" Ottomans there had existed a deep affinity for the messianic symbolism of their "Shiʿi" Safavid enemies makes for a complicated military history. For example, when the Ottomans defeated the Safavids in 1514 and captured the latter's capital at Tabriz, they did not consolidate their claims. Rather, they quickly left the region, because they feared that their own soldiers were susceptible to Safavid propaganda.[93] This case highlights the inadequacy of studying this period with labels such as Shiʿi and Sunni, based on doctrinal differences. To avoid being straitjacketed by these labels, we must pay more attention to patterned actions and practices of cultural actors—those "transient examples of shaped behavior"[94] of interest to ethnographers—that informed a common social experience and provided a common social spectacle.

The effectiveness of the Safavid dervish missionaries becomes obvious once seen against the backdrop of the spectacle of "deviant renunciation" that had spread across Anatolia, Iran, Transoxania, and India during this period.[95] There existed in large numbers bands of mendicant dervishes—variously referred to as Qalandars, Abdals, and Haydaris—who were mystics of a type quite unlike the princely Naqshbandi Sufis of Samarqand. Rather than hobnobbing with royalty and funding coups in pursuit of power and status, these renunciants strove to achieve the opposite effect of permanent social marginality. It was not necessarily class, birth, or even education that divided the conformist (*ba sharʿ*) from the deviant (*bi sharʿ*) mystics. Rather, it was how they lived, what they consumed, and the way they adorned their bodies, deliberately breaking as many of society's taboos as possible.

Sixteenth-century reports about these groups relate that instead of keeping beards, these mystics shaved off all of their facial and body hair.[96] They wore nose rings, pierced their bodies, carved out signs on their flesh, tattooed themselves, and went around naked, begging for food. They said they shaved all the hair on their face "to make the mirror of the face more brilliant."[97] They said they shunned clothing because that was the way of Adam, who wore nothing but a fig leaf when he was cast out from paradise. They slept on the ground and were awakened by a horn, the sound of the trumpet of Israfil, the angel who will announce the end of time and summon the dead. They eagerly awaited this moment, for they were already dead to the world, calling themselves the beheaded dead people (*ser buride murde*).[98] They did not adhere to the prescribed rituals of Islam.

Instead, they lit a great fire in the evening, told stories, took intoxicants, and danced in circles, holding hands and singing. They "carried lamps and played tambourines, drums, and horns, at the same time screaming."[99] Suffice it to say, if any of these raucous and unruly friends of God entered a village, city neighborhood, or military encampment, it would be difficult to take one's eyes off them. And, what would one see? In all his glory, Ali!

Ali's name or an image of his double-tipped sword Zulfiqar would be tattooed across their chests. They wore collars around their necks as slaves of Ali. They would carry a hatchet of Abu Muslim, the epic defender of the Alids, whose heroic deeds regaled and inspired people all over the region. Like Abu Muslim, they were ready to fight the enemies of Ali. They would swear vengeance for Ali's family by reciting apocalyptic verse by poets such as Nesimi and Khata'i.[100] They carried a horseshoe belonging to Duldul, Ali's famous mule.[101] When they begged for alms, they did so in the name of the King of Men (Shah-i Mardan), Ali. They would wear a tall conical hat with twelve gores signifying the twelve Imams, that is, Ali and his eleven rightful successors. On four sides of the hat would be written the Muslim profession of faith and the names of the Prophet, Ali, and his two sons, Hasan and Husayn.

In sum, these antinomian dervish groups were the bodily instantiation of the messianic myth of Ali. As they moved across the land, they reinscribed this myth in social memory, reminding all who saw and heard them of its key symbols and narratives. They were ideally suited to do so, for they cut a figure that was awesome and jarring, eye catching and repulsive, sacred and dangerous. One can imagine the worry they engendered among those in authority, because these ascetics—drugged, armed, and hard to control—were often very popular among those not in authority. They presented a dilemma for kings. While rulers boasted in proclamations and edicts how they had put an end to such groups, in practice they deftly accommodated these spectacular deviants and used their gripping displays of religiosity to enhance their own charisma.[102] Thus, when a screaming, naked dervish threw a piece of meat at Timur, the Lord of Conjunction wasted little time in declaring it an omen of victory.[103] For all he knew, it was a gift from Ali.

As much as any text of prose or poetry, it was the visual, aural, and somatic culture kept alive by these antinomian mystics that gave Alid symbols and narratives the force of truth. Through them, the fantastic and miraculous tales of Ali and his partisans were made substantial and real.[104] There was a parallel and related development in elite culture at this time, in which Ali's image as a hero of Islam was given a coherent symbolic and visual form. Beginning in the thirteenth century, after the Mongol invasion, Ali began to be depicted and painted in both historical and literary texts produced in Iran.[105] In the fifteenth century, Ali's painted image had developed standardized details—he was shown apart from the crowd as red-haired, veiled, and haloed, with his sword Zulfiqar and his mule Duldul. Notably, in European accounts, Shah Isma'il's physical descriptions match the painted image of Ali. The Safavid king was said to be a handsome and agile youth with red hair who, some said, veiled his face.[106] With the air thick with the expectation of the rise of Ali's heir and of Ali's own bodily return, the fact that the lore surrounding Shah Isma'il depicted him with features matching the popular and painted likeness of Ali is too striking to be ignored. Whatever may be the case, one thing is certain. Shah Isma'il had little choice in how he would be imagined and remembered. The Safavid dervish missionaries and soldier devotees had already decided on the messianic template. Shah Isma'il was destined to perform the role he had been born into as the legatee of Ali.

MAKING THE BODY OF IRAN SAFAVID

Shah Isma'il's conquests were achieved both by a whirlwind of savage violence and a scheme of flexible political accommodation. Later Safavid historians would have us believe that his first priority upon gaining the throne was the imposition of doctrinal Shi'ism on the largely Sunni population of Iran. But the situation at the time was far more complex and interesting. Shah Isma'il's main power base was his Qizilbash soldier devotees, who considered him to be their perfect guide and messiah. They were not in the least interested in changing their religious ways, many of which were informed by the deliberately deviant practices of antinomian dervish orders. There was an immediate need, on the other hand, to put a Safavid stamp on the administrative structures and sociopolitical arrangements of previous rulers. The early Safavid response to these conflicting needs was to use a religious idiom of power that was not doctrinal and legalistic but symbolic and corporeal. In many ways, this was to be expected of a Sufi organization with well-established rituals of initiation, incorporation, and submission of disciples. Accordingly, the initial Safavid domination of the body politic of Iran took place not by the imposition of a new code of law but via the enactment of a politics of the body.

The most visible symbol of the new order was the Safavid crown or *taj* known as the Taj-i Haydari (Crown of Haydar).[107] According to Safavid tradition, Ali had come in a dream to Shah Isma'il's father, Shaykh Haydar, in 1487 and given him instructions to make a distinctive taj. This consisted of a hat topped by a tall red baton with twelve facets (*tark*), around which a turban could be tied. The red crown, whose wearers began to be called Red-heads (Qizilbash), was worn by the Safavid order as a mark of devotion to Ali and to his heir incarnate, the Safavid perfect guide (*murshid-i kamil*). Although called a crown, it did not mark the leader of a group. Rather, its function was the opposite, to incorporate the wearer into the body of the group. As the Safavid order became militarized, this practice was extended into the political domain. To become a partner in the Safavid project, one had to replace one's headgear with the Safavid hat. If later Safavid court paintings are any indication, this requirement was most vigorously and broadly enforced in the time of Shah Isma'il, when courtiers of every rank wore the red taj.[108]

The donning of a new headgear must be seen as more than just a cosmetic change. The form of one's clothes, the shape of one's hat, and the type of symbols that decorated one's body were dictated by more than just aesthetic taste. Swapping one set of apparel for another meant adopting a new social personality and its attendant norms of comportment.[109] Moreover, the significance of such an act was widely understood and reported. European accounts of the Safavids, for example, describe the shape of the red Safavid taj and relate how it was used in formal ceremonies of submission involving the defeated Uzbek princes who, it was said, exchanged their green "caftans" for the red ones of the Safavids.[110] In effect, the imposition of the red Safavid crown must be seen within an ensemble of practices sustaining and sustained by a "highly corporeal religious imagination"[111]—that is, an imagination focused on bodily submission, incorporation, and destruction.

An important corporeal practice involved the ceremony of the Chub-i Tariqat (Stick of the Path).[112] In this ceremony, which one observer called a "wedding," courtiers were bonded to the Safavid shah by an officiant of the Safavid Sufi order. The rite was open to anyone the shah invited, including non-Muslims. The Venetian-Cypriote envoy Michele Membré, for example, was shown favor by Shah Tahmasb, the son of Shah Isma'il, when he was asked to participate in the ritual. Membré described his experience as follows:

> The *khalifa* [deputy] has a substantial wooden stick, and begins from the first to the last; one by one they all come for love of the Shah to the middle of the room and stretch themselves out on the ground; and the said *khalifa* with the stick gives them a most mighty blow on the behind; and then the *khalifa* kisses the head and feet of the one he has given the blow; then he himself gets up and kisses the stick and thus they all do, one by one; so, as I was sitting then came to be my turn, and the villain, who had a pair of cloth breeches, gave me a blow which still hurts.[113]

Much like the red Safavid crown, the stick of the Safavid *khalifa* melded the bodies of the shah's disciples into one obedient and orderly social body.

Another more grisly way of demonstrating loyalty to the shah consisted of the frenzied devouring of the body of his enemy. Reportedly, one victim of this ritual act was the Uzbek ruler Shaybani Khan, whose muddied and bloodied corpse was eaten by a stampeding crowd of Qizilbash soldiers when Shah Isma'il said "whoever among our sincere soldiers (*qurchiyan-i kathir al-ikhlas*) and special servants (*mulaziman-i kathir al-ikhtisas*) loves our imperial head (*sar-i navab-i humayun-i ma*) should partake of the flesh of this enemy."[114] It has been observed that this transgressive act of cannibalism was a demonstration of the Qizilbash disciples' loyalty to the shah in a deeply affirmative sense—by the consuming together of tabooed flesh—as well as in a negative sense, by the corporeal destruction of all other possibilities of sovereignty.[115]

These bodily rituals used to uphold Shah Isma'il's sovereignty can be used to make sense of the larger pattern of social accommodation and annihilation that occurred in his reign. It is well known that organized Sufi orders declined under Safavid rule.[116] However, this decline was gradual, and many mystical brotherhoods survived for generations. Their fate depended for the most part on how they responded to the new Safavid regime. For example, the important Ni'matullahi Sufi order, which spanned Iran and South India, thrived for over a century by accepting the Safavids' messianic claim. The Ni'matullahis seems to have paid for Safavid patronage in the ecumenical coin of "strangeness." Their founder, Shah Ni'matullah Wali, who has been called the Nostradamus of the East, was famous for his mystical and divinatory poetry, which was used to predict the end of time and change in religion and politics.[117] Under the Safavids, the Niʿmatullahis produced proof that Shah Niʿmatullah's verse had predicted the rise of the Safavids as the expected messianic order.[118] As part of the accommodation, the Niʿmatullahis not only retained control over their major shrine complex in Yazd but also received choice posts in Safavid religious administration, married into the Safavid royal family, and even played an important role in dynastic politics.

Not all Sufi orders were so fortunate. Not even being openly Shiʿi guaranteed an order's survival if its leaders refused to submit or developed dangerous ambitions. The Nurbakhshi brotherhood, for example, had strong Shiʿi leanings even before the rise of the Safavids.[119] This may have been why Nurbakhshis received favor from Shah Ismaʿil, who initially enlarged Nurbakhshi land holdings in Rayy. Even when Nurbakhsh's son was tortured to death by Ismaʿil for reasons that remain unknown, the family continued to hold sway in Rayy. It was only when Nurbakhsh's grandson, Shah Qawwam al-Din, began to build castles and fortifications during Shah Tahmasb's reign that he was arrested, executed, and the order suppressed. The suppression of a Sufi order meant the destruction of its shrine or its incorporation into an Alid-Safavid symbolic order. The place of Sufi shrines across Iran was taken over slowly during the sixteenth and seventeenth centuries by holy sites dedicated to the Shiʿi imams and their progeny. However, in the early Safavid period, shrine destruction and grave desecration appears to have been patterned not by a systematic imposition of juridical Shiʿism but by a logic of imperial conquest and local resistance.

When the Safavids conquered Baghdad, their soldiers desecrated the grave of the famous Sunni jurist Abu Hanifa.[120] His bones were dug up and burned. The same thing occurred with the graves of Naqshbandi figures, such as the famous saint and poet Jami, in Herat. One could argue that these acts showed a pattern of anti-Sunni acts of the Safavids. While there is no denying the dissonance between Qizilbash practices and those of Sunni Islam, such violence needs to be examined within the context of how armed resistance was punished and political vendettas settled. In the early Safavid period, this meant the destruction of the body of the local ruler or of the local holy site, which was often the grave of a revered saint linked to the ruler's sovereignty.[121] Moreover, this practice affected not only Sunnis but also rebellious Shiʿi, Ismaʿili, and even ghulat groups.[122] Thus, when some of the Qizilbash rebelled against Safavid imperial policies aimed at restricting their power within the realm, one of the ways they were punished was by the destruction of the shrine of Abu Muslim, the epic Alid hero who was a central figure in Qizilbash religious imagination.[123]

In sum, those who played by the new rules were incorporated into the Safavid symbolic order. Sunni and Sufi elites were encouraged to join the Safavid project on the condition that they demonstrated their loyalty by wearing the red headgear. Without the help of these established families, the Safavids would not have succeeded. This is why when Shah Ismaʿil defeated Shaybani Khan and wanted to conquer Samarqand, he chose to enlist Babur, a Timurid experienced and motivated in taking this important city in Transoxania. The way Babur received a message of friendliness from Shah Ismaʿil was again corporeal. Shah Ismaʿil returned to him his sister Khanzada Begum—rescued from the camp of the defeated Uzbeks—whom Babur had surrendered to Shaybani Khan in Samarqand ten years earlier.

BABUR THE QIZILBASH

Babur's memoir is mostly silent about the rise of Shah Ismaʿil, containing only six brief but mostly respectful mentions of him. Moreover, Babur does not allude to Shah Ismaʿil's messianic pretensions or openly disparage his religion. This is surprising, given the savage treatment meted out to the population of Timurid Herat under the Safavids. Unfortunately, we do not have Babur's account of the years in which Shah Ismaʿil came east, defeated the powerful Uzbeks, conquered Herat, and enrolled Babur in his plans to take Samarqand and Transoxania. There is a large gap in Babur's text from 1508 to 1519.[124] In the extant portions, Babur passes little comment on Shah Ismaʿil's heretical reputation. Instead, he reserves his most venomous remarks for the Uzbek Shaybani Khan. From Babur's perspective, the "Shiʿi" Shah Ismaʿil Safavid had done him a great favor by eliminating the "Sunni" Uzbek who had for so long shamed the Timurids with his subjugation of their territories in Transoxania and Khurasan. This again shows how doctrinal labels are of little use in understanding the politics of the time. Yet religious symbols and rituals played an important role in royal affairs. To resolve this paradox, we need to focus less on doctrine and more on practice. This shift in perspective makes clear how well attuned Babur and his fellow Timurids were to the "strange" rituals of the Safavids.

Shah Ismaʿil and his followers were not the only ones swept up in the messianic expectations of the time. Babur related how the people of

Herat, facing annihilation at the hands of the Uzbeks in 1507, also tried to seize the moment. But the Timurid princes of Herat were too refined and unwarlike to be given the role of divinely appointed saviors.[125] Rather, it fell to the lot of an important Mongol nobleman, Zu'n-Nun Arghun, to confront the massive Uzbek army. Babur described the manner of his selection and motivation:

> He held such a position of authority and importance in Herat that several Shaykhs and Mullas went to him and said, "We are in touch with the Qutb [*axis mundi*]. He has named you 'Lion of God,' (Hizibrullah) and you will conquer the Uzbeks." He swallowed this praise and, throwing a shawl around his neck, said prayers of gratitude. When Shaybani Khan had defeated the mirzas one by one at Badghis, Zu'n-Nun, believing those words to be true, faced Shaybani Khan at Kara Robat with a hundred or 150 men. A large contingent came forth, seized them, and took them away. Zu'n-Nun was executed.[126]

The unfortunate Zu'n-Nun Arghun was told that the hidden master saint of the age had named him the Lion of God (a famous title of Ali, recognizing his bravery in battle). Thus inspired, he rose up as a messianic champion to confront the Uzbeks with only a few hundred men. A miraculous victory was so widely expected that "the fortress was not made fast, battle weapons were not made ready, reconnoiterers and scouts were not sent to give information on the enemy's advance, and the army was not adequately prepared for battle."[127] The man responsible for this scheme was a courtier, Kamaluddin Husayn, whom Babur called a self-declared Sufi (*mutasawwif*). It was plausibly a dream vision of the mystically inclined Kamaluddin, known for his deep knowledge of sainthood and kingship and for the divinatory science of *jafr*, that set the whole "strange" affair in motion.[128] Babur admired the Mongol amir's bravery but called him "a bit of a fool" for falling for such flattery. Nevertheless, Babur had nothing disparaging to say about Shah Isma'il, whose reputation as Ali reborn was well known. In fact, when the Safavid "Lion of God" defeated the Uzbeks three years later and conquered Herat, Babur willingly put on the red, twelve-gored crown of Haydar and joined the rank of Shah Isma'il's Qizilbash devotees.

Babur was well aware that to join the Safavids meant becoming a disciple of the shah and submitting oneself to Qizilbash rituals. Indeed, some of these customs were not that different from Timurid norms practiced in court and camp. For example, the Timurids also paid attention to the design of their turbans. In his memoir, Babur described in detail the way his father used to tie his turban and how he always wore it when holding court, even in the heat of summer, when he would usually don the lighter Mongol cap.[129] The style of a man's turban signified his allegiance to a group. During battle, when soldiers deserted and crossed over to the opposing camp, they did so turban in hand.[130] Moreover, Babur was used to stringent bodily regimes that dominated the Timurid's Mongol-style court ceremonies.[131] His own military experience included expiatory and talismanic rites little different than those of the Qizilbash. He described battles in which fighting was "enjoined without armor"[132] and protective charms used.[133] His soldiers could be as rowdy and uncontrollable as the frenzied Qizilbash warriors. Discipline had to be imposed by shooting arrows into an unruly group or by summary dismemberment of two or three men. Once, such a disciplinary action led to the accidental death of a favorite storyteller of Babur's son, Humayun.[134] While we do not know what stories this unfortunate man used to tell the prince and his men, it would be surprising if they did not include the heroic tales of Lords of Conjunction such as Abu Muslim and Amir Hamza.[135]

Like the Safavids, Babur also followed the wartime practice of desecrating graves. In one of his punitive raids against the rebellious Yusufzai and Dilazak Afghans, he destroyed a local shrine commemorating a dervish named Shahbaz Qalandar, who, Babur said, had led these tribes into heresy (*ilhad*).[136] Nevertheless, religious deviancy was not an impediment for Babur in seeking an alliance with the most notorious "heretic" of his time, Shah Ismaʿil.

Babur had no delusions about Shah Ismaʿil's messianic claims. He mentioned how one of his cousins, a son of Husayn Bayqara, became "a devotee (*murid*) of Shah Ismaʿil" and "died astray in that heresy (*batalat o gumrahi*) in Astarabad."[137] When his own turn came, however, a contemporary chronicler politely wrote how Babur sent "eloquent ambassadors with generous gifts to the fortune-adorned threshold [of Shah Ismaʿil] and made manifest his sincerity and fealty."[138] In return, Shah Ismaʿil provided military assistance and promised Babur control over any territory he could take from the Uzbeks in Transoxania. With Qizilbash help, Babur was able to conquer Samarqand for the third time in 1511. However, this time he would rule not as a Timurid sovereign but as a Safavid satrap. His cousin, Mirza Haydar Dughlat, who had accompanied him as a child, described how the populace of Samarqand greeted Babur with a display of overwhelming joy. But their delight soon turned to consternation when they saw that he had adorned himself with the "garments" of the Qizilbash, which was "pure heresy, nay almost unbelief.... [The people] sincerely hoped, when he mounted the throne of Samarqand (the throne of the Law of the Prophet), and placed on his head the diadem of the holy Sunna of Muhammad, that he would remove from it the crown of royalty, whose nature was heresy and whose form was as the tail of an ass."[139]

Babur disappointed the people of Samarqand. He did not take off the Qizilbash taj, with its tall red baton sticking out like "the tail of an ass." Instead, he kept his agreement with Shah Isma'il and had coins struck with the names of the twelve imams and the Alid formula ʿali wali allah (Ali is God's appointee/friend/saint).[140] Babur could not fight off the Uzbeks without Safavid help. So he "overlooked the gross errors" of the Qizilbash.[141] We do not know what the Qizilbash did at Samarqand. But if their antics in Herat are any model to go by, it would have included extortion of treasure via torture; harassment of the clergy and lay people by forcing them to curse publicly the first three caliphs, who were considered rivals of Ali; and the desecration of the graves of Naqshbandi Sufi saints.[142] Babur could do little to check their aggression in the region and lost the support of the locals. For example, when the Safavid general Najm al-Din Thani ordered a general massacre (qatl-i ʿamm) of the people in the fortress of Qarshi, near Samarqand, which led to the killing of fifteen thousand people, including many locals, Babur could not prevent it.[143] Afterward, when the Uzbeks attacked Samarqand, he went out to fight them. Upon returning defeated to the city, however, he was "unable to get a firm footing upon the steps of the throne" and had to bid "farewell to the sovereignty of Samarqand."[144] A pro-Uzbek author, Ruzbihan Khunji, who was present in Samarqand during Babur's defeat, poured scorn on him for becoming a Qizilbash in the following verse:

> That horde scattered again from the gates of Samarqand
> Toward Hisar they fled like veiled women
> Babur enjoyed sovereignty till he remained a Sunni
> When he sided with a heretic (rafizi), he came to regret his decision.[145]

Such were the insults the descendants of Babur had to face. Although his later conquest of Hindustan seems like a redeeming accomplishment, this view reflects our perspective more than that of sixteenth-century Mughals. Mughal rituals of sovereignty and symbols of kingship were deeply informed by their knowledge of Safavid practices and of what Babur (and later his son Humayun) had to go through as disciples of the Safavid shah. Timurid sovereignty was severely undermined by Babur's discipleship to Shah Isma'il. As the next two chapters show, a considerable amount of ritual and symbolic effort came to be expended by Babur's son and grandson, Humayun and Akbar, to restore Timurid sovereignty. However, here, the final question that will detain us is: with the expulsion of Babur from Transoxania and the end of Timurid rule in Iran, what happened to the cultural memory of Timur Sahib Qiran? Did it disappear with the rise of Ali's heir? To answer this, we must examine how Shah Isma'il saw himself as a king. Although we do not have his own views on the subject, we can infer a great deal from the actions he took once he became the ruler of unified Iran.

SHAH ISMA'IL, THE LORD OF CONJUNCTION

While Shah Isma'il was considered to be the embodiment of Ali by his Qizilbash devotees, his own ambitions were much broader and more "universal." This can be seen in the way he named his sons. None of the Safavid princes have a Shi'i or Alid name. They do not even have Arabic Muslim names. Instead, they have names of heroes from the epics of pre-Islamic Iran, the *Shahnama* (Book of Kings) and the *Khawarnama* (Book of Khawar): Sam, Bahram, Tahmasb, Alqasp, and Rustam. Notably, this is in sharp contrast to how his successor, Shah Tahmasb, named his own sons after Alid figures.[146] Shah Isma'il's fascination with the *Shahnama* can also be judged from many other sources. As mentioned before, in his poetry Shah Isma'il called himself the reincarnation of Islamic figures as well as of those from pre-Islamic Iran celebrated in the *Shahnama*: "I am Faridun, Khusraw, Jamshid, and Zahhak; I am Zal's son (i.e., Rustam) and Alexander."[147] On the battlefield, he is said to have rallied his soldiers by shouting verses from the *Shahnama*. Oral legends of the manner of Shah Isma'il's birth bear a striking similarity to anecdotes about the birth of the hero Sam in the *Shahnama*.[148] The pervasiveness and seriousness of these references to ancient Iranian lore makes it difficult to dismiss them as mere rhetoric.

Even if we set aside the puzzle of why an Alid messiah would inspire his men by invoking champions of Zoroastrian Iran, it is more difficult to ignore the naming of princes after heroes of a pre-Islamic past. This is because naming was not merely a rhetorical practice. Rather, it was a cosmologically informed act—an act with "strange" consequences and one that had to be performed with consultation and care. Babur, for example, named one of his sons "Hindal" because the boy was born while Babur was on his way to conquer "Hind" (India), a good omen.[149] On the face of it, Shah Ismaʿil's deep commitment to the Iranian epic tradition is just as difficult to reconcile with his image as a promoter of doctrinal Shiʿism as are the shockingly deviant practices of his Qizilbash devotees—that is, until we remind ourselves that this was the age of Lords of Conjunction.

In this age, the "time" of kingship was based on the cyclical motion of the cosmos, which was thought to dictate the rise and fall of dynasties and religions. Moreover, sovereignty was shared by and rotated among Lords of Conjunction—both prophets and kings, saints and conquerors. It was widely accepted that the Arab Islamic past had provided the world its great prophets and the Zoroastrian Iranian past its great kings. Whether it was in works of astrological history or in oral epic literature, figures from these two pasts were considered equally "historical" and coexisted interchangeably in popular and political imagination.[150] There were certainly attempts to contain this confusion and to keep apart the two orientations in separate genres—the Arab Islamic one in the chronicle tradition and the Iranian Zoroastrian one in the epic and storytelling genre—but it would be a mistake to think that these attempts were successful, especially during this period. This is evident from the cultural production of Shah Ismaʿil's reign, which transcended these generic boundaries and blended the Iranian and Islamic orientations toward the past. This cultural production, moreover, was based directly on Timurid practices of kingship.

When Shah Ismaʿil captured Timurid Herat in 1510, he acquired the best artists, poets, and writers of the eastern Islamic world. To celebrate his centennial feat—the reunification of Iran—he commissioned not chronicles but paintings and epics. In terms of painting, the most famous of all Safavid works remains the illustrated Persian epic, the *Shahnama* (Book of Kings). Work began on it in the early 1520s under Shah Ismaʿil and was carried out for another twenty years or more under his successor Shah Tahmasb. The Safavid version of the *Shahnama* was produced and painted with such finesse, bringing together the "Turkmen" style of art associated with Shiraz and Tabriz with the eastern "Timurid" one of Herat, that to this day it remains unsurpassed as an example of Persian miniature painting. This was not merely a "secular" act of celebration, however. A painting in this pre-Islamic Iranian epic depicted the Prophet,

Ali, and his sons Hasan and Husayn together on a ship at sea, all wearing the Taj-i Haydari.[151] It was as if Iran and Islam had become one under the sign of the Safavids.

Given the high cultural import of the "Book of Kings," it is significant that in 1510 Shah Ismaʿil commissioned a "personalized" epic to celebrate his own heroic deeds in the versified form of the *Shahnama*. Appropriately, it was called *Shahnama-i Ismaʿil* (The Book of Kings of Ismaʿil).[152] In it, Shah Ismaʿil performs the role of the quintessential epic hero who was more than a match for the Iranian champions of yore: he makes a drinking cup out of Isfandiyar's skull, he uses the ring in Rustam's ear as his lasso, and he scalps Jamshid and uses the skin to fashion a war drum out of the latter's famous goblet (*jam*).[153] As far as Islamic symbols are concerned, the descriptions of Shah Ismaʿil contain heavy Alid and Sufi overtones: his sword is compared to Ali's sword Zulfiqar, he is called the monument (*yadgar*) of the Prophet's family and the star of the twelfth mansion of the zodiac, his position is equated with that of the mahdi, and his Sufis (*sufiyan*) and hereditary disciples (*muridan-i ajdad-i u*) are shown arrayed ready for battle.[154] His plans to conquer the world follow the plot of other Lords of Conjunction, both epic (Hamza and Ali) and historical (Alexander, Chinggis, and Timur); they include the territories of Shirvan, the two Iraqs (Persian and Arab), Egypt, Georgia, Syria, Rum, Khurasan, and India.[155] At one point, the story takes a legendary turn when the presence of demons (*dev o dad*) is reported in Isfahan and Shah Ismaʿil sends a troop of soldiers to fight them off.[156] But for the most part, the epic remains grounded in real events. This is not to say, however, that it is a historical narrative. The battle of Chaldiran against the Ottomans, which Shah Ismaʿil lost, is not mentioned.[157] The conquest of Samarqand, on the other hand, is mentioned, but Babur's name does not come up.[158] In short, as a mixture of fact and fiction, history and legend, this work defies characterization—unless, of course, we describe it as a narrative of "Lord of Conjunctionship" (Sahib Qirani).[159] Indeed, the epic constantly refers to Shah Ismaʿil as Sahib Qiran.

The large number of surviving manuscripts attests to the popularity of Shah Ismaʿil's epic among the kings and nobility of early modern India and Iran.[160] In many of these manuscripts, moreover, this epic is paired with the earlier, similar work on Timur, the Herati poet Hatifi's *Timurnama* (Book of Timur) on which it was modeled.[161] The literary practice of celebrating the achievements of a living or recently deceased king in an epic—as opposed to commemorating a legendary emperor like Alexander—had been pioneered by the Timurids. That Shah Isma'il wanted to continue this literary practice can be seen in his choice of Hatifi as the first author of his personal *Shahnama*.[162] Thus, the similarity between Timur and Shah Isma'il was not lost on posterity. His son Sam Mirza, a well-known writer and anthologist, also called Shah Isma'il the "late Sahib Qiran."

Later Iranian and Indian historians did not have a problem recognizing the value of Shah Isma'il's epic. They used it liberally as a source of poetry, beautiful phrases, and even to describe "mythical" moments such as the versified correspondence between the young shah and his guardian, in which Isma'il decides to make his initial messianic manifestation or "emergence" (*khuruj*).[163] Most telling, however, is the observation of the traveler Michele Membré, who visited Iran in the decade after Shah Isma'il's death. He wrote that "mountebanks" sitting in town squares would read from books the tales of the "combats of . . . Shah Isma'il."[164] Whether this book of stories was the above-mentioned epic of Shah Isma'il, we do not know. But we do know that much like Timur, the founder of the Safavid dynasty had become a legendary and messianic sovereign in his own right.

CONCLUSION

These were strange times indeed. Babur, the heir of Timur, became a devotee of Ali. Shah Isma'il, a son of Ali, became another Timur. If an artist of Timurid Herat was to depict our bafflement, he would do so with the stylized gesture of a forefinger raised to the lips. The goal of this chapter was to confound some of the received categories of Mughal historiography by bringing them into dialogue with those of Safavid historiography. This is necessary if we are to see what shape kingship was taking in the eastern Islamic world a hundred years after Timur.

What we find is a formative moment that was not yet part of either a Mughal future or a Safavid one. In this moment, a few major symbols were available for making a claim to power. One was Ali and another Timur. The Timurids, however, were by this time too weak to make effective use of either of these. Babur, for all his trying, remained a minor king for most of his life. The first quarter of the sixteenth century belonged instead to Shah Isma'il, the descendant of Ali who conquered Iran and assumed the trappings of Timurid kingship. Oddly, our knowledge of the two men is inversely proportional to their fame. Babur, an unknown prince in his time, is intimately familiar to us because of the "historical" memoir he left behind. Shah Ismaʿil, the famous conqueror, remains impossibly remote, as a Sufi king about whom we have more legends, poems, and rumors than "history." Between Babur's history and Shah Ismaʿil's myths, however, we have enough to develop a composite picture of kingship.

From Babur's detailed account, we get a sense of the ritual and symbolic realm a ruler had to negotiate. Even though he was a Muslim king ruling over a largely Muslim population, the aspect of religion that he had to interact with had little to do with law and doctrine. Instead, much of his time was spent in engaging with embodied symbols and performed myths. This aspect of kingship is difficult to recover from Babur's writing, however, without developing an appreciation of the learned cosmology and the embodied practices of the time. Rather than being separated by social strata, elite knowledge and popular practices coexisted in harmony, one often reinforcing the other. An aspect of this coexistence can be explained by the shared participation of all classes in the religious life of the period dominated by shrine-based Sufism. This is also evident in the way rulers like Babur had to share power, prestige, and material wealth with local Sufi families. These bonds between princes and mystics were not merely those of pragmatic politics; they were also reinforced by religious education and popular rites.

From such a world, then, it is not difficult to imagine the emergence of a figure like Shah Ismaʿil. As a regional Sufi leader with strong links to the local royal dynasty, he too was a product of the symbiosis of kingship and sainthood that had developed by this time. But he was not just a Sufi master. He was also born to perform a mythical role as Ali's messianic heir. As we saw in the last chapter, Timur and his immediate successors had also tried to engage with the messianic myth of Ali. But they had lacked the institutional wherewithal to deploy it effectively. Shah Ismaʿil, on the other hand, inherited an organization in which the Alid myth was already operationalized.

The Safavid missionary organization opens up a vista onto yet another realm of practice, that of antinomian mendicancy. These unruly mystics, notable for their affected marginality and exaggerated deviance, represented one more link between the wider social world and the realm of kingship. Many of the Alid symbols they kept alive provided a charismatic draw for kings, strong echoes of which can be found in the courtly paintings and royal epics of the time. In sum, we find a great deal of innovation in the style and practice of kingship, much of it derived from the institutions, cosmology, and rituals of the different types of Sufism that dominated the social and religious life of this period. There was a tremendous willingness to invent new rituals and symbols or to adapt old ones to new situations. Doctrinal religious categories of Islam preserved in texts did not drive or constrain kings and sovereigns as much as symbols that were embodied and performed. Accordingly, rulers valued doctors of religion and ritual specialists less for their interpretation of law and doctrine and more for their "strange" and socially inflected knowledge of time and cosmology.

These insights have the potential to change radically the way the story of Mughal kingship in South Asia is told. Seen from the perspective of South Asian historiography, the Mughals entering from Kabul appear as another Muslim dynasty that brought Sunni Islam to India. Once there, the Mughals are said to have softened their Islamic ways and adapted themselves to the practices of their Hindu subjects. In this version of history, little consideration is given to the flexible, innovative, and evolving nature of Muslim kingship that the Mughals brought with them from the extremely diverse religious and social environment of Iran and Central Asia. In other words, we need to question how rigidly doctrinal or legalistic were these Islamic institutions of rule to begin with and emphasize instead their foundation of symbolic and corporeal practices, which were readily adaptable to the social and religious situation in India. This, then, is the task taken up in the remaining chapters, which focus on the establishment of Mughal rule in South Asia.

{4} THE ALCHEMICAL COURT

THE BEGINNINGS OF THE MUGHAL IMPERIAL CULT

Humayun, one of the greatest kings in the world, had five lac [100,000] troops and 12,000 elephants. Then . . . he became so vain as to claim divine powers. His occasional appearance to the people was described as divine effulgence (*jalwa-i quddusi*). In his entire dominion and in his army, the Shariʿat was abrogated and heresy (*ilhad*) and evil prevailed. One day he called a meeting of his notables, soothsayers and astrologers and said he had seen in a dream that the moon, the sun and stars had come down to the foot of his throne. The soothsayers and astrologers said that the position of the heavenly bodies confirmed the purport of the dream and that the Sultan of Turkey, the Shah of Iran, the rulers of Turan and other kings would soon have to present themselves at his (Humayun's) court and accept his service, and their tenure of sovereignty will depend on his will.[1]

So wrote the Safavid ruler of Iran, Shah Tahmasb (r. 1524–1576), to his Ottoman rival, Sultan Sulayman (r. 1520–1566). The two had frequently corresponded with each other, but the exchange was rarely friendly, strained as it was by the violent struggle over border regions, the granting of asylum to traitors and princely defectors, and the memories of past battles and treacheries.[2] The taunts they hurled at each other were often couched in an idiom of piety and heresy. The Ottomans were at the time militarily stronger, and their sultan would not let the Safavid shah forget the terrible defeat his "heretical" father, Shah Ismaʿil, had suffered at Ottoman hands in 1514.[3] Shah Tahmasb, in response, adopted a tone of false humility and fatalism[4] and recounted the cautionary tale of the Timurid king of India, Humayun, son of Babur. Easy victory and sudden wealth had affected Humayun to the degree that he embraced divine pretensions. Soon, however, fate "tore off his robe of honor and sat him on the sackcloth of degradation,"[5] with Humayun losing his dominion to an upstart Afghan warlord. The crestfallen Timurid had little choice but to do what his father had done before him: seek aid from the Safavids. Shah Tahmasb's warning to his Ottoman rival was that he too could pay for his hubris and, like the great Humayun, end up as a beggar at the Safavid threshold; as he put it in verse, "From Hind came Humayun, my slave to be."[6]

Humayun provides a particularly illuminating specimen of sacred kingship in sixteenth-century Iran and India, because he experienced the same degree of highs as the Safavid Shah Isma'il in achieving divinity in the eyes of his followers and touched the same depths of lows as his father, Babur, in becoming a Safavid subordinate and disciple. Humayun's performance as a sanctified sovereign and his trials as a fallen prince not only provide us another case study of sacrality and sovereignty in this period but also open up a perspective on the Timurids' early attempts at adapting the institutions and practices of sacred kingship they had brought with them from Iran and Central Asia to the social milieu of sixteenth-century India.

HUMAYUN RECONSIDERED

Compared with the other "great Mughals" of India, Humayun has received relatively little scholarly attention.[7] This disregard is understandable, given that during his twenty-six-year reign (1530–1556) Humayun spent fifteen years (1540–1555) outside Hindustan after losing Delhi to Sher Shah of Sur, on the run from his enemies, wandering the wastelands of Sindh and Baluchistan, in exile in Iran, and in a struggle to take Kabul from his brother with the aid of the Safavids.[8] If Humayun was found wanting in politics, he certainly did not make up for it in cultural life, apart from his patronage of a few artists he brought with him from Iran and Kabul.[9] Unlike his father, he did not compose a brilliant memoir or leave behind some other intellectual artifact of note. His alleged lack of political acumen and cultural accomplishment thus leads to easy contrasts between him and his father: more indolent than athletic, more sentimental than pragmatic, and more of an epicure than a littérateur.[10] Humayun's greatest sin in modern eyes, it seems, was his deep interest in magic and astrology. Thus he receives mention today mainly for two things: for losing the fledgling Mughal empire in northern India to the Afghans and for the "strangeness" of his beliefs.[11]

But, as we have seen in the last chapter, Babur was also well accustomed to astrology and the occult and spent much of his early life on the run as a desperate prince. If one chooses to emphasize just these aspects of the father's royal career and read them with a presentist bias, he can be made to appear just as inane and inept as the son. In general, the accident of extant sources can make an inquiry into the "character" of individual kings from this period an arbitrary and somewhat futile exercise. It is more fruitful to focus instead on the character of kingship.

Kingship was a social institution, and kings were social beings. Whatever their individual preferences and religious outlooks, rulers had to contend with a set of socially governed norms of behavior, institutionalized knowledges, and forms of authority. Babur, whom much of modern scholarship takes to be a forthright Sunni Muslim and an eminently learned Timurid prince, had little choice but to patronize astrologers, pay close attention to local mythical lore, deploy "magical" techniques of power and, when circumstances demanded, submit to the "heretical" Sufi messiah-turned-king of Iran, Shah Isma'il. On the other hand, Shah Isma'il, who was a charismatic leader of a band of Sufi warriors with a reputation for ritual cannibalism, upon donning the mantle of sovereignty had to assume the "civilized" trappings of Timurid kingship. Instead of cataloguing these rulers under different ideal types of authority, it is more useful to take their differing and contradictory aspects—charismatic and rational, transgressive and conformist, performative and doctrinal, mythical and historical—and use them to imagine a composite and multidimensional picture of sacred kingship. Such a picture helps us rise above the textual confines of "orthodoxy" and "heterodoxy" to obtain a glimpse of the practical "doxa," that is, the concrete universe of the thinkable and doable within which kings and rulers conceptualized and inhabited their sovereignty.[12]

Such a shift in emphasis away from doctrine and words toward practice and performance is productive not only in theoretical terms but also in enabling an alternative historical narrative. It directs our focus away from the differences in character between Babur and Humayun and toward the commonalities and continuities between them. Since Babur died so soon after the conquest of Hindustan, it was Humayun who oversaw the setting up of an elaborate court with its symbolic forms and narratives of sovereignty. There is no a priori reason to view Humayun's articulation of sacred kingship as a magical-heretical break from Babur's rational-orthodox policies. In fact, one can argue for a considerable degree of continuity between the actions of father and son in the establishment of a Timurid dispensation in South Asia. An aspect of this continuity can be seen in the way both Babur and Humayun cultivated a relationship with the leaders of a popular mystical brotherhood, the Shattari Sufi order of northern India. The Shattaris were famous for their spiritual abilities and thaumaturgical accomplishments; that is, for their mastery of the planets and their knowledge of local yogic idioms of power.[13] If we are to make something of Shah Tahmasb's charge that Humayun's court was riddled with "soothsayers and astrologers" and that in his army "Shari'at was abrogated and heresy (*ilhad*) and evil prevailed," we need look no further than the Shattaris of Gwalior.[14]

THE CHANGING OF PATRON SAINTS

The last entry in Babur's annalistic account of his life, made a few months before his death, recorded that he received a visit from Shaykh Muhammad Ghawth Shattari (d. 1562) from the region of Gwalior, where the Sufi lived and ministered to his devotees. The holy man asked Babur to forgive a rebellious commander of Gwalior.[15] Babur held the Sufi in high regard and accepted his advice. In doing so, he prevented the local fortress from being handed over to the Timurids' Afghan-Rajput enemies. This was not the first time that the Shattari saint had given the new ruler of Hindustan political counsel. Two years earlier, Shaykh Ghawth had on his own initiative assisted Timurid forces in taking the fortress of Gwalior by sending a secret message from inside, warning that the fortress commander with whom the Timurids were negotiating at the time had subversive intentions. On that date, Babur noted in his diary, respectfully, that Shaykh Ghawth was a powerful (*'aziz*) Sufi leader with numerous disciples and companions.[16]

The mode of interaction between Babur and Shaykh Ghawth indicates that the Timurids consolidated their dominion over Hindustan in much the same manner as they had ruled Khurasan and Transoxania, by engaging with established networks of spiritual authority and embracing local idioms of affective knowledge. While in their ancestral dominions they had developed a symbiotic relationship with the Naqshbandis and, briefly, a subordinate one with the invading Safavids, in their South Asian territories they began by collaborating with local influential Sufis such as Muhammad Ghawth and his older brother Shaykh Phul (also Pul or Bahlul)[17] in order to establish themselves in the local political and moral economy.

The early Timurid-Shattari alliance was not accepted without criticism by those among the Timurid kin and nobility who were still closer, geographically and spiritually, to the Naqshbandis or by those who nursed rival claims of sovereignty. We know this from the chronicle of Mirza Haydar Dughlat, Babur's proud Mongol cousin, whose scathing criticism of the way Babur had become a disciple of the Safavid shah in his third and last bid to capture Samarqand was noted in the previous chapter. Mirza Haydar was present during the latter part of the Timurid conquest of India and witnessed Humayun's defeat by Sher Shah Suri in 1540, after which he sought his fortune in Kashmir and Tibet. From his account, which provides a rougher image of early Timurid experience in India than the more polished and revisionist chronicles of later Mughal times, we get a sense of how Humayun's relationship with the Shattari order was viewed by some Timurid insiders as a spiritual betrayal of the highest order that had brought ruin upon the dynasty.

Mirza Haydar related how, in the process of establishing this new religiopolitical alliance with the Shattaris, Humayun had alienated an old spiritual ally of the Timurids. This was the eminent Naqshbandi Sufi saint of Central Asia, Khwaja Makhdumi Nura, a grandson and successor of the famous Khwaja ʿUbaydullah Ahrar mentioned in the previous chapter. A learned and well-traveled man, Khwaja Nura had read philosophy and medicine with eminent scholars in Iran and Egypt and, traversing the Indian Ocean trade and pilgrimage routes, visited Hijaz and Gujarat before returning to Central Asia. Most rulers and nobles of his home region were said to be his devotees and depended upon his medicines and miracles for their health and well-being. He enjoyed, in the words of Mirza Haydar, a "hereditary claim to their veneration."[18]

For his part, Khwaja Nura worked hard to make good on this hereditary claim. He pursued men in power as much as they venerated him. When Babur became the ruler of Kabul, Khwaja Nura came to this city, and when Babur went to conquer Samarqand, the Sufi followed him there. After Babur's defeat by the Uzbeks, Khwaja Nura parted company with the disgraced Timurid, accepted the invitation of another ruler in Central Asia, and went north. In 1531, the year after Babur's death, the Naqshbandi Sufi decided to reestablish his links with the victorious and wealthy Timurid court in Hindustan. On his way, in Lahore, Khwaja Nura met Babur's younger son Mirza Hindal, who asked the holy man to stay, but the latter refused, stating his desire to proceed immediately to Humayun's court: "From the first, it had been my intention to wait upon the Emperor

[Babur]; therefore I must now go and condole with Humayun. Having performed this duty, should I return, I will accept your invitation."[19] However, when he arrived in Agra, the Khwaja found unexpectedly strong competition for Humayun's attention. In the words of Mirza Haydar:

> In those days a man named Shaikh Pul had appeared in Hindustan. Humayun desired to become his devotee because he had a great interest in the occult sciences (*ulum-i ghariba*), and a passion for invoking prayer spells (*ad'iyya*) and spirits (*taskhirat*). Shaikh Pul had donned the guise of a Sufi master (*shayyukhat*) and taught that spells and invocations were the best means to obtain one's true desire (*maqsud-i haqiqi*), and even that one's true desire should be the attainment of these means. Since [Humayun] had a temperament for such things, he soon became a disciple (*murid*). Furthermore, there was Maulana Muhammad Parghari who, though a religious scholar (*mulla*), was a very unscrupulous man, and plotted relentlessly to achieve his corrupt ends. That Shaikh [Pul] managed to enlist Mulla Muhammad in his cause. The Maulana began to work his charms on the emperor who fell for his flattery.[20]

Feeling slighted, Khwaja Nura left Humayun's court and headed back to Lahore, to the emperor's brother Hindal, also an aspirant to the Timurid throne. There he described a dream that foretold the destructive end of Humayun's dominion: "I have seen in a vision, a great sea which overwhelmed all who remained behind us in Agra and Hindustan; while we only escaped after a hundred risks."[21] According to Mirza Haydar, the scorned saint's prophecy came true three years later, when Humayun's Hindustan was "devastated," and, as the dream had predicted, Khwaja Nura managed to escape safely to Transoxania.

The case of Khwaja Nura highlights how Sufis imbued with hereditary charisma would attempt to exchange their symbolic capital for more tangible forms of wealth and influence. Such Sufis pursued power and status as much as any king or warlord, and the brotherhoods they belonged to sought to add new territories to their dominion much as an imperial dynasty would. While the worldly pursuits of saintly families were often portrayed in a spiritual light by their followers, their competitors, on the other hand, were not treated so generously. To this end, Mirza Haydar recorded that in contrast to Khwaja Nura Naqshbandi, who could offer sovereigns like Humayun spiritual succor and the purest of miracles, ersatz Sufis like Shaykh Phul Shattari could conjure up little more than "magic" and "sorcery." To prove his point, Mirza Haydar devoted several pages in his work to the miracles performed by the Naqshbandi saint before, during, and after his meeting with Humayun.[22] These examples of the Sufi's sacred power made it clear, from Mirza Haydar's perspective, that it was Humayun's neglect of his hereditary duty to venerate the Naqshbandi saint that led to the demise of his empire in Hindustan.

Why did Humayun abandon his ancestral relationship with the Naqshbandis and patronize the Shattaris instead? Perhaps it was simply because the Shattaris had a large following in Humayun's new dominion while the Naqshbandis did not as yet. But would Humayun and his contemporaries have viewed the matter in terms of such *realpolitik*? His cousin the chronicler certainly did not. Theirs was a phenomenological setting where the cadences of social and political life were linked to the rhythms of a cosmos kept in balance by the efforts of holy men. How could one abandon a spiritual counselor who was part of one's *nomos* (*namus* in Persian) with such facility? Yet given the evidence presented here and earlier, such switches and exchanges occurred with a frequency that renders most categories of sectarian affiliation and devotional loyalty useless in describing the religious life of the time.

The problem cannot be dismissed by describing this religious milieu as "fluid," a term that implies a lack of social institutions to anchor religious or communal identities. On the contrary, the Sufi orders of this period were extremely hierarchical entities with complex rituals of initiation, bodily markers of identity, and techniques of disciplinary control. How could social identities be fluid in the face of such entrenched and enforced institutions? The solution to this paradox lies in unearthing and taking seriously the social mechanisms and cultural practices that facilitated the switching back and forth across cultural boundaries or, to put it differently, enabled a simultaneity of multiple, conflicting bonds of moral community.

Two insights are crucial for pursuing this line of inquiry. First, it is important to recognize that in this milieu the local and the particular had a phenomenological precedence over the global and the universal. In other words, sacrality was grounded in geographies and embodied in personalities that were local, concrete, and highly visible. Engagement with such forms of sacrality could only occur via a process that was ritualistic, tactile, and performative. This engagement, however, exposed one to charges of irreligion, impiety, magic, and other forms of spiritual waywardness, charges made by rivals and those who stood to lose from the establishment of new sociomoral bonds. Although these charges were made with rhetorical reference to "universal" categories of doctrinal religion, in most cases their real referent was an intense competition that was local and particular. And as the jostling between the Shattaris and Naqshbandis during the early phase of Timurid rule in Hindustan shows, it was a struggle in which the stakes were simultaneously political and moral, territorial and spiritual, mundane and magical. With these observations in mind, we are ready to examine how the Shattari brothers' activities in the Timurid court and camp aided the dynasty to become one with its new dominions.

HUMAYUN AND THE SHATTARI BROTHERS

The Shattari hagiographical sources claim that both Shaykh Phul and Shaykh Ghawth enjoyed the enviable position of being the Sufi master (*pir*) of Humayun. The extant Timurid sources, mostly inimical toward the Shattaris, make it clear that the relationship between the Sufis and the Timurids had aspects to it that were less transcendental. Babur's interaction with the younger Shattari brother, mentioned above, highlights the Sufi's active role and initiative in matters of local war and politics. In Humayun's case, we know that the older brother, Shaykh Phul, acted as an important advisor. The significance of Shaykh Phul's position at court can be gauged by the fact that when Humayun left Agra to campaign in Gujarat, he left the Shattari shaykh behind to serve as his eyes and ears. For good reason, Humayun did not trust his younger sibling, Hindal, who had been left in charge of Agra in the emperor's absence. The Shattari saint was not a mere spy in the guise of a reclusive mystic, however. He accompanied the army on war campaigns and gave counsel on military affairs. For instance, when faced with a serious rebellion led by Timurid cousins, Hindal Mirza became impatient to do battle. For two months, the armies stood opposite each other, but Shaykh Phul would not permit military engagement, saying,

> "Be patient, for I am busy invoking the Divine Names (*ba daʿwat-i ismha mashghulam*). God willing, they will fall to pieces of their own accord." This placated Hindal Mirza. . . . [Then] the enemy grew impatient, mounted, and came to do battle. Hindal Mirza asked Shaykh Phul what should be done. "Since the enemy has mounted and come to do battle," replied the shaykh, "one must necessarily fight."[23]

While Humayun was still away from Agra, having conquered Gujarat and now campaigning in Bengal, the Afghan warlord Sher Shah Suri achieved a string of victories against the Timurids. By capturing the region of Bihar, Sher Shah was able to block Humayun's path from Bengal to Agra. Taking advantage of the situation, some Timurid rebels reached Hindal and planned a coup against Humayun. They offered Hindal the throne of Hindustan on the condition that he prove his commitment to break from Humayun with no chance of reconciliation. Hindal, the rebels stipulated, had to murder Shaykh Phul:

> "You kill Shaykh Phul so that we can be certain that you have turned against the emperor. Then we will obey you and have the khutba read in your name." Therefore Hindal Mirza said to [the rebel leader], "Come up with some ruse to have Shaykh Phul killed." They slandered Shaykh Phul by saying that he had sent weapons and letters to Sher Khan [the Afghan rival of the Timurids]. On this pretext they killed the shaykh and had the khutba read in Hindal Mirza's name.[24]

The way different Timurid sources related the event reveals the tension that the killing of Shaykh Phul had generated within the royal family. Humayun's sister, Gulbadan Banu, for example, tried to take Hindal's side in her memoir, written almost half a century later, and stated that Shaykh Phul was caught supplying weapons to the enemy and so had to be executed, but even she did not hide the fact that this execution created a great deal of distrust between the king and his younger brother.[25]

In sum, Shaykh Phul was a key political appointee and advisor to Humayun. However, his power was based not on the control of men and material but on his influence over the planets. Shaykh Phul was a renowned master of the Shattari procedure of invoking "divine names," a mystical technique involving the use of prayer formulae to muster the "spirit" powers of the planets.[26] Such sacred ability could not be gained by mere incantation, however. For the prayer formulae to work, the invoker's soul had to be in the purest of states.[27] While no reliable method exists to determine the purity of sixteenth-century Sufi souls, we are on relatively firmer ground when gauging the grandeur of saintly reputations.

Shaykh Phul's great charismatic repute was shared, and perhaps even eclipsed, by that of his younger brother, Shaykh Muhammad Ghawth. The latter had submitted himself as a young man to twelve years of grueling asceticism in the mountains of northern India, fasting, it was said, for days at a time.²⁸ It was the younger Shattari's work, *Jawahir-i Khamsa* (The Five Jewels), available in Arabic and Persian versions, which became a key Sufi guidebook across the Islamic lands and contained a long section on how to capture the power of the planets.²⁹ His spiritual status became so great that he was called Ghawth (Spiritual Succor), a title afforded to the axial saint of the age, a prophetlike entity who could intercede with the divine on humanity's behalf. Shaykh Ghawth had achieved this status because of a miraculous feat of phenomenal proportions. In 1526, the year Babur had ascended the throne of Delhi, Shaykh Ghawth had ascended to the throne of God.

Shaykh Ghawth's reputation rested on a miraculous trip to heaven that rivaled the ascension journey (*mi'raj*) of the Prophet himself.³⁰ The Shattari shaykh was said to have been physically taken by the angel Gabriel to journey from India through the seven heavens and witness the glory of God with his own eyes. Babur did not concern himself in his memoir with the source of the Shaykh Ghawth's power and glory. He simply made use of them. The Timurid, after all, had been used to dealing with this type of local charismatic figure, one wielding both spiritual and earthly authority, in Iran and Central Asia. What is notable here is the Shattari saint's age. At the time Shaykh Ghawth had first aided Babur in capturing the fort of Gwalior, the Sufi was less than thirty years old. His stature as a great mystic was not based on his years of experience but rather on the rapidity with which he had acquired spiritual prowess. This was generally true of the Shattari order, which was so named (*shattar* in Arabic means swift) because of its promise to provide an experience of divine rapture without undergoing the stages of self-discipline that other mystical brotherhoods required.³¹

By achieving a physical experience of divinity at so young an age and in so spectacular a fashion, Shaykh Ghawth had become the living proof of the efficacy of Shattari spiritual techniques. He imparted knowledge of his ascension experience as a "seal" to his initiates and disciples to finalize their initiation into the order.³² There are few indications that he faced any organized religious opposition in his early career. It was only after Humayun's defeat and exile, when Shaykh Ghawth had to escape to Gujarat, that the Shattari saint faced religious inquiry and persecution. He was challenged by other Sufis and ulama in Gujarat, possibly because of his growing influence on the ruler there, to retract his heretical claims or face punishment. Under severe pressure, Shaykh Ghawth recanted, agreeing that his ascension to heaven had really been a dream and not a bodily event.³³ This retreat into the realm of dreams, a domain of routinized miracles, allowed him to survive as a Sufi master in Gujarat.

Shaykh Ghawth returned to Mughal Agra in 1559, in the reign of Humayun's son, Akbar (r. 1556–1605), but was unable to regain his former status at court. Reportedly, the Shattari Sufi offered to become Akbar's spiritual master, but the royal chronicler mocked the shaykh for not recognizing that the real saint of the age was the Mughal emperor himself. Indeed, when Akbar's chronicles were written in the 1590s, the political and spiritual landscape had changed so much that the Shattari brothers were given but brief mentions and ridiculed as magicians and sellers of sainthood (*muta'-i wilayat mifarukhtand*).³⁴

Although the conflicting reports in later Timurid and Shattari sources limit the degree to which we can reconstruct the history of early Timurid-Shattari interaction, it is certain that the Shattari brothers played a brief but important role in making Humayun's claim to sacred kingship, a role for which they received little credit in later Mughal chronicles. In historical terms, it could be said that the Shattaris were just as marginal as Humayun. Their project, like that of their royal ally, had a promising beginning but an abortive end. Nevertheless, if we ignore the teleology of Mughal history and instead focus on the years before Humayun's defeat and long exile, the Shattaris provide an excellent lens for bringing into focus the sacred and sociological context in which the early Timurid dominion took shape in India.

THE "UNIVERSAL" SACRALITY OF "LOCAL" HOLY MEN

The two poles of history and hagiography around which sources from the period under study are clustered provide us with two distinct and contradictory images of the Shattaris. Near the historical pole they appear as worldly and ambitious men who, in the guise of holiness, were deeply involved in local matters of war and politics. The hagiographical narrative, by contrast, associates with them the most universal of sacred powers and the deepest of mystical mysteries. These two images seem impossible to reconcile unless we turn to the observation that although the holiness of holy men was often memorialized in universal terms of unrelenting piety and spectacular spirituality, it was often realized by their active role in the routine life of local society.³⁵ Such figures had a reputation that was often based on the religious imagination and social needs of their followers; they were "arbiters of the holy" and rallying points around which a "religious commonsense" developed from multiple strands of local religious practice. More importantly, in the absence of formal political hierarchies or officialdom, these holy men could serve as crucial "hinge" figures and articulate relationships between their local followers and supralocal lords.

This insight is especially salient for sixteenth-century northern India, where many lords were Turkish- and Persian-speaking Muslims—some, as in the case of Babur and Humayun, only recently arrived—while a majority of the populace and soldiery was not.[36] It was also a time where enough conversion to Islam had taken place for there to be significant communities of lay Muslims in some areas, but much of the population was incorporated into structures of Brahmanical religious traditions, followed anti-Brahmanical devotional sects, or participated in a wide range of local spirit cults.[37] The Timurids had little choice but to engage with local intermediaries in order to establish themselves in their new dominions and, importantly, raise local allies and recruits for their army. The Shattaris were Sufis of a type ideally suited to play such a role. They were saints whose claims to universal sacrality were firmly grounded in local social structures and the knowledges and memories they sustained.

The Shattari brothers were not only immensely popular local saints but also experts in the Arabic, Persian, and Sanskrit learned traditions. In other words, these Sufis used both elite intellectual traditions and popular local knowledges to demonstrate their command over Islamic and Indic idioms. This can be seen in Shaykh Ghawth's translation of the famous tantric yogic text *Amrta Kunda* from an earlier Arabic version into Persian and in his use of yogic formulae in his text on the invocation of "divine names," *Jawahir-i Khamsa*.[38] Moreover, his expertise in astrology and the knowledge of the cosmos it entailed enabled him to draw parallels between cosmologies derived from both traditions. Carl Ernst has argued that while later Shattari traditions sought to portray Shaykh Ghawth's interest in yogic spiritual knowledge as driven by a need to purify or Islamicize this knowledge, the original texts show no such attempt.[39] Rather, in his works Shaykh Ghawth treated the two knowledge systems of Islam and Hinduism as equally valid sources of cosmological truth and demonstrated their correspondence.

The process of later Sufi traditions attempting to recast the earlier role of Indian Sufis as carriers of the "sword of Islam" who subdued "Hindu" power and dismissed "Hindu" sacred claims is well documented.[40] There certainly developed in the sixteenth and seventeenth centuries Sufi hagiographic traditions in Persian that sought to downplay their local roots and, instead, establish pure genealogies linking their orders to an authentic and universal Islamic past. However, this written tradition represented only one part of the social dynamic involving Islam in South Asia and, arguably, the lesser part if one takes into account the popular memory of Muslim saints and the lived experience of their vast numbers of devotees, many of whom did not profess Islam. Indeed, it has been shown that many elite Sufi writings were inspired by the oral lore and popular memories surrounding Muslim saints, which were then later sanitized and disciplined according to conventions of genre and "universal" tradition.[41] There was, in other words, a tense and productive relationship between the written Sufi orientations to the past and the popular memories of their lay devotees. However, it was the popular tradition that did more to define the mold of sainthood, which shaped the social personalities of holy men like the two Shattari brothers. To see why this was the case, we need to examine the social process that turned ordinary—and sometimes completely imaginary—men into saints and messiahs in the region. A vivid example in this regard is that of a legendary Muslim saint, Sayyid Salar Masʿud Ghazi, the epitome of popular sainthood in northern India.

The fact that Salar Ghazi was a figment of collective imagination was no impediment either to the popularity of his shrine, which has existed at least since the fourteenth century, when Ibn Battuta visited the place and found it too crowded for comfort, or to his fame as a spiritually gifted nephew and warrior of the first Turkish conqueror of India, Mahmud of Ghazna (d. 1030). This imaginary warrior saint became so famous that the elite hagiographic Sufi tradition later adopted him as a bona fide saint and gave him a proper lineage and history in a text called *Mirat-i Masʿudi* (The Mirror of Masʿud, c. 1611). Indeed, as the first saintly conqueror of Hindustan, Salar Ghazi's personality was cast in a messianic image in this Persian-language hagiography, which compared his visage and attributes to that of Jesus.[42]

However, as Shahid Amin has shown, the bardic traditions surrounding Salar Ghazi portrayed him in a manner a great deal more concrete and complex.[43] While acknowledging his role as a founding Muslim warrior and conqueror, the bards also assigned to him the qualities of a local Indic hero, of a god descended to earth. In this popular version, the Muslim saint fights on the side of good and dies the death of an Indic epic warrior: in battle as a virgin on his wedding day. Salar Ghazi embraces martyrdom, according to the oral tales, when he goes to fight a tyrannical Hindu raja who had attacked his devotees, the local (non-Muslim and low status) herdsmen and their cows. In other words, he fights both as a Muslim saint spreading his faith and as an epic Indic god-hero responding to the dharmic call of "save the kine" (*gao guhar*), and, thus, he lays down his life simultaneously for Islam and cows. As Amin has pointed out, this odd conflation of the universal and the local—that is, the Muslim saint's martyrdom involving the saving of cattle—even lived on in a muted form in the recounting of Salar Ghazi's life in the elite Persian hagiography, a work that otherwise molded the narrative of the saint's life into a more "sanitized" Islamic form.[44] This correspondence between the written and the oral traditions suggests it was the latter that served as the inspirational source for the former. It also demonstrates the limits to which elite writing could discipline popular lore. Indeed, it was popular imagination that produced the socially, as opposed to the textually, "real" version of the saint.

The hagiographical and popular narratives surrounding saintly and epic figures like Salar Ghazi were the product of collective memory and thought. As such, they can only be made sense of by appreciating the "common" sense that gave them coherence and meaning. This can be seen in the way Salar Ghazi was granted powers that were not only supernatural but also supersocial. Among his miracles was the power to subvert, even if momentarily, social boundaries by throwing across them contradictory strands of moral community. Even today, since Salar Ghazi is thought to have sacrificed his life on his marriage day, his devotees commemorate him by forming a wedding procession on his death anniversary and, in the process, overcoming their religious and caste differences.[45] As Amin points out, however, this was not a "syncretism sans conflict."[46] On the contrary, the charisma embodied by Salar Ghazi was situated within memories of violence and predicated on acts of war.[47] The insight that Muslim saints from this period, in their social incarnations, sought neither intercommunal peace nor the uncompromising victory of orthodox Islam but rather enabled a culture of routinized war and violent coexistence is a nonintuitive one. Yet saints and holy men have been shown to play just such a social role in "frontier" settings, where social divisions, despite being strongly marked, often had to be transgressed because of the way organized violence and seasonal war structured the routines of social life.[48] It is crucial to develop an intuitive sense of this social dynamic if we are to appreciate how universal myths of sovereignty were adapted to such local settings.

Take, for instance, the case of the early sixteenth-century northern Indian messiah Sayyid Muhammad of Jaunpur (d. 1505), whose followers, known as the Mahdavis, were active before, during, and after Humayun's reign and played an important role in the millennial claims of his son and successor, Akbar.⁴⁹ Sayyid Muhammad had made the rather strong assertion that anyone who denied his messianic status could no longer be considered a Muslim. He preached asceticism and organized his followers, men and women, into residential communities called "circles" (da'ira) where all property and income were shared. He also declared the four dominant schools of Islamic jurisprudence defunct. His movement had a desultory career that took Sayyid Muhammad and his followers to Gujarat, Sind, and eventually to Safavid-controlled Afghanistan, where he died and was buried. His shrine was reported to have been attacked by Safavid forces but defended and saved by his followers. Sayyid Muhammad's successors kept the messianic movement alive for some generations despite facing severe persecution. The movement was politically and militarily active at the time of Humayun's exile. Islam Shah Sur (r. 1545–1554), the son of Sher Shah Sur, suppressed it violently, executing one of the movement's leaders and making another recant. Yet the Mahdavis survived in more quietist groups and were present at the court of Akbar.

Sayyid Muhammad is said to have received his deepest religious inspiration about Islam in a region largely populated by non-Muslims. According to Mahdavi tradition, as a youth he had fought for the last Sharqi sultan of Jaunpur, the Muslim ruler of a small kingdom in northern India, against a neighboring Hindu raja. This raja had become powerful enough to demand tax from the sultan, which the Muslim ruler would have paid had it not been for the exhortations of young Sayyid Muhammad, who lobbied instead for an armed response.⁵⁰ In the ensuing battle against the Hindu raja, Sayyid Muhammad is said to have led a band of fifteen hundred young *bairagis* (Hindu ascetics).

When Sayyid Muhammad struck the Hindu raja dead, his sword cleaved the enemy's chest open and exposed his heart. Islam's future messiah saw that on the raja's heart was carved the image of the Hindu god he worshipped. Sayyid Muhammad was stunned: if the power of belief in a false god could have such an effect on a non-Muslim heart, then what would devotion to the true God do to a Muslim one? He went into a long-lasting trance. This was the beginning of his spiritual quest, which led him to Mecca, where he declared himself to be the awaited messiah. Note the "strange" numbers that patterned the life of the Mahdavi leader. His trance lasted twelve years, the number of mansions of the zodiac and the number of Shiʿi imams in history. He became the messiah at age forty, the same age that the Prophet had received his first revelation. In effect, this hagiographical narrative portrays Sayyid Muhammad both as a staunch Muslim committed to advancing the cause of Islam in a radically revived form and as the leader of an open-status warrior group in which Hindu sadhus fought alongside Muslim Sufi warriors. Moreover, it suggests a religious imagination in which Muslims may have considered the gods of India to be false but did not doubt their sacred powers and the commitment of their brave devotees.

The living memory of great saints like Salar Ghazi and messianic figures like Sayyid Muhammad of Jaunpur was, quite plausibly, the model for aspiring holy men like the Shattari brothers. For one, the Shattaris' active and leading role in moments of war corresponds closely to the warrior-saint image. Their order even seems to have had institutionalized such a role for its leaders. The founder of the order in India, Shah ʿAbdullah (d. 1485), is said to have toured the country in the costume of a king, with his devotees in military dress carrying banners and beating martial drums.[51] Furthermore, Shattari knowledge of yogic traditions of sacred power served to root their spiritual reputation in local idioms. Even more indicative of the fact that Shaykh Ghawth had assumed the trappings of a local holy man is the fame of his herd of cattle, an Indic mark of sacredness, as witnessed in the legend of Salar Masʿud Ghazi. Shaykh Ghawth's bulls and cows were so renowned that when the Shattari saint returned to Agra after his long exile in Gujarat, the young emperor Akbar went to see the animals with his own eyes.[52]

These local and concrete bases of Shaykh Ghawth's sacred authority were the foundation for his universal claims of spiritual power preserved in his textual endeavors. In his written works, he used the sacred knowledge of Indian yogis alongside Arabic prayer formulae to draw down the angelic powers of the planets. A person who invoked these powers properly would possess, he asserted, "the miraculous ability of our Lord Moses, may peace be upon him, and our Lord Jesus, may peace be upon him, and become the guide and messiah of his age (*wa yakun hadiyan mahdiyan fi zamanihi*)."[53] This was, most likely, the promise the Shattari saint held out to young Humayun, who began to see himself as a manifestation of divinity.

With this context in mind, it is worth paying attention to the rumor that Humayun "used to cast a veil over his crown (*taj*), and when he removed it the people used to say, 'manifestation [of the Divine Light]' . . . and so he imposed upon the populace the requirement to prostrate before him with their foreheads touching the ground."[54] We must resist the temptation to dismiss such accusations of heresy merely on the grounds that no direct or confessional evidence such as formal decrees or royal chronicles corroborate them. Such claims of sacrality would have rarely been articulated in words and decrees. Rather, they would have been made manifest in a profusion of symbols, arranged and performed in a great theater of sovereignty.

THE SPECTACLE OF EMPIRE AND THE THEATER OF SOVEREIGNTY

In contemporary descriptions of Humayun's reign there is hardly a mention of an imperial bureaucracy, judiciary, or revenue service. In this regard, Humayun was not exceptional. Neither his Timurid predecessors nor his contemporary Safavids in Iran were much concerned with methods of "rational" administration.[55] Rather, the expectation from a great king and conqueror was that he would first and foremost perform his public role as an epitome of righteousness and awesome might. To this end, the foundational process of kingship depended less on tax collection and the establishment of a bureaucratic order and more on conquest and a patterned display of sovereignty. This process included the circulation of the sovereign through the realm with his grand entourage, hunting, conquering, and feasting, taking in the sights, sounds, and tastes of its various locales while imposing upon it a new order of color and rhythm.[56]

Consider the way how Babur, two years after his initial victory in Hindustan in 1528, had organized a royal feast. The guest list included his allies and ambassadors from Iran (Qizilbash), Central Asia (Uzbek), and India (Hindu).[57] In his memoir, Babur described in great detail the design of the canopy for the occasion, the arrangements made for the guests, who sat with whom, the distance between him and his noble visitors, and the types of gifts received and given. The carefully choreographed affair ended with a meal followed by a magnificent performance of Indian acrobats whose amazing feats, Babur admitted, were beyond the ability of Central Asian entertainers.

Local entertainment was not the only way to experience his empire. There was also the local cuisine. Indeed, Babur went to great lengths to "taste" his new dominions. In his first year in India, 1526, after he had defeated the Afghan Lodi Sultan Ibrahim, Babur commissioned the dead king's cooks to prepare Hindustani food for him. This was no frivolous pursuit. Babur was well aware of the risk of poisoning he was exposing himself to. Despite strict security measures, the former queen mother managed to convince one of the Indian cooks to mix poison in Babur's food. However, the king only ingested a few morsels of the tainted dish and survived after a night of violent retching.[58] He then had a dog eat the vomitus, and when the creature became sick, he ordered an investigation and uncovered the plot. Babur dubbed the incident a "strange" affair, an indication that fortune was on his side, and reported it in detail in a letter sent to Kabul.

Babur did not only adjust himself to local taste and style. He also modified his new dominions to suit his own sensibilities. His penchant for building distinctive Timurid-style gardens with fountains and running water and for planting melons and other fruits from his native land is well known. Another more somber practice in this regard was his desire to remove any spectacle that competed with his own performance of kingship. While touring Gwalior, he saw giant statues of Hindu deities carved into the mountains near Urwahi. He remarked in his diary, "Urwahi is not a bad place. In fact, it is rather nice. Its one drawback was the idols, so I ordered them destroyed (Turkish: *buzgaylar*; Persian: *viran bikunand*)."[59] Archaeological evidence shows that these statues were not destroyed; at most, their heads were removed.[60] There was more than just Islamic iconoclasm at work in Babur's actions, however. On the same tour, he had sealed alliances with local rajas and then gone to see the Hindu temples of Gwalior. He admired these buildings, even comparing one set of temples to the design of an Islamic madrasa. He also noted the "lower chambers," where idols were kept, but recorded no distaste or urge to destroy. Why were the idols on the mountainside "beheaded" but the idols in the temple's inner sanctum left untouched? The answer could well be that the giant statues, which loomed large over the landscape with their uncanny gaze fixed upon it, interfered with Babur's imperial performance and his own imperial gaze. Whatever the case may be, Babur, by feasting and arranging, tasting and observing, planting and building, had begun to merge his royal self with the landscape of his new dominion. But it was Humayun who upon ascending the throne gave this ritual process a formal, cosmological shape.

Humayun showed a great deal of inventiveness in the way he organized a ritual display of kingship. In order to make visible, classify, and regulate his court and realm, he commissioned a new range of material objects such as buildings, boats, drinking vessels, tents, and carpets, as well as symbolic practices such as calendars, games of chance, court ceremonies, uniforms, dress codes, and naming conventions. By all accounts, the result was an impressive affair. Even his usually critical relative Mirza Haydar could not contain his admiration for the spectacle of the imperial camp and army.

> When ... I entered [Humayun's] service in Agra ... it was after his defeats [by Sher Shah Suri], and when people said that compared with what it had been, there was nothing left of his pomp and magnificence. Yet when his army was arrayed for the Ganges campaign (in which the whole direction devolved upon me) there were still 17,000 menials in his retinue, from which circumstance an estimate may be formed of the rest of his establishment.[61]

Mirza Haydar thus noted with praise that Humayun possessed immense "natural talent and excellence" and that the emperor was "brave in battle, gay in feast and very generous ... a dignified, stately sovereign, who observed much state and pomp."[62] The emperor's shortcoming, from Mirza Haydar's perspective, was not that he neglected imperial administration but rather that he ruined himself by keeping company with pseudo-Sufis and profligate companions like the Shattaris instead of authentic mystics and pious men like the Naqshbandis.

Fortunately, Humayun's efforts in laying the symbolic foundations of empire are preserved in a panegyric work called *Qanun-i Humayuni* (Canons of Sovereignty, and a play on Humayun's name: Canons of Being a Humayun), composed by the famous Timurid historian Ghiyas ad-Din Muhammad Khwandamir (or Khvand Mir, d. c. 1537).[63] It is significant that Khwandamir composed this work. Not only was he the greatest Persian historian of his time, but he had also served both the Timurids and the Safavids, witnessing their cultural worlds up close.[64] Khwandamir was well aware of the competition for sovereignty between the two dynasties and understood the messianic idiom of sacrality and the stakes involved.

In his grand chronicle *Habib al-Siyar* (The Friend of Biographies), which he wrote in part under Timurid patronage and in part under the Safavids, Khwandamir took a neutral stance, leaving out the embarrassing moments of each dynasty's past and describing them both as equally worthy. However, in the *Qanun-i Humayuni* written for Humayun, he portrayed the Timurid monarch as the greatest and most sacred sovereign of the age. Moreover, steeped in Timurid cultural forms, Khwandamir remained true to his roots. He presented Humayun's entire imperial endeavor in classical Persianate style and a universal Islamic idiom. In his description of the emperor's "inventions" (*ikhtiraʿat*)[65] of kingship there was no mention of the Shattari Sufis and their local knowledge. Yet a close reading of Khwandamir's text shows that the cosmological basis of Humayun's new order corresponded well with the "strange" teachings of the Shattaris and their locally flavored idioms of sacrality.

THE CANONS OF HUMAYUN

Khwandamir's work began with a hierarchical view of the social order with Humayun at its apex. He was God's successor or caliph according to the Quranic tradition "and we made you regents (khala'if) on earth" (10:14). He was also a Lord of Conjunction (Sahib Qiran). As the head of God's ecumene on earth, Humayun's role was to provide succor to all its social constituents (see table 4.1).[66]

In this social hierarchy, the religious scholars of Islam, the ulama, were placed below both the political and spiritual aristocracy as defined by blood and kinship ties. It was these two hereditary groups—the ruling nobility and the Sufis/Alids (Shaykhs/Sayyids)—whose presence and efforts

TABLE 4.1

The Social Hierarchy Under Humayun as God's Caliph and Lord of Conjunction

SOCIAL GROUP	FUNCTION/POSITION
Nobles (umara') and ministers (wuzara')	Look after affairs of the world (umur-i jahani) and collect revenues (husul-i amwal)
Descendants of the Prophet (sadat) and Sufis (masha'ikh)	Fruits of the garden of sainthood (wilayat) and the planets of the heavens of guidance (hidayat)
Men of knowledge ('ulama') and distinction (fuzala')	Lights of gnosis (ma'arifat) and doors of beneficence (ifadat)
Judges (quzzat) and jurists (muftiyan)	Implement the law (shari'at)
Poets (shu'ara) and secretaries (arbab-i insha')	Adorn the emperor and his court
Farmers (dahaqin) and tillers (muzari'an)	Sustain the condition of the world through effort and organization
Merchants of land and sea (tujjar-i bahar o amsar)	Travel far and wide for commerce
Craft professions (muhtarifat) and market folk (ahl-i aswaq)	Practice a variety of manufacturing techniques

maintained order in the material and spiritual domains, respectively. Accordingly, they had an ontological precedence over scholars and men of knowledge. The kinship element is worth emphasizing, as these two groups intermarried in the early periods of the Mughal and Safavid empires. Humayun, for example, upon his return to power in Kabul reestablished his links with the Naqshbandis by marrying his sisters to important members of the Sufi family.[67] The Safavids too established marriage ties with leading Sufi and Sayyid lineages like the Ni'matullahis, who in turn played key religious and political roles in the empire.[68]

Furthermore, the word for religious scholars (ʿalim, pl. ʿulamaʾ) was not limited in this scheme to those who were masters of doctrinal or juridical knowledge. Rather, it included those who possessed an inner knowledge (maʿarifat) and thus provided benefit (ifadat) to the ruler. Their wisdom (hikmat) was considered to be broader than that of religious law, as evidenced by their higher status than that of the mere judge or jurist. This catholic definition of knowledge (ʿilm) was widespread in the region, especially so in Iran, which was at this time still largely Sunni. Indeed, Arab Shiʿi jurists, who were just beginning to trickle into the Safavid realm, had to compete for the title of ʿalim with an entrenched "estate" of scholarly families.[69] These incumbents, who were mostly Sunni but also Sayyid, not only prided themselves on their prophetic genealogy but also subscribed to a view of learning that included much more than just the study of Islamic jurisprudence and scriptural traditions. This view included not only mathematics, philosophy, and astronomy but also the occult sciences (ʿulum-i ghariba) and related "wisdom" (hikmat)—what today would be termed divination, astrology, alchemy, and magic.

Khwandamir certainly had such a perspective of religious knowledge in mind when he asserted that anyone familiar with the Prophet of Islam's life and customs would know that he used to take auguries from the names of men.[70] In this view, Humayun followed the prophet's tradition from a young age. Once, when Humayun was still a prince, his father left him in charge of Kabul while away on a campaign. During this time, the prince was out riding in the countryside when suddenly it occurred to him to take an augury from the names of the first three men that came his way. Although the prince's tutor, a certain ʿalim named Maulana Masihuddin Ruhullah, whose title indicated that he was also a physician,[71] suggested that one name should suffice for this exercise, Humayun was determined to pursue his original inspiration and seek out three men.

The first man the young prince met was called Murad Khwaja. *Murad* means goal or desire, which made this chance meeting a good omen. Soon afterward, Humayun saw another man carrying wood. His name turned out to be Dawlat Khwaja. *Dawlat* means fortune or dominion, another good omen. Humayun remarked that if the third person's name was Saʿadat, which means felicity and fortune, it would be a most amazing and fortunate coincidence (*ittifaq*). Within the hour, he came across a boy grazing cows whose name was indeed Saʿadat Khwaja. At this incident, all his servants were amazed and convinced that this prince destined for sovereignty (*padishah-i humayun fal*) would in little time, with the help of divine fortune (*saʿadat-i azli*), obtain the greatest ranks of dominion and fortune (*maratib-i dawlat o iqbal*).[72] Humayun was so taken by this augury that when he ascended the throne he used it to organize his court and administration. He divided his entourage into three divisions, each of which was named according to the auspicious names the emperor had come across that day (see table 4.2).[73]

TABLE 4.2

Imperial Administration Arranged According to Humayun's Augury

GROUP	MEMBERSHIP	FUNCTION/BENEFIT
People of Government and Dominion (Ahl-i-Dawlat)	The emperor's brothers (*ikhwan*), relatives (*aqraba*), nobles, ministers, and soldiers (*sipahiyan*)	Maintain rule, authority, and stability
People of Felicity and Fortune (Ahl-i Saʿadat)	Religious administrators (*sudur*), Sufi shaykhs, family of the Prophet, religious scholars, judges, men of learning (*fuzalaʾ*), poets, courtiers, and the imperial retinue (*mawali, ashraf, ahali*)	Increase eternal fortune (*irtiqaʾ ba darajat-i dawlat-i sarmadi*)
People of Object and Desire (Ahl-i Murad)	Lords of beauty and taste (*arbab-i husn o malahat*), the young masters of loveliness (*javanan-i sahib-i sabahat*), and musicians and singers	Satisfy the desire to meet beautiful youth and to hear the sound of the musical instruments: *chang, qanun,* and *ʿud*

Each of the three groups was assigned two days for court appearance, according to the astral auspiciousness of each day (see table 4.3).[74] Thus Humayun's schedule, which set the rhythm of empire, was marked both by the founding royal augury and by the auspicious positions of the planets. Moreover, each day just before dawn the royal drums (*naqqara*) announced the Time of Felicity (*nawbat-i saʿadat*), reserved for worship and meditation. Then at sunrise the Time of Dominion (*nawbat-i dawlat*) would be sounded, and at sunset the Time of Desire (*nawbat-i murad*).

TABLE 4.3

The Schedule of Humayun's Court Arranged According to the Planets

AUSPICIOUS GROUP	DAY OF THE WEEK	REASON
People of Felicity	Saturday and Thursday	The reason for this arrangement is that Saturday is related to the planet Saturn, the protector (*murabbi*) of shaykhs and ancient lineages (*khandanha-i qadim*). Also, Thursday is associated with Jupiter, which is the planet of the Prophet's family and religious scholars. On these days, the monarch meets with his managers of the system of knowledge and worship (*naziman-i manazim-i ʿilm o ʿibadat*).
People of Dominion	Sunday and Tuesday	The wisdom behind this is that Sunday is the day of the sun, which is associated with rulers and sultans, while Tuesday is the day of Mars, the lord of able soldiers. Thus the emperor devotes himself to governance on these two days, which are best suited for issuing royal edicts.
People of Desire	Monday and Wednesday	Monday is associated with the moon and Wednesday with Mercury. It is appropriate that in these two days one should associate with moonlike (*qamar paykar*) youths and increase beauty and adornment with a combination (*imtizaj*) of songs (*naghmat*) and melodies (*ilhan*) of instrument and voice.
Any and all	Friday	Finally, Friday (*jumʿa*), as its name indicates, brings together (*jamiʿ*) all mentioned affairs. The assembly on this day depends on the need of the moment.

In this organizational scheme, the three pillars of empire consisted of what would today be translated as "politics," "religion," and "entertainment." Presiding over all three types of activities was the duty of kings. Any error or imbalance in performing this duty would, it would seem, lead to disorder in the realm. While it may have been an "invention" of Humayun to use an augury to name these three realms of his dominion, such a division was not merely rhetorical but rather a well-established practice of kingship. This can be gauged from the difficulty Shah Tahmasb faced when he tried to upset this balance and was overzealous in his attempts to be pious.

Shah Tahmasb was well known for his many relapses into piety, during which he pronounced bans on alcohol, gambling, prostitution, and other vices throughout the realm.[75] In fact, it was during one of these episodes of repentance (*tawba*) that he gave up painting and his famed atelier. In doing so, he lost his leading artists to Humayun and inadvertently launched a brilliant era of Indo-Persian art. Most of Shah Tahmasb's pious proclamations were highly symbolic, as they mainly coincided with moments of war, when the Safavid realm was under threat. Moreover, that these decrees were repeatedly issued throughout Tahmasb's reign also points to the lack of intention or ability of the crown to implement such prohibitions. In one case, which Tahmasb related in his memoir, the shah had a dream in which the Prophet appeared and told him that if he wanted to be victorious, he should give up forbidden things (*manahi*). In the morning, Tahmasb discussed his dream with his chief minister and other nobility. They said, "we are willing to abstain from some of these forbidden acts but others, like drinking [wine], which is necessary for governance (*saltanat*), we cannot give up."[76] Shah Tahmasb was only able to convince his courtiers, most of whom, it should be remembered, were also his Sufi disciples, after he brought further oneiric instructions from the Prophet the next morning. In short, the institution of sacred kingship had a strong performative and transgressive element to it. Even fastidious Sufi kings like Shah Tahmasb could only exercise their piety within limits.

The *Qanun-i Humayuni* also makes it clear that the auspicious form and pattern of imperial decrees was as important, if not more, than their content and execution. This can be seen in how Humayun divided his court into twelve ranks. Khwandamir wrote that the number twelve was chosen because of its far-reaching cosmological and scriptural importance:[77]

1. The eighth heavenly sphere is divided into twelve signs of the zodiac, on which the movement of the sun, moon, and all the planets depend, as does the calculation of months and years.
2. Some affairs of the world are dependent on time (*zaman*), that is, the hours of day and night, and day and night each are divided into twelve hours when they are in a state of balance (*hal-i i'tidal*) at the beginning of the seasons of spring and fall.
3. It is also mentioned in the Quran (9:36) that "the number of months according to Allah is twelve."
4. The prophet Jacob also had twelve sons, which later became the twelve tribes of Israel (*asbat*), as mentioned in the Quran (7:160).
5. The Quranic verse says that Allah sent twelve chiefs (*naqib*, p. *nuqaba'*) to the people of Israel to explain his word to them.
6. The Prophet appointed twelve men of the Ansar to chiefdom (*naqabat*) on the night of 'Aqaba (an incident in the Prophet's twelfth year of prophethood).
7. The number of innocent imams also reached twelve.
8. The written form of the two Muslim confessions of faith (*kalamatayn shahadatayn*) also depends on twelve characteristics. Anyone who calculates the letters (*huruf*) of these two expressions will obtain this truth.

In this scheme, the number twelve connected everything: the organization of the heavens, time, the calendar, the tribes of Israel, the leaders of the Ansars of Medina, the innocent imams, and the letters constituting the Muslim profession of faith. As was discussed in the last chapter, such "strange" connections were not merely symbolic but indicated hidden ontological links that made up a unified cosmic plan. True knowledge, then, consisted of the ability to know, divine, and manipulate this plan. Such augury taking was a common ritual among kings. Not only were practices of divination and geomancy used before battle but also afterward, in moments of leisure. Humayun, for example, after his conquest of Gujarat, had played a game of chance—"divining arrows" or "lots"—setting himself up against his Safavid rival, Shah Tahmasb, to determine the relative strengths of their sovereignty.[78] When Humayun was in exile at the Safavid court, this particular event was related to Shah Tahmasb, conceivably by the Timurid's enemies. The shah was told that Humayun had written "his own name on twelve first-class arrows and that of Tahmasb on eleven low-class arrows," an arrangement favorable to Humayun. The Safavid sovereign asked Humayun for an explanation and chastised him publicly for his hubris. The latter was able to assuage the anger of his royal host only after gifting a huge sum in diamonds.

To appreciate the role of such divinatory practices in the Sufi customs of the day, it is worth noting the claims of the millenarian Hurufi (Letterist) Sufi order in vogue during the classical Timurid period in Iran.[79] The Hurufi founder, Fazlallah Astarabadi, had gone a step further than most mystics in claiming to decipher completely and comprehensively the order of "resemblance" in all created things and to possess divine omnipotence. The basis of Astarabadi's thaumaturgical system was the shape, diacritical markings, and numerological properties of the Arabic and Persian alphabet. Even though Khwandamir in his descriptions of Humayun's court does not explicitly invoke Hurufi conceptions, he points toward a similar form of knowledge, in which the occult powers of numbers and

TABLE 4.4

The Twelve "Golden Arrows" or Alchemical Ranks of Humayun's Entourage

ARROW OR LOT	IMPERIAL GROUP
12	The emperor
11	The relatives, brothers, and other sultans who serve the emperor
10	The greatest of shaykhs, the Prophet's family and men of knowledge, and the People of Felicity
9	The great nobles
8	The emperor's personal servants (*muqarriban*) and officers (*ichkiyan*) who hold rank (*mansab*)
7	Remaining (non-rank-holding) officers (*ichkiyan*)
6	Clan leaders (*sarkhilan-i qaba'il*) and elders (*yuzbigiyan*)
5	Unique young men of ability (*yakka-i javanan*)
4	Special servants (*tahwildan-i sift-i ikhtisas*)
3	Young men of the circle [possibly of the hunt] (*javanan-i jirga*)
2	Servants in waiting (*shagird-i pishgan*)
1	Porters (*darban*) and camel drivers (*sarban*)

letters were the bases of an esoteric and alchemical scheme at work behind the order of the world.

Thus each of the twelve ranks of Humayun's entourage was assigned a "golden arrow" (*tir-i mutalla'*) of varying quality (see table 4.4).[80] The purity of the gold in each arrow or rank increased from one to twelve. The ranking of the imperial court and camp had, in other words, an alchemical basis. All men were ordered according to the purity of their being, the most pure being the emperor. The first eleven ranks or arrows were assigned to the nobility, court, army, and servants. The twelfth arrow, the highest-ranking one, was reserved for Humayun, since it was "equivalent (*mawafiq*) to the measure (*'iyar*) of red gold and [belonged] to the quiver of the emperor." Red gold, it should be noted, was the purest form of gold that an alchemist could produce.[81] The number twelve also suggested both an astrological reference as well as a messianic one, as the twelfth imam was supposed to return as the messiah, the purest of beings who would inaugurate the last millennium.

A further alchemical reference in Humayun's scheme was the use of the four elements (fire, air, water, and earth) to organize all the imperial services, each with its own function and chief functionary (see table 4.5).[82]

TABLE 4.5

Humayun's Imperial Services Organized According to the Four Elements

IMPERIAL SERVICE	RESPONSIBILITY
The Service of Fire (Sarkar-i Atish)	All affairs in which the lighting of fire was involved, such as instruments of war; the chief of this service always wore red
The Service of Air (Sarkar-i Hava)	Jurisdiction over the domain of the imperial kitchen (*bavarchikhana*), stables (*astabal*), and the necessities of adornment and beautification
The Service of Water (Sarkar-i Abi)	All the affairs of drink (*umur-i sharbatkhana*), the digging of canals (*juryan-i nahr*), and oceangoing missions (*muhimmat-i bahar*)
The Service of Earth (Sarkar-i Khaki)	All matters pertaining to agriculture (*zira'at*), construction (*'imarat*), and the extraction of essences (*zabt-i khulasat*)

Having divided up his court and dominion based on such cosmological principles, the emperor then assumed his role as the central being and animating force of the realm. He did so by drawing down the powers of the planets into his body. Each day of the week was known to be associated with a particular planet, and each planet with a color. Thus, the emperor donned clothes that suited the planet that oversaw that day (see table 4.6).[83]

As the table shows, the color of Humayun's dress was not merely related to the planets but through them to a series of signs in Islamic history and cosmology. On Saturday, for example, he would use black to draw

TABLE 4.6

The Color of Humayun's Clothes Selected According to the Planets

DAY / PLANET / COLOR	COSMOLOGICAL CAUSE AND EARTHLY EFFECT
Saturday / Saturn / Black	The wearing of black creates awe (*haybat*). This is why the Prophet wore a black hat (*ʿamama*) the day he conquered Mecca. Abu Muslim (the messianic leader of the eighth-century Abbasid revolution in Khurasan) had at the time of his emergence (*khuruj*) ordered his followers that for a few days they should wear clothes of the same color. The day they wore black, their faces looked awesome, so this became the color of their emblems (*shaʿar*). Thus the Abbasids adopted this color for their clothes, flags, and other materials of rule (*asbab-i farman farmaʾi*).
Sunday / Sun / Yellow	The emperor wears yellow this day according to the Quranic verse (2:69), "yellow, intense is her color, she delights the beholders" and spreads the rays of the light of justice.
Monday / Moon / White or Green	If the moon is near its fullness (*sarhad-i badriyyat*), then he wears white. Otherwise, he wears green. The Quran (76:21) says that green is the color of clothes in paradise.
Tuesday / Mars / Red	Tuesday is associated with the bloodthirsty Mars (*bahram-i khun asham*), and its color has redness (*hamriyyat*) in it. Thus, the emperor wears red on the throne on this day, and evildoers receive their due and the doers of good, peace and security.

(*continued on next page*)

TABLE 4.6 (CONTINUED)
The Color of Humayun's Clothes Selected According to the Planets

DAY / PLANET / COLOR	COSMOLOGICAL CAUSE AND EARTHLY EFFECT
Wednesday / Mercury / Blue	Wednesday is related to the lord of the planets, Mercury (tir-i-dabir). Since its nature allows mixture (*imtizaj*), the emperor sometimes wears collyrium blue (*kuhli*), sometimes azure (*lajawardi*), and sometimes "alcheh" [a Turkish word for a type of blue silk].
Thursday / Jupiter / Brown	On Thursday, which is overseen by Jupiter (*birjis*), the emperor wears beige-brown (*nakhudi*, or the color of chickpeas) and sits with the People of Felicity.
Friday / Venus / Green or White	On Friday, which is associated with Venus (*nahid*), the emperor wears either green or white. Many ulama have commented that the color green is related to the prophets (*anbiya'*) and the Prophet's family (*ahl-i bayt*). The Prophet Khizr (Green) is so named because wherever he sat down, the ground would break out in greenery [a sign of fertility also associated in Iran with the Zoroastrian goddess Anahita or Nahid (Venus)]. It is said that once he sat on a white skin and it turned green. A green garment is considered the *khil'at* or robe of honor of Khizr. It is also related by historians that at the time when the Abbasid caliph Ma'mun made Imam Riza [the eighth Shi'i imam] his successor in the caliphate, he changed the black dress and banners of the Abbasids to the color green. The emperor himself has said that when he sees the Prophet in a dream, the latter is dressed in green.

upon the power of Saturn and appear as awesome as the Prophet during the conquest of Mecca in the seventh century and as fearsome as Abu Muslim when he manifested himself as the revolutionary defender of Alid sovereignty and overthrew the Umayyad dynasty in the eighth century.[84] On Friday, Humayun would wear green, the color of the Prophet's clothes, as the king himself had witnessed in his dreams. Humayun's daily routine was in effect a powerful spiritual act, similar to the Shattari technique of calling upon the power of the planets, which could revive in new earthly forms the spiritual powers of past prophets, saints, and messiahs.[85]

Not all of Humayun's rituals were so somber in tone, however. As a sacred sovereign, Humayun's role was to strike a balance between the other world and this one, between conquest and stability, between justice and mercy, and between piety and pleasure. Thus, when Humayun was in a good mood, he would gather his favorites around him on a celestially patterned "carpet of mirth." Round in shape and placed on a round wooden platform, the carpet was made of a series of concentric rings, each colored to signify one of the nine heavenly spheres and the two "elemental" spheres of fire-air and earth-water. Humayun would seat himself in the sixth circle of heaven, golden in color, associated with the sun. His courtiers would be assigned places according to an astrological scheme. For example, the nobles of Indian lineage (*hindi al-asl*) and Sufis would sit in the sphere of Saturn, and the Sayyids and ulama would sit in the sphere of Jupiter. When everyone was seated, lots were cast. Everyone picked from a bag a piece of paper that had the figure of a person drawn on it in various poses, such as sitting, standing, and sleeping. Each member of the assembly would then assume the pose that fell to his lot. Thus, "without doubt that gathering took on an exceedingly odd appearance and became a source of increased mirth and delight."[86] Even imperial entertainment, it seems, was patterned on cosmological principles.

In short, the *Qanun-i Humayuni* justifies Humayun's practices of kingship by relating them to alchemical and astrological traditions as well as prophetic and Quranic ones. The work was written in such a high literary style and panegyric tone that at first glance it appears that all these symbolic arrangements were little more than a pleasing aesthetic façade bearing little relationship to the particular facts of Humayun's imperial life. However, there still remain in Khwandamir's beautifully constructed prose traces of the "practical" ends of these practices. Some of these ends were geared toward entirely local and bodily needs. For example, we learn that one of Humayun's inventions was a new type of vessel for pouring wine. With a uniquely long and curving spout, this vessel solved a problem particular to India: the need to keep the royal drink free of the dust and flies that infested Humayun's new dominions. Not all practical ends were inspired by the ecological challenges of Hindustan, however. One of the most important symbolic inventions of the emperor had its provenance in Iran. This was the special *taj* (crown) that Humayun designed for himself and his followers.

THE AUSPICIOUS TAJ OF HUMAYUN

The *Qanun-i Humayuni* called Humayun's "crown" his chief invention (*saramad-i ikhtira'at*). Meant for both the emperor's use as well as his chosen courtiers, it consisted of several raised gores (*tark*) and a cloth (*ʿasaba*) wrapped around it. This sash had two openings in it, shaped in the figure of the number seven. The two sevens put together became seventy-seven, the numerical value of the word *ʿazza* (or *ʿizzat*, meaning honor, power, and glory). Hence Humayun called his headgear the Taj-i ʿIzzat (Crown of Power and Glory). The emperor's turban was produced in one color, while the turban of the rest of the court was of one color inside the sash and another color outside it. Khwandamir recorded that he was among those who had the honor of wearing it. A court poet wrote the following poem to give a chronogram for the establishment of this imperial practice:

> The head of religion-nurturing (*din parvar*) kings, Humayun,
> May his dominion increase at every moment (*har dam*).
> Among the people, the wearing of the Crown (Taj),
> Became customary due to his good invention (*az husn-i ikhtiraʿash*).
> Although it is called the Crown of Glory (Taj-i ʿIzzat)
> Its date was given by Crown of Felicity (Taj-i Saʿadat).[87]
>
> (939 AH)

Humayun's new taj, according to the chronogram in the poem above, was invented in 1532 (939 AH), that is, within two years of his ascension. The Taj-i ʿIzzat clearly bore both a mimetic and a competitive relationship to the Safavid headgear, the Taj-i Haydari, a symbol of their Sufi brotherhood. It was meant to enact a ritual of sovereignty similar to the Safavid one, in which the ruler was the object of ritual devotion of his courtiers and soldiers. It would appear that Humayun instituted this symbolic practice in response to the loss of glory and power that his father had experienced when he became a Safavid disciple. But to become an object of ritual devotion, Humayun had to first become sacred. Thus, his keen interest in the esoteric sciences—the *ʿulum-i ghariba*—especially his recourse to the thaumaturgic gifts of the powerful and charismatic Shattari saints, was a means to achieve a degree of sacrality that would surpass even that of the messianic Safavid Shah Ismaʿil.

It is worth noting Eva Orthmann's insight that at key moments in his astrological staging of power, Humayun may have equated his throne to the throne of God. Orthmann observed that when celebrating his birthday, Humayun had his throne placed outside the tent of the twelve zodiac signs—a space reserved for God's pedestal and throne in Islamic cosmology—where, as Khwandamir stated, even "the sun needed the help of the pedestal (*kursi*) to reach the King and prostrate before him."[88] Shah Tahmasb apparently recognized the nature of these performative assertions when he complained that Humayun "became so vain as to claim divine powers" and began to believe that "other kings would soon have to present themselves at his court and accept his service, and their tenure of sovereignty will depend on his will." What the Safavid shah did not mention was that this was precisely the transgressive type of claim to power that his father, Shah Isma'il, had made fifty years ago, a claim that still resonated with the Qizilbash soldiers and nobility who saw Shah Tahmasb as the messiah's heir.

HUMAYUN AT THE COURT OF SHAH TAHMASB

Shah Tahmasb was the leader of the Safavid Sufi order as well as the sovereign of Iran. Barely ten when he inherited the throne, he spent his first ten years of rule faced with a civil war fought among the rival Qizilbash lords. When he finally managed to establish himself on the throne, he still remained constrained by the powerful Qizilbash elite. He tried to control them with all the means at his disposal, with his power as king and with his charisma as saint. The practices of the Safavid court still entailed the ritual of imperial discipleship. Shah Tahmasb remained for his Qizilbash followers the perfect guide (*murshid-i kamil*), to whom they submitted corporeally in the ritual of the Stick of the Path (Chub-i Tariqat). There are also reports that the ritual cannibalism of Shah Isma'il's days was still referred to in the court of Tahmasb's son, Muhammad Khudabanda (r. 1578–88).[89] Unlike his father, however, Tahmasb developed a more subdued manner of publicly expressing his sacrality. Perhaps it had become necessary to do so after Shah Isma'il's disastrous defeat at the hands of the Ottomans in 1514 at Chaldiran.

In contrast to the "ecstatic" poetry of Khata'i, Shah Tahmasb wrote a "pious" memoir, calling it a *tazkira* after the established tradition of the Sufi biography. In it, he focused on his role as a Sufi leader and related a series of dreams in which the Prophet, Ali, and the eponymous founder of the Safavid Sufi order, Shaykh Safi al-Din, aided him in establishing a just order on earth.[90] In sum, the Safavid saint-monarch still nurtured his saintly and messianic legacy and knew precisely how to respond to Humayun's symbolic claims to sacred power. He got his chance when Humayun appeared in his court seeking aid and asylum.

Defeated by the Afghan Sher Shah Suri in 1540 and abandoned by his brothers, Humayun had wandered in Sind and Baluchistan in poverty and desperation, with a shrinking band of supporters, until his request for help was granted by the Safavids in 1544. Most of the Mughal sources portray the moment of Humayun's arrival in Safavid territory as one in which the Timurid sovereign was treated as a great emperor, at least as an equal to the Safavids.[91] The Safavid sources treated the matter, as is to be expected, as a submission of the Timurid to Safavid rule. We also have one Timurid eyewitness account, composed by Humayun's ewer bearer, Jawhar Aftabchi, whose narrative supports the Safavid version. Although Aftabchi describes Humayun's submission to the Safavids in a somewhat sanitized fashion, his account still provides important details of the rituals involved.

Aftabchi recorded that as Humayun neared the Safavid court, the Safavid shah organized a grand reception at a distance from the court in which his courtiers, nobles, and princes participated according to proper protocol. Shah Tahmasb's brother, Sam Mirza, then personally welcomed Humayun in ceremonious style. The two men approached each other on horseback until they were a distance of one arrow shot away from each other. They then dismounted and came forward on foot. The Safavid prince had brought for Humayun a robe and an unbroken colt. He personally dressed the emperor in the robe but, Aftabchi was careful to mention, without the taj. It is not clear from Aftabchi's description whether it was the Safavids who did not impose the taj on Humayun at this time or whether it was the Timurid who resisted wearing it. In any case, even if the Timurid was spared the ignominy of putting on the Safavid marker of submission at this stage, he still had to undergo another Safavid ordeal. He had to ride the unbroken horse that the Safavids had brought for him. In this endeavor, according to Aftabchi, he passed with flying colors: "The emperor got on the unbroken colt, and when he mounted the horse was calm, and so the Turcomans [Safavids] tested and found this emperor's fortune to be strong (*imtihan kardand ki dawlat-i in padishah qavi bud*)."[92] The welcoming ritual, in other words, included taking an omen or augury to gauge Humayun's sovereign status at the time.

Thus, appropriately dressed and cosmologically vetted, Humayun was presented to Shah Tahmasb, only to be immediately put on the spot. The first question the Safavid monarch put to him was, "will you wear the *taj*?" Humayun immediately replied, according to Aftabchi, "it is a crown of glory (*taj-i ʿizzat*), I'll certainly wear it."[93] In Aftabchi's account, Humayun referred to the Safavid crown with the same name that he had given his own imperial headgear—Taj-i ʿIzzat. This was perhaps Humayun's (or Aftabchi's) way of lessening the insult that Humayun had to undergo in this ritual of submission.[94] Humayun had little choice but to give up his own crown and instead wear the emblem of Safavid discipleship, much as his father had done before him.[95] Until now, most scholarly accounts have treated Humayun's submission to Shah Tahmasb as a conversion to Twelver Shiʿism. However, this interpretation is anachronistic, as it ignores the Sufi nature of Safavid court rituals and assumes a predominance of juristic Shiʿism at the Safavid court, which was still several generations away. This ritual submission, instead, was undergirded by Sufi practices and tinged with *ghuluww* (exaggeration): the shah put the Safavid Taj-i Haydari on Humayun's head with his own hands, at which time all the Qizilbash nobles present in the gathering broke out in good cheer, and "saying 'Allah, Allah' prostrated before their monarch, as was their custom."[96] For the Qizilbash, their Sufi king had broken the power of a great rival dynast and made him a disciple and slave.

After Humayun's submission, the Mughals abandoned Humayun's taj. This is understandable, as it had been symbolically superseded and negated by the Safavid shah. Its memory was preserved in Mughal painting, however. Whenever Humayun or one of his servants was depicted in later Mughal paintings, they were shown wearing Humayun's sacred headgear. However, this did not mean that the Mughal dynasty had withdrawn from the competition. Indeed, the practice of royal deification and imperial discipleship did not end with Humayun. The cosmology and rituals of the devotional cult enacted in the grandeur of Akbar's court were a variation on the themes originally elaborated by Humayun and a direct response to the Safavid model of sacred kingship. But that is an argument for the next chapter.

CONCLUSION

Guru Nanak (d. 1539), an Indian mystic, poet, and holy man based in Punjab, whose disciples (*sishiyas* or Sikhs) and followers later gave rise to a new religious tradition, woefully described the coming of the Mughals as a "marriage party of sin."[97] Sinful or not, the party was joined by many Indians, whether soldiers or commanders, mystics or saints. The Mughals, for the most part, welcomed them with open arms, because their rule depended on garnering the support of local intermediaries. Although the religions and languages of Hindustan were new to the Mughals in the early sixteenth century, the fact of ethnic and religious diversity and the ability to function within such a social environment was not. They had not come to India from a homogeneous "Islamic world," bringing with them a uniform conception of rule based on classical legal traditions of Islam. Nor did they simply take over such a legalistic structure from their Afghan predecessors in Hindustan. The law books of Islam certainly existed at the time—and they were copied, transmitted, and taught—but the same cannot be said for social and political institutions that would have allowed these normative texts to shape society and politics. Instead, the range of religious beliefs was wide and the complexity of practices bewildering. Furthermore, this was true as much in Safavid Iran as it was in Mughal India.

Despite the Safavids' strong Alid leanings, in Shah Tahmasb's time Iran had not yet become Shiʿa in any juridical sense of the word. Indeed, the shah for all his piety still had to contend with the transgressive religious practices of his Qizilbash generals, who could not imagine giving up wine and still perform the role of governors. To control them, the shah did not make recourse to ideals of Islamic law but to his power as a saint in regular oneiric communication with Ali, the Prophet, and Shaykh Safi al-Din, the founder of the Safavid order. Thus, when his brother challenged his power as a Sufi monarch by putting on the taj, Shah Tahmasb boasted that not one of his Qizilbash disciples went over to his rival because they all recognized only one master in pursuit of the Sufi way (*dar rah-i sufigari murshid yaki ra midanand*).[98] The Safavid shah had inherited a saintly status, marked by the taj that his disciples wore. Humayun, on the other hand, had to work to make his own taj sacred.

The knowledges and institutions available to a ruler like Humayun to give himself an aura of sacrality and saintliness were rooted in both elite Perso-Arabic and Sanskrit intellectual traditions as well as in local devotional practices and competition. That these traditions and practices were so elaborate, pervasive, readily available, and institutionalized—some would say even "commercialized"—can be seen in the reactions of holy men like Guru Nanak, who preached giving up all these trappings of the sacred—whether Islamic or Indic, Sufi or Yogi—in order to return to a simpler mode of devotion without form and color, text and ritual, master and idol.[99] Strong reactions such as these highlight the social power of these trappings and institutions, which could transmute saints into kings and kings into saints. Such was the idiom of sacrality and sovereignty, and it was one that was used and understood both locally and universally. The Shattaris, known for their royal and martial style of mysticism and their local sources of power, were ideally suited to help Humayun develop an imperial cult of devotion in Hindustan. They were not alone, however, and faced competition from the Timurids' old spiritual allies, the Naqshbandis, who saw the Timurid conquest of Hindustan as an opportunity to spread their networks of influence and, possibly, make up for the territory and followers they had lost to the Safavids in Iran.

This competitive dynamic enveloping Sufis and soldiers, mystics and kings, was the real, "practical" relationship between religion and politics, between Islam and kingship. Yet, it is easily missed if the focus remains only on normative ideals of scriptural religion or royal advice derived from Iranian and Greek literary traditions. In this vein, dismissing Humayun as eccentric and idiosyncratic because of his deep interest in astrology and other occult traditions is to miss the point that these forms of knowledge provided an important symbolic foundation for the nascent Mughal empire in India. Unlike his Safavid rival, Humayun had not been born a Sufi leader and, despite strenuous efforts, was not able to achieve the status of a saint or messiah in his lifetime. But his efforts provided his successors with the sacred and mythical resources they needed when making their claims of sacred sovereignty. Humayun's important contribution was not lost on posterity.[100] Indeed, the chronicles from the court of his son, Akbar, recorded that upon seeing the horoscope of his newborn son, Humayun "fell a'dancing in exultation and whirled around in ecstatic joy" (*az kamal-i shawq ba raqs midaramadand wa az ghayat-i shawq junbish-i dawri minamudand*) because he had realized that the "horoscope of this Light of Fortune [Akbar] was superior, in several respects and by sundry degrees, to that of His Majesty, the Lord of Conjunction (Timur)."[101]

To appreciate his role in the development of Mughal sacred kingship, Humayun need not be compared with his warlord father, Babur, or with his pious Safavid contemporary Shah Tahmasb. He need not even be compared with Shah Isma'il, the first successful messianic monarch of Safavid Iran. Rather, Humayun's contribution mirrors closely that of Shah Isma'il's father, the Sufi Shaykh Haydar, who, even though he failed in his bid for the throne of Iran, bequeathed a sacred institution to his successors in the form of a cult of devotees marked by a sacred emblem, the Taj-i Haydari. Much like Shaykh Haydar, it was Humayun's symbolic and sacred legacy that enabled his son to claim that he had been born the Lord of the Age and the messiah.

{5} THE MILLENNIAL SOVEREIGN

THE TROUBLED UNVEILING OF THE SAVIOR MONARCH

Events of the year 990 AH (1582)
... Some shameless and ill-starred wretches also asked His Majesty [Akbar] why, since a thousand years from the Hijrah were passed, he did not bring forward, like [the Safavid] Shah Ismaʿil the First, some convincing proof (burhan).
—ʿAbd al-Qadir Badaʾuni, *Muntakhab al-Tawarikh*

HUMAYUN HAD made a concerted attempt at creating an imperial cult modeled after the Sufi kingship of the Safavids of Iran.[1] More generally, this attempt was an enactment of the style of sacred sovereignty that had taken shape in the former territories of Timur, a style inspired by emergent Sufi institutions, enshrined in elite knowledges of astrology and alchemy, and enlivened by popular memories of saints and heroes. But Humayun failed. He had little to show for his efforts except a ruined reputation as a vain heretic who dabbled in magic. His sacred order was publicly undone when, as a refugee in Iran, he was uncrowned at the hands of the Safavid Shah Tahmasb. This symbolic subservience of Humayun to the Safavids haunted the Mughals for generations. Yet it is easily missed, because later Mughal history reconfigured this embarrassing memory. This reconfiguration, however, required more than an act of negation, elision, or distortion in a set of texts. It also called for an act of production, a grand performance of sacrality. This was a burden that fell on the shoulders of Humayun's son, Jalal al-Din Muhammad Akbar (r. 1556–1605). And, as is argued below, Akbar chose the sign-laden moment of the Islamic millennium to requite the wrongs inflicted by the Safavids on his dynasty and redeem the sovereignty of Timur's heirs in India.

To appreciate the significance of this millennial moment, we must penetrate the thick layers of modern historiography under which Akbar's social personality lies buried. This Mughal emperor is, deservedly so, the most well-known and extensively studied figure from sixteenth-century India. The administrative and cultural foundations of empire that were laid in his half-century of rule gave the region a political cohesion and historical direction that were felt well into the eighteenth century. Even the early colonial administrators of the East India Company initially turned to the grand framework of Akbar's reign, recorded in the imperial manual titled A'in-i Akbari (Institutes of Akbar), for knowing the land, its peoples, its productivity, and the principles to govern it. Besides his political accomplishments, however, Akbar's name today evokes his innovative experiments with the religious traditions of his realm. At the height of his reign, he is thought to have given up Islam, his religion of birth, and instituted in its place a new sacred order centered on the figure of the monarch.

Although commonly referred to as the Divine Religion (Din-i Ilahi) and thought of as an amalgam of Islam and Hinduism, Akbar's cult remains an enigma, with its precise nature and purpose still open to debate.[2] The official Mughal sources do not even give it a name, simply calling it discipleship (muridi), while other sources refer to it variously as Divine Religion (Din-i Ilahi), Divine Monism (Tawhid-i Ilahi), or Four Degrees of Devotion (Ikhlas-i Chahargana). Nevertheless, this indeterminacy surrounding Akbar's spiritual endeavors has not hindered their being mythologized in popular and textbook histories. Given the rise of fractious Hindu and Muslim nationalisms in modern South Asia, Akbar's "religion" is commonly imagined as a precocious attempt at social engineering to harmonize the sacred traditions of his realm. Whether critical or laudatory, such appraisals are often made within nationalist frames of thought based on anachronistic conceptions of "religion" and "state."[3] What they do reveal, however, is that of all the Mughals discussed until now, Akbar's reign is seen as the dawn of a new era in the history of India.[4] Such a strong focus on Akbar as a myth of beginnings has led, predictably, to a neglect of the historical processes that shaped him as a sovereign.

The religious controversy surrounding Akbar must be reinterpreted in light of the institutions and knowledges of sacred kingship that had developed in early modern Iran and India. We must make an effort to move beyond the largely synchronic and South Asian evaluations of Akbar's "religion" as a sum of his spiritual quest and involvement with the Sufi orders of his realm,[5] his enthusiasm for a pantheistic metaphysics,[6] and his political need to bind together a ruling class in India that was ethnically and religiously diverse.[7] While these elements were certainly relevant, they do not explain why Akbar's claim was made in an idiom of messianism and enacted with rituals of sainthood similar to the ones that the Safavids of Iran had deployed. To understand why, we must view the religious dynamic at Akbar's court through sixteenth-century eyes. We must take seriously the fact that Akbar used the first Islamic millennium to proclaim his sacrality and, as the opening quotation shows, in doing so was accused of mimicking the messianic project of the Safavid Sufi-monarch Shah Isma'il.[8]

THE MILLENNIUM IN MUGHAL INDIA

Made king at age thirteen, Akbar spent the first five years of his reign in the grip of powerful regents, court factions, and kin groups. Successfully breaking free of these political forces at the age of eighteen, he began the hard work of building alliances and establishing a stable equilibrium among his Turkish, Persian, and Indian nobility. Akbar also had to fight incessantly, at first to preserve his precarious patrimony and then to subjugate rival sovereigns and warrior chiefs across northern and central India. He excelled at war, deploying innovative tactics and inventing new technologies. Between 1561 and 1569, a number of important Rajput kingdoms were added to the Mughal realm. In 1573, Gujarat was conquered, and in 1576, Bengal. This was not for Akbar, however, a zero-sum game of territorial conquest. Rather, it was a remarkably successful campaign to recruit participants in a long-term project of empire building that remapped the political geography of South Asia. Two decades into his reign, Akbar had created under him a diverse ruling class of noblemen, warlords, clan chiefs, and minor kings who were assigned numbered ranks and incented to serve as salaried servants of the expanding Mughal imperial realm. The emperor had become without doubt one of the greatest sovereigns of the time.

It was at this juncture that Akbar turned to pursuits that can be termed "cultural." Illustrated works of history, poetry, and epics were produced on a scale and in a style that had no precedent. Imperial palaces, mausoleums, and urban complexes were erected of a size, number, and grandeur hitherto unimagined. Amid this frenzy of cultural production and experimentation, the emperor began his inquiry into the religious traditions of his realm. In 1575, Akbar established the House of Worship (*'Ibadat Khana*). In this novel venue, the emperor personally supervised late-night debates in which scholars of various traditions—Islam, Christianity, Brahmanism, Jainism, and Zoroastrianism—expatiated and defended their beliefs.[9] During these gatherings, Akbar allowed free-ranging discussion on all points of doctrine and metaphysics, not excepting even the most central tenets of Islam. As was to be expected, the discussions often became bitter and deeply acrimonious, but he continued with the project. Then, in 1579, scandal broke and controversy began raging publicly. The emperor's rivals used accusations of heresy to rally men to their cause.[10] In some cases, religious edicts were issued against Akbar. None of this seriously weakened his political position, however. The rebels were crushed and at least two of the unruly Muslim jurists reportedly put to death.[11]

Once political order had been restored, Akbar celebrated his victories in the year 1582. In terms of the Islamic Hijri calendar, it was only the year 990. But those familiar with astrology knew that in this year an important conjunction of Saturn and Jupiter had reoccurred in the same celestial position as it had near the birth of Islam and the end of the Sassanian-Zoroastrian dispensation—a once-in-a-millennium event.[12] Grand celebrations were held at court. New coins were issued with the word "thousand" (*alf*) stamped on them. Most significantly, a thousand-year history was commissioned, called *Tarikh-i Alfi* (Millennial History).[13] This voluminous chronicle, written in Persian, consumed the labors of a team of authors for more than a decade. As a work of history, it was an unremarkable synthesis of the established Arabic and Persian chronicle tradition. But as a symbol of the millennium, the chronicle had many notable attributes.

For one, the Millennial History began not from the birth of the Prophet or his famous migration (*hijra*) from Mecca to Medina but from the year of the Prophet's death. No explanation was given for this curious choice of beginning. Universal histories at the time usually began with the birth of Adam. Dynastic histories began with a founding figure. Similarly, the history of an individual monarch started with the year of his birth or ascension. The norm, in other words, was to imagine the past as beginning with the advent of a sacred being, an embodied presence. The Millennial History, by contrast, began with the end of a sacred being, an embodied absence. By doing so, it set up an expectation of a new beginning and a new being, that is, a new cycle of time. Since the chronicle ended with the reign of Akbar, one can surmise that it was the Mughal emperor who had filled this absence and fulfilled this expectation by inaugurating the new millennium. This observation is supported by the fact that in this work Akbar was declared to be the Renewer of the Second Millennium (Mujaddid-i Alf-i Thani).[14]

"Mujaddid," or Renewer, was a label that had seen frequent and mostly uncontroversial usage since the early Islamic centuries.[15] According to prophetic tradition, a Mujaddid was supposed to appear at the beginning of every Islamic century to renew or revive Islam. As this scriptural tradition about the centennial Mujaddid indicated, the label carried within it a conception of cyclical time. Overall, it was a more restrained way of making a claim of sacrality than that afforded by the more openly messianic category of mahdi. That it carried such a messianic meaning in the case of Akbar is suggested by the evidence adduced for his status as the millennial Mujaddid: an occult calculation based on the letters of the emperor's name and the apocalyptic science of *jafr*.[16] In this form, Mujaddid was a sacred title and a coveted one. Akbar was not alone to have laid claim to it. In fact, the label Renewer of the Second Millennium became widely applied to one of Akbar's most acerbic contemporary critics, the famous Naqshbandi Sufi, Shaykh Ahmad Sirhindi (d. 1624).

Before his association with the Naqshbandis, Sirhindi had been a young scholar employed at Akbar's court. It was much later, in the reign of Akbar's son Jahangir (1605–1627), that Sirhindi became prominent as a leader of a branch of the Indian Naqshbandi Sufis. His main teachings as a Sufi master were recorded and circulated in a compilation of letters (*maktubat*) he had written to his sons, disciples, and contemporaries, some of whom were noblemen at the Mughal court.[17] In these letters, Sirhindi's charge against Akbar, whom he did not mention by name, and his corrupt ulama (*'ulama'-i su'*), who also remain anonymous, is little more than a general outcry about the dismal state of Islam in the "previous century," that is, Akbar's reign. Processes of modern Muslim revivalism and nationalism later recast Sirhindi as an authoritative champion of Sunni Islam in South Asia, portraying him as a "reformer" who single-handedly defeated Akbar's nefarious designs against Islamic orthodoxy. However, there is little historical evidence of such a competition between the mystic and monarch or, for that matter, of Sirhindi's political significance.[18] What is evident is that Sirhindi had generated a storm of a controversy by making a grand mystical claim of power that also explicitly invoked the millennium.[19]

Sirhindi had maintained that at the end of the first thousand years of Islam, the Muslim community had lost its connection with the divine that had initially been established via the Prophet. He wrote that with the coming of the millennium, the first Arabic letter in the name Muhammad, "mim," had transformed into the letter "alif," changing "Muhammad" into "Ahmad."[20] It is notable that Sirhindi's own name was Ahmad, a fact that opened the possibility that he was in fact the awaited millennial being.[21] Nevertheless, he refrained from claiming this explicitly in his writing and only hinted at the possibility. He stated that with the millennial transformation of the Prophet into a purely spiritual being, Muslims were in need of a new spiritual mediator. This person—the millennial Renewer—would reestablish its link with divinity for the next thousand years, the final historical era before the end of time. Sirhindi made his bid for the millennium, dangerous and heretical as it was, in a language that was ambiguous and esoteric.[22] One could argue that much like the use of the divinatory science of *jafr* in Akbar's case, Sirhindi's link with the millennium also was cast using the hidden and mystical properties of the letters of his name.

As the examples of Sirhindi and Akbar show, occult and esoteric forms of knowledge that had been so central to Humayun's sacred claims were critical for all pursuers of the millennium, whether saint or heretic, Sufi or king. Indeed, later Naqshbandi hagiographies of Sirhindi explicitly broke down the distinction between mysticism and monarchy in describing his sovereign status. For example, one popular text from the eighteenth-century, *Rawzat al-Qayyumiyya*, related the following apocryphal story of how Sirhindi came to recruit Akbar's son and successor, the emperor Jahangir, as his disciple. At first, Jahangir had been advised by his powerful minister Asaf Khan to deal severely with Sirhindi, because the Naqshbandi Sufi had a hundred thousand followers willing to fight for his cause. If Jahangir was not careful, the minister had warned the emperor, he would face an armed Sufi uprising such as that of Shah Ismaʿil and his Qizilbash militant-devotees in the Safavid conquest of Iran. Jahangir followed his minister's advice and had Sirhindi imprisoned. However, soon faced with a massive rebellion and a debilitating disease, he saw the errors of his ways and released Sirhindi from prison. Sirhindi cured Jahangir's illness and made the emperor his disciple. In doing so, this legendary narrative implied, Sirhindi saved Islam and Jahangir his empire.[23] In short, the messianic path to sovereignty was a well-known and well-trodden one, used by warrior saints and kings in real life as well as in imaginative narratives of their lives and deeds.

Moreover, this way of making a sovereign claim was based on a highly embodied notion of sacrality.[24] This can be seen in the way both Akbar and

Sirhindi were cast in the cosmological mold of a millennial "being." Their claim to inaugurate a new era of history pivoted not on a new "doctrine" or interpretation of "law" but on taking the place—bodily and spiritually—of a sacred entity that had existed in the previous era or cycle of time.[25] Such a religious imagination is also evident in the case of another "messiah," mentioned in the previous chapter, the founder of the Mahdavi movement, Sayyid Muhammad of Jaunpur (d. 1505), whose followers had been active in Gujarat in Akbar's time and were also invited to the Mughal court for religious discussions. A Chishti Sufi and learned scholar of Islam, Sayyid Muhammad, in the year 1495, had declared himself the expected mahdi and his interpretation of Islam as superseding and annulling the existing schools of Islamic jurisprudence—making, in effect, everyone outside of the Mahdavi fold to be non-Muslim. His messianic assertion had also been based on a corporeal omen: the prophetic tradition (hadith) that the body of the Prophet will no longer remain in its earthly abode after a thousand years and thus necessitate the rise of the mahdi.[26] No wonder that Sirhindi was accused by his contemporaries of claiming prophetic status and making heretical assertions like those of the mahdi of Jaunpur.[27]

There was no shortage, in other words, of sacred beings in a thaumaturgical competition for the millennium. Therefore, when the emperor's courtier and critic ʿAbd al-Qadir Badaʾuni accused Akbar of trying to mimic the messianic claims of the Safavid Shah Ismaʿil, this was not merely a rhetorical reference to a distant historical figure. One of the Safavid founder's descendants was present at the Mughal court to provide powerful evidence of his sacral lineage. This was Shaykh ʿArif-i Husayni, referred to respectfully as "shah," whose miracles were famous across India. Even Badaʾuni narrated his spiritual feats (khawariq) with awe and admiration: Shaykh ʿArif could throw round pieces of paper into a burning fire and take out gold coins in their stead, distributing them to all present. He could walk out of locked rooms and transport himself across time and space. He was known to distribute summer fruits from distant lands during the winter, and winter fruits in the summer. Most importantly he was, as Badaʾuni put it mysteriously, a man of many sacred claims (sahib-i daʿiyya ast).[28]

One of these claims was that of being the messiah.[29] Shaykh ʿArif had the habit of going around with his face veiled and would not lift it even in the company of high-ranking officials. The veiling of the face, as we have seen earlier in accounts of Shah Ismaʿil and Humayun, was a mark of the awaited savior who had yet to manifest his true nature. Ali was also often described in epics and depicted in painting with his face veiled. Shaykh ʿArif took his veiling with the utmost seriousness. Once, when Akbar's courtier Shaykh Abul Fath tried to pull off his veil, Shaykh ʿArif became incensed and cursed the transgressor. Then he revealed his face but warned Shaykh Abul Fath that he would pay the price in a fortnight. Shaykh Abul Fath, Badaʾuni reported, died of severe diarrhea exactly fifteen days later. This is how Badaʾuni described Akbar's envy for Shaykh ʿArif's abilities: one day the emperor exclaimed to the descendant of Shah Ismaʿil, "Shah, either become like me, or make me like yourself" (*shah ya khud chun ma shavid ya ma ra chun khud sazid*).[30]

Such embodied notions of sacrality, in which one sacred being replaced another in space and across cycles of time, was also at work in the narrative of Akbar's birth in his chronicle, the *Akbarnama* (Book of Akbar). The chronicle asserted that the emperor had been born—or more precisely, reborn—to inaugurate the millennium. It maintained that the divine light that had impregnated the Mongol princess Alanquva "in the same way as did her Majesty (*Hazrat*) Miryam (Mary) the daughter of ʿImran (Amram)" had found its perfection in Akbar after being reincarnated through the ages in different sovereign bodies. This divine light,

> which took shape, without human instrumentality (*wasila-i bashari*) or a father's loins (*rabita-i sulbi*), in the pure womb of her Majesty Alanquva, after having, in order to arrive at perfection (*istikmal*), occupied during several ages the holy bodily wrappings of other holy manifestations (*malabis-i qudsi-i mazahir-i digaran*), is manifesting itself at the present day, in the pure entity of this unique God-knower and God-worshipper (Akbar).
>
> How many ages (*zaman*) have passed away!
> How many planetary conjunctions (*qiran*) occurred,
> That this happy star might come forth from heaven![31]

In preparation for this holy birth, the chronicle portrayed Akbar's father Humayun as bequeathing a rich legacy of omens and sacred premonitions to his heir. As noted earlier, the chronicle described how it was Humayun who first recognized that his son's astrological status was greater than that of Timur Lord of Conjunction. It also related the father's dreams, miraculous events surrounding the expectant mother (given the honorific title of Maryam Makani, meaning "Of Mary's Stature," or, more literally, in place of Mary), and the infant Akbar's ability to speak, Jesus-like, in the cradle.[32] Since much of this material was compiled in the mature years of Akbar's reign, it can be argued that it was invented to create a hagiographical picture of the saint king's birth. What we do know for certain is that the chronicle celebrated Humayun's knowledge of the occult, giving weight to his foresights regarding his heir's future greatness. In this vein, Humayun's cosmological "inventions" of kingship were listed with pride.

Notably, however, Humayun's crown (*taj*) received only a brief mention, and only as a novel artifact from his days as a prince and not as a symbol of sovereignty. Akbar's chronicle gave an earlier date for the invention of Humayun's crown than that given by the contemporary writings of Khwandamir.[33] Furthermore, it did not describe how Humayun had adorned his entourage with the crown and how he had lost it at the hands of the Safavid Shah Tahmasb, who had put on Humayun's head, instead, the turban of the Safavid disciple.[34] Akbar had certainly known about his father's imperial headgear and in fact had worn it himself as a boy. This is evident from one of the few extant miniature paintings from Humayun's reign, in which the young Akbar stands by his father, both wearing the taj.[35] Rather than highlight the ignoble end of Humayun's cult and its iconic headgear, the chronicle's focus remained, instead, on Akbar's program of imperial discipleship. What it did not hide was that this endeavor, unveiled at the turn of the Islamic millennium, had also run into trouble.

THE *AKBARNAMA*: THE TROUBLED UNVEILING OF THE SAINT KING

The official chronicle of Akbar's reign was commissioned in 1589 and completed in 1598, the fifth and final decade of Akbar's reign. By this time, the millennium and the accompanying controversy (1579–1582) had passed. The chronicle contained a detailed and reflective account of the entire episode. In general, the *Akbarnama* was a massive effort of remembering, commemorating, and synthesizing history that had taken an army of collaborators across the realm to complete.[36] The emperor had been personally involved in the project, helping to resolve conflicting historical reports and even selecting which episodes to depict in painting. By one estimate, the chief author Abul Fazl produced five drafts before he was satisfied with the outcome.[37] From what survives of the original manuscript presented to the emperor in two parts in 1596 and 1598, it can be seen that some written pages accompanying the paintings were pasted over existing pages of writing, suggesting a reordering of images and text even in the final version. This strenuous and deliberate collective endeavor was not, even though it may appear at first glance, merely or even primarily an exercise in public relations or imperial propaganda. Rather, it is better understood as an effort at making whole the meaning of a long and turbulent life that not only saw the creation of a vast empire of unprecedented sophistication, power, and wealth but also experienced in the process an inordinate amount of violence, strife, and criticism. This introspectiveness and self-reflexivity of the imperial chronicle has to be kept in mind as we read a long section in it that referred to the troubled unveiling of Akbar's sacred cult.[38]

The *Akbarnama* relates how in 1579 an imperial decree was issued, signed by eminent scholars of Islam, in which Akbar was declared the imam and mujtahid of the age.[39] These were unusual titles for a monarch, especially the technical category of mujtahid, which implied an authority to decide matters of religious doctrine. This term was normally reserved for an eminent scholar of Islamic jurisprudence qualified to use reasoned judgment or *ijtihad* to resolve thorny questions of law that had no obvious solution in scripture or legal precedent.[40] As a ruler, for Akbar to claim the status of a mujtahid was a particularly bold act but not entirely without precedent. There had been the infamous case of the Abbasid caliph al-Maʿmun (r. 813–833) in Baghdad, who had launched the so-called inquisition (*mihna*) in an attempt to coerce leading Muslim jurists to recognize him as the ultimate authority in matters of Islamic doctrine and law.[41] In fact, Akbar's courtier Badaʾuni compared Akbar to Maʿmun when he observed that "the emperor [Akbar] examined people about the creation of the Quran." The question of whether the Quran was eternal or created in time had been central in Maʾmun's "inquisition."[42] Nevertheless, what made the use of the label of mujtahid in Akbar's case especially baffling was the well-known fact that the emperor was unable to read and write.[43] What may have puzzled others was, however, a mark of the emperor's holiness according to the chronicle. Indeed, it quoted Akbar as declaring illiteracy a trait of the prophets: "The prophets were all illiterate. Believers should therefore retain one of their sons in that condition."[44]

The *Akbarnama* presented a spirited defense of Akbar's ability as chief mujtahid. It asserted that holding this status did not require the learning of "paper-worshipping scholiasts (*madrasa nashinan-i qirtas parast*)" mired in the blind imitation of tradition (*taqlid*) handed down in worthless texts; rather, it required someone with innate intelligence and supreme spiritual potential—pointing, in effect, toward the embodied nature of the emperor's sacrality.[45] According to the chronicle, the emperor had only a year ago experienced an episode of divine rapture (*jazaba-i shinakht-i izadi*) while hunting, which was witnessed publicly by all present.[46] Thus, the rank of a mujtahid, the chronicle asserted, was surely lower than that of a holy soul (*nafs-i qudsi*).[47] Recognizing Akbar as the embodiment of spirituality and saintliness, many of the wise and learned of the time approached him to come forth and play his due role in matters of religion and end the "confusion of religions and creeds."[48] Akbar at first declined, because he had chosen to throw a "veil over his world-illuminating spiritual beauty."[49] However, he changed his mind when he realized that even in his role as mujtahid—a position lower than that of the true leader of the spiritual world—he would still be able to remain behind a veil and a screen:

> When their ideas were brought to the sacred hearing, the world's lord [Akbar] for a while, from his love for a veil (*az niqab dusti*), did not accept the proposal, and the enlightened body had to have recourse to entreaty. Inasmuch as the granting of desires forms a part of the laudable character of that circumspect Seer (Akbar) and his profession is that of a Healer, it flashed upon the vision-portico of the farsighted one, the understander of beginnings, the attainer of ends, that to come forth from the position of commander-in-chief (*sipah salar*) of the spiritual world to this office and to apply his mind to it, was, in reality, an adorning of the veil and a choosing of a screen (*niqab guzidan*).[50]

The chronicle emphasized the emperor's hesitancy to make manifest his full spiritual potential. It was only out of a strong sense of duty to the realm that he accepted the role of mujtahid. In doing so, Akbar made it his goal, according to the chronicle, to end the unquestioned following of tradition (*taqlid*), which had only caused dissension and confusion, and in its place offer reasoned judgment (*ijtihad*). In accordance with his new responsibilities as both religious and temporal leader, the emperor decided to deliver personally a Friday sermon (*khutba*) at the imperial mosque.

The emperor's decision to partially unveil his saintly self on the pulpit, however, caused some unexpected problems. According to the chronicle, lies and calumnies began to spread through the realm. Notably, Bada'uni, the critic whose list of charges against Akbar is discussed below, compared this act of combining both temporal and spiritual authority in one's person to that of the Prophet and Timur Sahib Qiran:

As [Akbar] had heard that the Prophet... his lawful successors, and some of the most powerful kings, as Amir Timur Sahibqiran, and Mirza Ulugh Beg-i Gurgan, and several others, had themselves read the *Khutbah* [the congregational sermon during Friday prayers], he resolved to do the same, apparently in order to imitate their example, but in reality to appear in public as the Mujtahid of the age.[51]

Overall, the accusations against Akbar were many and contradictory. Some accused him of claiming to be divine. This charge arose because, the chronicle suggested, there were people at court who were inclined toward treating their spiritual guide as divine (*ghulat*); it was they who spoke of Akbar as the Manifestation of Truth (Mazhar-i Haqq).[52] The emperor's only fault in the matter was that he had tolerated these groups and their beliefs according to his policy of "universal peace" (*sulh-i kull*).[53] Similarly, the chronicle dismissed another accusation that Akbar was claiming to be a prophet of God. This misunderstanding occurred because the emperor had introduced new laws and publicly pointed out discrepancies in some received Islamic traditions. In the same vein, Akbar's decision to receive "all classes of mankind with affection" and his search "for evidence in religious matters from the sages of every religion and the ascetics of all faiths" was misconstrued by some as his stance against the "Din-i Ahmadi," that is, Islam. This particular accusation, the chronicle maintained, came from those who had been unable to defend the truth of their doctrines in open debate with the "Christian philosophers."

None of these accusations were valid, the chronicle asserted. In fact, the emperor was surprised when told that he was accused of claiming to be divine and that he was against Islam. How could this be the case, the chronicle implored, when Akbar had always cared for the Prophet's family and raised many Sayyids to high office, even waiving the requirement for them to prostrate before him? But the accusations did not stop there. He was accused by Sunnis of being a Shi'a. This was because he had shown favor to Persians, many of whom belonged to the latter sect. The chronicle noted the absurdity of this complaint in light of the fact that the emperor had also promoted Sunni Turks. But the bigotry of his enemies knew no bounds. Thus, when the emperor increased the rank of the Hindus, he was accused of adopting the religion of the Brahmans. In the end, the chronicle sums up three reasons for these "failed" accusations:

First—The sages of different religions (*milal o nihal*) assembled at court, and as every religion (*aʾin*) has some good in it, each received some praise. From a spirit of justice, the badness of any sect could not weave a veil over its merits.

Second—The season of "Peace with all" (*sulh-i kull*) was honoured at the court of the Caliphate [i.e., Akbar's court], and various tribes of mankind of various natures obtained spiritual and material success.

Third—The evil nature and crooked ways of the base ones of the age.[54]

In effect, the chronicle depicted Akbar as hurt at being misunderstood for taking a stance that was reasonable, equitable, and practical: patronize all classes of men who were loyal to the empire, inquire about the truth of all the sacred traditions of the world, and encourage debate to resolve matters of doctrinal difference among them. For all his efforts, however, he was branded variously as apostate, heretic, schismatic, and an enemy of Islam. He was, the chronicle maintained, none of the above. He was simply the supreme spiritual being of the age, the *peshwa* of the spiritual world who had been beseeched by many of his subjects to become their earthly guide as well as spiritual master.

Setting aside for the moment the question of the truth value of this apologia, it is worth noting that, even two decades after the controversial edict of 1579, the emperor did not retreat from his position as supreme spiritual guide of the realm. His authority in matters of Islam was held to be greater than that of any scholar. This stance was propounded even more clearly in the third volume of the chronicle, which laid out the "institutes" or "regulations" of Akbar's imperial administration. It contained "regulations for providing guidance" (*aʾin-i rahnamuni*), placed right after "regulations for the muster of people" (*aʾin-i didan-i mardum*), which stated in unambiguous terms that Akbar was both the temporal and spiritual leader of the realm. It was so, the chronicle maintained, that men and women came to him from all walks of life and religious traditions to obtain guidance, blessing, and miraculous cures:

> Many sincere enquirers, from the mere light of his wisdom, or his holy breath, obtain a degree of awakening which other spiritual doctors could not produce by repeated fasting and prayers for forty days. Numbers of those who have renounced the world (*arbab-i tajrid*), as *Sanyasis, Jogis, Sewras, Qalandars, Hakims,* and *Sufis,* and groups upon groups (*guruha guruh*) of such as follow worldly pursuits, as soldiers, tradespeople,

mechanics, and husbandmen, have daily their eyes opened to insight, or have the light of their knowledge increased. Turk and Persian, young and old, friends and strangers, the far and the near, look upon offering a vow to His Majesty as the means of solving all their difficulties, and bend down in worship on obtaining their desire. Others again, from the distance of their homes, or to avoid the crowds gathering at Court, offer their vows in secret, and pass their lives in grateful praises. But when His Majesty leaves Court, in order to settle the affairs of a province, to conquer a kingdom, or to enjoy the pleasures of the chase, there is not a hamlet, a town, or a city, that does not send forth crowds of men and women with vow-offerings in their hands, and prayers on their lips, touching the ground with their foreheads, praising the efficacy of their vows, or proclaiming the accounts of the spiritual assistance received. Other multitudes ask for lasting bliss, for an upright heart, for advice how best to act, for strength of the body, for enlightenment, for the birth of a son, the reunion of friends, a long life, increase of wealth, elevation in rank, and many other things. His Majesty, who knows what is really good, gives satisfactory answers to everyone, and applies remedies to their religious perplexities. Not a day passes but people bring cups of water to him, beseeching him to breathe upon it. He who reads the letters of the divine orders in the book of fate, on seeing the tidings of hope, takes the water with his blessed hands, places it in the rays of the world-illuminating sun, and fulfills the desire of the supplicant. Many sick people of broken hopes, whose diseases the most eminent physicians pronounced incurable, have been restored to health by this divine talisman (*ilahi tilism*).[55]

The chronicle maintained that it was this popular and widespread recognition of Akbar's spiritual status and the efficacy of his royal touch that compelled him, despite his hesitation ("why should I claim to guide men, before I myself am guided?"), to enroll disciples. People of all classes became the emperor's followers in droves. Accordingly, a proper ceremony was organized to bestow imperial discipleship on those whom the emperor saw fit. In this ritual, a novice supplicant took an oath and was awarded a special seal (*shast*) that had inscribed on it that "greatest of names" (*ism-i aʿzam*) and "holiest of talismans" (*tilism-i aqdas*), "Allah Akbar." This iconic utterance, *Allah Akbar*, served as the key emblem for the emperor's disciples. It was stamped on their seal rings and was used by them to greet each other. This greeting was the first item listing in the "regulations for disciples" outlined in the Institutes of Akbar.[56]

Recommendations for the Members of Akbar's Imperial Order of Disciples (*A'in-i iradat guzinan*)

1. The members ... on seeing each other, observe the following custom. One says "*Allahu Akbar*" and the other responds "*Jalla Jalaluhu.*" The motive of His Majesty, in laying down this mode of salutation, is to remind men to think of the origin of their existence, and to keep the Deity in fresh, lively, and grateful remembrance.
2. It is also ordered by His Majesty that, instead of the dinner usually given in remembrance of a man after his death, each member should prepare a dinner during his lifetime, and thus gather provisions for his last journey.
3. Each member is to give a party on the anniversary of his birthday, and arrange a sumptuous feast. He is to bestow alms, and thus prepare provisions for the long journey.
4. His Majesty has also ordered that members should endeavour to abstain from eating flesh. They may allow others to eat flesh, without touching it themselves; but during the month of their birth they are not even to approach meat. Nor shall members go near anything that they have themselves slain; nor eat of it. Neither shall they make use of the same vessels with butchers, fishers, and birdcatchers.
5. Members should not cohabit with pregnant, old, and barren women; nor with girls under the age of puberty.

The disciples were advised to salute each other in the following manner: one says "*Allahu Akbar*" and the other responds "*Jalla Jalaluhu.*" Both these Arabic salutations were, on the surface, in praise of Allah, but they also contained the emperor's name (Jalal al-din Akbar) within them. Thus, while their surface meaning was "God is Great" and "May His Glory be ever Glorious," their inner or hidden meaning could be, as the emperor's critics pointed out, a declaration of the emperor's divinity: "Akbar is God" and "May His Glory be ever Glorious."

It is worth noting that the regulations for disciples were set forth more as recommendations than as strictures, and they consisted of bodily practices rather than doctrines. Moreover, a common thread connecting these practices seems to be the notion of rebirth, that is, the transmigration of the soul. This is indicated by the regulations' emphasis on celebrating moments of birth and death, abstaining from meat during these celebrations, and avoiding men who had taken life and women who were unable to give life. All of these ritual acts and taboos seem to be based on a symbolic scheme designed to assist the recycling of the soul. This metaphysical concept was an important component not only of Indic religious traditions but also of the radical mystical traditions of Islam often labeled as *ghulat*.[57]

This, then, was the official description and justification of Akbar's sacred status and his devotional cult. It openly acknowledged his patronage of radical and antinomian Sufi groups who venerated him as divine; his support for the arguments of the Jesuit priests against their Muslim adversaries; his impatience with traditional Islamic law; his need to recruit and patronize men from all creeds and castes across India, Iran, and Transoxania; and, finally, his thinly veiled performance as the saintly guide and spiritual master of all humanity. Yet, despite all this, the chronicle maintained that Akbar had not turned away from Islam—that he was neither prophet nor deity. Taken together, these conflicting assertions seemed to say that Akbar was not against Islam or any other religious tradition, but rather, as the most sacred sovereign on earth, he was simply above them all.

In official terms, Akbar's sacred scheme was not presented as a "religion" meant to replace Islam. It did not have a centered theology or coherent doctrine. Yet it was founded upon the insistence that Akbar was the saint of the age. And this was an insistence coupled with a disdain for established textual traditions and scholasticism. One gets the sense that Akbar's sense of his own sacrality was highly imagistic, acted out with the help of visible and vocalized symbols (seals, talismans, and utterances) and tactile practices (breathing upon water, placing water in the sun, avoiding meat and barren women).[58] This way of engaging the sacred was consistent with saintly norms of comportment at the time. It also seemed particularly suitable for an emperor who was a supremely capable organizer of men and materials but who did so without recourse to reading and writing.

Akbar's illiteracy, which had been given a prophetic cast in his lifetime, has already been mentioned.[59] Moreover, the emperor was known to have loved working with his hands, making things, and inventing mechanical devices. He also possessed a prodigious memory, accurately remembering "the contents of books read to him, the details of departmental business, and even names of hundreds of individual birds, horses, and elephants."[60] All this evidence supports the notion that Akbar was uncomfortable with abstract thought but was a master of its concrete variety. The vast collection of books in his library, the large number and variety of texts produced at his court, and his alleged interest in religious "doctrines" belie the fact that Akbar was a *bricoleur extraordinaire*.[61] He was a dexterous intellectual handyman, imbibing and manipulating knowledge in a form that could be visualized, touched, embodied, and performed. Akbar's sense of the sacred was closer to that of the antinomian mystic and local "holy man"[62] than to the scholastic theologian and ordained cleric. Indeed, this was what the Jesuit priests who had come to convert him to Christianity discovered to their dismay.

THE JESUITS' ORDEAL AT AKBAR'S COURT

In 1579, the year Akbar was proclaimed the mujtahid of the age, the chief fathers of the Order of St. Paul in Goa received a royal edict requesting them to send Christian priests to his court: "I . . . ask you to send me two learned priests, who should bring with them the principal books of the law and the Gospel, so that I may learn the Law and what is most perfect in it. . . . And when I shall know about the Law and its perfection as I desire, they may go whenever they like."[63] The message caused quite a stir among the Portuguese. At the beginning of the sixteenth century, the Portuguese had established, chiefly through the means of armed naval aggression, a monopoly on the Indian Ocean and the lucrative spice trade across it. Although Akbar never openly challenged the Portuguese domination of the seas, he was an extremely powerful monarch whose expanding imperial interests frequently overlapped with those of the Portuguese and whose politics they could not ignore. The prospect of bringing such a great ruler into the folds of Christianity was certainly an exciting one for the devout Jesuits.[64] Jesuit missions aimed at converting monarchs and notables in the Indian subcontinent had neither been uncommon nor unsuccessful. Some kings in the Maldives and Ceylon—even a relation of the king of Bijapur—had been fruitfully converted. The Portuguese viceroy, however, was concerned about the missionaries being held as political hostages by the Mughals.[65] But the decision was left to the bishops, and religious fervor overcame political cautiousness. It was decided that three volunteers would be sent to the Mughal court in Fatehpur Sikri.

The three priests of the first Jesuit mission arrived at the Mughal court in February 1580.[66] Anthony Monserrate, forty-three years old, was considered the most mature and wise. Francis Henriquez, a couple of years younger than Monserrate, was of Persian descent—he had been converted to Christianity as a child in the Portuguese stronghold of Hormuz in the Persian Gulf—and was meant to serve as translator. Rudolf Acquaviva, only twenty-nine years old, was of high social standing and the most ascetic of the three.[67] From the Jesuits' own accounts, Akbar treated them with great respect and trust.[68] He had them tutor his son.[69] He visited their chapel, paid respect to the Bible, and even prayed in their manner.[70] The Jesuits were initially so surprised at their warm reception and at Akbar's "hands-on" approach to Christianity that they felt that the emperor, in his search for the one true faith, was more inclined toward their faith than any other.[71] Thus, when he asked them to participate in religious debate with his Muslim scholars, they did so with the utmost zeal and intellectual vigor.

The Jesuits claimed to be better prepared than their Muslim rivals. They had brought with them a Greek translation of the Quran and quoted from it to support many of their arguments.[72] Acquaviva took the lead in proving, according to him, the validity of the Christian scriptures and the fallacy of the Quran:

> We [the Jesuits] demonstrate all that we say of Christ by the testimony of the prophets of the past, thus their own book itself says many good things of Christ, but of Mahomet [Muhammad] none of the prophets that have gone have spoken. . . . And because we have here a translation of their book [the Quran], we cause them a lot of bother, and they cannot bear this, because the King tells them this many times to confound them.[73]

Since the Muslim scholars did not have a copy of the Bible, they were at a disadvantage, according to the Jesuits. Thus a suggestion emerged that the question of truth between Islam and Christianity should be settled not by reasoned debate but via an ordeal by fire.[74] The sources are not in agreement, however, about who made this suggestion.

The Jesuits initially wrote in their letters that the challenge came from their Muslim rivals and, although they were not afraid to die, they declined the ordeal because it was not the proper thing to do. Akbar's chronicle also recorded the incident but gave an account that contradicted the Jesuits' story. In the Mughal version, it was Acquaviva, praised as being "singular for his understanding and ability," who threw out the challenge to his Muslim adversaries:

> The Padre quietly and with an air of conviction said " . . . ! In fact, if this faction [Muslims] have such an opinion of our Book [the Gospel], and regard

the Furqan (the Qoran) as the pure word of God, it is proper that a heaped fire be lighted. We shall take the Gospels (*injil*) in our hands, and the ʿUlama of that faith shall take their book, and then let us enter that testing-place of truth. The escape of any one will be a sign of his truthfulness."[75]

The chronicle also recorded that the ordeal never came to pass, as the "liverless and black-hearted" Muslims refused to take up the challenge. This official Mughal version of events was contradicted by another eyewitness account written secretly by Badaʾuni, the emperor's critical courtier. Badaʾuni recorded that during the debates Akbar sent for a Muslim ascetic (*faqir*) with a reputation for spiritual enthusiasm. This man challenged the Christians to the ordeal, but it was the Jesuits' cowardice that prevented them from accepting the Muslim's challenge.[76] While all three accounts maintained that the rational debate between Islam and Christianity devolved into a challenge of ordeal by fire, they do not agree on who offered the challenge and who declined it. While the divergence among these narratives may be put down to spite, malice, and deceit, it may also be explained by another less obvious aspect of the episode: the Mughal emperor himself had been the chief proponent of this deadly competition.

Akbar had apparently harbored a desire to witness the ordeal by fire ever since he had heard about this practice from a lone Jesuit priest a few years prior. Monserrate, writing much later in life, revealed that the Christian practice of trial by ordeal had been described to Akbar by Julian Pereira, a Jesuit priest who had come from Bengal in 1578.[77] The fact that Pereira, a man "of more virtue than learning,"[78] had proposed an ordeal by fire may explain why Akbar had hoped that the Jesuits of the first mission would hold a practical demonstration of the truth of their sacred tradition. However, when the Christians demurred, he told them that his main motive in proceeding with the ordeal was to convince a "Mullah," whom the emperor severely disliked, to end his own life "in order not to arouse the people."[79] He wanted the Jesuits to go along with him in this scheme at least until the annoying man entered the fire. When the Jesuits still refused to cooperate, Akbar suggested other tactics. He proposed that they simply nod their heads at the appropriate time in public instead of verbally accepting the challenge. They still refused, so he suggested that they simply keep their silence and let him interpret it as a tacit agreement to go ahead with the ordeal. When the Jesuits remained unwilling to oblige, Akbar asked that they let him declare, in their absence, that they had accepted the challenge. The Jesuits, however, did not yield, and Akbar abandoned the scheme. From the Jesuits' account, it appears that it was Akbar who kept inciting them to accept the deadly challenge or at least pretend to until their adversaries entered the fire.

Even if the Jesuit account is discounted as biased—keeping in mind, though, that the other two Mughal sources were quite as embellished—there is no denying the fact that the ordeal by fire was proposed and encouraged at the House of Worship, where the emperor set the rules of the game. Why would Akbar, the most powerful sovereign of his age, go to such lengths to manipulate invited guests and eminent courtiers, asking them to die such grotesque and spectacular deaths? Clues to an answer lie in the complex relationship revealed by the Jesuits' ordeal between violent spectacle and sacred authority at Akbar's court. The episode of the ordeal by fire unsettles both the spiritual-theological and political-ideological interpretations of Akbar's "religious policy." It also forces us to reevaluate the official proclamations from Akbar's court about promoting "universal peace" (*sulh-i kull*), ending the "confusion of caste and creed," and privileging reason (*ijtihad*) over tradition (*taqlid*). This is not to say that there was no positive intent behind Akbar's quest to encourage peace among his subjects and impose order upon his realm. Rather, it is to argue that any interpretation of the pronouncements made in the emperor's name must be grounded in the practices and attitudes that underlay his mode of religiosity and notions of sacrality. To make sense of these practices and attitudes, it is worth examining the emperor's activities in a broader social context.

Akbar's embrace of the ordeal by fire is consistent with his pastimes outside the House of Worship in the more public arenas of the life of the camp. Here, too, we find evidence of the emperor's fondness for "hands-on" knowledge and public spectacle. As Monserrate recorded in one of his letters from the Mughal court:

> The King is considered by some to be mad, because he is very dexterous in all jobs, because I have even seen him making ribbons like a lacemaker, and filing, sawing, working very hard; he is the whole day with deer, pigeons, cocks, birds, cages, dances, fights of wild elephants, wild buffaloes, fights among men, mock quarrels and claims, and other pastimes.... I hold him to be astute and prudent, but a little excessive in the things I have related above.[80]

Indeed, the Jesuits had found Akbar's excessive fondness for *gladiatorii ludi* to be a roadblock to conversion. Akbar's zest for such spectacles is also recorded in his own chronicle. It described an incident, lavishly illustrated in a magnificent two-folio painting, in which a deadly fight between two Sannyasi (Hindu warrior ascetic) groups broke out at an encampment.[81] Even though Akbar eventually tried to stop the fighting, the chronicle reported that he was "highly delighted with this sport."[82] Incidences such as these were not random occurrences in the public life of a sovereign. It was, as was suggested earlier, the sovereign's role to gaze and impose order upon the realm. Moreover, seen from the pedestal of sacred kingship, this was a realm contiguous across culture and nature, court and camp, humans and animals. Both these aspects of the realm had to be brought under the sway of sovereign order. In this vein, observe how the regulations regarding man and beast were arranged in the imperial guidebook, the "Institutes of Akbar":

*The Arrangement of Akbar's Imperial Regulations
   Concerning Court and Camp*

Regulations for Admission to Court
Regulations for Making Obeisance
Regulations for Standing and Sitting
Regulations for the Muster of Men
Regulations for Providing Guidance
Regulations for Disciples and Devotees
Regulations for the Muster of Elephants
Regulations for the Muster of Horses
Regulations for the Muster of Camels
Regulations for the Muster of Cattle
Regulations for the Muster of Mules
Regulations for the Maintenance of Animal Health
Regulations for Animal Fights and for Betting

It was in the "Regulations for Providing Guidance" (*a'in-i rahnamuni*) that Akbar was declared the spiritual and temporal guide of all peoples regardless of caste, creed, or profession, who were all encouraged to become his disciples and devotees. Immediately after this regulation came those for managing the affairs of elephants, horses, camels, cattle, mules, and for arranging animal fights and public spectacles. These regulations were based on the detailed advice of the emperor, who routinely inspected, classified, and cared for his animals—and also enjoyed seeing them fight.

We get a similar picture from the classificatory zeal that the emperor showed in organizing his court and camp. Much as Akbar had arranged his nobility into dozens of numbered ranks (*mansabs*) based on merit and service, he had also organized his animals into groups by weight and food consumed; there existed thirteen weight ranges for elephants and six for other animals.[83] Finally, it is worth noting that in this milieu slavery served as another bridge across the culture/nature divide. Akbar is reported to have exchanged groups of heretics and rebels (exiles from culture) for horses and colts (exiles from nature).[84] Many of these aspects of Akbar's sovereign persona are also discernible in the religious debates that went on late into the nights in the House of Worship, where he alone served as spectator, referee, and judge.[85] It may explain why he brought from afar learned men of all stripes, to compete against one another in an arena specially built for this purpose, and why he goaded them to enter the ultimate contest, to fight to the death to uphold the truth of their beliefs.

Monserrate, a "sadder and wiser man,"[86] writing many years after his return from Fatehpur Sikri, lamented that Akbar's invitation to the Jesuits may have been motivated by something other than divine inspiration: "It may be suspected that Jalal-ud-din Akbar was moved to summon the Christian priests, not by any divine inspiration, but by a certain curiosity, and excessive eagerness to hear some new thing, or a design to devise something novel for the destruction of souls."[87] His bitterness at the failure of the Jesuit mission notwithstanding, Monserrate may have been correct to suspect that the Jesuits were invited to the Mughal court not to inform the emperor about the finer points of Christian doctrine. They were there to embody and perform their faith for his pleasure.

The argument above is not meant to dismiss Akbar's religious endeavors as mere spectator sport. Rather, it is meant to take seriously the sensuous and performative way in which the king preferred to "know" both the sacred and the profane. Akbar was not simply a detached observer of the sacred theater he had organized. He participated in it bodily. He not only prayed with the Jesuit priests, touched their holy relics, and meditated upon their sacred icons. He also performed similar participatory acts with other invitees to his court. For example, the Zoroastrian Parsis from Gujarat recorded that the emperor had put on their sacred cord and garb. The list of such reports is long: Akbar had memorized one thousand and one names of the sun in Sanskrit; he had, like his father Humayun, matched the color of his clothes to the planet of the day; he had practiced rites of "fire worship" in the Brahmanical and Zoroastrian style; he had modified his diet according to tantric principles to prolong his life; and he had shaved his head in preparation for letting his soul escape, so it could enter the body of another great sovereign.[88]

These reports bring us back to an earlier point made about Akbar's embodied notions of sacrality. Unable to read or write, the emperor had a preference for concrete thought and tactile knowledge. His understanding of the world was constructed more via the medium of things and sensuous signs and less from abstract concepts and ideas. A *bricoleur*, he assembled practical solutions from the materials at hand. These materials, as far as his subjects were concerned, were their religious identities expressed in acts and symbols, emblems and relics. Thus, Akbar's cult was built up from elements of the religious traditions he had experienced, arranged in new combinations and permutations. But these cultic elements must be understood primarily not as doctrinal or ideological but as somatic and talismanic. That is to say, they were not meant to be projected outward and imposed on his subjects. Rather, they were designed to be reflected inward and embodied by the saint king. Thus made sacred, he would become the ultimate holy man, venerated by his disciple-subjects throughout the realm, and thus would end the "confusion of caste and creed." And the most importune and efficacious time for this ritual enactment was, as any good astrologer would have known, the millennium.

BADA'UNI'S CRITIQUE: THE MILLENNIAL "MADNESS" OF KING AKBAR

The first Jesuit mission ended in 1582, but not before the Christian priests had seen the millennial celebrations at court. Acquaviva described them as follows:

> The court is much perplexed over the novelties introduced by the King each day, because among other things he seems to pay homage to creatures like the sun and the moon, and abstains from meat on Saturday night and entire Sunday.... In addition... he instituted a new festival called the Merjan [The Persian feast of the autumnal equinox] and commanded that all captains should appear in festive attire, and there was music and dancing.[89]

The Jesuits were not the only ones to remark on the bewilderment caused by Akbar's actions. Akbar's courtier Bada'uni also described it with relish in his secret chronicle, the *Muntakhab al-Tawarikh* (Selected Histories). Made public after the author's death (c. 1614), this book proved so scandalous that Jahangir banned it and had the late author's sons arrested to answer for their father's deed. The imperial ban, of course, had the opposite effect. According to the eighteenth-century chronicler Khafi Khan, the book sellers in the capital soon sold out of Bada'uni's work, which contained tales about Akbar that were "unmentionable" (*na guftani*).[90] This is not to say that the entire text was slanderous. In fact, much of Bada'uni's work was a conventional chronicle, and most of its mentions of Akbar were positive and respectful. The scandalous parts, however, were concentrated in the year of the millennium.

Bada'uni began his description of the "millennial" year 990 AH (1582) with Akbar proclaiming, "We have found out proofs for part of the reality of metempsychosis."[91] Metempsychosis, or transmigration of the soul, was, as discussed previously, a central tenet of both Indic cosmology and *ghulat* Sufi groups who espoused millennial beliefs, such as the Nuqtavis and Hurufis. It was used by the latter to deny Islamic eschatology and provide a metaphysical mechanism for the messianic soul to be reincarnated on earth. Having identified Akbar with this deeply heretical but powerful messianic concept, Bada'uni reported that as the new year according to the Persian calendar came up, Akbar believed that the period of the faith of Islam was now completed and "felt at liberty to embark fearlessly on his design of annulling the statutes and ordinances of Islam and of establishing his own cherished pernicious belief."[92] The emperor began to issue a series of decrees, which are only found in Bada'uni's account.

First, the emperor decreed that everyone perform the *sijda* (prostration) in front of the king, implying the divinity of the monarch. Then he allowed wine to be sold officially near the palace. Even though the wine was meant only for medicinal purposes, according to Bada'uni, in point of fact, "a shop for the benefit of drunkards was opened."[93] He quoted reports that "swine-flesh formed a component part of that wine, but God knows." He said that Akbar also tried officially to manage access to prostitutes just as he had tried to legalize wine selling, but all his efforts failed, and "drunkenness and debauchery" prevailed: "prostitutes of the imperial dominions . . . had gathered together in the Capital in such swarms as to defy counting or numbering. These he made to live outside the city, and called the place 'Shaitanpurah' [Devilsville]."[94]

The rest of Bada'uni's chronicle consisted of a list of similar actions of the emperor and his courtiers that would shock any pious person's sensibilities. For example, Akbar encouraged the shaving of the beard because "the beard drew its nourishment from the testicles . . . what could be the virtue and distinction of preserving it?"[95] He started to keep swine and dogs in the harem in order to look at them every morning as a religious service. Some of his courtiers started taking dogs—an animal considered impure by Muslims—to their dining tables, and a few even started "taking the dog's tongues into their mouths." Instead of performing ablution after having sex, as is normative Islamic practice, Akbar suggested that ablution be performed before having sex. Instead of avoiding silk and gold, as Muslim men are supposed to, he made the wearing of gold and silk mandatory. He forbade Islamic prayers, fasting, and the pilgrimage and allowed the day of resurrection and judgment to be openly doubted and ridiculed at court. He replaced the Islamic calendar with a Persian solar one and introduced Zoroastrian festivals at the court. He disapproved of the study of the religious sciences and promoted, instead, the study of philosophy. In short, according to Bada'uni, Akbar abandoned the entire normative order of Islam and instead instituted its diametric opposite in its place—all in the year of the millennium:

> The era of the Hijra was now abolished [in 990 AH/1582 AD]. . . . Reading and learning Arabic was looked on as a crime; and Muhammadan law, and the exegesis of the Quran, and the Tradition, and also those who studied them, were considered bad and deserving of disapproval. Astronomy, philosophy, medicine, mathematics, poetry, history, and epics were cultivated and thought necessary. Even the letters which are peculiar to the Arabic language . . . were avoided. Thus in pronouncing 'Abdullah, people ignored the initial letter *ayn* [specific to Arabic]; and for Ahadi they ignored the letter *ha* [specific to Arabic], etc.[96]

Bada'uni was deeply biased against the emperor and no doubt wrote to cause shock and revulsion. But there is no reason to dismiss his description of Akbar's millennial celebrations outright. Bada'uni's narrative contained most of the accusations that the official chronicle vehemently denied. It reflected what was widely believed about the emperor: that he had acted to end the order of Islam by inverting its symbolic order, even supplanting the signs and sounds of the Arabic alphabet. Also, the manner in which Bada'uni described the emperor's millennial celebrations resonated with the Jesuits' observations that some "believed the king to be mad" and that the "court is much perplexed over the novelties introduced by the King each day." Taken together, these two eyewitness accounts, which were poles apart ideologically—one of Akbar's Muslim scholar and the other of the Jesuit missionaries—both suggest that Akbar's actions confounded many and indicated an unhinged mind to others.

But it would not do to dismiss the emperor's behavior as pathological. There are two reasons for this caution. First, in the milieu under study there existed no sharp social distinctions between being absorbed in divinity and being pathologically narcissistic. In fact, as evidenced by the antinomian traditions of Sufism at the time, madness was a socially recognized station on the way to sainthood. There is no contradiction in saying that Akbar may have appeared an unbalanced fool to some and a saintly monarch to others.[97] Second, and more importantly, those who knew the cosmological significance of the millennium perceived a method in this "madness." If Akbar's transgressions followed a certain cultural logic, so did the accusations against him. The millennium was supposed to do away with the old symbolic order and usher in a new one. A sign of its coming was an inversion of social categories and an annulment of taboos. Bada'uni's critique of Akbar was meant to invoke these signs of the time. As an expert in astrology and a firm believer in the millennium, he portrayed Akbar not merely as a deranged king, but as the Antichrist. As he said in verse:

> I see in 990 two conjunctions,
> I see the sign of Mahdi and that of Antichrist;
> Either politics or religion must change,
> I clearly see the hidden secret.[98]

Indeed, Bada'uni's only difference with the emperor over the millennium was that he had given his allegiance to another messiah—or two!

BADA'UNI'S MANY MESSIAHS

Bada'uni is generally thought to provide a conservative Sunni perspective on Akbar. This interpretation is in need of significant revision, given the man's own millennial beliefs and writings. It is well known that Bada'uni spent most of his adult life as a courtier of Akbar but could not compete with Abul Fazl and his brother Fayzi, the poet laureate (*malik al-shuʿara*), for the emperor's favor. It is less well acknowledged, however, that Badaʾuni had deep sympathies for the Mahdavis, the messianic group already discussed in chapter 4, which had enjoyed a popular following in northern India in the first half of the sixteenth century and still had a presence in Gujarat in Akbar's time.[99]

By the time Akbar conquered Gujarat in 1572–1573, the Mahdavi movement there had entered a quietist phase.[100] After some initial tension, the emperor developed good relations with Mahdavis and even invited a leader of the group, Shaykh Mustafa Gujarati, to his court. Derryl MacLean has suggested that Akbar was evaluating Mahdavi millenarian ideology for his own political ends and that Shaykh Mustafa tried his best to convince Akbar to adopt the Mahdavi faith but failed.[101] If so, the Mahdavi's experience at Akbar's court was not that different from that of Jesuits and Zoroastrians, who had also thought for a time that Akbar had accepted their faith or was close to doing so. But, notably, the Mahdavis were the only "heterodox" Muslim group at the Mughal court, which had enjoyed the "orthodox" Badaʾuni's firm support.

In his chronicle, Badaʾuni wrote respectful biographical accounts of the four second-generation Mahdavi leaders that he had personally met: Shaykh ʿAlai, Shaykh ʿAbdullah Niyazi, Shaykh Abul Fath, and Shaykh Mustafa Gujarati. His account of the martyred Shaykh ʿAlai was by far the most detailed and hagiographical one. In it, Shaykh ʿAlai appeared as a pious Mahdavi who had organized his followers into an armed vigilante group in order to impose their version of Islamic law. Badaʾuni had been ten when he met Shaykh ʿAlai in 1550. This was the year the shaykh was killed by the Afghan ruler Islam Shah Sur (r. 1545–1554). Badaʾuni wrote about his memory of this dreamlike moment of meeting a living saint.[102] He then described the shaykh's defiant and fatal encounter with Islam Shah in emotionally charged detail: Shaykh ʿAlai is whipped and dies under the scourge, his body is trampled to pieces by elephants, and Islam Shah forbids the Mahdavis to bury the broken body of their leader and appoints guards to this effect. However, these orders are countermanded by divine providence:

> At that very time a vehement whirlwind arose and blew with so great violence, that people thought that the last day [*qayam-i qayamat*] had arrived, and great lamentation and mourning was heard throughout the whole camp, and men were in expectation of the early downfall of the power of Islam Shah. And they say that in the course of the night such a wealth of

flowers was scattered over the body of the Shaikh that he was completely hidden beneath them and was so to speak entombed in flowers.[103]

After this event, the child Bada'uni composed his first set of chronograms to commemorate the martyred Mahdavi shaykh.[104] These chronograms were short phrases that, when converted to a number using numerology, gave the year of the event. The chronograms Bada'uni composed to record the year of this Mahdavi saint's death were "Mindful of God" (Zakirullah) and "their Lord quenched their thirst with a drink" (*saqahum rabbuhum sharaban*), an extract from the Quran (76:21). Significantly, while Bada'uni praised this Mahdavi for his martyrdom, he criticized another member of the group, Shaykh Niyazi, for his moral weakness. Shaykh Niyazi had been unable to endure the torture and had recanted his Mahdavi beliefs.[105]

In 1574, as a courtier, Bada'uni met the Mahdavi Shaykh Mustafa Gujarati after the conquest of Gujarat and discussed Mahdavi beliefs with him in front of the emperor. He asked the Mahdavi shaykh about the messianic claims of another man, Sayyid Muhammad Nurbakhsh (d. 1464), who "also, in his time, had set up a claim to being the Mahdi, and had brought various troubles on himself thereby."[106] The shaykh was obviously upset about such questions, which implied that the Mahdavi founder may have made a false claim. Bada'uni assuaged the shaykh in private later that day: "To make amends for my fault I waited on him with my apologies, and asked him for forgiveness."[107]

To summarize, Bada'uni treated the Mahdavis with deep reverence in his chronicle. He did not hide the fact that he received mystical instruction from Mahdavis and that his father was a devotee as well.[108] Unlike the other Sunni ulama in the courts of Islam Shah and Akbar, Bada'uni did not condemn Sayyid Muhammad's claim to being the messiah but, on the other hand, treated his followers as upholders of the Sunni tradition. It is not surprising that at least one scholar believes Bada'uni to be a Mahdavi.[109] Given Bada'uni's sympathetic depiction of the Mahdavis in his chronicles, it is worth analyzing his writings about the Mahdavi movement in another work, entitled *Najat al-Rashid* (Salvation of the Rightly Guided). This book's name was a chronogram that gave its year of completion: 999 AH.[110]

In this long and rambling work, written at the end of the Islamic millennium, Bada'uni gave the early history of two messianic movements, the Mahdavis of India and the Nurbakhshis of Central Asia and Iran. Note that it was the competing messianic claims of the Mahdavi and Nurbakhshi founders that had interested him in 1574 during his discussions with the Mahdavi Shaykh Mustafa Gujarati. Writing in 1591, it seems that Bada'uni had found the answer, which allowed him to accept both the Mahdavi and the Nurbakhshi founders as divinely blessed saints whose messianic assertions were, according to him, beyond question or rebuke. This answer was based on a reinterpretation of the concept of metempsychosis or transmigration of the soul (*tanasukh*).[111]

In his discussion of metempsychosis, Bada'uni compared heretical (*malahida*) Muslim groups who subscribed to this phenomenon to Hindus and Buddhists, labeling them transmigrationists (*tanasukhiyya*). He condemned all these groups and presented an alternative—and "orthodox"—explanation of this phenomenon. He said that proper Sufi masters believe in "projection" of the soul (*buruz*), not in metempsychosis (*tanasukh*). The concept of *buruz* had first been put forth by Nurbakhsh, the fifteenth-century Sufi and messianic claimant mentioned earlier.[112] Following Nurbakhsh, Bada'uni asserted that the two spiritual mechanisms are distinct: in metempsychosis, the soul leaves a body that is dead in order to enter one that is ready to receive life; by contrast, in projection of the soul, the perfecting (*mukammil*) soul irradiates (*tajalli*) itself along with the perfect (*kamil*) soul and thus makes its existence complete (*mukammal*). Moreover, in projection, a soul never leaves a body to enter another, but instead it simply overpowers another soul in much the same way that the rays of a powerful lamp overcome the light of a weaker one.

Bada'uni wrote that many saints (*auliya'*) have performed projection on other complete souls in their own lifetimes, for if one believes that invisible spirits such as jinns can have the ability to control a weak soul, how can one say that prophets (*anbiya'*) and the pure ones (*asfiya'*) have a lesser ability than jinns? As an example, he related the story of an acquaintance of his, an Ottoman (*rumi*) nobleman, who once asked Bada'uni about the difference between projection and metempsychosis. This nobleman told Bada'uni that he had met and grown attached to a Sufi master in Egypt. When the Sufi was about to die, he promised to return after death in the form of a dervish in order to look after his disciple. His master's claim of metempsychosis upset the Turkish nobleman very much, for it implied his guide's beliefs had been beyond the pale of Islam. However, after listening to Bada'uni, he was content and happy to know that his master's beliefs were well within the boundaries of Islam and the realms of possibility.

According to Badaʾuni, the mechanism of soul projection explained why many saints, having reached a certain mystical stage, made claims of messianism or "being Jesus" (ʿiswiyyat) and brought down calamities upon themselves. According to him, men who made such claims were justified (maʿzur) and in the right (muhiqq), and Sayyid Muhammad Nurbakhsh of Badakhshan (of the Nurbakhshi order) and Sayyid Muhammad of Jaunpur (of the Mahdavi order) were two such men. He wrote that one must not be quick to judge such mystics, who have followed the mystical path all their lives and have discovered secrets unknown to ordinary men.

In his explication of the messianic claims made by the Mahdavi and Nurbakhshi leaders, Badaʾuni turned to a mixture of conjunction astrology and scriptural lore. In the case of Nurbakhsh, he noted that when the conjunction of the two farthest planets (Saturn and Jupiter) was in the sign of Scorpio, which was an omen for the religion of the nation, the lord of the age (sahib-i zaman) came forward. Immediately after relating the messianic career of Nurbakhsh, he began the story of the Mahdavi leader. Badaʾuni said that Sayyid Muhammad Jaunpuri declared himself the mahdi when he reached Mecca. Apparently, the people had asked the ulama of that region for a fatwa (responsa) on the truth of the hadith that "the honorable Prophet may peace be upon him has said, I will not remain in the pure and enlightened tomb [marqad] for more than *one thousand years*, and before the passing of one thousand years major signs of which the rise of the Mahdi is one must indeed be revealed [my italics]." In response, according to Badaʾuni, most of the hadith scholars of the region signed off on the worthiness of this hadith tradition except for one. This was the famous Jalal al-din Suyuti (d. 1505), a renowned scholar and exegete of the Quran based in Egypt, who wrote against the validity of this hadith mainly because he wanted to declare himself the mujaddid of the tenth century. Suyuti argued that the mahdi will appear somewhere in the fourth and fifth century after the millennium. Regardless, Jaunpuri made his claim on the basis of the above-mentioned hadith, and, upon doing so, he was asked to leave Mecca.

Badaʾuni also mentioned the famous Suyuti and his critique of the millennial hadith in his chapter on "the rise and fall of nations," which began with the following observation: "At the beginning of every few centuries, the affair [kar o bar] of religion has a peak and decline and thus the nation [ummat] of a prophet would exist for a thousand years. Such is what one may beneficially gather from some exegeses [tafasir]."[113] Badaʾuni went beyond Suyuti's answer about the timing of the millennium and quoted from memory a fragment from the writings of the renowned Andalusian mystic and metaphysician Ibn ʿArabi (d. 1240).[114] He related that Ibn ʿArabi once saw a group of people performing the circumambulation of the Kaʿba. One of these people saw Ibn ʿArabi and said to him that they were his ancestors. Ibn ʿArabi asked the man how long ago he had departed from this world. The man replied that it was some forty thousand years ago. Ibn ʿArabi was surprised and told him that even Adam was created less than seven thousand years ago. The man answered, "you are talking about the Adam who passed away near your time and was born at the beginning of these seven thousand years." Upon hearing this, Ibn ʿArabi suddenly recalled the Prophet's saying that "the Lord almighty has created a hundred thousand Adams and despite this the world is created and there is no escaping its destruction."

Badaʾuni did not critically examine the validity of the prophetic tradition quoted by Ibn ʿArabi. Instead, he simply juxtaposed Ibn ʿArabi's cyclical view of time to Suyuti's eschatological claims that the end of the world was going to occur between the thirteenth and fifteenth centuries of Islam.[115] In effect, he used Ibn ʿArabi's vast metaphysical authority to dilute the claims of Suyuti, whose well-known writings did not suit the messianic projects of the men that Badaʾuni supported. Furthermore, the way Badaʾuni used Ibn ʿArabi as a source of authority on the cyclical creation of the universe placed him against "traditional" Sunni doctrine. In this cyclical view of creation, a new Adam was born in every "cycle" of existence. As mentioned earlier, this was a well-known claim made by radical Sufi groups (*ghulat*) to deny traditional Islamic eschatology and was used to support the notion of the transmigration of the soul. Moreover, this view of time was based on the astrological theories of Abu Maʿshar, the famous proponent of conjunction astrology, who promoted Indic notions of cycles of time in Islamic astrology[116] and whose Arabic prayers to the sun were quoted in Akbar's Millennial History.[117] In short, Badaʾuni may have depicted the emperor as deviating from Islam, but he built his arguments for the millennium from the very same conceptual bases—conjunction astrology, repeating cycles of time, and the return of the soul—with the help of which Akbar's millennial status had been formulated.

To summarize, the "strange" millennial worldview in which saints and monarchs competed for the status of divinely incarnated saviors was invented neither by Akbar nor by his staunch critic Badaʾuni. Nor, for that matter, was it a happenstance of the sixteenth-century "syncretistic" Indo-Islamic environment. As the previous three chapters have shown, this view of temporality and sovereignty was part of the institutions of sacred kingship since the age of Timur. It resonated not only in the Indian empire of his successors but also in the territories of Safavid Iran, where, at the end of the sixteenth century, there was another millennial movement gathering strength that sought to end the dominance of the "Arab" order of Islam down to the very letters of the Arabic alphabet and resurrect in its place a "Persian" millennium.

THE MILLENNIUM IN SAFAVID IRAN

As described in chapter 3, in the beginning of the sixteenth century the Safavids had risen to power in Iran on the back of a messianic movement organized around a core of "exaggerated" Sufi beliefs in which the spiritual guide was treated as an Alid messiah and an embodiment of divinity. By the end of the century, however, the Safavids began to move away from their radical Alid stance and publicly adopted Imami Shi'ism. This shift was aimed at breaking the power of the unruly Qizilbash devotees of the Safavid saint king, famous for their messianic fervor, belief in metempsychosis, and red iconic headgear. Shah Tahmasb had spent most of his reign trying to achieve this objective but had been unsuccessful. It was Shah 'Abbas I (r. 1588–1629) who successfully launched a well-coordinated and large-scale effort to reorient the moral economy and political geography of empire. As part of this process, he took significant steps toward abandoning the Safavids' messianic image in favor of a more routinized Imami Shi'ism.[118]

Shah 'Abbas built a loyal military of Caucasian slave soldiers captured from neighboring Georgia, converted to Shi'ism, and trained by European military advisors. He abandoned the old imperial center of Qazvin for the new Safavid capital of Isfahan. He shifted focus away from the Safavid shrine-city of Ardabil toward the Shi'i spiritual center of Mashhad. During his reign, Safavid princes married the daughters of newly established Imami Shi'i ulama instead of marrying into the leading Qizilbash families, as had been the precedent. These strategic moves enabled him to reduce his dependence on the traditional tribal-warrior military groups of the Qizilbash. Thus, even the Qizilbash headgear began to be referred to as the Taj-i Ithna 'Ashari (Crown of the Twelver Shi'is).

Despite all of the above, however, the transition to Twelver Shi'ism in Safavid Iran was neither smooth nor unidirectional. The antinomian ethos of "exaggeration" (*ghuluww*) survived, shrouded in ambiguous cultural forms and nurtured in cultural sites that were difficult to police.[119] Indeed, in some cases, the Safavids themselves kept alive, albeit in tightly constrained forms, aspects of the millenarian cult that had brought them to power. For instance, the new Safavid imperial complex built by Shah ʿAbbas in Isfahan had a special chamber called the Tawhid Khana (House of Monism), which served as a retreat for Safavid devotees. It also served as a place of refuge and repentance for the Qizilbash. Those who had offended the shah would seek refuge here and ask for forgiveness, invoking in the process the affective bonds between disciple and master. But the extent to which the traditional disciples of the Safavid shah had been marginalized in the emergent imperial configuration at the end of the sixteenth century can be seen by how they served in the special corps of executioners at the court of Shah ʿAbbas.[120] Of a distinctive and terrorizing appearance, magnified by the tall hats they wore, these men were trained and deputed to perform public executions by eating alive the condemned enemies of their monarch. This was, perhaps, a ritualized commemoration of the transgressive practices that had made Shah Ismaʿil's soldier-devotees notorious a century earlier.

In general, violent spectacles that combined the sacred and the grotesque were an important aspect of public life in Safavid Iran. Like Akbar, Shah ʿAbbas enjoyed watching violent fights. Most famous of these are the ritualistic—and fatal—stick battles organized between urban neighborhoods and artisanal factions, in which the two sides would assume the names of defunct Sufi formations such as "Haydariyya" and "Niʿmatiyya."[121] These popular rituals were part of a large number of performative practices that came to inform the "passion plays" and Shiʿi commemorations of Husayn's martyrdom as they became institutionalized in Safavid times. In short, the performative culture of sacred kingship was intimately linked with popular religiosity, the life of the city, and military camps. Safavid attempts to change the former produced repercussions in the latter.

Thus, new millenarian tendencies arose to fill the gap left behind by the Safavid suppression of their messianic legacy. The most pronounced of these tendencies was the Sufi group known as the Nuqtavis, who nursed a deep enthusiasm for the millennium. The Nuqtavi movement had originally been founded in Iran in the years after Timur. The founder of the movement, Mahmud Pasikhani (d. 1427), was a native of Gilan; he termed himself the Millennial King (Padishah Hizara). The movement was a breakaway faction of the cabbalistic and politically active Hurufis, who were well known for their esoteric interpretations of the letters of the Arabic and Persian alphabets. The Nuqtavis were unique, however, in their exclusive focus upon the Persian alphabet or, more precisely, on the difference between the letters of the Persian and Arabic alphabets. The Nuqtavis (Pointilists) were called so because of their emphasis on the *nuqta* (point). A key significance of the *nuqta* in their doctrine was the disparity in the total number of diacritical points between the Arabic and Persian alphabet (calculated to be twelve, an astrologically significant number). In short, they derived much of their messianic metaphysics from Persianate astrological theories and the "strange" knowledge of ʿilm al-huruf (the science of letters).[122]

At the end of the sixteenth century, the Nuqtavis were loosely organized and displayed antinomian tendencies, perhaps reacting against the rigid "commercialization" of the Sufi orders of the time.[123] Their membership also reflected a blurring of ethnic and social barriers. Even though the Nuqtavis had a following among the urban craftsmen and the warrior Qizilbash, they also attracted many of the learned elite, including physicians and eminent poets. What links them to earlier *ghulat* groups is their belief in metempsychosis and cyclical time.[124] In Nuqtavi cosmology, historical time was divided into four cycles of sixteen thousand years. In each cycle there were eight thousand years of Arab rule and eight thousand of Persian rule, with the final cycle belonging to the Persians.[125] The Nuqtavis also subscribed to conjunction astrology and expected that the "greatest conjunction" was going to occur in the year 1582 (990 AH).[126] They expected that the era of Islam was coming to an end, opening the way for the dominance of the Persians and their religion under the guidance of a messiah.

The Nuqtavis had attempted but failed to proclaim the Safavid shah Tahmasb as their expected savior, the mahdi. When the Safavids broke with their messianic legacy and led a campaign (1571–1590) to bring unruly Qizilbash tribes under control, some warriors from these tribes began to follow the Nuqtavis. After Tahmasb's death, the Nuqtavis tried and initially succeeded in developing a positive relationship with Shah ʿAbbas I. He frequented their hospice in Qazvin and began to associate closely with a Nuqtavi named Dervish Khursaw.[127] Even though the court chroniclers later claimed that this association was for the purpose of surveillance, it is more likely that the shah was genuinely interested in the millennial doctrine of this increasingly popular group.

However, the growing popularity and temerity of the Nuqtavis alarmed Shah ʿAbbas, and he acted to suppress the group. Much of the confrontation between the Safavid shah and the Nuqtavis was expressed in competing interpretations of conjunction astrology. The Nuqtavis were expecting the Safavid dynasty to fall and to see in its place the rise of a Persian sovereign and messiah. The court astronomer also did his calculations and predicted that a conjunction of inauspicious planets indicated the imminent death of a royal personage. It was a sign that Shah ʿAbbas could not ignore. His court astrologer suggested a way out of the cosmic predicament, a way to make both the Nuqtavi prediction come true and also to save the Safavids' sovereignty. He recommended that the shah appoint a Nuqtavi devotee, a condemned man, to the throne of Iran for the three ill-fated days.[128]

The entire ceremony was carried out with the utmost seriousness. The shah prostrated himself in front of the Nuqtavi king and stood guard at the throne as master of ceremonies. All the grandees of the realm came to pay their respects to the newly enthroned monarch. It is worth comparing this ritual theater enacted by the Safavid shah and his nobility to the millennial celebrations at the court of Akbar. The former would have appeared no less perplexing and baffling—not to say tinged with madness—for outside observers than the latter. In any case, the Safavid astrologer's advice proved correct, and the three-day reign of the Nuqtavi monarch ended inauspiciously. He was dethroned, shot by firing squad, and strung up in public view. Returning to his throne at the start of the new millennium, Shah ʿAbbas launched an armed campaign against the Nuqtavis and extirpated the movement in Iran by the year 1593. As the shah's chronicler noted: "if anyone escaped punishment, they either fled to India or found themselves a corner and remained anonymous, so that in Iran the way of metempsychosis [*shivah-yi tanasukh*] was abolished."[129]

The Nuqtavis who escaped to India found refuge at the Mughal court, where some of their compatriots already led a comfortable existence. Akbar had for many years taken a deep interest in this radical Sufi group. The Safavid chronicler even suggested that both the Mughal emperor and his advisor, Abul Fazl, had been converted to the Persian millennial creed. "Travelers to India reported that it [the Nuqtavi heresy] existed there too, and that Shaikh Abuʾl-Fazl, the son of Shaikh Mobarak, a learned man in the service of the Mogul emperor Jalal al-Din Mohammad Akbar and esteemed by him, as a member of it. He had converted the Emperor to his latitudinarian ideas and seduced him from the path of the religious law."[130] It is not certain, however, who converted whom. In a letter to an important Nuqtavi, Akbar assumed the role of their spiritual patron, offering his guidance and blessings.¹³¹ Written in 1584, two years after Akbar's millennial celebrations, it was composed in the form of an edict (*farman*) and addressed the Nuqtavi Mir Ahmad Kashi as Akbar's disciple and agent in Iran. The letter used terminology specific to the Nuqtavis and asked Kashi to convince more of the group to become Akbar's devotees and to send regular reports on his progress. Most notably, the Mughal emperor told Kashi to send his greetings to Dervish Khusraw, mentioned earlier as a one-time confidant of Shah ʿAbbas and popular leader of the Nuqtavis in Qazvin.

After the Nuqtavi purge in 1594, in which Kashi met his end by being cleaved in two by Shah ʿAbbas's sword, Akbar wrote to the Safavid shah advising him to practice the policy of *sulh-i kull* (universal peace). The shah was asked to show more tolerance toward those of different faiths, even if they were believed to be in the wrong, and to exercise supreme caution before putting anyone to death, because it was akin to "demolishing a divinely built edifice" (*hadm-i bunyan-i rabbani*).¹³² The Safavid monarch did not receive the advice well, because Iskandar Munshi, the Safavid chronicler, explained the Mughal interest in the Nuqtavis by observing that Abul Fazl had made Akbar into a libertine (*wasiʿ al-mashrab*) in matters of religion.¹³³ Akbar and Abul Fazl's communiqués to the Nuqtavis as well as the protection and patronage the group received in India certainly point toward a long and active relationship between the Mughal court and the Iranian *ghulat* movement. This was a partnership built upon a shared adoration of pre-Islamic Persianate symbols. Both Akbar and the Nuqtavis privileged the use of the Iranian solar calendar, believed in the transmigration of the soul, and advocated a ritual veneration of the sun.

It was Badaʾuni who provided details of the Mughal-Nuqtavi relationship in India. He reported that in the year 1576 (984 AH) a man named Sharif Amuli, a Nuqtavi, came from Iran to India because "it is a wide place, where there is an open field for all licentiousness, and no one interferes with another's business."¹³⁴ Amuli declared himself a *mujaddid* (renewer) and gathered around himself some followers. When granted an audience with the emperor, he explained to Akbar the writings of the founder of the Nuqtavis, Mahmud Pasikhani, which according to Badaʾuni were "full of such droppings of heresy as no religion or sect would suffer."¹³⁵ Amuli impressed Akbar enough to be awarded a high rank and was made an officiant for the cult of imperial discipleship: he became "one of the apostles of His Majesty's religion in Bengal, possessor of the four degrees of Faith [i.e., imperial discipleship], and in his turn summoning faithful disciples to these degrees."¹³⁶ Three years later, Bada'uni related, Sharif Amuli was a key contributor to the theories that proclaimed Akbar as the messiah (*sahib-i zaman*) at the turn of the Islamic millennium. The Nuqtavi "brought proofs from the writings of Mahmud of Basakhwan [Mahmud Pasikhani, the Nuqtavi founder], that he had said that in the year 990 [AH] a certain person would abolish lies, and how he had specified all sorts of interpretations of the expression 'Professor of the true Religion,' which came to the sum-total of 990."¹³⁷ These predictions were corroborated by a certain Khwaja Maulana of Shiraz, a "heretic" and "*jafrdan*" (expert in *jafr*).¹³⁸ In the same vein, some Shi'as at court also supported this claim by quoting the following verses, which were said to have been composed by Nasir-i Khusraw, a tenth-century Isma'ili writer and poet:

> In 989, according to the decree of fate,
> The stars from all sides shall meet together.
> In the year of Leo, the month of Leo, the day of Leo,
> The Lion of God [Ali] will stand forth from behind the veil.¹³⁹

The Alid theories of the millennium that had once been at the core of Safavid sacral self-fashioning were now used to celebrate the resurrection of Timurid might, glory, and sovereignty under Akbar.

CONCLUSION

Akbar, like his ancestor Timur, had created an empire with a great diversity of sacred traditions and forms of moral community. This meant that he too had to inhabit a mold of sacred authority that drew upon multiple cosmologies often at variance with one another. Timur had performed the role of an heir of Chinggis Khan as well as of Ali. He had done so using a category that could encompass both these figures. This was the astrological concept of Lord of Conjunction, signifying a savior-conqueror marked by the planets, someone who would inaugurate a new era on earth. This was also, however, a saintly category claimed by those with mystical rather than physical powers. Timur was assumed to have both. In many ways, Akbar's claim of sacred sovereignty was enacted in a form similar to that of Timur. It drew upon conjunction astrology, messianic and millennial myths, and claims of royal and saintly authority combined in the person of the monarch.

There were important differences between the two Lords of Conjunction. Timur had performed this role but had been careful not to put it in words. It was only after his death that he was called Sahib Qiran and a sacred genealogy created linking him miraculously to Ali. He had, in other words, followed the norms of saintliness by not allowing his oral lore to be made officially public and collected in a written hagiography during his lifetime. Akbar, on the other hand, had been less circumspect. He had personally supervised the composition and illustration of his chronicle-cum-hagiography, the *Akbarnama*. It was this hubris to make explicit claims of sacred authority—in words rather than in deeds—such as calling himself the mujtahid of the age, which allowed Akbar's rivals to use accusations of heresy to attack him. These attacks may have harmed his reputation but did not dent his power. The norms of kingship he laid out were followed for more than two centuries.[140] More of his successors emulated him than not. Even after Akbar, the imperial chancellery marked all edicts and epistles with the condensed talismanic proclamation "Allah Akbar," and paintings from the imperial atelier were signed by artists declaring themselves to be the disciples of the king.

The goal of this chapter was to show that Akbar's style of sacred kingship was a variation on a historical theme. This is not to deny its inventive form and Indian content and context. Rather, it is to argue that this inventiveness built upon received institutional and narrative forms that were part of Timurid and Safavid legacies inherited by the Mughals. Moreover, these forms of sacred sovereignty were flexible enough to adapt to the requirements of the Indian milieu. The gift of Alid messianism offered by the likes of the Nuqtavis was important for the Mughals in their competition with the Safavids of Iran, but it made up only a part of the Mughal myth of sovereignty. India, unlike Iran, was not a land of Ali. It was the land of Rama. It was the story of this god-king descended to earth to rid it of evil and initiate a new utopian cycle of time that circulated in the streets and camps of the Mughal dominion. Like Ali and Chinggis Khan in Iran, in India it was Rama whom kings emulated and claimed to be embodiments of.[141]

No wonder that the story of Rama, the *Ramayana*, was translated into Persian and exquisitely illustrated in Akbar's atelier and that the Mughal emperor was called an avatar or reincarnation of Rama.[142] But what is striking is the degree to which the themes, plots, and imagery of the story of Rama matched those of the epics of Iran. Akbar's master artists, many of them from Iran, painted the Indian *rakshasas* (demons) fought by Rama in the same style as the Iranian *devs* (demons) destroyed by the Iranian hero Rustam in the *Shahnama*. Even Bada'uni, who had to bear the agony of translating the *Ramayana* into Persian verse for Akbar, could not resist equating these Indian and Iranian tales of sovereignty:

> And the opinion of this set of people [Brahmans] is that the world is very old, and that no age has been devoid of the human race, and that from that event 100 thousand thousand years have passed. And yet for all that they make no mention of Adam whose creation took place only 7,000 years ago. Hence it is evident that these events [of the *Ramayana*] are not true at all, and are nothing but pure invention, and simple imagination, like the Shahnamah, and the stories of Amir Hamzah, or else it must have happened in the time of the dominion of the beasts and the jinns—but God alone knows the truth of the matter.[143]

Bada'uni left open the possibility that these stories may have been true in another cycle of time. His conviction in a linear structure of time in which the birth of Adam had occurred "only 7,000 years ago" was quite feeble, as seen in his explanation of the transmigration of souls that drew upon the metaphysics of an Iranian Sufi master. Whether it was the notion of the returning soul or the conception of recurring time cycles, there was much in common between the Iranian heritage of the Mughals and that of their Indian polity. The two cultural systems were cemented further in the reign of Akbar, who began the practice of marrying Rajput princesses. It was such a Rajput queen, mentioned in the *Akbarnama* only by her title Mary of the Age (Maryam Zamani), who produced Akbar's heir. The queen—who despite being named after the mother of Jesus remained a Hindu—gave birth to the prince in the house of a local holy man, Shaykh Salim, a reclusive Chishti saint of Sikri.

The story of the Chishtis' success as a Sufi order in India and their alliance with the Mughals is well known.[144] As a young sovereign, well before he had discovered his own spiritual potential, Akbar had fallen deeply in the Chishtis' saintly debt. Heirless at the time, he had asked Shaykh Salim Chishti to pray for a son. When the Sufi's prayers came true, the Mughal emperor had a magnificent imperial city built near the site of the holy man's hermitage in Sikri and called it Fatehpur (City of Victory). Over the course of Akbar's long rule, Chishti Sufis became key spiritual and political allies of the dynasty and, as Muzaffar Alam has shown, in their writings celebrated the emperor as the "Caliph of the Age" and blessed him as a saintly sovereign.[145] Akbar also named his oldest son Salim, after the saint who had prayed for him and hosted his birth, and endearingly nicknamed the boy "Shaykhu Baba," or "Little Shaykh." From the moment of his birth, Prince Salim, the future emperor Jahangir, was part Timurid, part Rajput, and part Chishti. With the body of a king and the soul of a saint, he was a child of the millennium. And he too staked his claim of sovereignty in a messianic idiom that could be understood in both Iran and India.

{6} THE THRONE OF TIME

THE PAINTED MIRACLES OF THE SAINT EMPEROR

IN HIS half-century of rule, Akbar transformed the conquest state of Babur and Humayun into a wealthy, stable, and integrated empire. More than two generations witnessed the rise of a new social, political, and economic order that stretched from Kabul to Bengal and from Kashmir to Gujarat. The symbol of this new order was the Mughal emperor. When he died in 1605, Akbar was the greatest sovereign in living memory. This can be seen in the emotive reaction of Banarasidas, a Jain merchant who was nineteen at the time, to the news of the emperor's demise. In an account written in his later years, he reported that he had fainted, fallen down the stairs he had been sitting on, and injured his head. This sense of anomie was not merely the private emotion of a young man. It was collectively felt: bazaars shut down, and people buried their jewels, put on old clothes, and expected the worst. Banarasidas recounted, "The people felt suddenly orphaned and insecure without their sire. Terror raged everywhere; the hearts of men trembled with dire apprehension; their faces became drained of colour."[1] However, the transition of power to Akbar's son, Salim—who took the title of Jahangir (r. 1605–1627)—was a relatively smooth and nonviolent affair. An attempt to place Jahangir's seventeen-year-old son Khusraw on the throne was rejected by a majority of nobles, and the matter was settled within the palace precincts in a matter of days. Even when Khusraw fled to Punjab six months later, the new emperor was able to muster enough support to defeat and capture the rebellious prince quickly.

Jahangir was thirty-six years old at the time of his accession. He was already adept at maintaining an independent army and retinue as well as at negotiating complex political situations. In this respect, he had an advantage over his three predecessors—Babur, Humayun, and Akbar—who had all assumed the mantle of sovereignty at a young age with little skill or authority in handling a formidable array of male and female kin, court nobility, and other kingmakers. The problem facing Jahangir was of a different nature. In the last few years of Akbar's reign, he had been less than patient in waiting for the throne, openly rebelling and posturing against his "heretical" father's policies. Now, on the throne, Jahangir had to decide how much of Akbar's sacred legacy to embrace as a model for fashioning his own sovereign self.

As we saw in the last chapter, Akbar's foundational claim of sacrality, enunciated at the moment of the millennium, had embroiled the emperor in controversy. He was accused of attempting to undo the order of Islam and replacing it with his own religion. These accusations occurred in the wake of Akbar's attempts to seal his conquests and administrative accomplishments with a new set of courtly rituals and symbols. Despite this resistance, he went ahead with his project and instituted an order of disciples in which initiates swore to sacrifice their life, family, honor, and religion in the service of the emperor. Furthermore, this imperial cult was inaugurated at the moment of the first Islamic millennium, or, more precisely, in 990 AH (1582), when a conjunction of Saturn and Jupiter took place, indicating a great change in world affairs. In essence, Akbar celebrated his imperial achievements as a millennial being who had ushered in a new world order, as a Lord of Conjunction like his ancestor Timur, as a savior like the expected heir of Ali, as an avatar like Rama, as a messiah like Jesus, and as a Renewer of the Second Millennium (Mujaddid-i Alf-i Thani) of Islam. This was the millennial-messianic dispensation that Jahangir inherited, in which the monarch was a sacred figure towering above the religious and sectarian differences of his subjects. The question taken up here is how Jahangir dealt with his father's sovereign legacy. Did he reject it or make it his own?

JAHANGIR AND AKBAR:
FROM OPPOSITION TO MIMESIS

In the last five years of his reign, Akbar's political energies had mainly been consumed by attempts to rein in his rebellious heir.[2] In 1599, he had given Jahangir the assignment of dealing with the recalcitrant rana of Mewar, while he ventured south to the Deccan to expand the Mughal realm. Taking advantage of Akbar's absence from the capital, Jahangir abandoned his mission and, ignoring the entreaties of his grandmother, the empress mother, Hamida Banu Begum, the head of the dynasty in Akbar's absence, he assumed independent control of an imperial treasury and rich agricultural territories in Bihar. He then enthroned himself, issued coins and edicts as a sovereign, and enrolled courtiers as disciples.[3] To contain the crisis, Akbar left the Deccan campaign to his generals and hurried back. However, instead of directly confronting Jahangir, the emperor used trusted servants and family members as intermediaries to bring the wayward prince to heel. On the other hand, as Akbar's likely successor—the other two princes would succumb to wine and good living in 1598 and 1604[4]—Jahangir's transgressions knew no bounds. When Akbar called his old confidante and advisor Abul Fazl back from the Deccan to help him manage the situation, Jahangir had him waylaid and beheaded.

A later chronicler noted that by having Akbar's favorite minister murdered, "His Highness's [Jahangir's] bravery and manliness were noticed."[5] It was well known that Abul Fazl was at the center of Akbar's innovative efforts concerning the symbolic role of Islam—or lack thereof, depending on one's perspective—in formulating imperial policies. Accordingly, the assassination of Akbar's chief ideologue signaled to those opposed to the old emperor to see in his son a willingness to break from the tenor and style of the Akbari dispensation. This observation is corroborated by other evidence that Jahangir had set himself up against Akbar as a defender of Islam. Specifically, there exists a copy of an edict (*farman*) of 1601 in the prince's name in which he announced his opposition to his father's policies to "convert mosques into stables" and vowed to make every effort to reverse it: "At the instigation of some mischievous persons, my father [Akbar] has ... prohibited the performance of *namaz* (Muslim prayers) in congregation. He has converted many mosques into store-houses and stables. It was improper on his part to have acted in this manner."[6]

Whether Akbar had in fact desecrated mosques or forbidden Muslim prayers is debatable, but, as was shown in the previous chapter, he was widely accused of having harbored such ambitions. The Jesuit reports of the time also noted with cynicism, and more than a hint of disappointment, Jahangir's sudden turn toward Islam. This is how a contemporary Jesuit historian summed up the letters received from the third Jesuit mission (1595–1773) at the time of Jahangir's accession:

> All men hoped much from the new King [Jahangir], and especially the [Jesuit] Fathers, who believed that his accession would lead many to embrace the Christian faith. For up to that time he had been looked upon

almost as a Christian, and had been openly spoken of as such by his adherents. But these hopes were disappointed; for he had sworn an oath to the Moors to uphold the law of Mafamede [Muhammad], and being anxious at the commencement of his reign to secure their good will, he gave orders for the cleansing of the mosques, restored the fasts [*ramesas*] and prayers of the Moors. . . . Of the Fathers he took no more notice than if he had never seen them before.[7]

The Jesuits had been close to Jahangir ever since the first mission to the Mughal court in 1580. In his days as a rebellious prince, Jahangir had shown a deep fondness for Catholic art and commissioned many copies from the artists in his independent atelier. As Gauvin Bailey observed, Jahangir paid more attention than Akbar to the "iconic and talismanic" qualities of Catholic images and less to their narrative aspects.[8] Jahangir's stance changed toward the Jesuits when, as was mentioned earlier, at the time of Akbar's death he faced an opposing court faction that tried to put his son Khusraw on the throne. Khusraw's party was led by the Rajput Raja Man Singh, the prince's maternal uncle and the brother of Jahangir's first wife, Man Bai. The raja had been the most powerful general under Akbar and symbolized the eminence of Rajput kings in the Mughal empire.[9] According to the Jesuits, it was Jahangir's need to drum up support against such powerful "Gentile," that is, Hindu, noblemen that led Jahangir to reassure Muslims that he would undo many of the policies of Akbar that had benefited the Rajputs and hence style himself as a champion of Islam.[10]

The early part of Jahangir's own memoir, the *Jahangirnama* (Book of Jahangir), written in the informal and colloquial style of a diary (*ruznamcha*), corroborated the view of the Jesuits. Jahangir had begun his memoir according to the Islamic lunar calendar rather than the divine (*ilahi*) solar calendar of Akbar. He noted in the opening pages how his birth had been predicted by a renowned saint of the popular Chishti order and how, upon ascending the throne, he had molded himself according to the wisdom of sages who had foretold that Akbar's reign would be followed by the rise of a "Light of Religion [Nur al-Din]": "While a prince I heard from the sages of India (*danayan-i hind*) that when the time of Jalaluddin Muhammad Akbar Padishah's rule was over, one named Nuruddin [Light of Religion] would succeed to the rule. This had also remained in my mind, and therefore I named myself Nuruddin Muhammad Jahangir."[11]

While most of these sages remained anonymous in Jahangir's writings, he mentioned one Naqshbandi Sufi, Shaykh Husayn Jami, who had given him the following "good news" a few months before his accession: "I dreamed that the great saints have transferred the rule to that divinely chosen one [i.e., Jahangir]. Armed with this good news, be ready for such an occurrence."[12] The Jesuits had also reported rumors circulating at the time that eminent Sufis and astrologers had sent Jahangir omens, dreams, and prognostications that sovereignty was shortly to be his. These omens represented much more than sycophancy. Rather, they carried substantial symbolic capital and, as was discussed in the case of Babur in chapter 3, constituted cosmological gifts in an exchange economy that created obligations for the sovereign. From this perspective, these prophecies formed a strand of public opinion and political communication; they offered loyalty but also imposed certain demands on the ruler. Shaykh Husayn Jami, for one, was amply rewarded in cash by Jahangir when the former's prophecy came true.[13] To gauge the social import and political weight of such "strange" gifts, it is worth examining Jahangir's reactions to those that were not given to him.

There was, for example, the dire prediction of a Jain holy man named Man Singh (not to be confused with the high-ranking noble Raja Man Singh). He was a leader of the Sewra sect, described by Jahangir as "a group of Hindu heretics [*malahida-i hunud*] who always go about stark naked" and took sexual liberties (*fasad o bibaki*) with the wives and daughters of their followers.[14] This antinomian sage had been close to Akbar and "considered himself an expert in astrology and predictions [*ʿilm-i nujum o taskhirat*]." Jahangir related how at the time of Khusraw's rebellion, Man Singh had been asked by an important Hindu general and landlord of Bikaner, Rai Singh Bhurtiya, about the new emperor's chances of survival. The holy man had opined that Jahangir's rule would last no longer than two years. Upon hearing this, the general abandoned his post and returned home to await the outcome of the struggle between father and son. Upon victory, Jahangir forgave and reinstated his nobleman but cursed the Jain mendicant as "black tongued" (*siyah zaban*). He noted that within three or four months of issuing this ill-omened statement, the man's limbs fell off from leprosy, making his life so miserable that "death would have been preferable." When ordered to appear before the emperor, the leprosy-stricken Man Singh took his own life by poison. Men like Man Singh were, by dint of their spiritual status, masters of affective knowledge and controllers of local nodes of political communication. Their fate shows that the predictions of holy men had important consequences for their patrons and audience as well as for themselves.

An important case of a spiritual leader throwing his political weight against Jahangir occurred at the time of Khusraw's rebellion. In the province of Punjab, the young prince had come across the leader of the Sikh community, Arjan, fifth in the line of the Sikh gurus and compiler of the Sikh scriptures, the *Adi Granth*. Jahangir wrote: "Khusraw happened to halt at the place where [Arjan] was, and he came out and did homage to him. He behaved to Khusraw in certain special ways, and made on his forehead a fingermark in saffron, which the Indians (*hinduvan*) call *qashqa*, and is considered propitious (*shugun*). When this came to my ears I clearly understood his folly (*butlan*)."[15] When the prince lost his bid for the throne, the Sikh guru had to pay for this "folly" with his life.[16] His death too became a subject of circulating prophecies, used by some to celebrate Jahangir's defense of Islam. For example, Shaykh Ahmad Sirhindi—the Naqshbandi Sufi whose enthusiasm for the millennium was mentioned in the last chapter—wrote to the Mughal governor of Punjab, rejoicing at the news of the Sikh leader's death. In this letter, he also offered an oneiric omen in Jahangir's favor: "Before this infidel was killed, this humble one [Sirhindi] had seen a dream that the emperor (*badshah-i waqt*), has broken the wretched head of polytheism (*shirk*) and, truth be told, that Gentile (*gabr*) was the chief of the polytheists and the leader of the infidels."[17]

From the discussion above it may seem that Khusraw was to Hindus, Jains, and Sikhs what Jahangir was to Muslims. But it is important to note that these were more the expectations of ambitious holy men like Jami, Man Singh, Arjan, and Sirhindi than firmly held policies of either Jahangir or Khusraw. Clad in omens and blessings, these expectations structured the religiopolitical field within which the competition for sovereignty took place. The actions taken and alliances made by the Mughal father and son show how they formulated complex strategies within this field. For example, Jahangir as the "champion of Islam" had finished off his father's "heretic" ideologue Abul Fazl with the help of a Hindu raja. Later in his reign, he indicted for heresy the same Naqshbandi Sufi, Sirhindi, who had praised the emperor for the death of Guru Arjan. It is significant that the emperor did not turn Sirhindi over to a Muslim judge (*qazi*) to be prosecuted according to the *shariʿat*. Rather, he handed the Sufi over to his fearsome Hindu hunting companion Ani Rai Singhdalan (Commander Lion-Crusher) to be imprisoned.[18]

Conversely, at the time of Khusraw's rebellion a troop of Turkish soldiers on their way from Kabul to offer their services to Jahangir had, upon meeting Khusraw, thrown in their lot with the rebelling prince.[19] Thus it would be hasty to assume a simple or stable dichotomy between "Muslim" father and "Gentile" son. Rather, it is more feasible to conclude that, once made emperor, Jahangir learned his lesson quickly and abandoned the anti-Akbar stance he had cultivated briefly during his days as a rebellious prince.[20] Perhaps sitting on Akbar's throne had shown him the practical wisdom of his father in casting the net of sovereignty as wide as possible. Jahangir's embrace of a more "Akbari" attitude is also evident from the early pages of his memoir, where, alongside declaring himself the embodiment of Muslim prophecies, Jahangir proudly praised Akbar's personal qualities, his "universal" patronage of all systems of belief, his veneration of the "Great Luminaries" the sun and the moon, and last but not least his tradition of taking on imperial disciples.[21]

Jahangir's use of the institution of imperial discipleship is well attested in contemporary sources and well studied in modern scholarship. As we have seen, he started the practice while still a prince. When on the throne, he charged his "chief justice" (*mir-i ʿadl*) Shaykh Ahmad Lahori with the duty of vetting and initiating his disciples.[22] One of his generals, Mirza Nathan, described in his writings how as a young officer he had been inspired to become Jahangir's devotee.[23] Nathan had been seriously ill with a fever and unable to take part in battle when the emperor appeared to him in a dream, cured his serious illness, and enjoined him to fight. We also know that Jahangir enrolled as disciples eminent men of all backgrounds, granting this favor even to Sir Thomas Roe, the English ambassador from the court of King James I.[24] In effect, Akbar's millennial scheme was continued as an important institution by his son. Moreover, Jahangir was not the only one to use this ritual mode of binding men to the sovereign. When the rebellious Khusraw made his bid for sovereignty, he too had his officers swear oaths of discipleship. These oaths were not lightly taken. When Jahangir caught the rebels, he had them publicly impaled.[25]

Overall, the Sufi practice of inculcating loyalty and marking fealty that had been inflicted upon Babur by Shah Ismaʿil had, over the course of a century, become an institutional scaffolding of the Mughal imperial system. This had occurred gradually but deliberately. Babur had witnessed how the Safavids acted as both kings and saints, first absorbing his Timurid cousins and then him as their subordinates and disciples. However, having become a sovereign of import only toward the end of his life, Babur's sacred legacy was modest, limited to a few "ordinary" miracles remembered posthumously or inserted into his memoir. His son Humayun, on the other hand, had inherited a great conquest state. Subsequently, he had used his wealth and expertise in the occult to create a Safavid-like circle of devotees complete with cosmologically marked headgear. But Humayun lost his empire and had his imperial cult dismantled by Shah Tahmasb. The project did not die with Humayun's uncrowning, however. His son Akbar had successfully revived the scheme at the moment of the first Islamic millennium. In the process, he had claimed an unrivaled spiritual status and organized a cult of discipleship. Despite resistance from certain quarters, Akbar succeeded in institutionalizing his sacrality using the norms of sainthood. Thus among the Mughals, Jahangir was the first to inherit a fully functioning system of sacred kingship, in which the sovereign was both the political leader and spiritual chief of the realm. Upon ascending the throne, he became both the king of kings and the saint of saints.

A Sufi treatise from the period related how Jahangir jealously guarded his saintly preeminence. A prominent Sufi of the Naqshbandi order, Khwaja Khawand Mahmud, had apparently gotten into trouble with the emperor for trying to recruit one of his noblemen as a disciple. When the nobleman complained that he was being unduly pressured by the Sufi leader, the emperor asked Khwaja Khawand for an explanation. The Sufi was only able to avoid Jahangir's wrath by declaring himself an imperial disciple:

> The *faqir* [this humble one] is also your Majesty's *murid*, for there are two types of *murids*, i.e., *murid-i anabati* [a disciple to whom repentance (*tawba*) is administered] . . . and *murid-i shar'i* [disciples according to Islamic doctrine]. The former are these days rare; the latter discipleship relates to the obedience of the God's command, "Obey God and obey the Prophet and those who are in command among you." Since your Majesty is the emperor and is in command, I am your Majesty's *murid* [disciple].[26]

This account is from a hagiography of Khwaja Khawand written by his son. Its aim was to highlight the khwaja's wisdom in making Jahangir believe that the Sufi master had become his disciple while, in reality, only following the Quranic injunction to obey the sovereign. Whatever the factual validity of the anecdote, it gives us a sense of how being the disciple of the emperor could overlap and compete with being the devotee of another politically ambitious saint.

Jahangir's assumption of his father's style of sacred kingship can be seen most vividly in accounts of the religious debates he presided over between his Muslim scholars and the Christian priests of the third Jesuit mission. Much as they had with Akbar, the Jesuits believed they had a good chance at converting Jahangir to the Christian faith. Their letters from the time narrated how a year after his accession, the emperor had abandoned his exclusively Islamic stance and again developed an attitude toward Christianity that was reminiscent of his father's views—though there was no report of another ordeal by fire.[27] Jesuit accounts on the matter are corroborated by another report, that of the Muslim scholar and courtier ʿAbdus Sattar.

During Akbar's reign, ʿAbdus Sattar had been assigned to learn Latin and study the science, religion, and politics of the "Franks." He had worked with the Jesuits and translated several works on Christianity into Persian. He had continued this work under Jahangir, who mentions him in his memoir, noting with pleasure that ʿAbdus Sattar had presented him with a collection of works in Humayun's own hand on astrology and the occult—works that ʿAbdus Sattar had tried and found to be effective![28] Fortunately, ʿAbdus Sattar also composed an account of the religious disputations at court in a text called *Majalis-i Jahangiri* (The Assemblies of Jahangir).[29]

It has been suggested that ʿAbdus Sattar's *Majalis-i Jahangiri* was a work in the mold of Sufi texts known as *malfuzat* (utterances), which recorded the sayings of a saint.[30] It was most likely meant for a close circle of courtiers. In it, ʿAbdus Sattar called himself a disciple of the emperor, whom he referred to as spiritual master (*pir o murshid*), guide (*rahnuma*), and miracle worker. He described how Jahangir had ordered him to be present during religious disputations with the Jesuits, since he had knowledge of their language and texts. Once during these discussions, he had read his translation of the Bible with such enthusiasm that the emperor thought he had become a secret convert to Christianity. Jahangir's reaction is worth noting. He did not condemn ʿAbdus Sattar but rather stated that if the court scholar indeed had changed his religion, he should not be afraid to declare it for fear of punishment because "as you know full well that our [Jahangir's] sacred person is the 'Universal Manifestation' (*mazhar-i kull*), and that just as God is concerned with all His slaves . . . we too are concerned with all of His slaves."[31] Jahangir repeated his position at another point in the discussions, again declaring himself the Universal Manifestation (*ma mazhar-i kullim*) and giving ʿAbdus Sattar permission to change his religious affiliation from Islam to Christianity if he so desired.[32] The term Universal Manifestation (Mazhar-i Kull) had a resonance with Akbar's famous policy of Universal Peace (Sulh-i Kull). Its use shows that Jahangir had assumed the same "universal" spiritual status as his father, a status that placed him above all religious traditions and made him the ultimate arbiter of religious truth.

However, not all of our sources are in agreement on the matter of the emperor's status as a saint of saints or Universal Manifestation. Most significantly, Jahangir affected no such pretensions in his memoir. In fact, he did quite the opposite. In the *Jahangirnama*, which in the twelfth year of his reign was distributed across the empire and beyond as a model of sovereign behavior, the emperor offered a pious and humble image of himself. Jahangir's diary did not contain a single assertion that even came close to Akbar's claim of being the greatest spiritual being of the age. While Akbar's chronicles had described his every act as miraculous, Jahangir's writings did not contain even a few meager dream miracles of his own. If the *Jahangirnama* was meant to be a public account of how he performed his sacred sovereignty, it provides a jarringly subdued contrast to the grand claims of his father preserved in the *Akbarnama*. We know from the account of 'Abdus Sattar and the Jesuit missionaries that Jahangir had not retreated from the millennial and messianic sacrality his father had so assiduously instituted. But then why did he present such a modest and profane self-image in his memoir?

THE CASE OF JAHANGIR'S MODESTY

Jahangir's memoirs are often taken to be the official chronicle of his reign. This is understandable, given that he did not commission a formal chronicle like the *Akbarnama*, choosing instead to have his own diary completed, polished, and illustrated as a record of his rule.[33] This work was similar in many ways to a court chronicle. It followed an annalistic organization. It recorded the emperor's routine in the manner of a court diarist or news writer (*waqi'a navis*): promotions, grants, rewards, gifts given and received, types and number of animals hunted, and so on. Yet, for all these similarities, the Book of Jahangir did not belong to the same genre as the Book of Akbar.

The *Akbarnama* epitomized a style of writing in which historiography and hagiography were fused together to describe the life of a sovereign who possessed both royal and mystical qualities. Unsurprisingly, it was modeled after Timur's *Zafarnama* (Book of Victory).[34] The author of such a text was more than a courtier of the king or a historian of the dynasty. He was also a devotee and disciple of the patron and his family.[35] Thus

Akbar's closest disciple and the officiant of his sacred order, Abul Fazl, took it upon himself to describe in the Book of Akbar the cosmological significance and hidden truth of nearly every word and deed of his monarch cum messiah. The Book of Jahangir, on the other hand, was a first-person narrative. This was a rare form of self-expression. While kings and aristocrats were known to compose poetry, perform calligraphy, and paint, it was uncommon for a sovereign to keep his own diary or describe his own feelings in candid prose. Before Jahangir, we only know of Babur and Shah Tahmasb who wrote about themselves in such a manner.

That the "memoir" was not quite yet a genre in its own right—that it had no canon of its own—is evident from the fact that such rare works continued to be classified under other better-established forms of writing, like "chronicle" or "epic" (*nama*), "remembrances" (*tazkira*), "annals" (*waqiaʿ*), "daily affairs" (*ruznamcha*), and "regulations" or "norms of behavior" (*tuzuk*), all of which typically dealt with the life or deeds of someone other than the author. Furthermore, while there was no dearth of works containing elements of autobiography—letters, travelogues, pilgrimage narratives, eyewitness accounts in chronicles, professions of devotion in hagiographies of saints, personal confessions in works of ethics, and so on—texts nakedly devoted to one's own life were unusual. A reason for the rarity of self-referential writing was, plausibly, that it was considered bad form to discuss one's own life and accomplishments. Social etiquette dictated the use of profuse praise for others and abject humility for oneself. Thus, it was common to use expressions such as slave (*banda*) and worthless (*haqir*) for oneself and master (*mawla*) and icon or altar (*qibla*) for one's superiors. Overall, then, writing about oneself required the author to affect a high degree of modesty. When undertaken by a great sovereign, such a literary endeavor produced an effect that contrasted sharply with the panegyric and hagiographic tone of a royal chronicle.

There is no doubt that Jahangir followed the "modest" conventions of the "memoir" and maintained, to the degree he could, an air of being ordinary. At times, he used a humble expression to refer to himself: a petitioner at the divine court (*niyazmand-i dargah-i ilahi*).[36] He appeared subject to the same whims of nature and fortune as the common man, and he used the same remedies and protections against disease and danger that were available to everyone else. Once, when seriously ill, he wrote how it was his prayers at the Chishti shrine at Ajmer that cured him—a blessing he repaid by wearing a pearl earring as a sign of devotion to his patron saint buried there, Muʿinuddin Chishti.³⁷ Similarly, when during a hunt a lion charged at his group, Jahangir described how his servants pushed him over in their panic and trampled him: "I know for certain that two or three of them stepped on my chest getting over me."³⁸ He did not punish anyone but instead rewarded all those who helped subdue and slay the beast. Even when Jahangir's accomplishments were truly extraordinary, he clearly stopped himself from offering too great a detail or too high a praise. When, for example, a ferocious lioness jumped onto the back of his elephant, he swung around and, using his gun as a club, killed it with a single blow. This famous incident was depicted in multiple paintings over the next century by his descendants, but, in his own memoir, Jahangir gave it but a brief mention: "Since it is not seemly to write such things of myself (*chun az khud nivishtan khushnuma nist*), I will cut these reports short."³⁹ In effect, Jahangir's humble voice in the text traced the conventional grooves of genre and society.

Here, the important question to ask is why did Jahangir, a great sovereign and "Universal Manifestation," restrict himself to this intrinsically modest mode of self-expression? And, even more so, why did he conform to its conventions? In fact, there are rare but intriguing examples of autobiographical writings from the time in which these conventions were abandoned. Often it was done deliberately, to underscore the exceptional status of the author. This is especially true for works penned by men of great spiritual ambition, namely, saints and would-be messiahs. In Jahangir's reign, the most prominent example of such a case was that of the above-mentioned Naqshbandi Sufi Shaykh Ahmad Sirhindi. Sirhindi had described his spiritual achievements in his letters to his disciples and followers, which had been bound together and circulated during his life. Based on the contents of these volumes of letters (*maktubat*), the Sufi had been hauled up before Jahangir on charges of heresy. This is how the emperor described the "charlatan" (*shayyad*) Sirhindi's sacrilegious assertions:

> One of the pieces of nonsense he wrote for his disciples and believers was a book called *Maktubat* [letters], a miscellany of drivel (*jung al-muhammilat*) in which he had penned the basis of his claptrap that would lead to infidelity and apostasy. One thing he had written in his *Maktubat* was the following: "During my [spiritual] progress I chanced upon the stage of dual lights. I saw it was an extremely lofty and pleasant stage. I passed beyond it and reached the stage of the Faruq [the second Caliph Umar]. From the stage of the Faruq I crossed over to the stage of the Siddiq [the first Caliph

Abu Bakr]. Having written a description worthy of each, I became at one with the stage of Mahbubiyyat [the stage of "being the Beloved" traditionally associated with the Prophet]. It was seen as a stage of extremely brilliant light and color. I found myself reflected in the lights and colors, that is—[Jahangir exclaims] God forgive me!—I passed beyond the stage of the caliphs and ascended to the highest level."

Jahangir accused the Naqshbandi Sufi of setting up a network of "caliphs" to spread his heretical message. He thought it best to imprison Sirhindi until "the frenzy in his mind (*ashuftagi-i dimagh*) would settle down, as well as the uproar among the common folk (*shurish-i ʿawamm*)."

With the phrase "frenzy in his mind," Jahangir suggested that Sirhindi had temporarily lost his head, a condition common among overly enthusiastic mystics. However, Sirhindi certainly knew the risks he was taking by committing such "ecstatic" claims to paper. In one of his letters, he had written that to disclose even more of his spiritual achievements would mean "the throat would be slit and the gullet severed."[41] In other words, Sirhindi's statements in his letters were only muted versions of his visions of his own sacrality. What these visions were we may never know, except for the descriptions given by his disciples of their saint in a state of divine rapture. Here is how one of his chief disciples narrated the experience:

> Sometimes he [Sirhindi] summoned his advanced disciples (*khils ashab*), and explained his own chosen secrets (*asrar-i khassa*) and unveiled divine knowledge (*maʿarif-i makshufa*). He ordinarily tried to conceal those secrets with all his heart, but when he was explaining this divine knowledge, it was perceptible that he was encountering and receiving that spiritual state (*hal*). There were many who, when they heard this sublime divine knowledge from his pearl-scattering tongue, in gazing upon him at that very instant themselves experienced that divine knowledge. Most of the time that this revered one spent with his companions and others was in silence. His companions, from their extreme awe and wonder at him, did not even have the power to breathe. His control was at such a level that, in spite of the onslaught and frequency of numerous kinds of enrapturing visitations (*waridat-i mutanawwiʿa*), no external sign of the rapture of that revered one ever appeared. He was never seen to be agitated, to exclaim, to shout, or to cry out, except on very rare occasions. Occasionally he wiped away a tear or was close to weeping, and sometimes in the midst of explaining divine realities (*haqaʾiq*) his face became flushed.[42]

As a spiritually ambitious Sufi who had striven for recognition as a saint in his lifetime, Sirhindi epitomized, in his mystical and literary practices, a broader social institution at work. This was the institution of sainthood. The contender for this coveted spiritual status had to follow a dangerous ritual path, which involved breaking societal conventions and doctrinal taboos. The more "inviolable" the norm, the greater the spiritual reward existed for breaking it. We can see this at work in the stages of Sirhindi's spiritual ascension as he rose past, one by one, the eminent ranks of the first two caliphs of Islam to achieve a status equal to that of the Prophet himself. These stages and norms, by their aura of inviolability, circumscribed concentric circles of significance that could only be entered at the cost of overstepping strongly proscribed boundaries. Such transgressive acts and claims, however, exposed the actor to condemnation and ridicule. But this risk had to be taken because, in a paradoxical sense, the path to sacrality was paved with heresy and madness. This phenomenon was widely reflected in the social practices of the time, both in the antinomianism of naked, screaming mystics and in the bodily and violent excesses of royal life. We have already seen it at work not only in the messianic and prophetic claims of other Sufis, including Astarabadi, Nurbakhsh, Shattari, and Jaunpuri, but also in the sovereign reputations of monarchs such as Timur, Shah Isma'il, Humayun, and Akbar. Sufis and monarchs, in this milieu, were forged by similar ritual processes of sacrality and beholden to similar norms of saintliness.

An important aspect of these norms was that once sainthood was established, its true nature and full extent could only be communicated explicitly to the inner circle. At a distance from this core, the saint's miraculous accomplishments were typically expressed in ambiguous language and clothed in polyvalent symbols, poetic speech, and esoteric lore. This not only allowed the claimant to avoid condemnation by enemies and critics but also created a draw for potential followers to gain access to the inner circle. We can see such a pattern at work in Sirhindi's case, whose "public" letters contained only a diluted version—just a glimmer—of his "private" insights about his spiritual status. One could argue that Sirhindi had miscalculated: that the mystical content of his letters had not been vague enough to let him avoid charges of heresy. However, the fact that Sirhindi only spent one year in prison so that "the frenzy in his mind would settle down," after which he was released, granted a substantial purse, and given a prestigious appointment in Jahangir's entourage shows that his actions remained well within the socially accepted institution of sainthood.[43]

[184] THE THRONE OF TIME

Ambitious monarchs in this milieu had used similar methods for articulating the true extent of their sovereignty, manifestly to their inner circle and mysteriously to the wider world. Thus Timur had denied in public that he was a king even while his soldiers and successors celebrated him as a messianic Lord of Conjunction. Shah Isma'il had expressed his claim to be Ali's reincarnation in ambiguous verse even as his Qizilbash soldiers broke the strongest of taboos to prove their loyalty to him as the godsource. Humayun had assumed the status of *axis mundi* not by promulgating an edict but by staging his courtly performance according to astrological and alchemical principles. Even Akbar, who had declared his millennial and saintly status so explicitly at first, later adopted a more circumspect approach. In his regulations of 1601, Akbar forbade the practice of prostration before the monarch in public court (*darbar-i 'amm*) while still requiring it in private court (*darbar-i khass*), where only members of his inner circle were admitted:

> But as some perverse and dark-minded men look upon prostration as blasphemous man-worship, His Majesty [Akbar], from his practical wisdom, has ordered it to be discontinued by the ignorant, and remitted it to all ranks, forbidding even his private attendants from using it in the general assembly. However, in the private assembly, when any of those are in waiting, upon whom the star of good fortune shines, and they receive the order of seating themselves, they certainly perform the prostration of gratitude by bowing down their foreheads to the earth, and thus participate in the halo of good fortune. In this manner, by forbidding the people at large to prostrate, but allowing the Elect to do so, His Majesty fulfills the wishes of both, and shows the world a fitting example of practical wisdom.[44]

Much in the same vein, Jahangir too divided his imperial life into an inner and an outer existence. This division created two distinct social spaces in which the emperor lived and demarcated two symbolic realms in which he expressed himself. According to this scheme, the *Jahangirnama* was a description of Jahangir's outer (*surat*) and material (*zahiri*) world—of his public life and profane self. The self-effacement, modesty, and "profanity" built into the form of the "memoir" made it eminently suitable for the task of recording the uncontroversial daily routine of the emperor. It related the emperor's public audiences, hunts, pilgrimages, and travels. It recorded his interest in the flora and fauna, the fruits and foods, and the castes and tribes of his realm. In it, Jahangir noted down the stories and anecdotes of his empire both believable and incredulous, its miracles and marvels both good and bad, its religious practices both decent and absurd. In short, it described the empire and the emperor out and about in it. But the text contained no explicit references to his spiritual (*maʿni*) and inner (*batini*) self, his private audience hall, and his visions of his own sacrality.

Jahangir's memoir is completely silent about the deep debates the emperor had held with the Jesuits, in which he had assumed a status above all religions. Indeed, the *Jahangirnama* did not even mention the Christian priests. This partitioning of Jahangir's imperial self across two realms of existence and its implications for imperial cultural production was recognized by his courtiers and disciples. We can see this in the way ʿAbdus Sattar compared the *Jahangirnama* to his own hagiographical work on Jahangir's religious pursuits (*Majalis-i Jahangiri*). He called the former work an account of the emperor's activities of the day (*ruznamcha*) while terming the latter an account of the emperor's activities of the night (*shabnamcha*).⁴⁵ It was these nightly or private activities of the emperor, in which only the elect participated, that formed the explicit basis of Jahangir's sacred and saintly cult.

To summarize the argument, the lack of grand spiritual claims in Jahangir's memoir is not evidence either of his modesty or piety or of his abandonment of the Akbari tradition of sacred kingship. Rather, Jahangir's choice of a "modest" mode of narrating his daily routine is proof that he did not deign to express the true nature and extent of his spiritual status in prose. In fact, he had invented a whole other form of expression for that purpose, using a medium much better suited for recording talismanic qualities and conveying iconic messages. This was the medium of images. Jahangir's miracles and spiritual status—indeed, his millennial nature—are preserved in the innovative paintings he had his artists produce. Ironically, the Catholic missionaries may have unwittingly aided the emperor in this project when in their effort to convert the great "Mogor" to Christianity they had brought to him icons upon icons of the Messiah.

THE SACRED MEDIUM OF PAINTING

It is well acknowledged that painting was an important medium for Jahangir, one to which he applied a great deal of inventive energy.⁴⁶ This is saying a great deal in a cultural setting where the patronage and appreciation of art was already an established aspect of aristocratic life. In historical terms, the visual arts had become a powerful and necessary medium for the conception and enunciation of Muslim kingship from the Mongol period (the thirteenth century) onward.[47] In the fifteenth and sixteenth centuries, Timurid and Safavid princes were tutored in painting and as kings competed with one another in the commissioning of art.[48] Even if they could not afford to commission or purchase it, well-born men and women certainly knew how to appreciate it. Babur, for example, in his days as the impoverished ruler of Kabul, commented on the portrait technique of the famous Timurid painter Bihzad, noting that the master artist tended to draw "faces of beardless people badly by drawing the double chin too big."[49] But this art appreciation was not merely limited to evaluating the painted image. It also included gazing upon the world through the lens of art. Thus, when awestruck by the beautiful autumnal foliage of an apple sapling (*nihal-i sib*), Babur gushed that even "if painters had exerted every effort they wouldn't have been able to depict such a thing."[50] In sum, there had developed among the Persianizing elites of India and Iran a particular way of seeing their surroundings and themselves through the painted image. Among the Mughals of India, this visual paradigm was already highly evolved by the time of Jahangir.

Within this paradigm, not all paintings were accorded the same value. Those that depicted kings and prophets held a greater attraction for patron and artist alike. Along with scenes of courtly merriment and victories in battle, the Prophet's night journey to heaven had become a choice study for the painter's brush.[51] However, such imagery tended to run afoul of the long-held Islamic strictures against the making of graven images. To bypass these strictures, or at least to offer a counterrationale, there had developed in the fifteenth and sixteenth centuries an "Islamic art historical" narrative that gave painting a sacred dimension. This narrative consisted of traditions that located painting in the practices of ancient biblical prophets who were also revered in Islam.[52]

In these traditions, which are found both in the universal histories of the time—including the Millennial History of Akbar—as well as in prefaces to art albums, an important tradition was that of the Chest of Witnessing.[53] This story was told as a valid and sacred historical report passed down from the Companions of the Prophet. It related that after the Prophet's death, a set of his Companions were sent by the first caliph to the emperor of Byzantium. This Christian sovereign showed them a chest with thousands upon thousands of compartments, each containing an image of a prophet painted on silk. The Persian word used for "chest" in this tradition was the same as the word used for Ark of the Covenant, a "container of revealed truth."[54] The Byzantine emperor began by bringing out the image of Adam and continued one by one until he reached the last box, bringing out an image that was, the Companions attested, of the Prophet of Islam. When asked, the Christian emperor told the Companions that the Chest of Witnessing had been discovered by Alexander in Adam's treasury in the lands of the west. The prophet Daniel had taken it from Alexander and made copies of the images, which had come into Byzantine possession. In short, the Chest of Witnessing tradition maintained that the original images of the prophets had been given to Adam by God and were copied faithfully by Daniel, who, it was well known, possessed a gift of the occult. Image making according to this view was not just a form of idolatry but also an important aspect of both divine and prophetic practice. A related tradition held that although no one made images in early Islam, Ali had laid the foundation of calligraphy. It maintained that Ali had made designs (*raqam*) so refined that it amazed even the Chinese, who were widely considered to be masters of the aesthetic arts. As David Roxburgh has argued, such traditions sought to legitimize painting by associating it with calligraphy—already a sacred art—and by rooting the two artistic forms in the experience of early Muslim figures.[55]

The notion that painting was a "scriptural" art, one in which divine and sacred knowledge could be transmitted, was also conveyed through the story of the Iranian "false prophet" Mani (c. 216 to c. 276).[56] Mani's adherents were well-known "heretics" of early Islamic history. It was widely held that Mani had presented the (false) proof of his prophecy in painted images. The implication of this story, especially when it was told alongside the Chest of Witnessing tradition, was that even if Mani had been a false prophet, he had certainly been clever enough to make his claim in a medium that had the ability to enthrall people and had once been used by God and his true prophets. Thus, not all references to Mani and his art carried negative connotations. Indeed, the spellbinding aspect of Mani's legendary images was commonly used to celebrate the mastery of the visual arts. The title "Mani of the Age" was a coveted one for Muslim artists and, in the case of the Mughals, for Hindu ones too.

Overall, the notion of the sacred and talismanic quality of the painted image had filtered into the occult traditions of Islam. Images were commonly used in techniques of magic and drawn in manuals of talisman making. Paintings were an important aspect of books of divination (*falnama*), such as the famous one painted for the Safavid Shah Tahmasb in 1550.[57]

In at least one strand of Islam's mystical tradition, that of the millenarian Hurufis of Iran and Central Asia and their important offshoots such as the Bektashis of Anatolia, the painted image and the calligraphic alphabet even served as scripture.[58] Thus, despite the doctrinal restrictions against image making in Islam, in early modern India and Iran not all associations with the visual arts were negative or profane for Muslims. Indeed, when the Jesuits appeared at the Mughal court, they reacted with surprise that there existed among the nobility and the populace a much better attitude toward holy images than that of the protestant "iconoclasts" of Europe.[59]

It should not be surprising, then, that we find in the *Jahangirnama* strong evidence that painting for Jahangir meant much more than mere aesthetics and representation. Consider, for example, his reference to the art when he narrated his father's first victory in battle. Akbar had gone up against Hemu, a powerful Hindu general who had served the rival Afghan Sur dynasty during Humayun's reign. Hemu had posed a major threat to the nascent Mughal empire at the time when Akbar ascended the throne. His defeat and capture was for the young Akbar, thirteen years of age, a great accomplishment. When the injured and half-dead Hemu was presented after the battle to the youthful emperor, his regent told Akbar to cut off the enemy's head. Jahangir related that Akbar refused to do so, and quoted his father's explanation: " 'I have already torn him to pieces,' His Majesty [Akbar] said. And then he explained: 'One day, in Kabul, I was practicing drawing with Abdul-Samad Shirin-Qalam [the Sweet Penned]. I drew a picture of a person with disjointed limbs. One of those nearby asked who it was a picture of. I said, "It's a picture of Hemu." ' "[60] In other words, Akbar refused to perform the execution because he had already done so in a painting. This was one of Akbar's many miracles described in the *Akbarnama*.[61] Akbar's chronicle also related that on the way to battle he had had an effigy of Hemu filled with gunpowder and lighted up during a fireworks display for the army.[62] This too turned out to be another royal miracle. According to the chronicle, what seemed like an entertainment for soldiers was in reality the miraculous destruction of a vile enemy. That is to say, as a saintly being, the millennial monarch had a thaumaturgic ability to impose his will on the world. Images and likenesses crafted by him had a talismanic effect.

While Jahangir mentioned his father's miraculous images in his memoir, he did not list any of his own. In this he was following, as was argued above, the "modest" convention of his self-authored text. There is, however, extant a series of Jahangir-era paintings that, in their unique and intricate symbolism, present a highly sacred image of Jahangir's imperial self. While his memoir mainly narrated the worldly doings of the emperor, these paintings referred to his mystical achievements. These paintings, it will be argued, constituted the space where Jahangir performed his miracles.

THE PAINTED MIRACLES OF JAHANGIR

To understand the basis of Jahangir's approach to the visual arts, it is necessary to appreciate the high bar his father had set. Although the Timurids and Safavids had long been connoisseurs of painting, the number and quality of paintings produced under Akbar was and remained unrivaled. To get an idea of scale, just the illustrated epic *Hamzanama* (The Book of Hamza) produced for Akbar had fourteen hundred poster-sized paintings and took ten years to complete.[63] Indeed, no Muslim ruler of the time could outdo Akbar either in conquest or in the production of visual and aesthetic monuments to celebrate sovereignty. These grand achievements may have been the reason Jahangir did not try to compete with his father on similar terms, keeping instead a diary, something his illiterate—perhaps dyslexic—father had not been capable of. Similarly, in the sphere of art Jahangir distinguished himself from his father in both style and content. Instead of commissioning grand illustrated histories or epics, he ordered a series of highly innovative paintings, arranged in albums, which broke the mold of the Persian miniature tradition.[64]

Many of these Jahangiri paintings are thought to date from or after the period when Jahangir moved his court to Ajmer for three years (1615–1618).[65] Ajmer was a place of great spiritual significance for the Mughals because of the shrine of Mu'inuddin Chishti (d. 1230), the patron saint of the dynasty.[66] It is plausible that the spiritual and sacred content of these paintings executed at Ajmer may have been inspired by the charisma of the Chishti saint buried there. However, it is also noteworthy that the relationship between Jahangir and Mu'inuddin Chishti is rendered very differently in his art than in his memoir. While in the *Jahangirnama* the emperor called himself a slave and disciple of the thirteenth-century Chishti saint, in his paintings he made no such submission. This can be seen clearly in a pair of exquisite paintings, designed to be placed on the facing pages of an imperial album, in which Jahangir interacts with the Chishti Sufi (figures 6.1 and 6.2).[67]

On the left side, with the whole painted page devoted to him, the Sufi saint Mu'inuddin Chishti stands holding a globe with a keyhole, a key that

FIGURE 6.1 Shaykh Mu'in al-Din Chishti holding a globe (detail from folio). The Minto Album. Painted by Bichitr, c. 1620.

Source: CBL In 07A.14. © Trustees of the Chester Beatty Library, Dublin.

FIGURE 6.2 Jahangir holding a globe (detail from folio). The Minto Album. Painted by Bichitr, c. 1620.

Source: CBL In 07A.5. © Trustees of the Chester Beatty Library, Dublin.

points up and away from the keyhole, and a crown. His walking stick temporarily resting against his shoulder, he uses both hands to hold this collection of objects, as if waiting to give them to someone. The explanatory Persian script on the globe says "The key to the conquest/opening (*fath*) of the two worlds is entrusted (*musallam*) to your hands." On the facing painting is Jahangir, also a sole figure. He has in his hand the same globe and key, but the key now points down toward the keyhole. Jahangir holds these objects confidently with his right hand while keeping his left one on the hilt of his sheathed sword. The same statement in Persian about the "key to the conquest of the two worlds" appears in this painting but separate from the globe on the top left corner of the page. This statement serves, along with the globe and the changed direction of the key, to link the two paintings together and indicate the flow of the visual narrative from the Sufi to the emperor.

These twin paintings have several features that distinguish them from other works depicting Jahangir's interactions with holy men. To begin with, most such paintings portrayed actual meetings of Jahangir with Sufis and mendicants who were his contemporaries.[68] The famous Muʿinuddin Chishti, however, had lived five hundred years before Jahangir, so the meeting between the two could not have occurred in ordinary space and time. Thus, it is notable that in these paintings the saint and the monarch do not appear on the same page. This compositional technique serves to avoid the question of hierarchy. Both sovereigns are rendered independently, each a master of his domain. That they are equivalent figures is also indicated by how they appear suspended in a similar sacred space, silhouetted against a solemn darkness pierced only by the light of their respective halos. Finally, what the saint offers Jahangir is not a prayer or token of grace. Rather, it is a key to the mastery of two worlds, the material *and* the spiritual. The word used to explain this transaction, *musallam*, means to entrust, to give custody, to give up possession, to make whole. It conveys a sense of permanency. Thus, the most eminent Sufi saint of India gives up his position as master of the two worlds to Jahangir. In essence, this pair of images does not merely depict a Sufi blessing a king. Rather, it constitutes an act of succession from Muʿinuddin Chishti to Jahangir: the substitution of one saintly being by another.[69]

There are a number of Jahangiri paintings with characteristics similar to the ones discussed above. These features, which serve to unite them while distinguishing them from traditional Persian miniatures, can be summarized as follows:

1. The portrayal of a royal action taking place on a mythical or metaphysical plane.
2. The recurrence of mythological symbols from different religious and cultural traditions spanning India, Iran, and Europe.
3. Comments written directly on the painting in a minute but legible Persian script to explain its complex symbolism.

Given their inventiveness and sharp formal break from received artistic trends, it can be argued that these paintings belong to an emergent genre of visual culture. Linked by a shared symbolism, style, inspiration, and even the location and period in which they were produced, they can only be appreciated when studied together. These images also bear a complicated relationship to Jahangir's memoir. Rather than being representations of events or royal qualities mentioned in the emperor's writings, they add to the text and at times even contradict it. Indeed, if in his candid memoir Jahangir was an "ordinary" king, in these sacred images he becomes the saint of the age, with all the spiritual and thaumaturgic power that the position entailed.[70] Armed with this insight, we are ready to explore the inner recesses of Jahangir's sovereign existence and witness a record of his miracles.

JAHANGIR THE THAUMATURGE

Take, for example, the miniature in which Jahangir stands atop the globe of the earth shooting an arrow at the severed head of a dark-skinned man impaled on a lance (figure 6.3).[71]

Two *putti* hover above Jahangir, handing him a sword and arrows. Two owls are also present; one is perched on the head, while the other is hanging dead, lower down on the lance. A gun rests against the foot of the lance. The Persian commentary written on the painting tells us that the disembodied head belonged to Malik ʿAmbar, an enemy general of Abyssinian slave origins. Malik ʿAmbar had become the power behind the throne of the Nizamshahi dynasty of Ahmadnagar in the Deccan. Jahangir despised him, because he had kept the Mughals from extending their dominion southward. While there were many engagements between Mughal forces and Malik ʿAmbar's army, the latter was only temporarily defeated but never captured or killed. In this sense, this painting's depiction of the impaled head of Malik ʿAmbar is not a factual event. The painting is not completely devoid of historical reality, however. For it does portray an

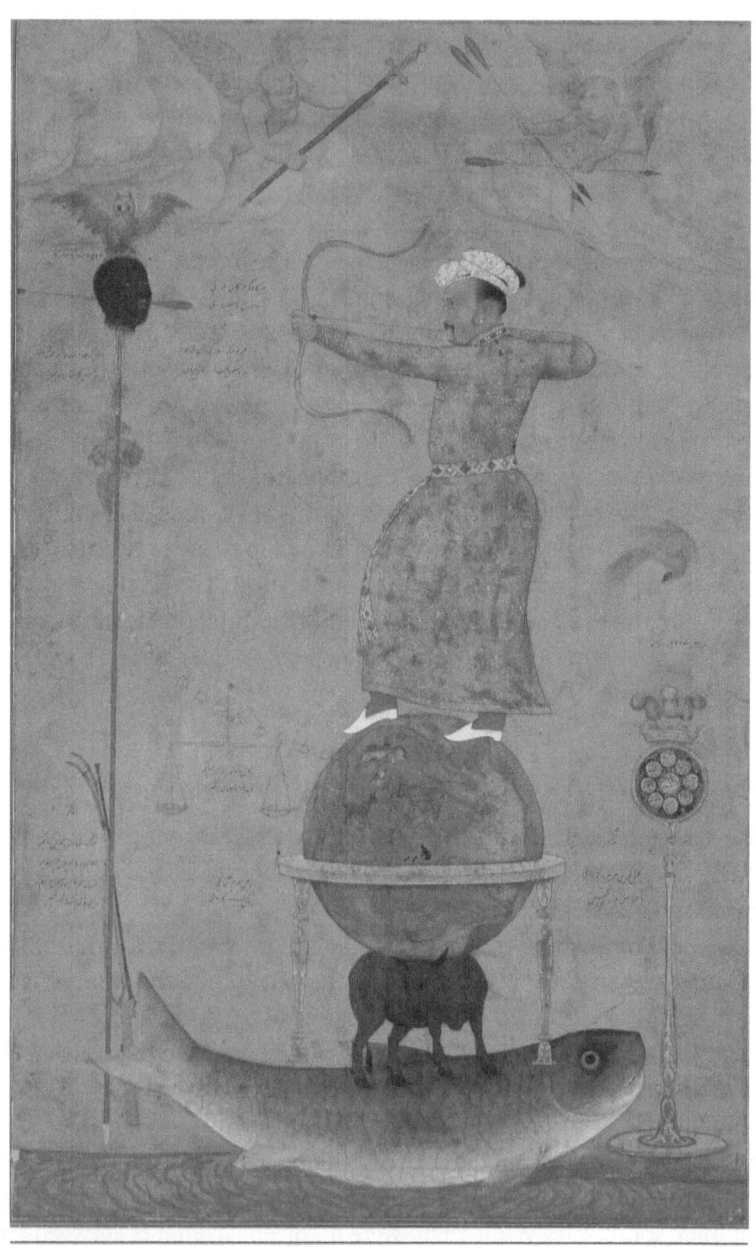

FIGURE 6.3 Jahangir shoots Malik ʿAmbar (detail from folio). Painted by Abuʾl Hasan, c. 1620. Gouache on paper, 25.8 × 16.5 cm.

Source: CBL In 07A.15. © Trustees of the Chester Beatty Library, Dublin.

incident mentioned in the *Jahangirnama*. This event involved the killing not of Malik ʿAmbar but of an owl.[72]

The owl incident occurred while Jahangir was in Ajmer in 1617.[73] It was the evening before the Mughal army was about to set out under the leadership of Jahangir's son Prince Khurram, the future Shah Jahan, to confront Malik ʿAmbar. At twilight, an owl alighted on the palace roof. Jahangir was immediately informed of this ominous occurrence. An owl was a symbol of violent death.[74] The matter was serious enough for the emperor to act personally. He immediately sent for his gun. Although the light was failing, Jahangir, a keen marksman, was able to bring down the ill-omened bird. This owl is one of the two depicted in the painting, with its neck bent, hanging above the royal matchlock that ended its life.

The dead bird and the gun are the only two things that relate the image to an event mentioned in Jahangir's memoir. The remaining ensemble of symbols, including the live owl perched on Malik ʿAmbar's head, constitute an act set on a metaphysical plane. First of all, Jahangir occupies a position reserved for the saint of the age, the pole or axis (*qutb*) of the world. That this world is not merely a material entity but the center of the cosmos is made evident by the presence of the cosmological symbols of the fish-bull.[75] Jahangir, in other words, maintains the balance of the cosmos, as the commentator states: "Through the felicity (*yumn*) of the Divine Shadow's coming, the earth is raised up on to the Fish-bull."[76] Similarly, it is because of Jahangir's sovereign presence that the world is at a messianic peace with "the lion drinking milk from the goat's teat"[77]—an image whose significance will be discussed in detail below.

From this elevated spiritual position, Jahangir reverses the ill effects of the owl's presence in the royal abode. He acts as the cosmic agent through whom the forces of light and good are channeled against the powers of darkness and evil—the owl and Malik ʿAmbar—as the commentary states: "Your enemy-smiting arrow has driven from the world [Malik] ʿAmbar, the owl which fled the light."[78] Jahangir enjoys abundant supernatural assistance. Angels hand him ammunition. A phoenix (*huma*) preserves his throne by alighting on the imperial Timurid genealogy. However, it was not sufficient for Jahangir merely to kill the owl that sat on his palace roof. The curse had to be turned back on the enemy. Thus an owl—the live one in the painting—finds its rightful place on the head of the accursed Malik ʿAmbar. Much in the way that the young Akbar had drawn a dismembered Hemu and burned his effigy before battle to miraculously destroy the enemy, Jahangir attempted to curse and kill Malik ʿAmbar through a talismanic painting.

It is worth emphasizing that in following such "magical" practices, Jahangir was not acting out of mere superstition. Rather, he was beholden to the institution of sacred kingship he embodied. For one, the practice of observing birds near a king or ruler for signs of evil omens, called *tatayyur*, was common at the time.[79] It belonged to a range of divinatory and cosmological knowledge such as astrology, geomancy, and dream interpretation, which structured the lives of the elite and learned. Furthermore, such knowledge was especially important for rulers and sovereigns, because it indicated the health of the body politic and the rise and fall of dynasties. Thus when a lunar eclipse occurred, a well-established sign of evil, Jahangir recorded it in his memoir and noted that he gave away fifteen thousand rupees in alms—a huge sum by the standards of the day—to propitiate its dark effects.

Similarly, Jahangir also recorded in detail another "celestial phenomenon," the appearance of a long-tailed comet in the winter of 1618. He noted the opinion of astrologers that "its appearance indicates a weakness among the kings of the Arabs and domination of them by their enemies." Although the emperor did not say anything else on the matter, his close confidante and secretary Muʿtamad Khan provided a great deal more detail.[80] This is how he described the ill effect of the comet of 1618 on Jahangir's dominions:

> Throughout the vast realm of India, it caused epidemic and cholera the likes of which had never been seen before. People had never heard of such disease or read about it in the trustworthy books of India. These dire conditions became manifest within one year of its appearance and remained so for eight years. And it was its influence that caused confrontation and animosity between Jahangir and his nobility. This violent state of affairs lasted for the next seven or eight years causing untold blood to be spilt and countless homes to be destroyed.[81]

As if to give a concrete example of the effects of this celestial phenomenon, the next report in both the *Jahangirnama* and the narrative of Muʿtamad Khan recorded a massive infestation of rats in the province of Qandahar. This plague destroyed all crops, orchards, and stores of grain, ending only when there was nothing more for the rodents to feed on. This, then, was a king's perspective on the comet's effects. To get a saint's of point of view, we have to turn to the mystical letters of Shaykh Ahmad Sirhindi.

One of Sirhindi's disciples had written to him asking about the messianic significance of the same celestial phenomenon, the comet of 1618. The Naqshbandi Sufi's rambling reply evaluated a number of interpretations.[82] He began by noting that such a twin-tailed comet was indeed expected to presage the coming of the mahdi. This phenomenon, he wrote, had reoccurred many times before in history at moments of great changes in world affairs: at the time of Noah and the flood, when Abraham was thrown into the fire, when Pharaoh and his people were destroyed, and when the prophet John (the Baptist) was killed. However, Sirhindi concluded that this particular comet did not indicate the imminent appearance of the mahdi. This was because the mahdi, according to Sirhindi's calculations, was scheduled to manifest himself at the end of the current Islamic century, out of which only twenty-eight years had yet passed (that is, it was 1028 AH, and the mahdi would not appear until 1100 AH). Nevertheless, Sirhindi speculated that even if the comet was not a sign of the mahdi's manifestation, it could very well be a sign of his physical conception. He wrote that if this was the case, it would soon be confirmed by many of the same signs that had once accompanied the conception and birth of the Prophet of Islam:

> Thus it is written that when [the Prophet's father] 'Abdullah's seed (*nutfa*), which was the substance of the Prophet's form, peace be upon him, lodged itself in [the Prophet's mother] Amina's womb (*rihm*), all the idols of the world fell down, and all the devils stopped their work. The angels turned Satan's [Iblis's] throne upside down and threw it in the sea and tormented him for forty days. And the night when the Prophet was born, an earthquake shook Xerxes' palace and its fourteen pinnacles fell. And the [Zoroastrian] fire of Persia that had been burning continuously for *a thousand years* died out. [my italics]

Sirhindi's letter shows how well he was attuned to cyclical and millennial interpretations of history and their implications for embodied sovereignty.[83] His interpretation of the celestial phenomenon had a strong political undercurrent: if all the idols of the world fell down at the time of the Prophet's physical conception, and if the thousand-year flame of Zoroaster's religion died out at his birth, the conception of the mahdi in the first century of the Islamic millennium could also spell doom for the religiopolitical order of the day. Overall, the widespread focus on a sign in the sky shows that it was a weighty matter of religion and politics. It could be used to explain natural and political disaster, develop claims of power, motivate followers, and threaten enemies. But under no circumstances it could be dismissed as meaningless.

In this vein, it is worth noting that Jahangir's ritual action against a dark omen at a moment of war and rebellion was similar in many ways to his Iranian Safavid contemporary Shah ʿAbbas's response to an astrological threat. As was discussed in the previous chapter, Shah ʿAbbas temporarily abdicated his throne to defend himself from the evil influences of a planetary conjunction and to turn back the dire predictions of the millenarian Nuqtavi brotherhood.[84] Jahangir had continued to patronize Nuqtavis in Mughal India. For example, Sharif Amuli, a Nuqtavi from Iran mentioned in the last chapter, received a high rank and even served as a provincial governor. In both Safavid and Mughal kingship, then, such divinatory knowledge was related to the cosmological right to rule. A commoner may have ignored an owl on his roof or a comet in the night sky, but a sovereign could not, especially during a moment of war and rebellion. The owl for Jahangir, like the conjunction for Shah ʿAbbas, was a cosmological sign that required immediate and forceful ritual action. The only difference in the two cases was that while Shah ʿAbbas had organized a ritual theater for the purpose, Jahangir had encapsulated the ritual in a painting.

JAHANGIR THE RENEWER

If there is any doubt that the painting just discussed constituted a ritual act, it should be dispelled when we examine another formally similar image (figure 6.4).

In this painting, Jahangir, once again the *axis mundi*, shoots an arrow at a naked, emaciated, dark-skinned old man.[85] The explanatory script states that this is an "auspicious image of His Supreme Majesty [Jahangir] whose arrow of kindness destroys *dalidar* from this world and recreates the world anew with his justice and fairness." Although the commentary is in Persian, the word used for the target of Jahangir's arrow is the Hindi word *dalidar*, derived from the Sanskrit *daridra*, meaning poverty. Under this word, the Persian gloss states, "that is, the 'person of poverty' (*shakhs-i iflas*)."

In some Hindu religious traditions, Daridra is the goddess of poverty and misfortune, the contrasting sister of Lakshmi, the goddess of wealth.[86]

FIGURE 6.4. Emperor Jahangir triumphing over poverty (detail from folio). Attributed to Abu'l Hassan (Nadir al-Zaman), c. 1620–1625. Opaque watercolor, gold, and ink on page, 23.81 × 15.24 cm.

Source: Los Angeles County Museum of Art, Nasli and Alice Heeramaneck Collection, Museum Associates, purchase M.75.4.28. Digital Image © 2009 Museum Associates / LACMA / Art Resource, N.Y. Image Reference: ART391108

In the Diwali festival, one of several "Hindu New Years," people rid their homes of poverty (Daridra) in order to start anew with prosperity (Lakshmi). Accordingly, the use of this word in the painting indicates that Jahangir is performing a type of renewal ritual. This is supported by the commentary, which states that the emperor is recreating the world (*jahan*) anew with justice. But neither this painting nor the memoir explains why the king must perform this renewal ritual for the world. Nevertheless, a clue may be found in the association of the Diwali festival with a key symbol of Hindu kingship: Rama.

Diwali in northern India was, and still is, a commemoration of the coronation of Rama upon his victory over the demon Ravana. The story of Rama and its importance for Indic kingship was well known to the Mughals.[87] Rama was a god-king, an avatar of Vishnu, who inaugurated a new cycle of time by ridding the world of demons, corruption, and disorder. It is for this reason that Akbar, at time of his millennial claim, was declared to be a reincarnation of Rama. In light of these facts, *dalidar* here may not simply refer to poverty but to evil, darkness, and a corrupt world order. The biblical sign of messianic peace—the lion and the lamb living in harmony—at Jahangir's feet once again reinforces Jahangir's actions to renew the world. Finally, below the globe of the earth, we witness another story of cosmic rebirth. The fish, the Matsya avatar of Vishnu, carries Manu on the waters of the flood, which, much like the biblical flood, inaugurated a new cycle of time in Indic cosmology.

There does not seem to be an event in the *Jahangirnama* that directly connects the text to this image. However, from his memoir it is evident that Jahangir vigorously observed many important Indic customs of kingship. These included annual rituals such as the solar and lunar weighing ceremonies (*jashn-i wazn-i shamsi o qamari*), in which the ruler was weighed against precious metals, which were then distributed among the needy. He also gave alms to Brahmans as propitiatory acts during times of war and rebellion. He held private spiritual counsel with Hindu mendicants, the most famous being the ascetic Jadrup.[88] Furthermore, Jahangir participated in the major festivals of the Hindu calendar, including Diwali and Holi. Finally, Jahangir was well aware of the cyclical dimension of time that formed the cosmological substrate of these Indic rituals. In describing the Hindu festival of Holi, Jahangir remarked that "the lighting of fires of the last night of the year is a metaphor for burning the old year as though it were a corpse."[89] Jahangir's arrow of light in the painting performs a similar function, as he puts an end to disorder and inaugurates a new cycle of time.

Overall, it is important to recognize that Jahangir's ritual art bore an important relationship to the experience, practice, and embodiment of sacred kingship. To develop a textured sense of what this means, it is worth paying attention to Gauvin Bailey's insights on the way Mughal artists drew inspiration from popular culture and religious festivals for their depictions of Jesus. When Mughal artists were ordered to illustrate a Persian narrative of the life of Jesus, they not only copied scenes from European oil paintings and engravings but also rendered them from the lively street theater, full of gimmicks and contraptions, which the Christian priests had regularly organized for the Indian populace.[90] These religious parades sometimes attracted thousands of people and were often enjoyed by the emperor himself. In the report of one such parade, we learn that the decorations at the Christmas crib featured a portrait of Jahangir:

> A [mechanical] ape which squirted water from its eyes and mouth, and above it a bird which sang mysteriously . . . and a globe of the world supported on the backs of two elephants . . . and above this a large portrait of the King [Jahangir] which he sent us when he was a prince . . . and next to this figure was placed a large mirror at the front of the crib . . . [At the gates] was the Angel, i.e., Gabriel, with many angels.[91]

In effect, Jahangir participated in the Christmas pageant organized by the Jesuits through one of his paintings. Through this participation, the Jesuits' religious festival became a venue for the articulation of Jahangir's sovereignty. This articulation occurred via sacred icons and symbolic juxtapositions. In other words, it made use of a visual form very similar to the ones we have seen in the last two paintings: the depiction of Jahangir above the globe of the world, framed by angels, and paired with prophetic and messianic figures. The similarity between the elements of Jahangir's talismanic paintings and the way his figural presence was arranged within this popular parade indicates how Mughal artists may have used popular events and public spectacles as models on which to base their portrayals of the emperor's miraculous qualities.

Furthermore, these connections between the world of popular spectacles and the art of imperial self-fashioning shed new light on the significance of animal imagery in Jahangir's paintings. Specifically, this was the imagery of predator and prey lying together in harmony. In some paintings it was a lamb, in others a goat or an ox alongside a lion, but the theme was instantly recognizable as one of sacred sovereignty and messianic justice. In a classic essay, Ebba Koch observed that the source of this iconic image was the picture of "peace among animals under the rule of the Messiah" that had graced the Jesuits' printed Bible.[92] She also noted that the peaceful coming together of the hunter and hunted—leopard and deer, hawk and dove, and so on—was an ancient myth of Iranian kingship that had survived in Mughal court panegyrics.[93] To these insights we must add, however, that this Mughal vision of messianic peace was more than just pompous mimicry of received images and texts. The notion may well have been part of biblical and ancient Iranian traditions, but Jahangir, his populace, and his painters saw this miracle manifest itself in nature all around them.

The emperor's memoir contains a large number of observations concerning the marvels of nature. These marvels and inexplicable occurrences, much like the popular religious spectacles, were both a source of popular entertainment as well as sacred wonder. To begin with, consider the episode concerning a lion and a mendicant:

> A lion was brought from the royal lion house to be made to fight an ox. Many people had gathered to watch. There was also a group of yogis, and the lion approached one of the yogis, who was naked, in a playful manner, not in rage, and knocked him to the ground. Then, just as though it were copulating with a female of its own kind, it mounted him and began to hump. It did the same thing the next day. It has acted like this several times. Since before now no such thing had ever been seen, and it is exceedingly strange (*ghara'ib-i tamam dasht*), it is recorded.[94]

The emperor had wanted to enjoy a fight between a lion and an ox in the company of a crowd, which included a band of naked Hindu ascetics. However, the affair suddenly took a strange turn. The episode was termed marvelous not simply because of the puzzling fact that the beast had changed its nature and tried to consort with a man but because it occurred in the presence of the sovereign. In other words, it took on cosmological significance and became an omen to be interpreted. As was argued in chapter 3, "strangeness" was an important category of knowledge for kingship, one to which sovereigns devoted a great deal of time and attention, because it related to the health of the body politic and, consequentially, to the health and power of the sovereign. This was not only a "magical" worldview but also a "scientific" one, reflecting a "humoural understanding of polity."[95] In this view, the monarch held the status of chief natural philosopher, and news writers were required to report to him strange occurrences in the animal, vegetable, or mineral world, so he could determine their significance for his dominion.

Jahangir noted, for example, how in his reign leopards and lions had begun to mate successfully in captivity. Such wondrous phenomena, the emperor observed, had not been witnessed even in the time of his father.[96] Indeed, Jahangir's dominion had become so full of felicitous signs in nature that the emperor could not help but state—ever so humbly—that in his reign wild beasts had lost their wildness: "During the felicitous reign of this petitioner at the divine court [i.e., Jahangir] wildness has been eliminated from the nature of wild beasts to such an extent that lions have become tame and roam in packs among people, without restraints or chains, and they neither harm them nor run away."[97]

How these phenomena were used to celebrate Jahangir's sovereign health can be seen in the gift given him by his son. Prince Dawarbakhsh presented the emperor with a pair of animals that seemed to have overcome their wild natures and opposing tendencies to bond with each other. A lion and a goat had apparently fallen in love:

> The lion got along so well with the goat that they were kept in the same cage and the lion exhibited great affection for the goat. The lion would take the goat in its embrace in the manner that animals couple and hump it. When an order was given for the goat to be concealed, the lion cried out and showed great distress. . . . Then the first goat was brought, and the lion exhibited the same love and affection as before, falling on its back, taking the goat on its chest and licking it on the mouth. Never before had any animal, tame or wild been seen that kissed its mate.[98]

This was indeed a "strange" affair by the standards of any era. However, we must do more than laugh at it. The wondrous interest of the emperor and his entourage in it may explain why it was only in Jahangir's time that the image of "the lion drinking milk from the goat's teat" became a painted icon of sovereignty. In sum, the medley of symbols in Jahangir's sacred paintings—animals and angels, condemned men and holy ones, chains of justice and arrows of light—were more than just reflections of elite ideals, written theories, or literary tropes of sovereignty. Rather, they drew their strength from popular practices and public spectacles that framed the performance and shaped the experience of sacred kingship.

These signs signified, by their materialization in culture and nature, the embodied sovereignty of the ruler. And this is why they graced the emperor's talismanic paintings.

JAHANGIR THE SEER

The paintings previously discussed show Jahangir following the tradition of sacred kingship established in the time of his father. The monarch, in this tradition, was a source of immense spiritual power, with which he could perform miracles, sustain the balance of the cosmos, inaugurate new cycles of time, and impose his will on the world by mere allusion. Moreover, this inner strength of the king drew sustenance from the truth of not one but many sacred traditions, and not just from their doctrines but also from their practices and symbols. Kingship, in other words, was above all religions. However, a skeptic may take issue here that these paintings are nothing more than the product of court sycophants, of painters eager to praise the emperor. Indeed, how do we know that these innovative works of art bear the stamp of Jahangir's own imagination and desire?

The proof, fortunately, is available in a unique cultural artifact from this period: the visual record of an imperial dream (figure 6.5). In this painting, Jahangir stands atop the world embracing his contemporary, Shah ʿAbbas of Iran. Many of the symbols in this painting connect it to the two already discussed: the globe, the lion and the lamb, and a miraculous event—the oneiric meeting of Jahangir and Shah ʿAbbas. According to the commentary on the painting, Jahangir saw a dream in which Shah ʿAbbas appeared in a wellspring of light (*chashma-i nur*). He ordered his artist to paint the dream quickly before the approaching Persian New Year (*nawruz*). To render Shah ʿAbbas's portrait accurately, the artist interviewed people who had visited Iran and seen the Safavid ruler. Finally, the painting is also marked by a verse that spontaneously came to Jahangir's "miraculous tongue":

> Our Shah came in a dream, and so gave us joy
> The enemy of my dream is the one who woke me up

Most art historical interpretations of this painting ascribe it to Jahangir's anxiety over losing the border province of Qandahar, in present-day Afghanistan, to the Safavids.[99] These political and psychological interpretations

FIGURE 6.5 Allegorical representation of Emperor Jahangir and Shah ʿAbbas of Persia (detail from folio). The St. Petersburg Album. Painted by Abuʾl Hasan, c. 1618. Opaque watercolor, gold, and ink on paper, 23.8 × 15.4 cm.

Source: © Freer Gallery of Art, Smithsonian Institution, Washington, D.C.: Purchase F1945.9a.

overlook the important fact that in Jahangir's time the dream was a medium of miracles and prophecy.

As was discussed in the case of Babur's oneiric visions, the dream in Islamic culture, both learned and popular, was considered to be a part of prophecy.[100] The appearance in a dream of God, the Prophet, a saint, or a king was considered a source of blessing and instruction. For example, in his memoir, Jahangir mentioned a dream in which his late father appeared and told him to free Mirza Aziz Koka, a nobleman who was at the time imprisoned in the fearsome Gwalior fort.[101] Jahangir followed his dead father's directive and freed the man. It has already been mentioned how Jahangir himself was known to appear in the dreams of his officers. In sum, dreams were substantial and real events that played an important role in social discourse. Jahangir's emphasis on having his dream depicted realistically underscores this point. The people and elements in his dream were real, not imaginary or metaphorical, even if they had only come together in a higher spiritual realm opened up by dreaming.

It is worth noting, however, that this particular dream is not mentioned in Jahangir's memoir. This is significant because Jahangir referred to the Iranian ruler many times, calling him endearingly "my brother" (*baradaram*), and he even included copies of letters sent by Shah ʿAbbas. This gap between the memoir and the painting strengthens the impression that Jahangir had reserved this new visual genre for the expression of his deepest mystical thoughts and actions. From the phrase in Jahangir's verse "gave us joy" or more literally "blessed our time" (*khushwaqt kard*), it appears to be a friendly visit. From Shah ʿAbbas's pose, it seems like a brotherly submission. If two of Jahangir's forefathers—Babur and Humayun—had submitted themselves to the ritual discipline of the Safavids, this oneiric miracle of his seemed to have undone and reversed that bond. Shah ʿAbbas was now the recipient of Timurid charisma and *barakat*.

JAHANGIR THE MILLENNIAL BEING

There is another striking painting that has much in common in terms of style, theme, and symbolism with the one depicting Jahangir's dream. In it, too, kings whom Jahangir had never met in person appear before him, and the same giant halo surrounds him (figure 6.6). Do we not see here another one of Jahangir's dreams? In this painting, Jahangir no longer stands on the globe of the earth as he did in the other images.[102] Instead,

FIGURE 6.6 Jahangir preferring a Sufi shaikh to kings (detail from folio). By Bichitr, c. 1625. Opaque watercolor, gold, and ink on paper. 25.3 × 18.1 cm (10 × 7 1/8 in.).

Source: © Freer Gallery of Art, Smithsonian Institution, Washington, D.C.: Purchase F1942.15a.

he sits on a giant hourglass. The poetry above and below the painting sets the scene:

> The King of the outer (*surat*) and inner (*ma'ni*) domains is, by the grace of God,
> Nur al-Din Jahangir ibn Akbar Padishah.
> Although outwardly (*dar surat*) kings stand before him,
> Inwardly (*dar ma'ni*) he always turns his gaze towards dervishes.

Here we have an explicit statement of Jahangir's sovereignty over the world in all its aspects, its material and outward form as well as its spiritual and inward dimension. The world's greatest monarchs and mystics pay him homage. In the competition for Jahangir's attention, the kings are disappointed, while the Sufi is rewarded.

The visual hierarchy makes clear that the Sufi is above the kings and Jahangir above them all. The Sufi whom he rewards with a book was the leader of the Chishti brotherhood in Jahangir's time. The kings who stand before him include King James I of England and, apparently, the Ottoman Sultan.[103] But there are other symbols and actions that the verses do not explain. Instead of the globe of the earth with a lion and lamb on it, we have an hourglass with a pair of angels writing on it. The *putti* above Jahangir have broken their arrows in despair. What are we to make of these differences and changes from the images discussed earlier?

Although there is no detailed commentary to aid our understanding, there is one line of writing on the lower half of the hourglass. It is a prayer written jointly by two angels. And in it we may have the clue to the significance of the hourglass. The angels have written: "Allah Akbar! Oh King, may your age endure a thousand years." The angelic prayer of a thousand-year life, juxtaposed with Akbar's talismanic sign (Allah-u Akbar), marks Jahangir as a millennial being. Jahangir, adorning the throne of Time, inaugurates the new Islamic millennium. The running sands of the hourglass show that the millennium has already begun. The struggle to bring order to the world is over. With the kings of the world at Jahangir's feet, the *putti*'s heavenly arrows are no longer needed. The emperor blesses the new millennium as he would bless a new year, by patronizing holy men. In short, Jahangir upholds the millennial-messianic dispensation that he inherited from his father.

From his memoir we know that under Jahangir, as it had been under Akbar, one of the rituals of imperial discipleship involved the veneration of the sun and the moon.[104] This may explain why the emperor's halo in the last two paintings consists of the disc of the sun and the crescent of the moon. When Jahangir referred to the sun and the moon in his memoir, he addressed them as His Holiness the Greater Luminary (Hazrat Nayyir-i Aʿzam) and His Holiness the Lesser Luminary (Hazrat Nayyir-i Asghar), respectively. That is to say, the emperor addressed the sun and the moon as holy beings. The personification of these two heavenly bodies is also evident in Jahangir's paintings. In figure 6.5, we can see two angelic beings peek out from below the halo, one on each side. In figure 6.6, however, they are no longer present under the sun and the moon. Instead, they are to be found further below, inscribing Jahangir's millennial status on the hourglass. The two "angels" appear to be the embodiments or agents of the sun and the moon, blessing the emperor's "time."

The idea that these two heavenly bodies were beings worthy of veneration was not merely an Indic practice taken up by the Mughals. Rather, it was an integral part of the Illuminationist (Ishraqi) philosophy of the famous thinker Suhrawardi (d. 1191), which was in vogue at the time. Indeed, Suhrawardi had composed prayers in Arabic to ask the sun for knowledge and salvation.[105] But he was not the only Muslim authority on the subject. Another major figure in this regard was Abu Maʿshar (d. 886), a Persian philosopher and mathematician of the Abbasid period who became the most famous astrologer of medieval times. As was noted previously, Abu Maʿshar's Arabic prayers to the sun were quoted in the first volume of the *Tarikh-i Alfi* (Millennial History) commissioned by Akbar.[106] Incidentally, it was in the same work that the emperor was also declared to be the Renewer of the Second Millennium (Mujaddid-i Alf-i Thani). Abu Maʿshar was a great proponent of the science of conjunction astrology, which he used to divide historical time into millennial cycles. He was also deeply influenced by Indic notions of cyclical time and bequeathed the idea to both the Islamic and Christian worlds in the science of astrology.[107] The sun and the moon, then, were for Mughal kings luminous beings responsible for the changing cycles of time and the vicissitudes of kingship. Sovereignty, especially of the millennial order, could not be had without paying heed to these heavenly bodies.[108]

CONCLUSION

There survive a pair of Jahangir's portraits from around 1614, one now in Paris and the other in Delhi, that depict his messianic genealogy.[109] In one

Jahangir holds a portrait of his father, Akbar, and in the other, a portrait of his "mother," the Virgin Mary. For Jahangir, such images were not only expressive but also operative—not only allegorical but also talismanic. In other words, this type of innovative art was both a record of and a medium for the emperor's miraculous self. As such, it was meant for those in the know, the inner circle of disciples. By contrast, the emperor's memoir was a "public" document—somewhat formulaic in its self-effacing and "pious" tone—copied at various stages of writing and sent across the realm. The paintings portrayed what could not be stated in the memoir. This scheme followed an established Sufi hagiographical practice. The saint's miracles were only disclosed to his closest disciples and sons. Although they may become part of the oral lore surrounding the saint in his lifetime, they were committed to paper and made public in a hagiography (*tazkira*) only after his death. A saint who strayed from this custom caused controversy and invited accusations of heresy. This held true as much for the famous Naqshbandi leader Shaykh Ahmad Sirhindi, who made a millennial claim in Jahangir's reign, as it did for the emperor Akbar. Both men had become the focus of religious controversy because they claimed their sacredness explicitly and publicly in writing. Jahangir, it seems, was much more cautious in following the norms of saintliness. Or, one could say, he was much more inventive. Instead of writing down his miracles, he had them painted.

It should come as no surprise, then, that the painted image played a central role in the Mughal institution of imperial discipleship. Akbar had revived Humayun's cult of disciples but not his cosmologically inflected headgear, the Taj-i ʿIzzat (Crown of Glory). Instead, each supplicant was given upon initiation a small painted likeness (*shabih*) of the emperor, which could be pinned on or wrapped within one's turban. Although no such portrait has been found from Akbar's reign, we possess several copies of tiny portraits of Jahangir that were rendered for this purpose.[110] In these paintings, Jahangir is shown haloed and framed by a window. The window indicated that he was performing the famed *jharoka-i darshan* (window of veneration) ceremony, in which the sovereign showed a glimpse of himself from a distant palace balcony to his subjects. These tiny portraits were, in other words, painted rituals. They encapsulated in visual form the sacred manifestation of the saint-emperor to his disciples.

{7} CONCLUSION

THE GRAFFITI UNDER THE THRONE

It is also a sign of auspiciousness and divine guidance that at the beginning of every millennium a world ruler should come into existence to eradicate rebellion and ignorance from the world, just as the rising of this star was predicted 565 years ago by Afzal al-Din Hakim Khaqani:

"They say that every thousand years there comes into this world one who is privy to the people of perfection. One came before this, but we had not yet been born; one will come after this, but we will have sunk into grief."

On the third day after his birth, His Majesty the Emperor Akbar went to the palace to feast his eyes on the baby's [the future Shah Jahan's] world-adorning beauty and such a celebration was held that the eyes of the world were dazzled.

—Muhammad Hadi (c. 1720), Preface to the Jahangirnama

AS THE chroniclers and astrologers of Shah Jahan (r. 1627–1658) were keen to point out, their sovereign too had been born on the eve of the first Islamic millennium.[1] Upon his enthronement, the emperor styled himself as the Second Lord of Conjunction, openly embracing his millennial legacy and asserting his oneness with Timur. Shah Jahan's predecessors had also pursued the memories of their Timurid past. Jahangir, for instance, had lavishly rewarded the sweet-tongued visitor from Samarqand, Abdul Razzaq Mutribi, for his eyewitness account of the physical condition and miraculous nature of Timur's black-stoned sepulcher, on which was inscribed the legend of the luminous conception of the Lord of Conjunction's ancestor.[2] Shah Jahan, however, went even further. He became the Second Lord of Conjunction and acted forcefully to reclaim his Timurid patrimony. At the height of his reign, he launched an ambitious military effort to reconquer his ancestral homeland. The logistically difficult campaign bore little fruit, even though three of Shah Jahan's sons—first Murad Bakhsh, then Aurangzeb, and finally Dara Shikoh—led a massive army for two years across the hardscrabble landscape of Afghanistan and Central Asia.[3] Nevertheless, Shah Jahan's willingness to stake considerable prestige, life, and treasure on the project shows that for him the label Lord of Conjunction was much more than a fanciful evocation of memory.

In twentieth-century scholarship, however, Shah Jahan is known not for his millennial and messianic self-fashioning but rather for establishing an "Islamic political culture."[4] The scholarly evidence adduced for this switch in Mughal imperial style is substantial and on the face of it straightforward: upon ascending the throne, Shah Jahan abolished the practice of prostration before the sovereign as an explicit break from the "un-Islamic" ways of Akbar and Jahangir; he reinstituted the formal patronage of the annual overseas Hajj pilgrimage from India to Hijaz that had been abandoned by Akbar; and he began to implement the Islamic strictures against the building and repair of non-Muslim places of worship, namely Christian churches and Hindu temples.[5] Even the emperor's trim beard as depicted in imperial portraiture—unlike the elegant moustaches sported by Akbar and Jahangir—may be taken as evidence of his growing orthodoxy.[6] All this is generally attributed to a pressure upon Shah Jahan to conform to a rising Islamic sentiment, a backlash against the liberal—if not libertine—practices of his forefathers led by the Sunni Muslim intelligentsia of the empire, notably the leaders of the ostensibly shariʿa-minded Naqshbandi Sufi order. Under such pressure, it is thought that he abandoned the controversial practice of accepting noblemen and gentlemen officers as disciples and instead revived the custom of incorporating them as "sons of the emperor's household."[7] According to this argument, Shah Jahan placated orthodox Muslim sentiment by transforming the Mughal imperial paradigm from one of Sufi devotion (*muridi*) to one of adoptive kinship (*khanazadgi*).

So, we may ask, what manner of sovereign was Shah Jahan—millennial and saintly or Muslim and sanctimonious? If seen as the latter, his reign appears as the beginning of the end of the style of sacred kingship that had evolved among the Timurids and Safavids of India and Iran, a mode that drew extensively upon the universal knowledges of astrology and alchemy as well as the widespread institutions and embodied practices of a shrine-centered sainthood. The end, in this view, came finally with Shah Jahan's successor, Aurangzeb, who is even more well known—some would say notorious—for his lifelong pursuit of a forbidding and austere form of Islam that had little place for wine, women, and merriment—nor, more significantly, for music, mysticism, and astrology. This view of a steady recentering of Mughal kingship around a staid scriptural Sunnism from the middle of the seventeenth century onward finds a parallel, it must be noted, in the scholarship on Safavid Iran, in which a juristic Shiʿism finally triumphs over the Alid and Sufi mores of the Safavids. In sum, the established narratives of the second century of Mughal and Safavid kingship in India and Iran, respectively, follow similar paths that steadily lead toward an Islam of the sedate, conformist, and scholastic jurist and away from that of the enthusiastic, transgressive, and performative mystic.

These narratives, however, are in need of some reconsideration. While there is no denying that Aurangzeb in his half-century-long reign began to abandon the customs of his ancestors and displayed a fondness for a more scripturally motivated Islam, this did not mean that the ways of empire changed irrevocably according to his wishes or that he did not feel the pressure to inhabit the broader, more universal conception of sacred kingship that had inspired his forefathers. Similarly, while it is certain that juristic Shiʿism took hold in Iran over the seventeenth and eighteenth centuries, this process did not merely involve the imposition of a new doctrine by fiat on the Iranian population. It also required the gradual molding of abstract Shiʿi ideals to fit the symbolic and institutional contours of a shrine-centered Sufism in Iran. To examine these dynamics in India and Iran for the remainder of Mughal and Safavid history and to explore their interconnections merits a separate book-length study. What can be highlighted in these final pages, nevertheless, are new lines of inquiry that should inform such an effort. These new perspectives, it is hoped, will complicate the received views and reveal significant threads of continuity in the manners and modes of sacred kingship through the seventeenth century and later.

THE EMPEROR'S CHOICE

One can begin, for example, by examining Shah Jahan's paradoxical choice of successor. If the emperor was such a champion of Islamic purity, it is puzzling that he threw his weight so completely behind his free-thinking son Dara Shikoh rather than his shariʿa-minded one, Aurangzeb. Dara Shikoh was well known for his passionate pursuit of a unified understanding of Islam and Hinduism derived from the metaphysics of

Sufism and Vedanta.⁸ As in the days of Akbar, such an eclectic quest for universal wisdom then was not exclusively an Indian phenomenon. Many prominent Iranian intellectuals—such as the notable philosopher and enigmatic alchemist Mir Findiriski—were also drawn to India at this time in pursuit of ancient Indic cosmological knowledge and bodily practices such as yoga and vegetarianism.⁹ The work that captures this universalistic spirit most aptly is the encyclopedic *Dabistan-i Mazahib* (School of Religions), written during Shah Jahan's reign by a member of a Zoroastrian sect living in India.¹⁰ The *Dabistan* provides a fascinating and comparative—even if at times a highly embellished—account of the established "world religions" of its day. It also describes in detail some of the more recent saintly and messianic movements in Iran and India, including the divine (*ilahi*) pursuits of Akbar. Its sectarian polemics aside, the *Dabistan* shows that during Shah Jahan's reign the memory of Akbar's millennial experiments was still alive beyond the courtly circles, as were a few of the bygone emperor's committed devotees.¹¹

There is much to indicate that as an heir to the throne Dara Shikoh had broadly followed an Akbari scheme of sovereignty. The prince had kept company with antinomian Hindu and Muslim mystics, explored and written about the parallels among the different religions of the realm, and attempted to rally the Rajput nobility to his side in the competition for the throne against Aurangzeb. The latter, however, was the better military strategist and commander. Upon victory, Aurangzeb had his brother executed on the pretext of abandoning Islam. Dara Shikoh was charged with, among other things, using the Sanskrit expression *Prabhu* to venerate God and of holding himself to be above the ritual Islamic requirements of praying and fasting. As we have seen, such accusations had also been leveled against Akbar, but with much less success.¹² So the question remains: if Shah Jahan had desired a return to juristic Islam in his realm, then why did he anoint a successor well known for his disdain of such a program?

Shah Jahan's choice—or his predicament, as the case may have been—might make more sense if we begin with the assumption that he, like his ancestors before him, had been enacting multiple scripts of sovereignty. If the previous chapters are any guide, in order to interpret these scripts and see how they fit and functioned together it is not enough to pay attention to formal pronouncements, official edicts, and polite literature bound by conventions of genre. We must also look for a performative engagement with embodied and "strange" discourses of sovereignty. In doing so, it will become clear that the possibilities available to Shah Jahan and his successors in molding their social personalities were far too complex to fit into neat categories of orthodoxy and heterodoxy.

Take Aurangzeb's "orthodox" position on music, for example, over the "funeral" of which he was said to have presided. It was reported in some sources inimical to Aurangzeb that his musicians had taken out a symbolic procession, carrying their instruments on a bier, in protest over the emperor's ban on music as un-Islamic. When told of this, Aurangzeb is said to have remarked, "bury it so deep under the earth that no sound or echo of it may rise again."[13] As Katherine Butler Brown has recently argued, this report was most likely a later polemical exaggeration. Her critical reading of contemporary sources indicates that Aurangzeb's gradual renunciation of music was less a matter of imperial policy and more a troubled and "private" affair, having to do with his personal efforts at piety, manly comportment, and bodily self-control. Aurangzeb's self-denial, Brown suggests, was a way for the emperor to guard himself against his weakness for elite courtesans skilled in music, a weakness he had struggled against since his days as a prince and that continued to haunt him late in his half-century-long reign.

If Aurangzeb had not been as puritanical a ruler and colorless an individual as he styled himself or was made out to be, Dara Shikoh's reputation as a spiritually absorbed and magnanimously liberal prince also needs to be qualified. According to a recent study by Rajeev Kinra, Shah Jahan's chosen successor was critiqued for his fickleness, arrogance, self-centeredness, and materialism by the very mystics and saints that were said to be his constant companions and spiritual guides.[14] While much work still needs to be done to make sense of Dara Shikoh's contradictory impulses, one thing is certain. He and Aurangzeb did not neatly balance each other out in a dualistic scheme of piety and transgression, bigotry and liberality, or law and sainthood. Rather, the two princes seemed to have staked their sovereign claims against each other by taking multiple, shifting positions within such poles. Indeed, such a performance is evident in Shah Jahan's own engagement with Islam and the millennium.

FROM DISCIPLES TO SONS

If Shah Jahan had abandoned discipleship as an imperial practice, did he consider himself any less sacred than his ancestors? Given his resurrection as the Second Lord of Conjunction and the open celebration of his millennial birth, it is unlikely that he did. The issue, then, is how his sacrality was embodied and enunciated, if not through the medium of discipleship. Here, it is worth turning to a series of astute observations made by the late John Richards. Richards noted that under Shah Jahan the newly revived paradigm of hereditary service still required Mughal nobles and functionaries to uphold the core values of discipleship—that is, loyalty, devotion, and sacrifice in the service of the emperor—but that these values were no longer cultivated on the basis of discipleship's "intense emotional aspect," which had previously accompanied a courtier's submission, body and soul, to a charismatic sovereign.[15] Moreover, Richards suggested that this decrease in the devotional requirements of imperial service had most likely resulted from the success of the empire.

To be sure, by Shah Jahan's time the empire had reached its apogee, with the emperor well established as its most sacred symbol. So many were clamoring to join imperial service that the initiation mechanism could be made less personal and more mediated. Further, the imperial household had expanded into a bureaucratic institution made up of individuals of varied status who had served the emperor personally or came from families that had served his forefathers. The principle of hereditary familial service thus became dominant.[16] To join the empire, moreover, one could attach oneself either directly to the imperial household or to that of a major Mughal nobleman who was already one of the emperor's "sons." This "patrimonial-bureaucratic" vision of empire was reflected, according to Stephen Blake, in the patterned urban life of Shah Jahan's new capital, Shahjahanabad (City of Shah Jahan), which was built in Delhi between 1639 and 1646. Here, major Mughal nobles maintained a "household" modeled after the imperial one, with a full complement of military personnel, artisanal workshops, and other features of civic life. The imperial city functioned, in an ideal sense, as a vast extended family tied together by client-patron relationships extending outward from the emperor, who appeared as "the pivot of a hierarchical, nested series of realms."[17] In effect, a strong case can be made that under Shah Jahan the Mughal empire completed a major symbolic and institutional shift, in which sovereign charisma came to be formally dispersed in a graded and mediated fashion and in which the idiom of kinship superseded the practice of discipleship. Nevertheless, it remains to be seen what, if anything, this shift had to do with the revival of an "Islamic political culture."

To begin with, it is far from certain that the notion of kinship espoused by the Mughals met the juristic standards of Sunni Islam any more than the deviant practices of discipleship. Take, for instance, how Jahangir described in his memoir the manner in which his sister Shakarunnisa Begum, a younger agnate sibling, was transformed into his "mother."

> After Danyal's birth, a daughter was born of Bibi Dawlatshad, and she was named Shakarunnisa Begum. Since she was brought up in the lap of my exalted father's care, she turned out very well, good-natured and innately compassionate toward all people. From her infancy and childhood until now she has been constant in her love for me. Rarely does such affection exist between brother and sister. The first time, as is customary, they squeezed my sister's breast and a drop of milk came out, His Majesty my exalted father said to me, "Baba, drink this milk so that in reality this sister of yours may be like a mother to you." The Omniscient knows that from the day I drank that drop of milk I have felt within myself, along with sisterly and daughterly affection, that type of love that children have for mothers.[18]

The use of milk to create obligations of kinship certainly had the sanction of Islamic law in a few restricted instances. However, most uses of milk kinship in Muslim societies, historically, have transcended these restrictions and been governed more by unwritten custom and symbolic reasoning.[19] By the same token, in the case of Jahangir and his sister/mother no "law" was invoked. Rather it was "custom" that made use of milk as a sublime substance to thicken the familial bond, as it were, between the imperial half-siblings. The crucial issue, of course, is whether such practices were used outside of the immediate Mughal kin in order to expand the imperial household.

Little scholarship exists on the question of how courtiers and officers were incorporated as "sons" into the imperial household. The reigning assumption has been that kinship was a convenient expression for describing the incorporation of courtiers into a gentlemanly club of sorts, which required them to conform to proper norms of comportment or *adab*.[20] Furthermore, it is thought that this assimilation took place via polite ritual protocols such as gift exchange and ceremonial robing. While generally valid, these views need to be qualified by evidence that there was more bodily substance behind this filial idiom, at least in certain important cases. There exists, for example, an account of such a case by Niccolao Manucci, a Venetian adventurer who had served in the entourage of Dara Shikoh. Mannuci described how the Mughal prince compelled the powerful Raja Sarup Singh to fight on his side against Aurangzeb by making the Rajput lord his "son":

> To gain more securely to his side, he (Dara) allowed his wife to send for the rajah [Sarup Singh] to her harem, where with soft words the princess once more begged for his aid and gave him many presents, the chief being a string of pearls of great value that she threw over his neck. She addressed him as her son, and said she looked on him as in the place of her son Sulaiman Shukoh. Then she did a thing never done before in the Mogul's empire—that is [to] say, she offered him water to drink with which she had washed her breasts, not having milk in them, as a confirmation of her words. He drank with the greatest acceptance and swore he would be ever true, and never fail in the duties of a son.[21]

Manucci's report appears breathless and gossip laden. Yet his account of the bonding rite between the Mughal princess and the Rajput raja does not stray far from Jahangir's description of the custom of milk kinship. It merely adds a ritual step in which water is transubstantiated into milk by contact with the princess's breasts. Accordingly, the Venetian's exclamation that this was "a thing never done before in the Mogul's empire" need not be given undue weight, for Manucci had apparently not heard that Dara Shikoh's grandfather had also tasted the milk of his younger half-sister in a similar ritual of familiarity. Although such reports are rare, and understandably so, they do point toward the important role of female kin in the affairs of empire, a subject on which the imperial chroniclers and artists are all too often silent.[22] It is tempting to speculate that the assertion of kinship and "domesticity" at the height of empire may have had something to do with the ambitions of Mughal women who had found their roles circumscribed within the phallocentric paradigm of discipleship.[23]

Ultimately, the custom of kinship was no less sacred and "strange" than that of discipleship. If the former was able to replace the latter, it is because the two were similar enough in form and content as to be interchangeable. Both kinship and discipleship were corporeal and tactile ways of adhering to or inhering in the body of the sovereign. And in this milieu, when sainthood had become hereditary and kingship saintly, the disciple could well become son and kin. With this in mind, let us return to the question raised earlier but still unanswered of how Shah Jahan's sacrality was enacted if not through the medium of discipleship. The answer lies less in Shah Jahan's official proclamations and more in his embodied

CONCLUSION: THE GRAFFITI UNDER THE THRONE [219]

performance of sovereignty. To judge a performance, it is reasonable to begin with a study of the stage on which it took place. In Shah Jahan's case, this means an examination of his imperial architecture.

THE *JHAROKA*: A WINDOW INTO SHAH JAHAN'S WORLD

Shah Jahan is famous today for building the Taj Mahal, the iconic tomb he shares with his beloved wife Mumtaz Mahal. Nevertheless, his strongest statement in terms of imperial architecture, as Ebba Koch has described so vividly, was the construction of formal, hypostyle public audience halls (*diwan-i khass o ʿamm*).[24] Shah Jahan had these large pillared halls built in all major palaces, both the old ones in Agra and Lahore and the new one in Delhi. As permanent structures, they replaced and reconfigured the open courtyard spaces that had been used for public audiences in the days of Akbar and Jahangir. Moreover, these halls were carefully designed to emphasize and enhance the presence of the sovereign. Upon entry, one's gaze immediately fell on the figure of the emperor, framed by a canopied platform, the "window" or *jharoka* throne.

The *jharoka-i darshan*, or "viewing window," had originally been on the outer palace wall from where the emperor, at least since the days of Akbar, showed himself at sunrise to his people and devotees, who waited to receive and reciprocate his vision (*darshan*). In this imperial ritual, as the Sanskrit word *darshan* implies, the sovereign assumed a sacrality akin to that of a deity venerated in a temple.[25] It is significant, then, that during Shah Jahan's reign, and especially in his new audience hall in Delhi, the covered throne platform or baldachin assumed the name and form of the jharoka. This ornately decorated stone and marble structure, with a distinctive curved *bangla* canopy, was now called the "window" of public and private audience (*jharoka-i khass o ʿamm*), named after the new imperial audience hall in which it was placed.

In his new capital, the emperor's daily routine linked together the meaning of the two "windows." Shah Jahan first displayed himself at dawn at the "window of veneration," after which he immediately proceeded to the "window of audience," where he assembled his court. With his noblemen and servants arrayed in front of the jharoka throne in a strictly graded hierarchy, the emperor exchanged gifts, received foreign dignitaries, and conducted the business of empire. It was here that he celebrated the important festivals of the solar Persian New Year (*nawruz*), the accession anniversary (*julus*), and the annual weighing of the emperor against silver and gold (*jashn-i wazn-i shamsi o qamari*). In effect, with its formalization in imperial architecture under Shah Jahan, the jharoka became the very center of the empire and, indeed, in Shah Jahani paintings, its very image.²⁶

Given its central significance in the emperor's sovereign performance, it should be expected that the place and orientation of the jharoka throne in Delhi was cosmologically marked.²⁷ The public audience hall containing the jharoka was laid out in such a way that it had a wider nave or space between the center columns, leading one's eyes to the jharoka at the end. Crucially, this design took its inspiration not from existing palaces of Indian or Iranian stock but from the columned prayer halls of mosques. As Koch has shown so well, the evidence for this link exists both in the physical similarities between the layout of a hypostyle mosque and the imperial audience chamber as well as in the converse relationship between the orientations of the two types of buildings. A pillared prayer hall of a mosque was designed to be "read" in the direction of the *mihrab* or prayer leader's niche, which was, in turn, aligned westward in India toward the Kaʿba in Mecca, the focus or *qibla* of Muslim prayer. Shah Jahan's audience hall in Shahjahanabad, on the other hand, was aligned in a precise counterimage, with the throne jharoka taking place of the prayer leader's niche and oriented eastward to the place of the rising sun.²⁸ The significance of this cosmological orientation and its implication for Shah Jahan's sacral status was hinted at by his chroniclers. The emperor, they wrote, was the *qibla-i hajat* (focus of supplication) whom the people turned to in need, and his jharoka was the rising place of the sun of the spheres of sovereignty and the caliphate (*matlaʿ-i khurshid-i asman-i dawlat wa khilafat*).²⁹

It must be emphasized that unlike the chroniclers' cryptic allusions, the proportional and patterned relationship between Shah Jahan's imperial audience hall and the mosque prayer hall must have been openly and immediately apparent to those in his presence. This is because of the master principle of "symmetry" or *qarina* that underlay Shah Jahan's architectural paradigm. The emperor was well known for imposing a rigid formalization and precise aesthetic formulation on all his art and architecture. Indeed, the high degree of order in Shah Jahan's buildings contrasts with the exuberant architectural creations of Akbar's days and, consequently, enables a sharper set of meanings to manifest itself. The analogies that we today must strive to discover and "read" in Shah Jahan's buildings would have intuitively "appeared" to those in attendance at his court. They would have known that just like a mosque's prayer hall pointed axially toward divinity's earthly manifestation in the cosmos (the Ka'ba), the imperial audience hall referred axially toward divinity's celestial manifestation in the cosmos (the sun), and just as a prayer leader in the mihrab niche embodied the divine locus or *qibla*, the Mughal sovereign on the jharoka throne embodied the divine light of the sun. It is significant that Shah Jahan, even decades after he had taken an "official" turn toward Sunni Islam, was still elaborating upon the sacred schemes of his predecessors, in which the sun served as a key embodiment of divinity and guarantor of sovereignty.

The sun in Shah Jahan's analogical scheme was not a chance occurrence or marginal presence but a central and structuring cosmological principle. It is worth exploring why this was the case. A plethora of signifying practices surrounded this "planet" in Mughal and Safavid imperial milieus. As all astrologers knew, the sun was the planet of kings. The most important festival for kingship, moreover, was the Persian New Year, or nawruz, celebrated at the vernal equinox.[30] Despite the common knowledge that nawruz had been a custom of pre-Islamic kings of Iran, its celebration remained indispensable for Muslim rulers, who had their court savants find ways of justifying its continued observance. In Safavid Iran, for example, despite the spread of Twelver Shi'ism, nawruz was still celebrated with great fanfare even if it fell on the days of mourning in Muharram.[31] In fact, it was Shi'i jurists who legitimized nawruz celebration as a commemoration of Ali's saintly and spiritual sovereignty.[32] Here is a case of the "conversion" of doctrinal Shi'ism to the modes of sacred kingship.

In the Mughal case too there had remained a sustained focus on the sun.[33] Humayun had identified himself with the sun while orchestrating his courtly theater. Akbar's court rituals had also revolved around the sun. He is said to have memorized 1,001 names of the sun in Sanskrit, and his Millennial History listed Arabic prayers to the sun composed by Abu Ma'shar, the father of Islamic astrology.[34] The sun, along with the moon, had featured prominently in Jahangir's "talismanic" images as a halo framing the emperor.[35] In a similar vein, Shah Jahan's astrologers emphasized numerological connections between the emperor's name, the name of Timur, the title Lord of Conjunction, and the number of days in the cycle of the sun.[36] From paintings, we know that Shah Jahan's army carried a flag emblazoned with the symbol of the sun on a lion's back, a reference perhaps to the horoscope of the ideal ruler.[37] Finally, Shah Jahan had observed both the Iranian nawruz as well as the Indian solar and lunar "weighing" festivals, in which the sovereign was ritually balanced against bags of gold and silver, respectively, which were then distributed among the poor. In fact, Shah Jahan's Sunni scholars in India had justified this "Hindu" tradition just as their Shiʻi counterparts in Iran had sanctioned the "Zoroastrian" one of nawruz, by finding analogies for it in Islamic prophetic custom.[38]

Yet while this jumble of practices shows that the sun was an important factor in Shah Jahan's performance of sovereignty, it is still not clear why this heavenly body was treated as an axial manifestation of divinity in the emperor's theater of sovereignty. We need an answer, in other words, that matches the precision and formalism of this master aesthetician, who abhorred chaos and randomness in his designs. There must have been a foundational cosmology at work that assigned a singularly pivotal role to the sun and drew sustenance from the most ancient and universal of wisdom. The oldest "wisdom of old"[39] (*hikmat al-atiq*) that met these requirements belonged to the "first sage"[40] and the "father of philosophers,"[41] Hermes Trismegistus.

Few studies of the Mughal era mention Hermes, the "Thrice Great" or "Triplicate in Wisdom." Yet, this modern neglect belies his importance for early modern India and Iran, when he was considered an antediluvian prophet and identified variously with the biblical Enoch and the Idris of the Quran. Hermes was a figure of great interest to those pursing an "eternal truth" in the form of a unified cosmology and universal chronology of existence that transcended known differences in various scriptural traditions. Although there was no self-declared Hermetic School in Islam, the number of prominent Muslim thinkers and mystical groups who saw themselves as building upon the universalistic teachings of Hermes is truly vast. From the mysterious Brethren of Purity (Ikhwan al-Safa) of the tenth century and the Illuminationist philosopher Suhrawardi of the twelfth to the activist millenarians like the Nuqtavis and the quietist gnostics of the "School of Isfahan" in early modern times, all referred to the wisdom of Hermes in their endeavors to unveil once and for all the deepest mysteries of the cosmos.[42] Unsurprisingly, most works of the occult sciences began with an attribution or dedication to the prophet Hermes.

The diverse admirers of this ancient sage and prophet agreed that he had been the first to whom the science of the stars was "revealed." As Abul Fazl noted in the *Akbarnama*, it was Hermes who "guided men to the reverence of the Great Light (the sun) [Nayyir-i Aʻzam]."[43] Abul Fazl's source for this observation was the renowned astrologer Abu Maʿshar, whose "discovery" and mastery of the Hermetic arts, it was widely believed, had enabled him to revive the astral sciences in Islam. The author of the *Dabistan* also credited Hermes with teaching mankind to venerate the sun.[44] Although Muslim practitioners of this ritual, such as the emperor Jahangir, qualified it by professing that "one should recognize that the real mover and creator in all forms and times is God," in effect, the sun in esoteric Hermetic cosmology was treated as the demiurge, the principal manifestation of divinity beneath the sphere of the fixed stars, or the second or visible God.[45] It is this central and divine significance of the sun in the teachings attributed to the ancient Hermes that may explain why this heavenly body served as a sacred locus for Shah Jahan, anchoring his jharoka throne and orienting all those present before it toward divinity.

There was an important difference between Shah Jahan's ritual schemes and those of his predecessors, however. Before his time, these rites surrounding the sovereign had been enacted in a circumscribed fashion, in seclusion with only the elect present (in a ritually isolated space) or from a distant palace window at dawn (at a ritually isolated time). Now, however, they were performed in a space and time that was permanent and public. Instead of abandoning or further circumscribing the imperial cult of discipleship with its "strange" requirement of solar veneration, Shah Jahan had expanded and instituted it within an enduring structure and constant performance. In a sense, the protean "cult" of the holy man from the days of Akbar had been transformed by Shah Jahan into the "church" of the sacred sovereign, enshrined in the solar-aligned jharoka. Individual devotion of the few was no longer required; it was replaced with public veneration by all.

Seen from this perspective, it appears that even if imperial discipleship came to an end under Shah Jahan, the style of sacred sovereignty that had engendered it did not. Besides the use of solar symbolism, some of the other key practices of the earlier institution—such as rewarding loyalty with an "auspicious likeness" of the sovereign—remained active under Shah Jahan, who gifted his miniature portraits in public court audiences at the jharoka throne.[46] Importantly, however, Shah Jahan's organization of sacred kingship was not meant to replace Islam or to displace it. Its goal remained, just as it had been in the ritual orders of his predecessors, to raise the body of the sovereign above the constraints of any one sacred tradition.[47] If this seems contradictory and confusing, it should not. This sublime and transcendental body of the sovereign was not Shah

Jahan's mortal and Muslim one, which remained subject to the strictures and scriptures of Islam. It was, rather, his eternal and millennial body.

SHAH JAHAN'S TWO BODIES

It was in his tenth regnal year that Shah Jahan is thought to have taken a definitive turn toward Islam. Scholars have found the evidence for the emperor's submission to scriptural norms in, among other things, his decision to have the chronicles of his reign organized according to the lunar Islamic calendar.[48] For the first ten years of Shah Jahan's rule, his chronicler, the Iranian scribe Qazvini, had used the solar divine (*ilahi*) calendar, which had been calculated in Akbar's reign but recalibrated by Shah Jahan's master astrologer. Qazvini's work, composed in highly ornate Persian prose, was already so vast that if printed today it would run to more than a thousand pages. Nevertheless, Shah Jahan had work stopped on these chronicles and begun on new ones that predominantly made use of lunar Hijra dates. It is important to note, however, that most other imperial business proceeded according to the cycles of the sun. The solar calendar was made subservient to the lunar one, it seems, mainly for the writing of history. It was as if Shah Jahan had decided, in the tenth year of his sovereignty, to order the domain of history writing according to the dictates of Islam. This emperor's "orthodox" attitude toward the new chronicles is also apparent in the way they fall silent about the emperor's supervision of the "forbidden" art of painting and portraiture.

The earlier chronicles had described in detail the personal direction Shah Jahan gave to his artists and painters.[49] The revised chronicles, by contrast, elided references to the emperor's involvement with the visual arts. But this change did not imply that Shah Jahan had abandoned his passion for painting. On the contrary, his artists continued to produce them in abundance in the highly polished and formal style favored by the emperor till the end of his reign. These works of art have a clear sense of historicity. They show Shah Jahan evolving from a mustachioed young prince at his father's side to an enthroned and bearded sovereign and then graying gracefully over time. Thus, as had been the case with the solar divine calendar, Shah Jahan did not proscribe the practice of painting and portraiture but only the historical mention of the emperor's participation in it.

At first this may seem like a duplicitous attempt at keeping up Islamic appearances. But there is another way to make sense of the textual revi-

CONCLUSION: THE GRAFFITI UNDER THE THRONE [225]

sions in Shah Jahan's chronicles concerning the "cycles of the sun" and the "auspicious likeness of the emperor." It is to place these actions within a larger scheme of enactment. This scheme is better understood as a separation of imperial life into two domains of genre and practice: a textual domain that conformed to the norms of scriptural Islam and a visual and performative one that transgressed it. In the previous chapter, we saw the way Jahangir had attempted to bifurcate his imperial self in his memoir and paintings. Shah Jahan had also done something similar but in a much more elaborate and formal manner: even as his chronicles were being edited according to Islamic traditions, his throne was being built according to millennial ones. There was, in effect, a "strange" cultural logic at work, dividing Shah Jahan's imperial practice into spheres of conformity and transgression. To appreciate the practical outcome of this logic, let us turn once again to the site of Shah Jahan's throne and pay close attention this time to its ornamental scheme.

Early on in his reign, the emperor had begun to restrict the decoration on his palaces and other buildings to vegetal, geometric, and calligraphic patterns.[50] In conforming to well-known Islamic prohibitions against the depiction of animate beings, he sharply broke from the tradition of Jahangir and Akbar. While his father and grandfather had adorned their rooms and halls with images of animals, humans, and angels, Shah Jahan had strictly abstained from using figural art as decoration. Nevertheless, as Koch pointed out, in one crucial instance he deviated from these Islamic conventions and created a space saturated with figural imagery. This exceptional site was the elaborate new jharoka throne in Delhi.

Visible even today, the wall immediately behind the Delhi jharoka is richly covered with birds and animals. Rendered in semiprecious stones set into marble plaques, these exquisite images provide a fine example of the *pietre dure* inlay technique of Italian origin that Shah Jahan had been so fond of. In similar materials, toward the top of the wall and centered on the jharoka, there also exists a figure of a man playing a musical instrument surrounded by wild animals. The precise meaning of this elaborate scene behind the throne remains an open question, although Koch suggested that for the Mughals it may have stood for the Islamic myth of the prophet-king Solomon (*Sulayman*), known for his powers over animals and nature. For the argument at hand, however, the more relevant question is why Shah Jahan permitted figural imagery at this location while banishing it from others.

The solution Koch offered for this puzzle was that Shah Jahan had confined these deviant images to the jharoka because here "they could be best defended as instruments of rulership."[51] This is a wonderful insight. But it must be stripped of its apologetic tone. Otherwise, we are in danger of treating the throne as if it were a marginal site where Shah Jahan could quietly follow the wayward traditions of his ancestors. We cannot assume, in other words, that the space surrounding the jharoka was somehow less public and significant than the other buildings where Shah Jahan displayed his conformity with Islam. In fact, as we have seen, the jharoka throne was the symbolic center of the empire and its most prominent location. If Shah Jahan had taken an unequivocal turn toward Islam, he surely would have exhibited his convictions here. That he did not and instead treated the throne as above the juristic norms of Islam cannot be dismissed as a defensive and cautious act. Rather, it must be seen as a sharply enunciated statement of the emperor's sacrality. The unique ornamentation surrounding the throne marked it as a place set apart. Sacred in the classic anthropological sense of the word, it was both a space and a state of exception that was above the constraints of the ordinary.

Ever the aesthete, Shah Jahan had tried to achieve a perfect, performative balance between his Muslim and millennial heritages. He did so by dividing the space and time of his sovereignty as neatly as he could into distinct spheres of practice. When dealing with "time," he made his chroniclers conform to Islamic tradition but had his astrologers and artists transgress it. Similarly, in terms of "space," he had his architects follow norms of juristic Islam in decorating his imperial buildings except for the jharoka. Thus isolated spatially and temporally, the emperor's "profane" world, which he shared with all his "ordinary" subjects, could be placed under the order of Islam. But simultaneously, this symbolic scheme liberated his "sacred" world and raised it to another order of being. The essence of this sacrality, moreover, was concentrated at the jharoka, a transcendent site uniquely reserved for and singularly linked with the sublime body of the sovereign. In a critical sense, this bond between the throne and the sovereign body was transformative. The one transmuted the very essence of the other. Off the jharoka, the emperor had the mortal body of an ordinary Muslim. But upon it, he became the Millennial Sovereign. Put simply, the connection between the two was not merely physical but also alchemical. Indeed, the evidence of this "strange" bond lies preserved in Shah Jahan's talismanic art.

THE GRAFFITI UNDER THE THRONE

It is well known that Shah Jahan had avidly pursued the style of art pioneered in Jahangir's atelier. There are numerous miniature paintings from his time that show the emperor surrounded by the same saintly and messianic symbols that are a signature of his father's sacred art. In these Shah Jahani images, the emperor always appears haloed with a solar nimbus. At times, he stands atop the globe of the earth. Often, lions and lambs lie together in peace at his feet, and chains of justice hang in the background. There even exist group portraits in which Shah Jahan's bygone ancestors appear together out of time, as if in a dream. It should be noted that in Jahangir's era, such symbols and narrative themes had only appeared in paintings that depicted occurrences on a higher "metaphysical" plane, such as the dreams and miracles of the sovereign. However, in an innovative move, Shah Jahan also had these sacred symbols adorn the depiction of his "earthly" and "historical" scenes.

A large number of paintings accompanying the text of Shah Jahan's revised chronicles, the *Padshahnama*, have reached us in good condition.[52] Given that these images illustrate major historical events, it is tempting to read them as straightforward assertions of a political program with an ideological message. This temptation must be resisted, however, for most art historical evidence indicates that these images were not incorporated into a finished chronicle during Shah Jahan's reign. According to Milo Beach, it was probably more than half a century later that the text and art were combined for the first time.[53] The reasons for this delay in putting together a finished illustrated chronicle can only be guessed at. Certainly, the high quality of these paintings and the care with which they were preserved shows that they were prized possessions of Shah Jahan. But in all probability, the emperor lost his throne to his rebellious son Aurangzeb before he could use these paintings to adorn the history of his reign. Aurangzeb was not interested in these paintings, it is thought, because of the high status they accorded to his brother and heir to the throne, Dara Shikoh. Thus, despite their high value, these works of art did not serve a public political role in Shah Jahan's time or later, and perhaps they were never meant to. As Beach noted, some of these images had in all likelihood been commissioned independently and not as illustrations for the chronicle. There is little value in pursuing just a utilitarian political interpretation of these paintings. Instead, it is more fruitful to apply some of the lessons from our analysis of Jahangiri "talismanic" art.

FIGURE 7.1 Jahangir presents Prince Khurram with a turban ornament. Folio 195A. Painted by Payag, c. 1640.

Source: RL OMS 1641. The Royal Collection © 2005, Her Majesty Queen Elizabeth II.

CONCLUSION: THE GRAFFITI UNDER THE THRONE [229]

In the *Padshahnama* paintings, the jharoka appears in about a third of all extant images, making it the most frequently depicted imperial site. It is significant, then, that the sacral paraphernalia of Jahangir's miraculous paintings appear only in the jharoka scenes and only under the throne. For example, in figure 7.1, Jahangir presents Prince Khurram with a turban ornament. It shows Shah Jahan as the young prince Khurram receiving a precious gift from Jahangir, who is seated on the jharoka. Both father and son are haloed. Below the emperor are two Muslim holy men, one holding a sword for the emperor and the other a scroll. Under them is the globe of the earth and, further down, a lion and ox lying blissfully together. The occasion is indeed a momentous one. The prince had just received the title of Shah Jahan, or King of the World.

Art historians have puzzled over the materiality of the symbols under the throne in this painting and others like it in the *Padshahnama*. Were they actually painted at the site of the jharoka? Or were they only part of the painted image of the jharoka? Until now, most interpretations have assumed that these symbols must have been physically present in Shah Jahan's court. For, if not, the thinking goes, then why would artists add them to an otherwise historical scene?[54] However, as the next painting (figure 7.2) shows, the issue merits a rethinking.

In this image, which at first glance appears similar to the previous one, Jahangir is still the emperor. He welcomes his victorious son, Prince Khurram (Shah Jahan), upon his return from military campaigns in the Deccan. This too is an occasion to celebrate. But, surprisingly, the symbols under the jharoka are not celebratory. See figure 7.3 for a closer look at the area under the jharoka.

Instead of messianic peace and absolute justice, there exists now a bleak picture of corruption and cruelty. Drawn without color or background and scratched out with the barest of lines are perpetrators and victims of vile and violent acts. A well-fed and bearded man—an official perhaps—leans on a staff while taking a bag of money disdainfully from a thin man bent in subservience. Below them, a strongly built man—a watchman perhaps—raises his cane to beat back two naked and emaciated beggars. One of the victims asks for mercy with his hands drawn together, while the other, who looks like a child, tries to crawl away from the blows. What are we to make of this graffiti under the throne?

The first thing to note is that this scene is too dismal to have actually adorned the physical site of the jharoka. It must be seen only as a part of the painted image. As such, it adds a second metaphysical layer

FIGURE 7.2 Jahangir receives Prince Khurram from his return from the Deccan. Folio 49A. Painted by Murar, c. 1640.

Source: RL OMS 1611. The Royal Collection © 2011, Her Majesty Queen Elizabeth II.

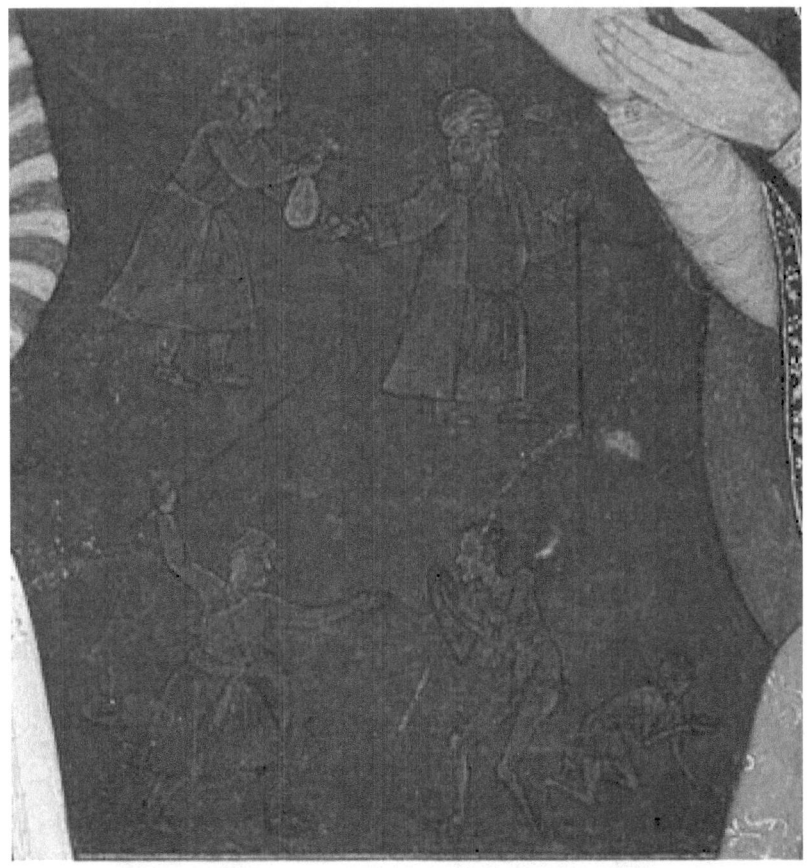

FIGURE 7.3 [Detail from 7.2] Jahangir receives Prince Khurram from his return from the Deccan (detail from folio). Folio 49A. Painted by Murar, c. 1640.

Source: RL OMS 1611. The Royal Collection © 2011, Her Majesty Queen Elizabeth II.

of meaning, just as the sacred symbols did in Jahangir's talismanic art. But why do the symbols signify corruption and disorder here, instead of justice and peace? A clue to this change in mood may be found in the position of the sovereign's body with respect to the jharoka. In all other *Padshahnama* jharoka scenes that are marked by saintly and messianic symbols, the sovereign is always shown in the center of the painting, in his rightful place on the throne. Here, however, the emperor has done

FIGURE 7.4 Shah Jahan with Asaf Khan (detail from folio). The Late Shah Jahan Album. Painted by Bichitr, c. 1650. Opaque watercolor and gold on paper mounted on paperboard, 36.9 × 25.3 cm.

Source: © Arthur M. Sackler Gallery, Smithsonian Institution, Washington, D.C.: Purchase—Smithsonian Unrestricted Trust Funds, Smithsonian Collections Acquisition Program, and Dr. Arthur M. Sackler, S1986.403.

something unexpected. In his enthusiasm to embrace his victorious son, Jahangir has stood up and moved to one side, leaving the jharoka empty. The bond between the body of the sovereign and the throne is broken. The consequences of this sovereign act are terrible. The world under the throne has been thrown off balance—from light and order into darkness and chaos. In other words, the symbols under the jharoka add a millennial dimension to an otherwise earthly and historical setting. They depict the miraculous nature of the throne and its "strange" bond with the body of the sovereign.

Shah Jahan continued his father's legacy of creating miraculous and millennial art. Indeed, he elaborated upon it, using it to "unveil" the higher, hidden nature of the jharoka and the sovereign who sat upon it. That this sovereign was a being infused with divine light can also be seen in another portrait of the emperor. In this painting (figure 7.4), from above the clouds "God the Father" showers a ray of light upon the emperor's halo. A dove—the "Holy Ghost"—descends upon him.[55]

By taking the position of messiah in this "Holy Trinity," Shah Jahan reveals that he is a millennial sovereign. Yet while the heavenly light links him with divinity, another transaction entangles him in the world below. The emperor stands with his most prominent minister, Asaf Khan, who presents him with the gift of a jewel. What must Shah Jahan give back in exchange that exceeds the value of this earthly gift? Do we not see here the emperor disbursing his sacrality to—and through—a "son of the imperial household"?[56]

THE DENOUEMENT

It is finally time to ask: did it all come to an end with Shah Jahan? The fallen emperor spent his last days a prisoner in his own palace, having lost his empire to his usurper son. When the "pious" Aurangzeb first celebrated his enthronement, he did so strictly according to the traditions of his ancestors. On the selected day, he waited behind a screen for a signal from his astrologers, who had calculated the most auspicious time for the ceremony. At exactly three hours and fifteen minutes from sunrise, we are told, the new sovereign sallied forth and ascended the jharoka throne, his performance accompanied by a burst of music from the imperial band and a whirl of movement from a troupe of female dancers.[57]

Over the course of his reign, however, Aurangzeb gradually gave up his central role in the theater of empire.[58] He abandoned the jharoka audiences, the nawruz celebration, and the weighing festivals. He gave up listening to musical instruments, stopped patronizing artists, and even tried to put restrictions on his astrologers—forbidding them one year from issuing almanacs. On the other hand, he began to devote a great deal of energy supervising a vast new compendium of Islamic jurisprudence that still bears his name—the *Fatawa-i Alamgiri*.[59] Unsurprisingly, Aurangzeb's dogmatic regulations against non-Muslims have become legendary—and so caricatured by his modern admirers and detractors that they do not bear repeating. What is worth emphasizing, though, is how little Aurangzeb was able to change the order of things.

Despite his exhortations to the contrary, Aurangzeb's sons still celebrated the Persian New Year and had themselves weighed against gold and silver on their solar and lunar birthdays.[60] Astrologers continued to dominate public and private affairs.[61] Music was patronized and enjoyed throughout the realm.[62] Poets wrote raunchy satires on the duplicity of the ruling elites.[63] Naked mendicants roamed the streets mocking the pious and the powerful.[64] Hindu officials enrolled in droves as "sons" of the emperor, and Muslim soldiers found employment in the armies of Hindu rebels.[65] The empire promoted agriculture—and its tax base—by granting virgin forest land to Muslim shrines and Hindu temples.[66] Mughal nobles of both religions celebrated one another's festivals in the military camps.[67] And in the cities, if Dargah Quli Khan's colorful account of mid-eighteenth-century Delhi is anything to go by, the nightlife remained alive with twirling eunuchs and winking boys.[68]

Indeed, if the stark and literalist political perspective from the imperial center is tempered with a sensitive cultural view from the marches and margins of empire, a very different picture of Aurangzeb and his "waywardness" begins to emerge. Although today he is thought of as the most orthodox Muslim among the Mughals, in the age of Timur he must have appeared as the most deviant of sovereigns. For, as has been the central argument of this book, the script of sovereignty that the ruler was expected to perform was written not in the imperial court but in the wider reaches of the ecumene and the diverse imaginations of its denizens.

Such an account—or accounting—of Aurangzeb's long rule has yet to be written. But when it does, it must take into consideration the great price the last of the "great" Mughals had to pay for his break from the tradition of Timurid sacred kingship. Even his archenemies quoted the principles of his forefathers to hector him. Take the letter, for instance, of the famous Maratha rebel and king Shivaji, whose uprising forced Aurangzeb

CONCLUSION: THE GRAFFITI UNDER THE THRONE [235]

to spend the last two decades of his life encamped in the south, engaged in a vain and expensive war. Written in Persian, the letter addressed the emperor in the politest of terms and chided him gently for imposing the lawful but despised *jizya* (poll tax on non-Muslims) to fund his war efforts. Moreover, it reminded Aurangzeb how his ancestor Akbar had become the "world's spiritual guide":

> That architect of the fabric of empire, Akbar Padishah, reigned with full power for 52 years. He adopted the admirable policy of universal harmony (*sulh-i-kull*) in relation to all the various sects, such as Christians, Jews, Muslims, Dadu's followers, sky-worshippers . . . materialists, atheists, Brahmans and Jain priests. The aim of his liberal heart was to cherish and protect all the people. So, he became famous under the title of *Jagat-Guru*, "the World's spiritual guide."[69]

It was not just Aurangzeb's foes who derided him for sullying the honor of the house of Timur. His own sons continued to defy his new vision of empire in their own preparations for the throne. One of the Mughal princes, also named Akbar, first joined forces with the rebellious Marathas and then later fled to the Safavid court in Isfahan to seek refuge. In doing so, however, Prince Akbar repeated the mistake of Babur and Humayun and revived the ignominious memory of Timurid subservience to the Persian line of Sufi kings. This memory had been kept alive in Iran and, indeed, had become part of the Safavid performance of sovereignty.

In a letter to Aurangzeb, the Safavid Shah Sulayman (r. 1666–1694) mocked his Indian counterpart's inability to subdue Shivaji.[70] The shah offered to come to Aurangzeb's aid, just as his ancestor Shah Tahmasb had once helped Humayun regain the throne of Hindustan. This bluster not only embellished Safavid correspondence. It also adorned their halls of public audience. It was Shah Sulayman's predecessor, Shah ʿAbbas II (r. 1642–1666), who had commissioned giant wall murals for the audience hall of the Chihil Sutun (Forty Pillar) palace in Isfahan, one of which depicted Humayun at the court of Shah Tahmasb (see figure 7.5; Humayun is the one seated, left, on the carpet).[71]

There were three other murals, one displaying the foundational victory of Shah Ismaʿil over the Uzbeks and the remaining two showing asylum-seeking Uzbek rulers at the court of later Safavid sovereigns.[72] Generally, these murals celebrated the Safavid court as a refuge for Muslim sovereigns. Specifically, Humayun's presence in these Chihil Sutun murals was

FIGURE 7.5 Isfahan. "Shah Tahmasb and Humayun." Mural from the audience hall of the Chihil Sutun Palace.

Source: Photograph courtesy of Mohammad Sarraf.

meant to remind visitors—such as Prince Akbar when he arrived there in 1688—of the historical superiority of the Persian dynasty over the Indian Timurids. That this superiority was political as well as spiritual was also evident from these paintings.

Besides the expected courtly entertainment with wine, song, and dance, the mural with Shah ʿAbbas I (see figure 7.6) also reveals a more transgressive subtheme. While the shah, his protection-seeking guest, and most of their attendees stare out consciously from the painting, a few in the crowd on the lower right side remain absorbed in what seem to be shockingly bizarre acts right in front of the sovereign. First, a man with a turban and a fearsome moustache—a Qizilbash master—raises a cane to hit a youth. Below them another young man, who seems either drunk or delirious from pain, is supported by two others and taken further down. There, at the bottom of the image, another youth lies flat on the floor on his back looking comfortable and relaxed. He has his head on the lap of another man who, while looking knowingly out at us, drops a piece of fruit in the youth's open mouth.

According to an insightful analysis by Kathryn Babayan, this subsection of the mural depicts not random acts of hedonism but a series of initiatory stages through which the youth are being made to pass.[73] These violent and transgressive acts, in other words, represent the Sufi rites of passage that had dominated the Safavid court in its early days. The beating stick is the first clue. It refers to the Stick of the Path (*Chub-i Tariqat*) ritual, discussed earlier, with which courtiers were made to bond with the body of the Safavid shah and shaykh. Upon passing this initial stage, the mural shows the young devotees as thoroughly intoxicated and "losing themselves" in devotion to their spiritual master. In doing so, they are rewarded with the fruits of mystical union with the Beloved. This "disciplining" takes place, moreover, under the gaze of the shah. Everyone present, including the audience inside and outside the painting, are made aware of the conditions for receiving the sovereign's largess. They too must become his devotees and disciples.

Shah ʿAbbas I may have put an end to the dominance of his Qizilbash devotees at the end of the sixteenth century, but half a century later, in an increasingly Shiʿi Iran, the Safavids still publicly and proudly commemorated their messianic Sufi origins. Thus, their shah continued to remind Aurangzeb that he was a hereditary slave of the Safavids. According to Manucci, this was indeed the message that Shah ʿAbbas II relayed to Aurangzeb via the latter's ambassador. The Venetian also described

FIGURE 7.6 Isfahan. "Shah 'Abbas the Great and the Uzbek Vali Mohammad Khan." Mural from the audience hall of the Chihil Sutun Palace.

Source: Photograph courtesy of Mohammad Sarraf.

a "wonder" that the Safavid shah reportedly performed to impress the Mughal ambassador. The shah had a chained lion brought to him. He then grabbed the beast by the mane, made it submit, and told the ambassador to "write this too to Aurangzeb."[74]

This was the world of sovereignty that Aurangzeb had to live and compete in. In India, Shivaji reminded him that he was no longer the "spiritual guide of the world," as his great-grandfather had been, while from Iran the Safavid shahs taunted him that he was still their servant and disciple. It is understandable that whatever his personal inclinations toward Islamic law and piety may have been, the Mughal emperor could not completely abandon the messianic modes of performance devised by his ancestors. As Manucci later reported, Aurangzeb also provided public evidence of his miraculous nature: "Aurangzeb, as proof of his justness and to advertise his good deeds, sends out every day to walk through the principal square a fierce lion in the company of a goat that has been brought up alongside it from birth. This is to show that his decisions are just and equal, without any bias."[75] This live enactment of "the peace among animals under the rule of the Messiah" indicates that Aurangzeb may have forsaken the sacred art of his ancestors but not, altogether, their art of being sacred.

CONCLUSION

Although the disintegration of the Mughal imperial center began soon after Aurangzeb in the early eighteenth century, the institutional shell of Mughal kingship survived for more than a century. Eventually made politically powerless and at times humiliated, impoverished, and even tortured by different regional or invading forces, the ruling Mughal dynast remained the exclusive symbol of sovereignty.[76] It was as if the throne of Hindustan could only be occupied by an heir of Timur. Even the English East India Company continued to enact this myth by formally drawing its authority from the Mughal dynasty until the rebellion of 1857.[77] Thus, even though attenuated, the modes and styles of sacrality described in this book did not immediately vanish with the decline of Mughal power. Their slow decline may yet have something to tell us about Islam in South Asia and the changes it underwent in British India and later.

To this end, it is worth observing that the reformist wave that culminated in the Islamic madrasa or college of Deoband and created a new social role for the ulama of South Asia gathered strength in an age that saw the end of Mughal monarchy and, more generally, the waning of Muslim sacred kingship.[78] In effect, with the rise of colonial rule the learned scholars of Islam, the ulama, had to reorient themselves in a world that had lost a master symbol, a sacred center—the body of a Muslim sovereign—and the networks of patronage and influence tethered to it. Without a Muslim ruler to look up to, they turned inward toward reform of the Muslim self. They became an "estate" that interacted with and depended upon the average Muslim in a way that had not been the case in the Mughal era.

This shift in social structure, it is important to add, led to a substantial change in the ritual use of knowledge (ʿilm) and in the social role of its purveyor, the ʿalim, who no longer had to serve, please, or oppose a Muslim sovereign. This transformation also dissolved major genres of knowledge and modes of practice that had sustained the institution of sacred kingship. This book has been an effort to recover some of these lost modes and genres that had once anchored notions of sovereignty. Accordingly, it has broached the subject of power and authority from two aspects that seem starkly alien to modern and reformist views of Islam: sacred kingship and charismatic sainthood. It is only by taking these forgotten elements as central to notions of authority in early modern Islam that we can appreciate the extent and nature of modern reform. The preceding pages provided a glimpse of the "unreformed" episteme in which Muslim kings enacted schemes of holiness and even of divinity, aided by the knowledge of the ulama and inspired by the performance of the saints.

NOTES

1. INTRODUCTION: ISLAM AND THE MILLENNIUM

1. The label "Timurid" is used in this study to refer to the descendants of Timur (d. 1405), who ruled in early modern Central Asia, Iran, and India. The term "Mughal" refers to the subset of the Timurids who established a dynasty in India. However, it is important to note that the Mughals were given this name by others, because of their Mongol heritage. They continued to identify themselves as heirs of Timur.
2. Examples of such views are too many to list. See, however, Annemarie Schimmel and Burzine K. Waghmar, *The Empire of the Great Mughals: History, Art, and Culture*, trans. Corinne Attwood (London: Reaktion Books, 2004); Sri Ram Sharma, *The Religious Policy of the Mughal Emperors* (London: H. Milford for Oxford University Press, 1940); Saiyid Athar Abbas Rizvi, *A History of Sufism in India*, 2 vols. (New Delhi: Munshiram Manoharlal, 1978).
3. Saiyid Athar Abbas Rizvi, *A Socio-Intellectual History of the Isna Ashari Shiʿis in India*, 2 vols. (New Delhi: Munshiram Manoharlal Publishers, 1986).
4. The classic account of this historical development is that of J. Spencer Trimingham, *The Sufi Orders in Islam* (New York: Oxford University Press, 1998). For an updated view, see Nile Green, *Sufism: A Global History* (Malden, Mass.: Wiley-Blackwell, 2012). I would like to thank Nile Green for sharing an early draft of his book. For a sense of the new "corporeality" that imbued the Sufism of this era, see Shahzad Bashir, *Sufi Bodies: Religion and Society in Medieval Islam* (New York: Columbia University Press, 2011).
5. Kathryn Babayan, *Mystics, Monarchs, and Messiahs: Cultural Landscapes of Early Modern Iran* (Cambridge, Mass.: Harvard University Press, 2002); Rula Jurdi Abisaab, *Converting Persia: Religion and Power in the Safavid Empire* (London: I. B. Tauris, 2004); Said Amir Arjomand, *The Shadow of God and the Hidden Imam: Religion, Political Order, and Societal Change in Shiʿite Iran from the Beginning to 1890* (Chicago: University of Chicago Press, 1984); Colin Paul Mitchell, *The Practice of Politics in Safavid Iran: Power, Religion, and Rhetoric* (London: I. B. Tauris, 2009).
6. For a developmental view of Shiʿi rituals in early Safavid Iran, see Jean Calmard, "Shiʿi Rituals and Power II: The Consolidation of Safavid Shiʿism: Folklore and

Popular Religion," in *Safavid Persia: The History and Politics of an Islamic Society*, ed. Charles P. Melville (London: I. B. Tauris, 1996).

7. See Shahzad Bashir, *Messianic Hopes and Mystical Visions: The Nurbakhshiya Between Medieval and Modern Islam* (Columbia: University of South Carolina Press, 2003), 31.
8. See, for example, A. Azfar Moin, "Challenging the Mughal Emperor: The Islamic Millennium According to ʿAbd al-Qadir Badayuni," in *Islam in South Asia in Practice*, ed. Barbara Metcalf (Princeton, N.J.: Princeton University Press, 2009). This issue is also dealt with in detail in chapter 5.
9. An anthropological work that I have found helpful in thinking through the relationship between cosmologies and social structure is Mary Douglas, *Natural Symbols: Explorations in Cosmology* (London: Routledge, 2003).
10. A good exposition of cyclical theories of time as they persisted in messianic Sufi circles in early modern Iran exists in Babayan, *Mystics, Monarchs, and Messiahs*. The ancientness of such views of time and eschatology are explored in Norman Rufus Colin Cohn, *Cosmos, Chaos, and the World to Come: The Ancient Roots of Apocalyptic Faith* (New Haven, Conn.: Yale University Press, 1993).
11. D. Pingree, "Kiran," in *The Encyclopaedia of Islam*, 2nd ed., ed. P. Bearman et al. (Brill, 2011), http://www.brillonline.nl; David Pingree, "Historical Horoscopes," *Journal of the American Oriental Society* 82, no. 4 (1962): 487–502; David Pingree, *The Thousands of Abu Mashar* (London: Warburg Institute, 1968); David Pingree, "Astronomy and Astrology in India and Iran," *Isis* 54, no. 2 (1963): 229–246; E. S. Kennedy, "Comets in Islamic Astronomy and Astrology," *Journal of Near Eastern Studies* 16, no. 1 (1957): 44–51; David Pingree and C. J. Brunner, "Astrology and Astronomy in Iran," in *Encyclopaedia Iranica Online* (December 15, 1987), http://www.iranicaonline.org; E. S. Kennedy, "Ramifications of the World-Year Concept in Islamic Astrology," *Actes, International Congress on the History of Sciences* 10 (1962): 23–43; E. S. Kennedy, "The Exact Sciences in Timurid Iran," in *The Cambridge History of Iran: The Timurid and Safavid Periods*, ed. Peter Jackson and Laurence Lockhart (Cambridge: University Press, 1986), 568–580; E. S. Kennedy, David Edwin Pingree, and Mashaʾallah, *The Astrological History of Mashaʾallah* (Cambridge, Mass.: Harvard University Press, 1971).
12. For a survey of the attitudes and debates on astrology in Western Christendom, see Laura Ackerman Smoller, *History, Prophecy, and the Stars: The Christian Astrology of Pierre d'Ailly, 1350–1420* (Princeton, N.J.: Princeton University Press, 1994), 25–42.
13. There are many studies of astrology in Europe. For example, Smoller, *History, Prophecy, and the Stars*; Eugenio Garin, *Astrology in the Renaissance: The Zodiac of Life* (London: Routledge & Kegan Paul, 1983); Anthony Grafton, *Cardano's Cosmos: The Worlds and Works of a Renaissance Astrologer* (Cambridge, Mass.: Harvard University Press, 1999).
14. The enduring critique of the "Orientalist" mentality remains that of Edward W. Said, *Orientalism* (New York: Pantheon Books, 1978).
15. The classic study is that of Norman Rufus Colin Cohn, *The Pursuit of the Millennium: Revolutionary Millenarians and Mystical Anarchists of the Middle Ages*, rev. and expanded ed. (New York: Oxford University Press, 1970).
16. See Sanjay Subrahmanyam, "Turning the Stones Over: Sixteenth-Century Millenarianism from the Tagus to the Ganges," *Indian Economic and Social History Review* 40, no. 2 (2003): 129–161.

1. INTRODUCTION: ISLAM AND THE MILLENNIUM [243]

17. Khaliq Ahmad Nizami, *Akbar and Religion* (Delhi: Idarah-i-Adabiyat-i-Delli, 1989); Saiyid Athar Abbas Rizvi, *Religious and Intellectual History of the Muslims in Akbar's Reign, with Special Reference to Abul Fazl, 1556-1605* (New Delhi: Munshiram Manoharlal, 1975).

18. Abu al-Fazl ibn Mubarak and Henry Beveridge, *The Akbar Nama of Abu-l-Fazl: History of the Reign of Akbar Including an Account of His Predecessors*, 3 vols. (1 and 2 bound in one) (Calcutta: 1897–1921; repr., Lahore: Sang-e-Meel, 2005), 1–2:68–115. Please note that the page and note numbers in the reprinted edition are different from those in the original edition. For the Persian, see Abu al-Fazl ibn Mubarak, *The Akbarnamah*, ed. Maulawi ʿAbd-ur-Rahim, 3 vols. (Calcutta: The Asiatic Society of Bengal, 1877–1886), 1:23–40. An excellent discussion of Akbar's horoscopes can be found in Eva Orthmann, "Circular Motions: Private Pleasure and Public Prognostication in the Nativities of the Mughal Emperor Akbar," in *Horoscopes and Public Spheres: Essays on the History of Astrology*, ed. Günther Oestmann, H. Darrel Rutkin, and Kocku von Stuckrad (Berlin: Walter de Gruyter, 2005).

19. In general, there is a dearth of comparative and theoretical scholarship on the institution of kingship in Islam. However, for the early medieval period of Islamic history, see the richly textured analysis by Aziz al-Azmeh, *Muslim Kingship: Power and the Sacred in Muslim, Christian, and Pagan Polities* (London: I. B. Tauris, 1997). There is also a useful collection of essays on kingship in South Asia, including some on the Mughal empire, in John F. Richards, ed., *Kingship and Authority in South Asia* (Delhi: Oxford University Press, 1998).

20. In this scholarly view, the emphasis remains on a "theory" of politics derived from "scriptural," "juristic," or "philosophical" texts of Islam authored by the "men of the pen" or the ulama, who, it is thought, provided a check against the excesses of kings. See Ann K. S. Lambton, *State and Government in Medieval Islam: An Introduction to the Study of Islamic Political Theory: The Jurists* (Oxford: Oxford University Press, 1981); Antony Black, *The History of Islamic Political Thought: From the Prophet to the Present* (New York: Routledge, 2001); W. Montgomery Watt, *Islamic Political Thought: The Basic Concepts* (Edinburgh: Edinburgh University Press, 1968); Patricia Crone, *Medieval Islamic Political Thought* (Edinburgh: Edinburgh University Press, 2004); Ram Prasad Tripathi, "The Muslim Theory of Sovereignty," in *Some Aspects of Muslim Administration* (Allahabad: Central Book Depot, 1964). Alternatively, those who believe that Muslim rulers had a more catholic and liberal outlook point to the universal and pragmatic norms preserved in the royal advice literature that often related the stories of pre-Islamic Persian kings and made only vague references to Islam or Allah. For a bibliography of Persian royal advice literature, see Z. Safa, "Andarz," in *Encyclopaedia Iranica Online* (December 15, 1985), http://www.iranicaonline.org. For a discussion of a "secular" code of ethics in Mughal times based on the political writings of Nasir al-Din Tusi, see Muzaffar Alam, *The Languages of Political Islam: India, 1200-1800* (Chicago: University of Chicago Press, 2004).

21. The classic account of sacred kingship in medieval Europe is Marc Bloch, *The Royal Touch: Sacred Monarchy and Scrofula in England and France* (London: Routledge & Kegan Paul, 1973). Another enduring work is Ernst Hartwig Kantorowicz, *The King's Two Bodies: A Study in Mediaeval Political Theology* (Princeton, N.J.: Princeton University Press, 1957). A recent view is that of Paul Kléber Monod, *The Power of*

Kings: Monarchy and Religion in Europe, 1589-1715 (New Haven, Conn.: Yale University Press, 1999). Also see Gábor Klaniczay, *Holy Rulers and Blessed Princesses: Dynastic Cults in Medieval Central Europe* (Cambridge: Cambridge University Press, 2002). Thanks to Alison Frazier for referring me to Klaniczay's work. In addition, studies of kingship that use cultural anthropology to understand the performative role of kings include Clifford Geertz, *Negara: The Theatre State in Nineteenth-Century Bali* (Princeton, N.J.: Princeton University Press, 1980); and Nicholas B. Dirks, *The Hollow Crown: Ethnohistory of an Indian Kingdom* (Cambridge: Cambridge University Press, 1987).

22. For a comparative perspective on how monarchs in different cultures publicly performed a "script" of sacred kingship, see Clifford Geertz, "Centers, Kings, and Charisma: Reflections on the Symbolics of Power," in *Local Knowledge: Further Essays in Interpretive Anthropology* (New York: Basic Books, 1983).

23. Emile Durkheim's classic text is *The Elementary Forms of Religious Life*, trans. Karen E. Fields (New York: Free Press, 1995). For a concise exposition of how Durkheim dealt with the "sacred" in his writings see Mary Douglas, *How Institutions Think* (Syracuse, N.Y.: Syracuse University Press, 1986). It is also noteworthy that Durkheim's notion of the "sacred" overlaps with Max Weber's concept of "charisma." See Raymond Aron, *Main Currents in Sociological Thought*, 2 vols. (New York: Basic Books, 1967), 2:224.

24. Michael T. Taussig, *Defacement: Public Secrecy and the Labor of the Negative* (Stanford, Calif.: Stanford University Press, 1999). I would like to thank Halide Velioglu for discussing the nature of the "public secret" and for referring me to this work by Taussig.

25. Maurice Godelier, *The Enigma of the Gift* (Chicago: University of Chicago Press, 1999), 171.

26. To follow a historian of medieval Islamic popular culture, "Much of what Western historians have written about the societies of the medieval Near East has rested upon the deceptively firm foundations of a particular textual tradition—that of chronicles, biographical dictionaries compiled by religious scholars, rarefied works of legal and religious scholarship, the literary legacy of accomplished poets and belletrists. But the story of medieval Islamic culture is . . . cluttered with a bewildering variety of texts, including stories of saints' lives, accounts of the splendors of one city or region or another, personalized recounting of dream visions, rhapsodies on the qualities and even the supernatural powers of popular texts . . . [which serve to] undermine, or at least to mute and to make contingent, the authority of that Islam that has been as much a construct of medieval ʿulama as of modern historians." Jonathan Porter Berkey, *Popular Preaching and Religious Authority in the Medieval Islamic Near East* (Seattle: University of Washington Press, 2001), 10.

27. While most writing on Islamic history tends to privilege the view from the center—that is, the view of the keepers of tradition—it is the view from the edge, that is, the perspective of the new converts or, more broadly, the consumers of tradition, that does more to explain how the "center" actually forms. See Richard W. Bulliet, *Islam: The View from the Edge* (New York: Columbia University Press, 1993).

28. See Talal Asad, "The Idea of an Anthropology of Islam," in *Occasional Papers, Center for Contemporary Arab Studies, Georgetown University* (1986).

29. See Clifford Geertz, *Islam Observed: Religious Development in Morocco and Indonesia* (New Haven, Conn.: Yale University Press, 1968).
30. See Victor Witter Turner, *The Ritual Process: Structure and Anti-Structure* (Chicago: Aldine, 1969).
31. Alam, *The Languages of Political Islam*.
32. Juan R. Cole, "Iranian Culture and South Asia, 1500–1900," in *Iran and the Surrounding World: Interactions in Culture and Cultural Politics*, ed. Nikki R. Keddie and Rudolph P. Matthee (Seattle: University of Washington Press, 2002).
33. Sanjay Subrahmanyam, "Iranians Abroad: Intra-Asian Elite Migration and Early Modern State Formation," *Journal of Asian Studies* 51, no. 2 (1992): 340–363; Aziz Ahmad, "Safawid Poets and India," *Iran* 14 (1976): 117–132; S. Nayyar Wasti, "Iranian Phycisians in the Indian Sub-continent," *Studies in History of Medicine and Science* 2, no. 4 (1978): 264–283; Abolghasem Dadvar, *Iranians in Mughal Politics and Society, 1606-1658* (New Delhi: Gyan, 1999).
34. On the place of "Islam" in the study of South Asian history, see Barbara D. Metcalf, "Presidential Address: Too Little and Too Much: Reflections on Muslims in the History of India," *Journal of Asian Studies* 54, no. 4 (1995): 951–967. For an overview of the scholarly debates on the rise of modern religious communalism in South Asia, see Peter Van der Veer, *Religious Nationalism: Hindus and Muslims in India* (Berkeley: University of California Press, 1994); C. A. Bayly, "The Pre-History of 'Communalism'? Religious Conflict in India, 1700–1860," *Modern Asian Studies* 19, no. 2 (1985): 177–203.
35. See, for example, Nikki R. Keddie and Yann Richard, *Roots of Revolution: An Interpretive History of Modern Iran* (New Haven, Conn.: Yale University Press, 1981).
36. Metcalf, "Presidential Address."
37. Abd al-Qadir ibn Muluk Shah Bada'uni, *Muntakhab-ut-Tawarikh*, 3 vols. (Calcutta: 1864–1869; repr., Osnabruck: Biblio Verlag, 1983), 2:246; Abd al-Qadir ibn Muluk Shah Bada'uni et al., *Muntakhabu-t-Tawarikh: by 'Abdul Qadir bin-Muluk Shah Known as al-Badaoni*, 3 vols. (Calcutta: 1884–1925; repr., New Delhi: Atlantic, 1990), 2:253.
38. See Lisa Balabanlilar, "Lords of the Auspicious Conjunction: Turco-Mongol Imperial Identity on the Subcontinent," *Journal of World History* 18, no. 1 (2007): 1–39; Lisa Balabanlilar, *Imperial Identity in the Mughal Empire: Memory and Dynastic Politics in Early Modern South and Central Asia* (London: I. B. Tauris, 2012). I would like to thank Lisa Balabanlilar for sharing an early draft of her work.

2. THE LORD OF CONJUNCTION: SACRALITY AND SOVEREIGNTY IN THE AGE OF TIMUR

1. Western interest and scholarship in Timur has a long history. The most updated scholarly account of his political and military career is by Beatrice Forbes Manz, *The Rise and Rule of Tamerlane* (Cambridge: Cambridge University Press, 1999).
2. Most of Shah Jahan's predecessors in India had used Lord of Conjunction among their titles, but he alone made it part of his name.
3. Milo C. Beach, Ebba Koch, and W. M. Thackston, *King of the World: The Padshahnama: An Imperial Mughal Manuscript from the Royal Library, Windsor Castle* (London: Azimuth Editions, 1997), 26–27.

4. The astrologer celebrated the fact that Shah Jahan's greatness as Lord of Conjunction the Second can be found in the numerical properties of the name of the first Lord of Conjunction, Timur, with the following verse: "Shah Jahan is the Sahib Qiran of the world, indeed / For, the 'Second' is also evident from the signs that revealed the 'First'" (*andar jahan bashad az an sahib qiran shah jahan / kiz bayyinat-i awwalin thani hamigardad ʿayan*). Farid Ibrahim Dihlavi, "Karnama-i Sahib Qiran-i Thani Zij-i Shah Jahani," British Library, London, MS Or 372, 4b. For a description of this work, see Charles Rieu, *Catalogue of the Persian Manuscripts in the British Museum*, 3 vols. (London: British Museum, 1883), 2:459.

5. These cabbalistic numerical calculations implied an ontological connection between the two men. This type of "mystical" knowledge was widely used at the time and part of a complex, interrelated set of divinatory sciences. See Gernot Windfuhr, "Jafr," in *Encyclopaedia Iranica Online* (December 15, 2008), http://www.iranicaonline.org. By "resemblance," it is implied that at work here was an episteme akin to the one outlined by Michel Foucault for sixteenth-century Europe, when divination was part of erudition. See Michel Foucault, *The Order of Things: An Archaeology of the Human Sciences* (New York: Vintage, 1973), 17–45.

6. John Richards says that Shah Jahan "spent forty million rupees in an attempt to conquer kingdoms whose total annual revenues were no more than several million rupees." John F. Richards, *The Mughal Empire* (Cambridge: Cambridge University Press, 1993), 133.

7. These "spurious" memoirs of Timur are discussed in Irfan Habib, "Timur in the Political Tradition and Historiography of Mughal India," *Cahiers d'Asie centrale* [En ligne], no. 3/4 (1997), http://asiecentrale.revues.org/index500.html. For an English translation of this work, see Abu Talib Husaini, *The Mulfuzat Timury or Autobiographical Memoirs of the Moghul Emperor Timur*, trans. Charles Stewart (London: Oriental Translation Committee, 1830).

8. The early nineteenth-century manuscript, with four illustrations, one depicting Firangi (Western Christian) ambassadors in Timur's court dressed like contemporary Englishmen, is Abu Talib Husaini, "Malfuzat-i Amir Timur," British Library, London, MS Or 158. For a description see Rieu, *British Museum*, 1:177–178.

9. See Beatrice Forbes Manz, "Tamerlane's Career and Its Uses," *Journal of World History* 13, no. 1 (2002); Sholeh Quinn, "Notes on Timurid Legitimacy in Three Safavid Chronicles," *Iranian Studies* 31, no. 2 (1998): 149–158; Cornell Fleischer, *Bureaucrat and Intellectual in the Ottoman Empire: The Historian Mustafa Ali (1541–1600)* (Princeton, N.J.: Princeton University Press, 1986), 281.

10. My goal is not, however, to provide a history of Timurid politics and administration or even a description of Timurid court culture. That topic is treated well in existing scholarship. See Beatrice Forbes Manz, *Power, Politics, and Religion in Timurid Iran* (Cambridge: Cambridge University Press, 2007); Manz, *Tamerlane*. For the refinements of the Timurid court, see Thomas W. Lentz and Glenn D. Lowry, *Timur and the Princely Vision: Persian Art and Culture in the Fifteenth Century* (Los Angeles: Los Angeles County Museum of Art, 1989).

11. The observation that the charisma of a leader draws its power from the collective desires of the group is supported by both Weberian and Durkheimian sociology. It goes against the common-sense notion of charisma being inherent in an individual "flashing out" to touch everyone around him or her. See Max Weber, *On Charisma*

2. THE LORD OF CONJUNCTION [247]

and Institution Building, trans. S. N. Eisenstadt (Chicago: University of Chicago Press, 1968), 3–42. For a succinct elaboration of the Durkheimian position, see Mary Douglas, *How Institutions Think* (Syracuse, N.Y.: Syracuse University Press, 1986), 97–99. For the relationship between Durkheim's "sacred" and Weber's "charisma," see Raymond Aron, *Main Currents in Sociological Thought*, 2 vols. (New York: Basic Books, 1967), 2:224.

12. David Morgan, *Medieval Persia, 1040-1797* (London: Longman, 1988), 93.
13. The classic scholarly treatment of the Mongols is by David Morgan, *The Mongols* (Cambridge, Mass.: Blackwell, 1990). A concise and up-to-date introduction to the Mongol conqueror can be found in Michal Biran, *Chinggis Khan* (Oxford: Oneworld, 2007). For a study of court culture, see Linda Komaroff and Stefano Carboni, eds., *The Legacy of Genghis Khan: Courtly Art and Culture in Western Asia, 1256-1353* (New York: Metropolitan Museum of Art, 2002). For a readable and imaginative account by an anthropologist, albeit one written for a general audience, see J. McIver Weatherford, *Genghis Khan and the Making of the Modern World* (New York: Crown, 2004).
14. For the long-lasting influence of the *yasa* among the Uzbeks of sixteenth-century Central Asia, see Ken'ichi Isogai, "Yasa and Shariʿa in Early Sixteenth-Century Central Asia," *Cahiers d'Asie centrale [En ligne]*, no. 3/4 (1997), http://asiecentrale.revues.org/index476.html. For a view of the competition and coexistence between Buddhism and Islam under the Mongols, see Johan Elverskog, *Buddhism and Islam on the Silk Road* (Philadelphia: University of Pennsylvania Press, 2010).
15. See H. R. Roemer, "Timur in Iran," in *The Cambridge History of Iran: The Timurid and Safavid Periods*, ed. Peter Jackson and Laurence Lockhart (Cambridge: University Press, 1986), 43.
16. It is generally acknowledged that the expression "Sahib Qiran" became widely adopted as a royal title used in courtly forms of address and prose texts—as opposed to mainly in panegyric court poetry—after Timur. See T. W. Haig, "Sahib Kiran (a. and p.)," in *Encyclopaedia of Islam*, 2nd ed., ed. P. Bearman et al. (Brill, 2009), http://www.brillonline.nl. One scholar has pointed out that the expression appeared on coins only after Timur. See G. P. Taylor, "On the Symbol 'Sahib Qiran,'" *Journal and Proceedings of the Asiatic Society of Bengal* 6 (1910). While the term became extremely popular after Timur, it can be found earlier in the poetry of Masʿud Saʿd Salman (d. 1121), Khaqani (d. 1190), Nizami (d. 1209), Saʿdi (d. 1283/1291?), and Hafez (d. 1390) and in the chronicle *Jamiʿ al-Tawarikh* of the Ilkhanid minister and historian Rashid al-Din (d. 1318). See "Sahib Qiran," in *Lughatname-i Dehkhoda [Dehkhoda Dictionary CD-ROM]*, ed. Ali Akbar Dehkhoda (Tehran: Daneshgah-i Tehran, 2002). For a recent review of the use of the expression "Sahib Qiran" by kings, see N. S. Chann, "Lord of the Auspicious Conjunction: Origins of the Sahib-Qiran," *Iran and the Caucasus* 13, no. 1 (2009): 93–110. The Ilkhanid ruler Arghun (d. 1291), whose son Ghazan was among the first Mongol rulers to convert to Islam, also called himself Sahib Qiran. See Anne F. Broadbridge, *Kingship and Ideology in the Islamic and Mongol Worlds* (Cambridge: Cambridge University Press, 2008), 44. Given Arghun's use of an astrological title, it is worth pointing out his deep interest in astrology, alchemy, and other occult sciences. In fact, he died from an elixir of life meant to make him immortal. See Charles Melville, "The Mongols in Iran," in *The Legacy of Genghis Khan: Courtly Art*

and Culture in Western Asia, 1256-1353, ed. Linda Komaroff and Stefano Carboni (New York: Metropolitan Museum of Art, 2002), 55.
17. "Thick description," advocated as an ethnographic technique by Clifford Geertz, needs little introduction. See Clifford Geertz, "Thick Description: Toward an Interpretive Theory of Culture," in *The Interpretation of Cultures* (New York: Basic Books, 1973). Today, Geertz's programmatic statements on "culture" provoke criticism, but for a good defense of "thick description" and its advantages in interpreting unfamiliar texts from a distant past, see Stephen Greenblatt, "A Touch of the Real," in *The Fate of "Culture": Geertz and Beyond*, ed. Sherry B. Ortner (Berkeley: University of California Press, 1999). For a reassessment and reinstatement of the concept of culture, see William H. Sewell, "The Concept(s) of Culture," in *Beyond the Cultural Turn: New Directions in the Study of Society and Culture*, ed. Victoria E. Bonnell and Lynn Avery Hunt (Berkeley: University of California Press, 1999).
18. I have modified the translation slightly from Ibn Khaldun and Walter Joseph Fischel, *Ibn Khaldun and Tamerlane: Their Historic Meeting in Damascus, 1401 AD (803 AH)* (Berkeley: University of California Press, 1952), 35–36. For the Arabic, see Ibn Khaldun, *Taʿrif bi-Ibn Khaldun wa-Rihlatuhu Gharban wa-Sharqan* (Lebanon: Dar al-Kitab al-Lubnani, 1979), 412–413.
19. For the research Ibn Khaldun did before Timur's arrival see the commentary in Ibn Khaldun and Fischel, *Ibn Khaldun and Tamerlane*, 82.
20. The Jewish physician and astronomer Ibn Zarzar, mentioned by Ibn Khaldun, was a famous intellectual who served both Muslim and Christian rulers of Spain. See the commentary in ibid., 80–81.
21. The *New Oxford Dictionary of English* (1998) defines millenarianism as "the doctrine of or belief in a future (and typically imminent) thousand-year age of blessedness, beginning with or culminating in the Second Coming of Christ." As eschatology, the idea is not limited to Christianity, however. Variations of it can be found in messianic traditions of a number of religious traditions. See Norman Rufus Colin Cohn, *Cosmos, Chaos, and the World to Come: The Ancient Roots of Apocalyptic Faith* (New Haven, Conn.: Yale University Press, 1993).
22. In a classic essay, Scarcia-Amoretti noted that in the Timurid and Safavid period of Iranian history, "it is indisputable that there was a rapprochement on the concrete plane which occurred at a time when, as all scholars admit, there was a 'return' to the myth of the ideal sovereign, a 'true Caliph', and consequently to a renewal of the hope in the advent of a leader in spiritual affairs and so too in religious affairs. This eagerly awaited leader was the Mahdi, a figure who was variously delineated and characterised in the different areas and *madhahib* proclaiming and anticipating his coming." B. S. Amoretti, "Religion in the Timurid and Safavid Periods," in *The Cambridge History of Iran*, ed. Peter Avery, Gavin Hambly, and Charles Melville (Cambridge: Cambridge University Press, 1968), 610. On the idea of the *mahdi* in Islam, see W. Madelung, "Mahdi," in *The Encyclopaedia of Islam*, 2nd ed., ed. P. Bearman et al. (Brill, 2011), http://www.brillonline.nl.
23. For a succinct account of the factors that went into the making of the "messianic age" of Islamic history, see Shahzad Bashir, *Messianic Hopes and Mystical Visions: The Nurbakhshiya Between Medieval and Modern Islam* (Columbia: University of South Carolina Press, 2003), 31–41.
24. Its pervasiveness in written and oral cultures around the world has led social

scientists to use millenarianism as an analytical category for the study of social movements "that have been animated by the idea of a perfect age or a perfect land." See Sylvia L. Thrupp, ed. *Millennial Dreams in Action: Studies in Revolutionary Religious Movements* (New York: Schocken, 1970), 11. Often, though not always, millenarian movements were a form of political protest by marginalized and oppressed groups. See Peter Worsley, *The Trumpet Shall Sound: A Study of "Cargo" Cults in Melanesia* (New York: Schocken, 1968); E. J. Hobsbawm, *Primitive Rebels* (Manchester: Manchester University Press, 1971). Sometimes this millenarian "enthusiasm" of the masses was harnessed for war, as was the case during the first crusade, when many of Europe's poor left their homes to fight what they thought was the last battle before the end of time. See Norman Rufus Colin Cohn, *The Pursuit of the Millennium: Revolutionary Millenarians and Mystical Anarchists of the Middle Ages*, rev. and expanded ed. (New York: Oxford University Press, 1970). However, it must be noted that the theory of millenarianism as merely a collective reaction to social deprivation has its strong critics. See Mary Douglas, *Natural Symbols: Explorations in Cosmology* (London: Routledge, 2003).

25. See, for example, Shahzad Bashir, *Fazlallah Astarababi and the Hurufis* (Oxford: Oneworld, 2005); Bashir, *Messianic Hopes*. Also, see Amoretti, "Religion in the Timurid and Safavid Periods."

26. For such a case study of Safavid Iran, see Kathryn Babayan, *Mystics, Monarchs, and Messiahs: Cultural Landscapes of Early Modern Iran* (Cambridge, Mass.: Harvard University Press, 2002).

27. Ibn Khaldun wrote, "The common people, the stupid mass, who make claims with respect to the Mahdi and who are not guided in this connection by any intelligence or helped by any knowledge, assume that the Mahdi may appear in a variety of circumstances and places.... Many weak-minded people go to those places in order to support a deceptive cause that the human soul in its delusion and stupidity leads them to believe capable of succeeding. Many of them have been killed...." Ibn Khaldun, *The Muqaddimah, an Introduction to History*, abridged and ed. N. J. Dawood., trans. Franz Rosenthal (Princeton, N.J.: Princeton University Press, 1969), 259.

28. Ibn Khaldun, *Muqaddima Ibn Khaldun*, ed. Ihab Muhammad Ibrahim (Cairo: Maktabat al-Quran, 2006), 19.

29. Astrology declined as an elite science first in seventeenth-century Europe and then slowly around the world as the results of the scientific revolution destroyed its intellectual foundations. Moreover, it was in the seventeenth century that the very category of "magic" as we understand it came into being, i.e., as false religion or bad science. Keith Thomas, *Religion and the Decline of Magic* (London: Penguin, 1991), 335–424.

30. There are a number of bibliographical and technical studies on astrology and the occult in Islamic traditions. For unpublished Arabic sources, see Toufic Fahd, *La divination arabe: Etudes religieuses, sociologiques et folkloriques sur le milieu natif de l'Islam* (Paris: Sindbad, 1987). Rigorous technical studies, translations, and overviews of Islamic astronomy and astrology include E. S. Kennedy, David Edwin Pingree, and Masha'allah, *The Astrological History of Masha'allah* (Cambridge, Mass.: Harvard University Press, 1971); David Pingree, *The Thousands of Abu Mashar* (London: Warburg Institute, 1968); David Pingree, "Astronomy and Astrology in India and Iran," *Isis* 54, no. 2 (1963): 229–246. For the pre-Mongol period, see George Saliba,

"The Role of the Astrologer in Medieval Islamic Society," in *Magic and Divination in Early Islam*, ed. Emilie Savage-Smith (Aldershot: Ashgate/Variorum, 2004); David Pingree and C. J. Brunner, "Astrology and Astronomy in Iran," in *Encyclopaedia Iranica Online* (December 15, 1987), http://www.iranicaonline.org.

31. The most influential vernacular treatise in seventeenth-century England, William Lilly's *Christian Astrology* (1647), was a translation of the work of Abu al-Hasan ibn Abi al-Rijal (d. c. 1035, known in Europe as Albohazen). Thomas, *Religion and the Decline of Magic*, 336. Discussions of Islamic astrology's influence on European thought can be found in Eugenio Garin, *Astrology in the Renaissance: The Zodiac of Life* (London: Routledge & Kegan Paul, 1983); Laura Ackerman Smoller, *History, Prophecy, and the Stars: The Christian Astrology of Pierre d'Ailly, 1350-1420* (Princeton, N.J.: Princeton University Press, 1994).

32. Indeed, Thomas argued that astrology was, in a way, the precursor of today's social sciences. Astrology's decline in the seventeenth century was related to the increasing mass of astronomical evidence that gradually eroded elite confidence in the structure of the Ptolemaic cosmos. Nevertheless, this decline was desultory and unpredictable at the time. English ship owners, for example, continued to consult astrologers before buying insurance for their ships. Thomas, *Religion and the Decline of Magic*, 368.

33. See J. Samso, "Masha'allah," in *The Encyclopaedia of Islam*, 2nd ed., ed. P. Bearman et al. (Brill, 2011), http://www.brillonline.nl.

34. When Abu Ma'shar's work was translated into Latin in the thirteenth century, his ideas had a major impact on shaping the intellectual basis of Christian millennial theories. J. M. Millas, "Abu Ma'shar," in *The Encyclopaedia of Islam*, 2nd ed., ed. P. Bearman et al. (Brill, 2011), http://www.brillonline.nl.

35. This is how David Pingree puts it: "A Saturn-Jupiter conjunction takes place about every 20 years; a series will occur in the signs of one triplicity for about 240 years, that is twelve conjunctions; and they will have passed through the four triplicities and begin the cycle again after about 960 years. When they shift from one triplicity to another, they indicate events on the order of dynastic changes. The completion of a cycle of 960 years, which is mixed up with various millennial theories, causes revolutionary events such as the appearance of a major prophet. The ordinary course of politics is dependent on the horoscopes of the vernal equinoxes of the years in which the minor conjunctions within a triplicity take place." Pingree, "Astronomy and Astrology in India and Iran," 245.

36. Ibn Khaldun, *Muqaddimah*, 261. For the Arabic, see Ibn Khaldun, *Muqaddima Ibn Khaldun*, 349.

37. Ibn Khaldun, *Muqaddimah*, 259.

38. Ibn Khaldun, *Muqaddima Ibn Khaldun*, 348–352.

39. Ibid., 351. Jafr originated as an occult technique for predicting the overthrow of the enemies of the Shi'a and the rise of the savior. Toufic Fahd, "Djafr," in *The Encyclopaedia of Islam*, 2nd ed., ed. P. Bearman et al. (Brill, 2011), http://www.brillonline.nl. Jafr drew upon and overlapped with a variety of divinatory techniques, including numerology, astrology, and scriptural traditions. See Windfuhr, "Jafr."

40. For example, it is well known that Mash'allah merged the astrological theory of Saturn-Jupiter conjunctions with Zoroastrian millenarian traditions. These

traditions held that a savior, called the Saoshyant, will rise at the beginning of every millennium after Zoroaster to usher in a new era and renew the teaching of Zoroaster. Cohn, *Cosmos*, 103.

41. For a detailed eleventh-century comparison of the various theories on the age of world, including Islamic, Christian, Jewish, and pre-Islamic Iranian and Indian ones, see the work by the brilliant polymath Muhammad ibn Ahmad Biruni, *The Chronology of Ancient Nations: An English Version of the Arabic Text of the Athar-ul-Bakiya of Albiruni*, trans. Eduard Sachau (London: Published for the Oriental Translations Fund of Great Britain & Ireland by W. H. Allen and Co., 1879).

42. Such a conception of time can also be understood as "figural," to quote Erich Auerbach, who reminds us that, unlike in symbolism and allegory, "in a figural relation both the signifying and the signified facts are real and concrete historical events" and that "the interpreter had to take recourse to a vertical projection of this event on the plane of providential design by which the event is revealed as a prefiguration or a fulfillment or perhaps as an imitation of other events." See Erich Auerbach, "Typological Symbolism in Medieval Literature," *Yale French Studies* 9 (1952): 5–6. Benedict Anderson used Auerbach's conception of the figural to describe messianic time as "a simultaneity of past and future in an instantaneous present." See Benedict Anderson, *Imagined Communities: Reflections on the Origin and Spread of Nationalism*, rev. and extended ed. (London: Verso, 1991), 24. For a discussion of the concept of messianic time in history and theory, see Kathryn A. Woolard, "Is the Past a Foreign Country? Time, Language Origins, and the Nation in Early Modern Spain," *Journal of Linguistic Anthropology* 14, no. 1 (2004): 57–80. A similar conception of the past seems to have animated classical Islamic historiography: "Unlike the neutral reader of today, who harbors few specific expectations of how things might or should develop, the medieval reader was primarily interested in seeing where all this was leading to—whether events . . . would truly fulfill earlier prophecies and whether the religious lesson truly exists." Tayeb El-Hibri, *Reinterpreting Islamic Historiography: Harun al-Rashid and the Narrative of the Abbasid Caliphate* (New York: Cambridge University Press, 1999), 53. Few, however, have taken seriously the role astrology played in keeping alive an explicit formulation of messianic time. But see Babayan, *Mystics, Monarchs, and Messiahs*; Bashir, *Hurufis*.

43. Ibn Khaldun and Fischel, *Ibn Khaldun and Tamerlane*, 36.

44. Timur professed his modest position as a subordinate to the Chinggisids to other people as well. See John E. Woods, "Timur's Genealogy," in *Intellectual Studies on Islam: Essays Written in Honor of Martin B. Dickson*, ed. Michel M. Mazzaoui and Vera B. Moreen (Salt Lake City: Univeristy of Utah Press, 1990), 102.

45. John E. Woods, "The Rise of Timurid Historiography," *Journal of Near Eastern Studies* 46, no. 2 (1987): 81–108.

46. See Sharaf al-Din Ali Yazdi, *The Zafarnamah*, ed. Muhammad Ilahdad, 2 vols. (Calcutta: Asiatic Society Bengal, 1887), 1:199, 211; Nizam al-Din Shami, *Zafarnamah: Tarikh-i Futuhat-i Amir Timur Gurkani*, ed. Panahi Simnani (Tehran: Bamdad, 1984), 61.

47. Note, however, that E. G. Browne suggested that Timur received the honor of being called Sahib Qiran when he overthrew his rival Sultan Husayn in 1370. Edward G. Browne, *A Literary History of Persia*, 4 vols. (Cambridge: The University Press, 1929), 2:185. This assumption, I believe, needs to be reexamined. Browne did not give a

precise citation but the 1887 Calcutta edition of the *Zafarnama* he used does not contain such a statement; neither do the manuscript versions I consulted in the British Library. The source for this error may have been an eighteenth-century abridged translation from Persian via French into English that paraphrases Yazdi's poetry, stating erroneously that during Timur's coronation ceremony "they gave him the title of Sahib Qiran." See Sharaf al-Din Ali Yazdi, *The History of Timur-Bec*, trans. John Darby, 2 vols. (London: Printed for J. Darby [etc.], 1723), 1:131. The actual verse carries no such meaning. For one, Yazdi's poetry is more likely rhetorical, not descriptive, and even if read descriptively, it states that "they showered him with gold and pearls and called him King Sahib Qiran" (*zar o goharash bar sar afshandand, u ra shah sahib qiran khwandand*) with the word "king" (*shah*) being the new operative term, as the event was clearly described by Yazdi as a coronation ceremony, and not the term "Sahib Qiran," which the chronicle uses to refer to Timur from the beginning. See Yazdi, *The Zafarnamah*, 1:211. Note that John Woods has also argued that in the revised chronicles Timur alone appears as the absolute sovereign and that the Chinggisid puppets on the throne are no longer called the "King of Islam" (*Padishah-i Islam*). See Woods, "Timur's Genealogy," 115–117.

48. John Woods calls it Timur's legal fiction. See Woods, "Timurid Historiography," 105.
49. "Le maintien à la tête de l'empire timouride d'un khan fantoche de sang gengiskhanide s'explique sans doute autant par des motifs propitiatoires que par des scrupules juridiques ou un calcul politique." See Jean Aubin, "Comment Tamerlan prenait le villes," *Studia Islamica* 19 (1963): 87.
50. See Broadbridge, *Kingship and Ideology*, 132–135.
51. Manz, *Tamerlane*, 15.
52. Marshall G. S. Hodgson, *The Venture of Islam*, 3 vols. (Chicago: University of Chicago Press, 1974), 2:428–436.
53. See the 1523 version of Sharaf al-Din Ali Yazdi, "Zafarnama (b)," British Library, London, MS Add 7635, 326a, 565b. Such towers can also be seen in another copy completed in 1552, see Sharaf al-Din Ali Yazdi, "Zafarnama (c)," British Library, London, MS Or 1359, 120a, 329a. This celebration of Timur's cruel displays of sovereignty were not just a matter of painting; Safavid and Mughal rulers kept this wartime tradition alive more than a century after Timur.
54. Ibn Khaldun and Fischel, *Ibn Khaldun and Tamerlane*, 47. Ibn Khaldun, *Ta'rif*, 428.
55. See J. Spencer Trimingham, *The Sufi Orders in Islam* (New York: Oxford University Press, 1998); Nile Green, *Sufism: A Global History* (Malden, Mass.: Wiley-Blackwell, 2012). For a description of shrines and their architecture from this period, see Sheila S. Blair, "Sufi Saints and Shrine Architecture in the Early Fourteenth Century," *Muqarnas* 7 (1990): 35–49. For a perceptive study of how shrines began to organize urban space, see Ethel Sara Wolper, *Cities and Saints: Sufism and the Transformation of Urban Space in Medieval Anatolia* (University Park: Pennsylvania State University Press, 2003). This did not mean, however, that an antinomian antisocial strain of mysticism did not sustain itself. See Ahmet T. Karamustafa, *God's Unruly Friends: Dervish Groups in the Islamic Later Middle Period, 1200–1550* (Oxford: Oneworld, 2006).
56. This phenomenon is not as extensively studied as it should be. But see Simon Digby, "The Sufi Shaykh and the Sultan: A Conflict of Claims to Authority in Medieval India," *Iran* 28 (1990): 71–81.
57. Ibn Arabshah had as a child accompanied his father, a scholar, when he was forced

to relocate to Samarqand after the fall of Damascus and work in Timurid imperial service.

58. Ibn Arabshah quoted and translated in Maria E. Subtelny, *Timurids in Transition: Turko-Persian Politics and Acculturation in Medieval Iran* (Leiden: Brill, 2007), 13. A variant translation is in Ahmad ibn Muhammad Ibn Arabshah, *Tamerlane*, trans. John Herne Sanders (Lahore: Progressive Books, 1976), 322. For the Arabic, see Ahmad ibn Muhammad Ibn Arabshah, ʿAjaʾib al-Maqdur fi Nawaʾib Taimur, ed. Ali Muhammad Umar (Cairo: Maktabat al-Anjulu al-Misriyah, 1979), 348.

59. For the concept of *ghuluww* and its historical relevance, see Marshall G. S. Hodgson, "Ghulat," in *The Encyclopaedia of Islam*, 2nd ed., ed. P. Bearman et al. (Brill, 2011), http://www.brillonline.nl. Those who subscribed to this view were often called *ghulat* or *ghali*, meaning exaggerators. It was a worldview that persisted in Iran well into the early modern period. See Babayan, *Mystics, Monarchs, and Messiahs*, xlv–xlvi, *passim*. How these soldiers came to view Timur as their spiritual master is not known. The Timurid chronicles do not mention the phenomenon. One can only speculate, but it is plausible that Timur's spy network, which included Sufis and wandering mendicants, was used to spread the legend of Timur's sainthood and messianic potential. See Ibn Arabshah, *Tamerlane*, 300. This method of spreading messianic propaganda (*daʿwa*) was well known in Islamic Iran, at least since the successful eighth-century rebellion organized by Abu Muslim in the name of Alids against the reigning Umayyad dynasty, which resulted in the Abbasid dynasty's rise to power. A similar tactic was used during the Mongol period to pressure the young Ilkhanid ruler Ghazan (d. 1290) to convert to Islam and to propagate his image as the messianic reviver of Islam using reports of black banners, an emblem of Abu Muslim's call to arms. See Charles Melville, "Padshah-i Islam: The Conversion of Sultan Mahmud Ghazan Khan," in *History and Literature in Iran*, ed. Charles Melville, *Pembroke Persian Papers* (British Academic Press, 1990).

60. For one, the literary sources from the period give us few accounts of shamans and often present the conversion of Mongol kings to Islam mostly at the hands of the learned men of Islam. See Reuven Amitai-Preiss, "Sufis and Shamans: Some Remarks on the Islamization of the Mongols in the Ilkhanate," *Journal of Economic and Social History of the Orient* 42, no. 1 (1999): 27–46. Also see Devin A. DeWeese, *Islamization and Native Religion in the Golden Horde: Baba Tükles and Conversion to Islam in Historical and Epic Tradition* (University Park: Pennsylvania State University Press, 1994).

61. See Sholeh Quinn, *Historical Writing During the Reign of Shah ʿAbbas: Ideology, Imitation, and Legitimacy in Safavid Chronicles* (Salt Lake City: University of Utah Press, 2000), 49.

62. See note 47, above. Also, see Woods, "Timur's Genealogy," 115–117.

63. Sharaf al-Din Ali Yazdi, "Zafarnama (a)," British Library, London, MS Add 18406, 3a. This comment is found not in the main chronicle but in a prologue (*iftitah* or *muqaddima*), which was written separately and perhaps meant for another unfinished work but sometimes accompanies the *Zafarnama* manuscripts. See Woods, "Timurid Historiography," 100–101.

64. See Pingree and Brunner, "Astrology and Astronomy in Iran."

65. See Hossein Ziai, "Al-Suhrawardi, Shihab al-Din Yahya b. Habash b. Amirak, Abu ʾl-Futuh," in *Encyclopaedia of Islam*, 2nd ed., ed. P. Bearman et al. (Brill, 2008), http://www.brillonline.nl.

66. Shahpur Shahbazi, "Flags i. Of Persia," in *Encyclopaedia Iranica Online* (December 15, 1999), http://www.iranicaonline.org.
67. See ibid. The Castilian ambassador Ruy Gonzalez Clavijo noted that the symbol of the lion and the sun was the standard of the king of Samarqand before Timur. Ruy Gonzalez de Clavijo, *Narrative of the Embassy of Ruy Gonzalez de Clavijo to the Court of Timour at Samarcand, A.D. 1403-6*, trans. Clements R. Markham (London: Printed for the Hakluyt Society, 1859), 124.
68. Sharaf al-Din Ali Yazdi, *Zafarnamah*, ed. Abbasi Muhammad, 2 vols. (Tehran: Amir Kabir, 1957), 1:13. Also, see Woods, "Timurid Historiography," 105. The idea of the cyclically appearing renewer or *mujaddid* is, in my opinion, a "weaker," routinized, and more "orthodox" variant of the idea of the cyclically reappearing millennial savior. Also, see E. van Donzel, "Mudjaddid," in *The Encyclopaedia of Islam*, 2nd ed., ed. P. Bearman et al. (Brill, 2011), http://www.brillonline.nl.
69. See Peter Parkes, "Fosterage, Kinship, and Legend: When Milk Was Thicker Than Blood?," *Comparative Studies in Society and History* 46, no. 3 (2004); Peter Parkes, "Milk Kinship in Islam: Substance, Structure, History," *Social Anthropology* 13, no. 3 (2005). I would like to thank Thomas Trautmann for these references. Also, see Lawrence Krader, *Social Organization of the Mongol-Turkic Pastoral Nomads* (The Hague: Mouton, 1963). For robing as a practice of bodily incorporation, see Stewart Gordon, ed. *Robes and Honor: The Medieval World of Investiture* (New York: Palgrave, 2001); Stewart Gordon, ed. *Robes of Honour: Khilʿat in Pre-Colonial and Colonial India* (New Delhi: Oxford University Press, 2003).
70. Ali was a dominant symbol of Islam in Iran well before the spread of juridical Shiʿism beginning in the sixteenth century. The literature on Ali is vast. For a bibliography, see I. K. Poonawala and E. Kohlberg, "ʿAli b. Abi Taleb," in *Encyclopaedia Iranica Online* (December 15, 1984), http://www.iranicaonline.org.
71. See note 54, above.
72. See Woods, "Timur's Genealogy." Also, see Denise Aigle, "Les transformations d'un mythe d'origine. L'exemple de Gengis Khan et de Tamerlan," *Revue de Mondes Musulmans et de Méditerranée* 89–90 (2000): 151–168.
73. See V. V. Bartold, "Ulugh-Beg's Private Life and Scholarly Occupations," in *Four Studies on the History of Central Asia: Translated from the Russian by V. and T. Minorsky, Volume II, Ulugh-Beg* (Leiden: E. J. Brill, 1958); Beatrice Forbes Manz, "Ulugh Beg," in *Encyclopaedia of Islam*, 2nd ed., ed. P. Bearman et al. (Brill, 2008), http://www.brillonline.nl. The mentioned tombstone can be seen in Lentz and Lowry, *Timur and the Princely Vision*, 28.
74. Translated from Aigle, "Mythe d'origine," 153. There are in fact two inscriptions on the stone with slightly different wordings but with essentially the same message.
75. In Islamic eschatology, Jesus is expected to appear at the end of the world. He is sometimes conflated with the mahdi figure, and at other times he is expected to appear after the mahdi and aid him in his battle against the Antichrist. See Madelung, "Mahdi."
76. Woods, "Timurid Historiography," 101.
77. Chinggis Khan was widely acknowledged to be a Lord of Conjunction. For example, a later Ottoman historian remarked that there had only been three Lords of Conjunction in world history, Alexander, Chinggis Khan, and Timur. See Fleischer, *Bureaucrat and Intellectual*, 281.

78. Amoretti, "Religion in the Timurid and Safavid Periods," 616.
79. The votive offerings the Mazar-i Sharif shrine attracted made it one of the most "profitable" shrines of the region. See Subtelny, *Timurids in Transition*, 208–214.
80. Amoretti, "Religion in the Timurid and Safavid Periods," 616.
81. The classic example of a figure from this period who defies categories but whom multiple sectarian and mystical traditions claimed as their own was the preacher and mystic Husayn Va'iz-i Kashifi, famous for writing the *Rauzat al-Shuhada*. A combination of formal Shi'i doctrine and oral lore, this work later became the master text for Shi'i ceremonies commemorating the martyrdom of Ali's son, Imam Husayn, and his family in the battle of Karbala. Kashifi wrote voluminously, producing, for example, a mystical exegesis of the Quran based on the inner symbolism of its letters and words, a famous work on chivalry (*futuwwa*) laying out the mystical code of conduct for artisanal fraternities, and a rendition of Indian animal fables entitled *Anwar-i Suhayli*. For an overview of Kashifi, see Maria E. Subtelny, "Husayn Va'iz-i Kashifi: Polymath, Popularizer, and Preserver," *Iranian Studies* 36, no. 4 (2003): 463–467.
82. For a succinct review of the sources of Alid loyalty, see Hodgson, *Venture of Islam*, 2:495–500.
83. The Isma'ilis constitute a major branch of Shi'ism. Their teachings, metaphysics, rituals, and organizational techniques deeply informed the Sufism of this period. See Farhad Daftary, *The Isma'ilis: Their History and Doctrines* (Cambridge: Cambridge University Press, 1990).
84. Ibn Arabshah, *Tamerlane*, 313.
85. The *Alinama* is mentioned in Aigle, "Mythe d'origine," 162. For a description and bibliography of the popular literature on Ali, see Poonawala and Kohlberg, "'Ali b. Abi Taleb."
86. Two lavishly illustrated seventeenth-century versions of the *Khawarnama* are in the British Library, one in Persian and the other a "freely rendered" translation in Deccani Urdu, see Muhammad bin Husam al-Din, "Khawarnama," British Library, London, MS IOIslamic 3443; Kamal Khan Rustami, "Khawarnama Dakkani," British Library, London, MS IOIslamic 834. For a description, see Hermann Ethe, *Catalogue of Persian Manuscripts in the Library of the India Office*, 5 vols. (Oxford: Printed for the India office by H. Hart, 1903), 1:560–562.
87. Ch. Pellat et al., "Hamasa," in *Encyclopaedia of Islam*, 2nd ed., ed. P. Bearman et al. (Brill, 2008), http://www.brillonline.nl.
88. This welcoming scene appears in both the illustrated *Khawarnamas* mentioned earlier. See Rustami, "Khawarnama Dakkani," 541b; Muhammad bin Husam al-Din, "Khawarnama," 359a, 61a.
89. She was the wife of Muhammad Ibrahim Adil Shah, who became ruler of Golconda in South India in 1626.
90. In the dedication, the Shi'i patroness, Khadija Sultan Shehrbano, is called "a slave girl of the five pure beings (*kanizak-i panj tan pak*) of the Prophet's family." See Rustami, "Khawarnama Dakkani," 543b. The five pure beings according to Shi'i tradition are the Prophet, his daughter Fatima, his son-in-law Ali, and their two children Hasan and Husayn. This style of dedication shows that this "legendary" and "entertaining" epic also had transcendental value for the patron.
91. For a good overview of the religious epic tradition in Iran, see Rasul Jafariyan,

Qissah Khvanan dar Tarikh-i Islam va Iran ([Iran ?]: Dalil, 1378 [1999]). Also, see Pellat et al., "Hamasa."

92. For Abu Muslim, see G. H. Yusofi, "Abu Moslem ʿAbd-al-Rahman b. Moslem Korasani," in *Encyclopaedia Iranica Online* (December 15, 1983), http://www.iranicaonline.org. For Mukhtar, see G. R. Hawting, "Al-Mukhtar b. Abi ʿUbayd al-Thaqafi," in *Encyclopaedia of Islam*, 2nd ed., ed. P. Bearman et al. (Brill, 2008), http://www.brillonline.nl.
93. Manz, *Tamerlane*, 66–106.
94. Ibn Arabshah, *Tamerlane*, 321. Ibn Arabshah, ʿAjaʾib, 346.
95. Gonzalez de Clavijo, *Narrative*, 171.
96. Clavijo also described how Timur destroyed all bridges over the river Oxus and placed a tight control over boat crossings so that none of his valuable captives could escape back to their own countries. Ibid., 120.
97. For a study of how some of these narratives informed conceptions of Islam in Europe at the time, see Margaret Meserve, *Empires of Islam in Renaissance Historical Thought* (Cambridge, Mass.: Harvard University Press, 2008). Thanks to Denise Spellberg for referring me to this work.
98. Johannes Schiltberger, J. Buchan Telfer, and Filip Jakob Bruun, *The Bondage and Travels of Johann Schiltberger, a Native of Bavaria, in Europe, Asia, and Africa, 1396–1427* (London: Printed for the Hakluyt Society, 1879).
99. Ibid., 65. The "Molwa who was an Infidel priest" will remain a mystery unless one accepts the translator's interpretation that it referred to the *mulhids*, a pejorative term meaning heretic that was often used for Ismaʿili and certain other Shiʿi and Sufi groups. An alternative explanation could be that it is a corruption of the word "mawla," meaning lord or guide, and that it refers to a saintly figure. The "three kings before they were baptized" is a reference to the biblical Magi and may refer either to Zoroastrians or Hindus, as might the reference to the fourth group, who "believe in fire." In all, the description indicates the bewildering array of religious rituals, myths, and symbols that Schiltberger had come across.
100. Poonawala and Kohlberg, "ʿAli b. Abi Taleb."
101. Bricolage refers to the way signs belonging to disparate groups are brought together in an organic relationship in the operation of "mythical thought." See Claude Levi-Strauss, *The Savage Mind* (Chicago: University of Chicago Press, 1966), 16–36. Bricolage does not exists only in "primitive" cultures but is all around us even in "civilized" forms. See Paul Christopher Johnson, "Savage Civil Religion," *Numen* 52 (2005): 289–324. Also, see Marshall David Sahlins, "*La Pensée Bourgeoise*: Western Society as Culture," in *Culture in Practice: Selected Essays* (New York: Zone Books, 2000).
102. As Levi-Strauss remarked, "Mythical thought . . . builds ideological castles out of the debris of what was once a social discourse." Levi-Strauss, *The Savage Mind*, 21.
103. See Ibn Taymiyya and Muhammad Umar Memon, *Ibn Taimiya's Struggle Against Popular Religion: With an Annotated Translation of His Kitab Iqtida as-Sirat al-Mustaquim Mukhalafat Ashab al-Jahim* (The Hague: Mouton, 1976).
104. He said that Shiʿi scholarship was akin to that of Christians and Jews who could not substantiate their religious traditions with strong *isnads* or verifiable chains of authority to the original historical statement.
105. Ibn Taymiyya, *Minhaj al-Sunnah al-Nabawiyya fi Naqd Kalam al-Shʿia wa al-Qadariyya*, 4 vols. (Bulaq, Misr [Cairo]: al-Matbaʿa al-Kubra al-ʾAmiriyya, 1904 [1322 AH]), 4:12.

106. For his attack on astrology, in which he admits the influence of the planets but condemns any attempt to harness their powers, see Yahya J. Michot, "Ibn Taymiyya on Astrology: Annotated Translation of Three Fatwas," in *Magic and Divination in Early Islam*, ed. Emilie Savage-Smith (Aldershot: Ashgate/Variorum, 2004).
107. See, for example, Josef W. Meri, *The Cult of Saints Among Muslims and Jews in Medieval Syria* (Oxford: Oxford University Press, 2002).
108. See Manz, *Timurid Iran*, 185. Also, Jafariyan, *Qissah*, 132.
109. As Jalal al-Din Suyuti (d. 1505), an Egyptian scholar, discovered when he was stoned by the crowd for criticizing the stories of their preacher. Jonathan Porter Berkey, *Popular Preaching and Religious Authority in the Medieval Islamic Near East* (Seattle: University of Washington Press, 2001), 25. For a sense of the competitiveness of the Iranian storytelling environment, see Jafariyan, *Qissah*, 12–18.
110. In discussing texts that today would be assigned to popular or "low" culture, Jonathan Berkey says, "Literary works such as these wreak havoc on the project of cultural archaeology, since they were acknowledged, sometimes even composed, by some representatives of high culture, and so confuse the stratigraphy of the literary remains." Berkey, *Popular Preaching*, 10.
111. The epic of Hamza was especially important in the "frontier culture" of thirteenth- and fourteenth-century Anatolia, where the two religious traditions in confrontation were Christianity and Islam. See Cemal Kafadar, *Between Two Worlds: The Construction of the Ottoman State* (Berkeley: University of California Press, 1995), 63.
112. See, for example, the numerous and lively paintings for the *Hamzanama* produced in the late sixteenth century at the Mughal court in India. John William Seyller and W. M. Thackston, *The Adventures of Hamza: Painting and Storytelling in Mughal India* (Washington, D.C.: Freer Gallery of Art; Arthur M. Sackler Gallery Smithsonian Institution, 2002).
113. G. M. Meredith-Owens, "Hamza b. ʿAbd al-Muttalib," in *The Encyclopaedia of Islam*, 2nd ed., ed. P. Bearman et al. (Brill, 2011), http://www.brillonline.nl.
114. However, note that even antinomian mendicants were not necessarily of low birth or devoid of learning. See Karamustafa, *God's Unruly Friends*.
115. Amoretti, "Religion in the Timurid and Safavid Periods," 616.
116. The text is in Arabic, edited and annotated by Shahzad Bashir, "The Risalat al-Huda of Muhmammad Nurbakhsh (d. 869/1464)," *Rivista Degli Studi Orientali* 75, no. 1/4 (2001): 119.
117. See Bashir, *Messianic Hopes*, 80–82.
118. Belief in *tanasukh* or metempsychosis often attracted charges of heresy and rebellion, as the concept was identified with the extremist or *ghulat* Shiʿi sects that had revolted against the caliphate in the early centuries of Islamic history. In essence, *ghulat* had become a trope for schism and rebellion of the worst kind. See D. Gimaret, "Tanasukh," in *The Encyclopaedia of Islam*, 2nd ed., ed. P. Bearman et al. (Brill, 2011), http://www.brillonline.nl. Hodgson, "Ghulat." Also see note 59, above.
119. See Bashir, *Messianic Hopes*, 98–99.
120. Ibid., 100; Bashir, "Risalat al-Huda," 51.
121. Nurbakhsh's theories became part of a popular Sufi text, written by one of his disciples, Muhammad Lahiji, as a commentary on a famous Sufi work. See Muhammad ibn Yahya Lahiji, *Mafatih al-Ijaz fi Sharh-i Gulshan-i Raz*, ed. Muhammad Riza Barzigar Khaliqi and Iffat Karbasi (Tehran: Zavvar, 1992).

[258] 2. THE LORD OF CONJUNCTION

122. Bashir, *Messianic Hopes*, 63.
123. Based in southern Iraq, he gathered Arab tribesmen around him and built a reputation as a master of thaumaturgic ʿ*ulum-i ghariba* (occult sciences). The movement is described in Amoretti, "Religion in the Timurid and Safavid Periods." For more detail, see Shahzad Bashir, "Between Mysticism and Messianism: The Life and Thought of Muhammad Nurbaks (d. 1464)" (Ph.D. diss., Yale University, 1997), 35–45.
124. Bashir, "Muhammad Nurbaks," 41.
125. Famous for developing a comprehensive "cabbalistic" system of letter symbolism and magic, he founded an order that became known as Hurufi (Letterist). A sayyid from an eminent family, his father was the chief judge of Astarabad. Hurufi teachings greatly influenced Sufism and became enshrined in the Bektashi order in Anatolia, which ministered to the spiritual needs of the Ottoman crack infantry, the Janissary. See Bashir, *Hurufis*.
126. Ibid, 56.
127. "*khaqan-i ordudar agar az jan nagardad il-i man; sahib qiran-i ʿalam-am bar il o bar ordu zanam*." Quoted in Aliriza Zakavati Qaraguzlu, *Junbish-i Nuqtawiyya* (Qum: Nashr-i Adyan, 1383 [2004]), 32.
128. This was an argument made by ʿAbd al-Qadir Badaʾuni, a supposedly "orthodox" historian and religious scholar at the Mughal court in the late sixteenth century. Badaʾuni wanted to defend the validity of overlapping messianic claims of Nurbakhsh and the Indian Mahdi of Jaunpur. This issue is discussed in detail in chapter 5. Also, see A. Azfar Moin, "Challenging the Mughal Emperor: The Islamic Millennium According to ʿAbd al-Qadir Badayuni," in *Islam in South Asia in Practice*, ed. Barbara Metcalf (Princeton, N.J.: Princeton University Press, 2009).
129. Consider, for example, the number of places where Ali's grave is supposed to exist: "Some authorities claim that it is located at the Baghdad quarter of Kark or at Hella [in Iraq], while others place it in various spots outside Iraq, including Medina, Damascus, Ray [Iran], and Mazar-e Sharif (in Afghanistan)." Poonawala and Kohlberg, "ʿAli b. Abi Taleb."
130. See Catherine B. Asher, "A Ray from the Sun," in *The Presence of Light: Divine Radiance and Religious Experience*, ed. Matthew T. Kapstein (Chicago: University of Chicago Press, 2004). Also, see Saiyid Athar Abbas Rizvi, *Religious and Intellectual History of the Muslims in Akbar's Reign, with Special Reference to Abul Fazl, 1556–1605* (New Delhi: Munshiram Manoharlal Publishers, 1975).
131. Sabine Schmidtke, "The Doctrine of the Transmigration of Soul According to Shihab al-Din al-Suhrawardi (Killed 587/1191) and His Followers," *Studia Iranica* 28 (1999): 237–254.
132. "Kitab Jamasp fi Tawaliʿ al-Anbiyaʾ," British Library, London, MS Add 7714. For a description, see Rieu, *British Museum*, 2:461.
133. Our knowledge of Jamasp's life and times is as vague as that of Zoroaster (roughly 1000 BCE). Jamasp was famous for his knowledge of the future, and Zoroastrian apocalyptic texts attributed to him were well known in Iran before and after the coming of Islam. For a *Jamaspnama* in Pahlavi with a French translation, see E. Benveniste, "Une apocalypse Pehlevie: le Zamasp-Namak," *Revue de l'Histoire des Religions* 106 (1932). Also, see M. Boyce, "Ayadgar i Jamaspig," in *Encyclopaedia Iranica Online* (December 15, 1987), http://www.iranicaonline.org.

134. The Zoroastrian *Jamaspnama* also starts with an explicitly millennial theme: The king Vishtasp asks Jamasp how long will their pure religion last, and what will happen after that? Jamasp replies that it will last a thousand years and begins to describe the calamities that will then befall the people of Iran. See the French translation of the Pahlavi in Benveniste, "Zamasp-Namak," 358–359.
135. "Kitab Jamasp fi Tawaliʿ al-Anbiyaʾ," 24b–25a.
136. Ibid., 33b–34a.
137. Shami, *Zafarnamah*, 6. Also, although little is known about the chronicler Shami's life, one of his titles was *vaʿiz* (preacher), which suggests that he was familiar with popular, oral narratives portraying the early heroes of Islam. See Woods, "Timurid Historiography," 85. Note that Duldul was originally the Prophet's mule but later ridden by Ali according to tradition. See, Suliman Bashear, "Riding Beasts on Divine Missions," *Journal of Semitic Studies* 36, no. 1 (1991): 62. I would like to thank Denise Spellberg for alerting me to this study.
138. See Amoretti, "Religion in the Timurid and Safavid Periods."
139. A good description of the bewildering array of religious practices and "magical" techniques followed by or ascribed to Timur, including praying Mongol-style to the Everlasting Sky, is in Aubin, "Tamerlan." Also, see Subtelny, *Timurids in Transition*, 12–13.

3. THE CROWN OF DREAMS: SUFIS AND PRINCES IN SIXTEENTH-CENTURY IRAN

1. It was argued in chapter 2 how these "mythical" and historical figures from Islamic and non-Islamic pasts were equivalent and interchangeable as sources of sacred sovereignty when seen through the lens of conjunction astrology and the millennial-messianic worldview it engendered. The political history in Iran after Timur can be found in John E. Woods, *The Aqquyunlu Clan, Confederation, Empire: A Study in Fifteenth/Ninth-Century Turko-Iranian Politics* (Minneapolis, Minn.: Bibliotheca Islamica, 1976); Roger Savory, "The Struggle for Supremacy in Persia After the Death of Timur," *Islam* 40 (1965): 35–65; Maria E. Subtelny, *Timurids in Transition: Turko-Persian Politics and Acculturation in Medieval Iran* (Leiden: Brill, 2007).
2. Since the principle of primogeniture did not exist, and since most rulers had multiple wives from different noble lineages, a fierce competition for sovereignty took place among half-brothers who then would draw upon their maternal kin in their bid for power. An excellent discussion of these issues exists in Maria E. Subtelny, "Babur's Rival Relations: A Study of Kinship and Conflict in Fifteenth-Sixteenth Century Central Asia," *Der Islam* 66 (1989). For the importance of maternal kin in Turkic kinship, see Lawrence Krader, *Social Organization of the Mongol-Turkic Pastoral Nomads* (The Hague: Mouton, 1963). The political role this allowed women to play was substantially greater than had been the case in the pre-Mongol period. See, for example, Maria Szuppe, "La participation de femmes de la famille royale a l'exercise du pouvoir en Iran safavide au XVIe siecle," *Studia Iranica*, no. part I (1994): 211–258. The Timurid prince Zahir al-Din Babur's comments on the prestige of his Chinggisid maternal kin and the obligations and rights of his stepmother and

[260] 3. THE CROWN OF DREAMS

brother highlight the complicated politics surrounding these relationships. Zahir al-Din Mirza Babur and W. M. Thackston, *The Baburnama: Memoirs of Babur, Prince and Emperor* (New York: Modern Library, 2002), 241–242.

3. The concept of the "civilizing process" is that of Norbert Elias, *The Civilizing Process* (Oxford: Blackwell, 1994). In a more recent programmatic call, Elias argued that "a theory of social processes must diagnose and explain those long-term and unplanned, yet structured and directional trends in the development of social personality structures that constitute the infrastructure of what is commonly called 'history.'" See Norbert Elias, Robert van Krieken, and Eric Dunning, "Towards a Theory of Social Processes: A Translation," *British Journal of Sociology* 48, no. 3 (1997): 355. Although such a historical sociology has yet to be attempted for the Timurid milieu and beyond in India and Iran, the "international" long-term influence of what is called the Timurid cultural renaissance suggests that such a study would be rewarding. To get a sense for how the Timurids set the "taste" and "style" of kingship for this milieu, see Maria E. Subtelny, "The Timurid Legacy: A Reaffirmation and a Reassessment," *Cahiers d'Asie Centrale* 3–4 (1997): 9–19; Maria E. Subtelny, "Arts and Politics in Early Sixteenth-Century Central Asia," *Central Asiatic Journal* 27, no. 1–2 (1983): 121–148; Subtelny, *Timurids in Transition*; Gulru Necipoğlu, "From International Timurid to Ottoman: A Change of Taste in Sixteenth-Century Ceramic Tiles," *Muqarnas* 7 (1990): 136–170; Thomas W. Lentz and Glenn D. Lowry, *Timur and the Princely Vision: Persian Art and Culture in the Fifteenth Century* (Los Angeles: Los Angeles County Museum of Art, 1989).

4. For surveys of the political histories of these empires, see John F. Richards, *The Mughal Empire* (Cambridge: Cambridge University Press, 1993); Andrew J. Newman, *Safavid Iran: Rebirth of a Persian Empire* (London: I. B. Tauris, 2006).

5. The most comprehensive work on Babur's life that makes extensive and excellent use of the Timurid ruler's poetry as well as his prose writings is Stephen F. Dale, *The Garden of the Eight Paradises: Babur and the Culture of Empire in Central Asia, Afghanistan, and India (1483–1530)* (Boston: Brill, 2004). A shorter, more comparative treatment of Babur as a "frontier warrior" or *ghazi* of Islam can be found in Ali Anooshahr, *The Ghazi Sultans and the Frontiers of Islam: A Comparative Study of the Late Medieval and Early Modern Periods* (London: Routledge, 2009).

6. Shah Ismaʿil's political career is traced in Ghulam Sarwar, *History of Shah Ismaʿil Safawi* (New York: AMS Press, 1975). Also, see Jean Aubin, "L'avenement des Safavides reconsidere," *Moyen Orient & Ocean Indien* V (1988): 1–126; Jean Aubin, "Shah Ismaʿil et les notables de l'Iraq persan," *Journal of the Economic and Social History of the Orient* 2, no. 1 (1959): 37–81; Roger Savory, "The Consolidation of Safawid Power in Persia," *Islam* 41 (1965): 71.

7. For a treatment of how Shah Ismaʿil's messianic legacy shaped Safavid politics, see Kathryn Babayan, *Mystics, Monarchs, and Messiahs: Cultural Landscapes of Early Modern Iran* (Cambridge, Mass.: Harvard University Press, 2002). Also see Colin Paul Mitchell, *The Practice of Politics in Safavid Iran: Power, Religion and Rhetoric* (London: I. B. Tauris, 2009), 19–67.

8. For example, in the decades before the rise of Babur and Shah Ismaʿil, the "Sunni" ruler of the short-lived Aqqoyunlu dynasty of western Iran, Uzun Hasan, was portrayed by his courtiers as the fulfillment of many of the same types of prophecies that Timur and his sons had been. He was called the renewer (*mujaddid*)

3. THE CROWN OF DREAMS [261]

of the ninth-century Hijri, much as Shahrukh had been called the renewer of the eighth-century. Uzun Hasan's rise was said to have been mentioned in the Quran. There were suggestions made that he had taken the place of the Shi'i Imam. He had reportedly also seen a dream in which all of the great Sufis of the region had raised him to the throne. Finally, much as Timur had, he also embraced Mongol myths of sovereignty. See Woods, *Aqquyunlu*, 82–83, 89; Newman, *Safavid Iran*, 10.

9. Dale, *Garden*, 1.
10. Babur referred to Timur simply as "Timur Beg" (Lord Timur). There are no obvious answers for why Babur did not call Timur a Sahib Qiran. But it is worth noting that Babur's memoir is incomplete and unfinished, with major gaps from 1508 to 1519 and 1520 to 1525 and large portions extant only in draft form. See Thackston's comments in the translator's preface, Babur and Thackston, *Baburnama*, xix. Babur's work may have had a different story to tell if it had reached its final state. Indeed, he had apparently begun to revise and polish the text in India but did not complete the project. One can speculate that if Babur's work had gone through the social machinery that produced stylized hagiographies and chronicles, it may have assumed a different style. However, Babur could not afford to maintain an elaborate entourage of poets and literati until late in life, after his conquest of Delhi. Overall, having Babur's writing in a "raw" and unembellished form is both a blessing and a nuisance for historians, as it affords a look at the inner workings of the sixteenth-century writing process but at the expense of leaving us with an unbalanced and unfinished work.
11. In fact, autobiographical writing such as Babur's was not the ideal genre for narrating one's spiritual accomplishments or making explicit claims of sacrality. This point is developed further in chapter 6, where the memoirs of Jahangir, Babur's great grandson, are discussed.
12. Gulbadan and Annette Susannah Beveridge, *The History of Humayun (Humayun-Nama)* (Delhi: Idarah-i Adabiyat-i Delli, 1972), 31.
13. The word *mentalité* is used here in the sense of the French Annales school, with its concern for the sociohistorical basis of beliefs and mental structures. The classic account in this vein remains Marc Bloch, *The Royal Touch: Sacred Monarchy and Scrofula in England and France* (London: Routledge & Kegan Paul, 1973).
14. The idea of the marvelous and miraculous spanned many genres of Islamic literature, including cosmology, cosmography, Quranic exegesis, and travel literature. For a bibliography, see Alice C. Hunsberger, "Marvels," in *Encyclopaedia of the Qurʾan*, ed. Jane Dammen McAuliffe (Brill, 2009), http://www.brillonline.nl. The attitude was not limited to the Persianate world but widespread across early modern Asia and Europe. See Jorge Flores, "Distant Wonders: The Strange and the Marvelous Between Mughal India and Habsburg Iberia in the Early Seventeenth Century," *Comparative Studies in Society and History* 49 (2007): 553–581.
15. It is worth noting that even in England it was only gradually in the seventeenth and eighteenth centuries that messianic claims became a sign of madness. Keith Thomas observed that "in the sixteen century the claims of a would-be prophet would always be seriously investigated, even if ultimately exposed as groundless, but by the eighteenth century the majority of educated men concurred in dismissing them a priori as ridiculous." Keith Thomas, *Religion and the Decline of Magic* (London: Penguin, 1991), 172–173.

16. Babur and Thackston, *Baburnama*, 8. Zahir al-Din Mirza Babur, W. M. Thackston, and Abdur Rahim Khan, *Baburnama: Chaghatay Turkish Text with Abdul-Rahim Khankhanan's Persian Translation* (Cambridge, Mass.: Department of Near Eastern Languages and Civilizations, Harvard University, 1993), 12. Note that in quotations from Babur's memoir, the language inside the brackets is Turkish unless stated otherwise.
17. Babur's memoir is rightly hailed as a rare and remarkably frank first-person account in Islamic literary history. Whatever its qualities as a literary product, however, in terms of genre it is close to the "court diary" that kept track of events (*waqi'a*) on a regular basis. Babur seems to have polished the earlier parts of this diary into more of a narrative, but the later parts remain organized in an annalistic diary format. Usually it was such a court diary that was turned into a chronicle at the end of a great king's reign. In the case of Babur this never happened, although variations in the extant versions—including the addition of some "miracles"—indicate that the process was attempted, possibly after Babur's time. One can speculate that by the time Babur became wealthy enough to afford a proper chronicler, he was in the last few years of his life and did not get around to doing it. The issue of Babur's memoir, its audience, nature, genre, etc., is a complicated one that still remains to be addressed adequately, but one cannot treat it as unique. Shah Isma'il's son, Shah Tahmasb, who was Babur's contemporary, also composed a memoir in Persian, but he called it a *tazkira*, a term used for a biographical dictionary or the life of a saint. See Tahmasb Safavi, *Tazkira-i Shah Tahmasb*, ed. A. Safari (Tehran: Intisharat-i Sharq, 1363 [1984]). No comparison between the two texts exists as far as I know.
18. This is to recall Levi-Strauss's observation that mythical thought is not illogical but hyperlogical in that it allows no event to remain meaningless, i.e., be without a cause or effect. It is not prior to "scientific thought" but exists alongside it in an all-encompassing demand for order and systemizing "what is immediately presented to the senses." Claude Levi-Strauss, *The Savage Mind* (Chicago: University of Chicago Press, 1966), 11.
19. Babur and Thackston, *Baburnama*, 260.
20. See Gernot Windfuhr, "Spelling the Mystery of Time," *Journal of the American Oriental Society* 110, no. 3 (1990): 401–416; Gernot Windfuhr, "Jafr," in *Encyclopaedia Iranica Online* (December 15, 2008), http://www.iranicaonline.org. For an example of how classical Persian literature was shaped by cosmological patterns, see Ziva Vesel, "Reminiscences de la magie astrale dans les Haft Peykar de Nezami," *Studia Iranica* 24 (1995): 237–254. Georg Krotkoff, "Colour and Number in the Haft Paykar," in *Logos Islamikos: Studia Islamica in Honorem Georgii Michaelis Wickens*, ed. G. M. Wickens, Roger Savory, and Dionisius A. Agius (Toronto: Pontifical Institute of Mediaeval Studies, 1984).
21. Babur and Thackston, *Baburnama*, 52. Babur, Thackston, and Khan, *Baburnama (polyglot)*, 86–87.
22. Babur and Thackston, *Baburnama*, 106. Babur, Thackston, and Khan, *Baburnama (polyglot)*, 180–181.
23. Maria E. Subtelny, "A Taste for the Intricate: The Persian Poetry of the Late Timurid Period," *Zeitschrift der Deutschen Morgenlandischen Gesellschaft* 136, no. 1 (1986): 56–79.
24. See Babur and Thackston, *Baburnama*, 407.

3. THE CROWN OF DREAMS [263]

25. Babur patronized astrologers. See discussion below. Babur's son, Humayun, had a tutor who trained him in finding and deciphering omens, as discussed in chapter 4. Shah Isma'il's Ottoman rivals also used such services. See Cornell Fleischer, "Seer to the Sultan: Haydar-i Remmal and Sultan Suleyman," in *Cultural Horizons*, ed. Jayne L. Warner and Talat Sait Halman (Syracuse, N.Y.: Syracuse University Press, 2001). A family of astrologers served the Safavids. See 'Ali Asghar Mossadegh, "La famille Monajjem Yazdi," *Studia Iranica* 16, no. 1 (1987): 125–129. The Hurufi leader Fazlallah Astarabadi, discussed in the previous chapter, claimed to be a perfect master in manipulating such patterns and controlling the universe. See Shahzad Bashir, *Fazlallah Astarababi and the Hurufis* (Oxford: Oneworld, 2005). Protective prayers, talismans, and counterspells were also deployed before critical battles. Babur gives one such prayer in Arabic, which he used before attacking to retake Kabul from rebels. This prayer, which seems to be a variation on the famous Quranic "throne verse" (*ayat al-kursi*) has interesting additions, such as providing protection from animals. Babur and Thackston, *Baburnama*, 239. Babur, Thackston, and Khan, *Baburnama (polyglot)*, 418–419. For Timur's long-lived reputation for clairvoyance, see chapter 2, note 61.
26. Babur and Thackston, *Baburnama*, 252. Babur, Thackston, and Khan, *Baburnama (polyglot)*, 440.
27. Edward G. Browne, *A Literary History of Persia*, 4 vols. (Cambridge: The University Press, 1929), 2:185. Sharaf al-Din Ali Yazdi, *The Zafarnamah*, ed. Muhammad Ilahdad, 2 vols. (Calcutta: Asiatic Society Bengal, 1887), 1:310.
28. For example, Husayn Bayqara, the last Timurid ruler of Herat, had an encounter with a dervish named Baba Khaki, whose "gifts" prepared the Timurid for the conquest of Herat. Subtelny, *Timurids in Transition*, 63. See below for a discussion of Babur's Sufi-enriched dreams during his conquests of Samarqand.
29. The French sociologist Marcel Mauss used the term "system of total services" or "total social fact" to describe a system of transactions between individuals in a society in which a valuable good or service is exchanged "in a somewhat voluntary form by presents and gifts, although in the final analysis they are strictly compulsory." Such a "total" system touches multiple cultural spheres—economic, religious, political, and aesthetic—and provides a type of social contract. Marcel Mauss, *The Gift: The Form and Reason for Exchange in Archaic Societies* (New York: W.W. Norton, 1990), 5–6. For an exposition of how the idea of the "gift" is linked to collective notions of the "sacred," see Maurice Godelier, *The Enigma of the Gift* (Chicago: University of Chicago Press, 1999).
30. Babur begins his memoir with a description of the valley of Fergana. The section below is based on Babur and Thackston, *Baburnama*, 3–7. Babur, Thackston, and Khan, *Baburnama (polyglot)*, 3–11.
31. This was Shaykh Burhanuddin Ali Qilich al-Marghinani (c. 1135–1197), the author of *Al-Hidaya fi Furu' al-Hanafiyya* (Guidance in the Branches of Hanafism). Note that Margilan is also called Marghinan is some Arabic sources.
32. The words of "exorcist" used by Babur in Turkish are *jinngiraliq, jinngiralar*. His sixteenth-century Persian translator uses *jingarahgi, jingarhai* in Persian. Babur, Thackston, and Khan, *Baburnama (polyglot)*, 6–7. Jinns are "fiery" beings mentioned in the Quran sometimes translated as "genie" in English.
33. He was called padishah in Kabul in the year 913/1507–1508. "Up to this time the descendants of Temur Beg had been called mirza, even when they were ruling. At

[264] 3. THE CROWN OF DREAMS

this time I ordered that they call me padishah." Babur and Thackston, *Baburnama*, 260. Babur, Thackston, and Khan, *Baburnama (polyglot)*, 455.
34. Babur and Thackston, *Baburnama*, 149. Babur, Thackston, and Khan, *Baburnama (polyglot)*, 256–257.
35. The sociological concept of "knowing" the country in order to rule it, used in this section, is taken from C. A. Bayly, "Knowing the Country: Empire and Information in India," *Modern Asian Studies* 27, no. 1, "Special Issue: How Social, Political and Cultural Information Is Collected, Defined, Used, and Analyzed" (1993). Also see C. A. Bayly, *Empire and Information: Intelligence Gathering and Social Communication in India, 1780-1870* (Cambridge: Cambridge University Press, 1996).
36. Babur and Thackston, *Baburnama*, 153. Babur, Thackston, and Khan, *Baburnama (polyglot)*, 264–265.
37. Babur and Thackston, *Baburnama*, 156. Babur, Thackston, and Khan, *Baburnama (polyglot)*, 270–271.
38. Khizr was especially important in Sufi traditions, prophetic lore, and epic traditions, appearing at moments of peril, often in dreams, to guide saints and conquerors—the most notable example being Alexander the Great. See A. J. Wensinck, "al-Khadir (al-Khidr)," in *Encyclopaedia of Islam*, 2nd ed., ed. P. Bearman, et al. (Brill, 2009), http://www.brillonline.nl; John Renard, "Khadir/Khidr," in *Encyclopaedia of the Qurʾan*, ed. Jane Dammen McAuliffe (Brill, 2009), http://www.brillonline.nl.
39. Babur and Thackston, *Baburnama*, 158. Babur, Thackston, and Khan, *Baburnama (polyglot)*, 274–275.
40. Babur and Thackston, *Baburnama*, 164. Babur, Thackston, and Khan, *Baburnama (polyglot)*, 284–285.
41. Babur and Thackston, *Baburnama*, 165. Babur, Thackston, and Khan, *Baburnama (polyglot)*, 286–287.
42. The Turks were famous for their rainmaking ability. It was widely reputed that this was a special power taught to the Turks by the biblical prophet Japheth, the son of Noah from whom Turks were believed to have descended. Eyewitness accounts of this phenomenon exist as early as the eleventh century. An Arabic "dictionary" of the Turkish language written in the eleventh century gives a detailed description of this unique ability of the Turks. The author, a Turk, noted that: "I myself witnessed it in Yagma. It was done to put out a fire that had broken out. Snow fell in the summer!—by the grace of God most high—and put out the fire in my presence." See Robert Dankoff, "Kasgari on the Beliefs and Superstitions of the Turks," *Journal of the American Oriental Society* 95, no. 1 (1975): 77.
43. Besides the Tokhta Buqa Sultan mentioned in the text, the other two were Ali Dost Taghayi, a falconer who had served Babur's father, and Khwajagi Mulla Sadr, an able warrior and seal keeper of Babur's father, who besides being skillful with the rain stone was a scholar, composer, and expert falconer. In short, these were not shamans or religious specialists but noblemen and warriors. Babur and Thackston, *Baburnama*, 19, 59.
44. Ibid., 439. Babur, Thackston, and Khan, *Baburnama (polyglot)*, 768–769.
45. In this case, the Uzbek rainmaking plan did not bear fruit, and they were routed by the Safavids, according to Babur. Babur and Thackston, *Baburnama*, 422. Babur, Thackston, and Khan, *Baburnama (polyglot)*, 738–741.
46. In fact, an argument can be made that learning and education was where this

attitude came from. See note 25 above on how princes were trained in such knowledge and patronized scholarly experts in it.
47. For Babur's account of Ulugh Beg's observatory in Samarqand, see Babur and Thackston, *Baburnama*, 58.
48. Ibid., 286.
49. See H. J. J. Winter, "Persian Science in Safavid Times," in *The Cambridge History of Iran: The Timurid and Safavid Periods*, ed. Peter Jackson and Laurence Lockhart (Cambridge: University Press, 1986).
50. Babur and Thackston, *Baburnama*, 413.
51. For an example of how astronomical and medical knowledge was used in public discussions and debate on sociopolitical conditions in eighteenth-century South Asia, see Bayly, *Empire and Information*, 247–283.
52. For example, Babur described how he changed the timing of battle because of astrological concerns: "The reason for my anxiousness was so that on the day of battle the Pleiades would be between the two armies. If the day had passed, the Pleiades would have been behind the enemy for thirteen or fourteen days. Such considerations were futile, and I hastened the battle for naught." Babur and Thackston, *Baburnama*, 104. In general, Timurid chronicles give many examples of how an astrological prediction threw a powerful army in disarray and brought ruin on the king.
53. Babur related, "I don't know whether it was of their own fear or whether they were trying to scare the men, but in any case Qisimtay, Shah-Mansur Barlas, and all who came from Bayana [where Rana Sangha had struck up camp] could not say enough of the audacity and ferocity of the Infidel's army (*kop sitayish o taʿrif kildilar*)." Ibid., 377. Babur, Thackston, and Khan, *Baburnama (polyglot)*, 664–665.
54. Babur and Thackston, *Baburnama*, 379.
55. Ibid., 381.
56. Ibid., 394. Babur, Thackston, and Khan, *Baburnama (polyglot)*, 692–693.
57. For a useful discussion of anthropological literature on how such "magical" thought and action is better interpreted with reference to social structures, cultural forms, or "language games" and not necessarily as a reflection of individual intent or intelligence, see Stanley Jeyaraja Tambiah, *Magic, Science, Religion, and the Scope of Rationality* (Cambridge: Cambridge University Press, 1990). The classic work of social history in this regard remains the study of early modern England by Thomas, *Religion and the Decline of Magic*. Many of Thomas's insights were based on structure-functionalist understandings of the relation between collective thought and social structure pioneered in E. E. Evans-Pritchard, *Witchcraft, Oracles, and Magic Among the Azande* (Oxford: Clarendon Press, 1950). Although structure-functionalism has fallen out of vogue in anthropology, many of Evans-Pritchard's insights were congruent with the still fashionable philosophy of the later Wittgenstein. For an excellent discussion, see Mary Douglas, *Edward Evans-Pritchard* (New York: Viking, 1980).
58. In other words, "ritual" here invokes the strand of anthropological theory that sees collective rites as a mechanism for structuring society, organizing collective activity, and concentrating group consciousness. The literature on this topic is vast. A classic work is Victor Witter Turner, *The Ritual Process: Structure and Anti-Structure* (Chicago: Aldine, 1969).

59. The ecumene can be thought of as a patrimonial political order consisting of a collection of communities participating in a shared moral discourse of rights and obligations. See Bayly, *Empire and Information*, 181n6.
60. It is well acknowledged that kingship in premodern times had a strong performative element to it, but few recognize it as an itinerant role performed outside the stylized setting of the palace court. For a sense of how mobile the institution of Mughal kingship was, see Jos Gommans, *Mughal Warfare: Indian Frontiers and Highroads to Empire, 1500-1700* (London: Routledge, 2002), 100-111.
61. Babur and Thackston, *Baburnama*, 300.
62. The king and his collaborators and competitors all tapped into flows of information fed by formal postal systems and intelligence-gathering mechanisms as well as by regular movement of people due to trade, pilgrimage, and seasonal migrations, which carried news and information across vast distances. It is important to remember that even though a large ratio of the population was illiterate at this time, people were literacy aware, and written information could easily be replicated and disseminated in oral form and vice versa. This argument, made by Bayly for eighteenth-century Mughal India, which also lacked a strong centralized administration, applies to Babur's period as well. Bayly, *Empire and Information*.
63. Bayly describes social knowledge of use to authority as consisting of two types: (a) patrimonial knowledge, i.e., the deep local knowledge of the "magnates and nobles" who knew particular regions because they ruled them or had deep influence over them; (b) affective knowledge, i.e., "the knowledge gained through participation in communities of belief and marriage and through religious affiliation and association with holy men, seers, astrologers and physicians." Rulers established their writ by cooperating with status groups formed on the basis of both types of social knowledge, patrimonial and affective. See ibid., 17.
64. Bayly makes a similar argument for late Mughal India, see ibid. For a general discussion on how social memory was shaped in premodern cultures, based on examples taken from European history, see James Fentress and Chris Wickham, *Social Memory: New Perspectives on the Past* (Oxford: Blackwell, 1992), 87-143.
65. Dale, *Garden*, 64.
66. For a discussion of Khwaja Ahrar's political activism and how it was remembered in Timurid Iran, see Jurgen Paul, "Forming a Faction: The Himayat System of Khwaja Ahrar," *International Journal of Middle East Studies* 23, no. 4 (1991): 533-548.
67. Khwaja was a title of respect used for Sufi masters and their descendants.
68. Babur and Thackston, *Baburnama*, 65. Babur, Thackston, and Khan, *Baburnama (polyglot)*, 110.
69. There is some indication that Babur's childhood religious education may have been in the hands of Khwaja Qazi. Babur and Thackston, *Baburnama*, xxxviii-xxxix, 227.
70. Ibid., 93. Babur, Thackston, and Khan, *Baburnama (polyglot)*, 158-159.
71. Babur and Thackston, *Baburnama*, 98. Babur, Thackston, and Khan, *Baburnama (polyglot)*, 168-169.
72. Babur and Thackston, *Baburnama*, 99. Babur, Thackston, and Khan, *Baburnama (polyglot)*, 168-169.
73. See Zahir al-Din Mirza Babur and Annette Susannah Beveridge, *The Babur-nama in English (Memoirs of Babur)*, 2 vols. (London: Luzac & Co., 1921), 1:132n2.

74. Babur and Thackston, *Baburnama*, 138. Babur, Thackston, and Khan, *Baburnama (polyglot)*, 242–243.
75. Babur and Thackston, *Baburnama*, 138–139. Babur, Thackston, and Khan, *Baburnama (polyglot)*, 242–243. Note that this dream does not appear consistently in the different extant versions of the Turkish manuscripts and is absent from the later Persian translations of the Mughal period. On this basis and other reasons, it was judged "spurious" by Annette Beveridge. See appendix D in Babur and Beveridge, *The Babur-nama*, 2:ix–xvi. There is no way to decide whether the dream was narrated by Babur or whether it was added by one of his descendants or devoted courtiers. Even if the dream is a later addition, it is an indication of how miracles began to be attributed early on to Babur in the context of his struggles to acquire Samarqand. Note that the saint Khwaja Ahrar played a similar "legendary" role in the "spurious" memoirs of Timur, mentioned earlier, that were "discovered" in the reign of Shah Jahan, who also launched an attack on Transoxania in the middle of the seventeenth century. For a reference to this memoir of Timur, see note 7, chap. 2.
76. Note that Babur even had a nobleman called Khwabbin (Dream Seer). Babur and Thackston, *Baburnama*, 192. Babur and Beveridge, *The Babur-nama*, 255.
77. The literature on the theory of dreams in Islam is vast. For a succinct summary of the notion of dreaming in Islam, see Leah Kinberg, "Dreams and Sleep," in *Encyclopaedia of the Qur'an* (Leiden: Brill, 2001). For a literature review, also see A. Azfar Moin, "Partisan Dreams and Prophetic Visions: Shiʿi Critique in al-Masʿudi's History of the ʿAbbasids," *Journal of the Oriental American Society* 127, no. 4 (2007): 415–428.
78. See Leah Kinberg, "Literal Dreams and Prophetic Hadiths in Classical Islam—A Comparison of Two Ways of Legitimation," *Der Islam* 70 (1993).
79. This phase was referred to as *qazaqliqlar* in Turkish and *zaman-i qazaqi* in Persian, meaning literally the "days of being a Cossack" or, more appropriately, the time of political vagabondage. For a good discussion of the topic, see Dale, *Garden*, 99–108.
80. For a sense of how Shah Ismaʿil's messianism was reflected in early Safavid sources, especially in the rhetoric of the chancellery documents and imperial correspondence, see Mitchell, *The Practice of Politics in Safavid Iran*, 17–46. The oral lore surrounding him survived long after his death in the storytelling and "romance" traditions. See Amelia Gallagher, "The Transformation of Shah Ismail Safevi in the Turkish Hikâye," *Journal of Folklore Research* 46, no. 2 (2009). A good survey of scholarship on the topic also exists in Barry Wood, "The Shahnama-i Ismaʿil: Art and Cultural Memory in Sixteenth-Century Iran" (Ph.D. diss., Harvard University, 1997), 1–33.
81. These accounts were by ambassadors or merchants who had been in the region during the reign of Shah Ismaʿil or later. Some even claimed to have seen him. However, they mainly relate the stories and rumors circulating about the mysterious child ruler of Iran. Yet barring a few errant plots and muddled names and dates, these accounts are consistent with what we know from other chronicles of the period. In fact, these European accounts based on oral reports and bazaar gossip may in fact be more valuable in constructing Shah Ismaʿil's popular image than any royal chronicle. Palmira Brummett, "The Myth of Shah Ismail Safavi: Political Rhetoric and 'Divine' Kingship," in *Medieval Christian Perceptions of Islam*, ed. John Victor Tolan (New York: Routledge, 1996).

82. Shah Ismaʿil's father, Shaykh Haydar was a nephew and son-in-law of Uzun Hasan, the last powerful Aqqoyunlu king. Shah Ismaʿil's maternal grandmother and wife of Uzun Hasan was Despina, daughter of the last emperor of Trebizond, a small remnant of the Byzantine empire on the southern coast of the Black Sea. Despina had been married to Uzun Hasan in a political alliance by her father to seek military assistance from the Aqqoyunlu ruler in case of an Ottoman invasion of Trebizond, which bordered Ottoman and Aqqoyunlu territories. As part of the marriage pact, however, Despina kept her Christian faith and reportedly raised her three daughters as Christians. Accordingly, from European accounts, we hear that Shah Ismaʿil's mother was named Martha. See Charles Grey, ed., *A Narrative of Italian Travels in Persia, in the Fifteenth and Sixteenth Centuries* (London: Hakluyt Society, 1873), 4. Safavid chronicles, however, give her the Muslim name Halima and do not mention her Christian mother. See Sarwar, *History of Shah Ismaʿil Safawi*, 24n22. Overall, Shah Ismaʿil's Sufi and royal descent shows the diversity of this "borderland" region and the flexibility in making political alliances across religious and sectarian divides. The way Persian chronicles erase this complexity to create a clean genealogy and smooth narrative also shows the care needed in reconstructing this history. For a review of the Persian chronicle tradition treating the early years of Shah Ismaʿil, see Alexander H. Morton, "The Early Years of Shah Ismaʿil in the *Afzal al-tavarikh* and Elsewhere," in *Safavid Persia: The History and Politics of an Islamic Society*, ed. Charles P. Melville (London: I.B. Tauris, 1996). Also, see Jean Aubin, "Chroniques persanes et relations italiennes. Notes sur les sources narratives du regne de Sah Esmaʿil Ier," *Studia Iranica* 24 (1995): 247–259.
83. Grey, *Italian Travels*, 187.
84. Ibid., 47.
85. Ibid., 61.
86. For a discussion of and review of literature on how the Alid lineage of the Safavids was created and polished over time, see Kathryn Babayan, "Sufis, Dervishes, and Mullas: The Controversy Over Spiritual and Temporal Dominion in Seventeenth-Century Iran," in *Safavid Persia: The History and Politics of an Islamic Society*, ed. Charles P. Melville (London: I. B. Tauris, 1996), 122–123.
87. Grey, *Italian Travels*, 115.
88. Roger Savory, "The Office of Khalifat al-Khulafa Under the Safawids," *Journal of the American Oriental Society* 85, no. 4 (1965): 497–502.
89. Said Amir Arjomand, "Religious Extremism (*ghuluww*), Sufism, and Sunnism in Safavid Iran: 1501–1722," *Journal of Asian History* 15 (1981): 1–35; Jean Aubin, "La politique religieuse des Safavides," in *Le Shiʿisme imamite* (Paris: Presses universitaires de France, 1970). See chapter 2, notes 59 and 118, above, for a discussion of ghulat. It would be incorrect, however, to characterize ghulat as a doctrinal sect. Generally, these ideas did not become broadly systemized into a set of independent or long-lived doctrinal institutions. Despite the popularity of ghulat symbols, they were mainly held in opposition to the well-established doctrines of scriptural Islam. Nevertheless, ghulat conceptions were widely accommodated in the teachings and practices of Sufism and even informed metaphysical doctrines of Shiʿism. See Babayan, *Mystics, Monarchs, and Messiahs*, xlv–xlvi, *passim*.
90. See, for example, G. G. Arnakis, "Futuwwa Traditions in the Ottoman Empire: Akhis,

Bektashi Dervishes, and Craftsmen," *Journal of Near Eastern Studies* 12, no. 4 (1953): 232–247.

91. V. Minorsky and Shah Ismaʿil I, "The Poetry of Shah Ismaʿil I," *Bulletin of the School of Oriental and African Studies, University of London* 10, no. 4 (1942).
92. Irène Mélikoff, "La divinisation d'Ali chez les Bektachis-Alevis," in *Au banquet des Quarante. Exploration au cœur du Bektachisme-Alevisme* (Istanbul: Isis, 2001). John Kingsley Birge, *The Bektashi Order of Dervishes* (London: Luzac Oriental, 1994), 68.
93. The Ottoman Sultan Selim I was given counsel after the battle of Chaldiran in 1514, in which the Safavids were defeated, that it was too dangerous to remain in the territory of an enemy leader who is revered by so many Ottoman soldiers. Birge, *Bektashi Order*, 67.
94. Clifford Geertz, *The Interpretation of Cultures* (New York: Basic Books, 1973), 10.
95. Ahmet T. Karamustafa, *God's Unruly Friends: Dervish Groups in the Islamic Later Middle Period, 1200–1550* (Oxford: Oneworld, 2006).
96. This composite and hypothetical portrait of renunciant dervishes in the sixteenth century is based on the descriptions provided in ibid., 65–84.
97. The Timurid ruler of Herat, Husayn Bayqara, tried to stop this practice of shaving all facial hair among some young men and qalandars of his realm. Ibid., 59.
98. Ibid., 83.
99. Ibid., 71.
100. Nesimi was a famous Hurufi poet. Khataʾi, as mentioned earlier, was the penname of Shah Ismaʿil.
101. Frederick De Jong, "The Iconography of Bektashiism: A Survey of Themes and Symbolism in Clerical Costume, Liturgical Objects, and Pictorial Art," *Manuscripts of the Middle East* 4 (1989): 10.
102. The Aqqoyunlu ruler Uzun Hasan, for example, boasted about suppressing heretic Qalandar and Haydari dervishes in a letter to an Ottoman prince. Karamustafa, *God's Unruly Friends*, 58.
103. See note 27.
104. Many of these legends are still alive in the oral traditions of Alavi groups in the region. See Ziba Mir-Hosseini, "Faith, Ritual, and Culture Among the Ahl-e Haqq," in *Kurdish Culture and Identity*, ed. Philip G. Kreyenbroek and Christine Allison (London: Zed Books, 1996).
105. Serpil Bagci, "From Text to Pictures: ʿAli in Manuscript Painting," in *From History to Theology: Ali in Islamic Belief*, ed. Ahmet Yasar Ocak (Ankara: Türk Tarih Kurumu, 2005).
106. His physical description is given in Grey, *Italian Travels*, 111, 202. It was Giovanni Rota, writing in 1504 or 1505, who reported that Shah Ismaʿil is adored as a prophet and keeps his face covered and veiled. Quoted in Aubin, "L'avenement des Safavides," 39.
107. A short history of the Safavid "taj" along with pictures is given in Barbara Schmitz, "On a Special Hat Introduced During the Reign of Shah ʿAbbas the Great," *Journal of Persian Studies* 22 (1984): 103–112.
108. Ibid., 104.
109. This was true broadly across the greater Persianate world, which included even non-Muslim areas, such as early modern South India, where courtly dress followed Persian fashion and differed, for example, from dress worn for temple ceremonies. See Phillip

B. Wagoner, "Sultan Among Hindu Kings: Dress, Titles, and the Islamicization of Hindu Culture at Vijayanagara," *Journal of Asian Studies* 55 (1996): 851–880.

110. Reportedly, Shah Ismaʿil said to the sons of the defeated Uzbek Shaybani Khan: "I will spare your lives, and allow you to return to your country on condition that you wear the red caftan, and that this river [Oxus] be your boundary." The young men replied, "Sire, we are content with what pleases your majesty, and will give in our submission." Grey, *Italian Travels*, 117.

111. The phrase and the argument is that of Shahzad Bashir, "Shah Ismaʿil and the Qizilbash: Cannibalism in the Religious History of Early Safavid Iran," *History of Religions* 45, no. 3 (2006): 255. The innovative practices of body symbolism that shaped the religious culture of this time remain understudied, but see Shahzad Bashir, *Sufi Bodies: Religion and Society in Medieval Islam* (New York: Columbia University Press, 2011); Scott Kugle, *Sufis and Saints' Bodies: Mysticism, Corporeality, and Sacred Power in Islam* (Chapel Hill: University of North Carolina Press, 2007).

112. Alexander H. Morton, "The Chub-i Tariq and Qizilbash Ritual in Safavid Persia," in *Etudes Safavides*, ed. Jean Calmard (Paris: Institut Français de Recherche en Iran, 1993).

113. Michele Membré, *Mission to the Lord Sophy of Persia (1539–1542)*, trans. Alexander H. Morton (London: School of Oriental and African Studies, University of London, 1993), 42–43.

114. Quoted in Bashir, "Shah Ismaʿil and the Qizilbash," 243.

115. See ibid. These reports of battlefield cannibalism exist only for the reign of Shah Ismaʿil. We do not find them before or after his realm. Later, in the reign of Shah ʿAbbas, when the Qizilbash had lost their power and were replaced as a military force by an army of slave soldiers, the ritual devotees of the shah had been reduced to services such as the torture of the shah's enemies by eating them alive.

116. While it is true that Iran became Shiʿi under the Safavids and organized Sufism declined, the process was a complex and desultory one and took more than a century after the reign of Shah Ismaʿil.

117. Hamid Algar and J. Burton-Page, "Niʿmat-allahiyya," in *The Encyclopaedia of Islam*, 2nd ed., ed. P. Bearman, et al. (Brill, 2011), http://www.brillonline.nl. E. G. Browne noted that even though Shah Niʿmatullah's poetry has little artistic merit, it had, nevertheless, remained popular for its apocalyptic message and divinatory potential. Browne, *A Literary History of Persia*, 3:468.

118. The Niʿmatullahi prediction regarding the rise of the Safavids appears in *Jamiʿ-i Mufidi*, a history of Yazd written in 1679 by Muhammad Mufid Mustaufi Yazdi. See the introduction in Jean Aubin, *Majmuʿah dar Tarjumah-ʾi Ahval-i Shah Niʿmatullah [Materiaux pour la biographie de Shah Niʿmatullah Wali Kermani]* (Tehran: Anjuman-i Iranshinasi-ʾi Faransah dar Tihran, 1982), 7–8. In this work, which is based on earlier Niʿmatullahi writings, Shah Ismaʿil is depicted as Ismaʿil the Guide (*hadi*) who manifested himself as the deputy of the messiah (*naib-i mahdi*) in 909 AH. The author states that before Ismaʿil's manifestation (*khuruj*), Iran was in a dismal state because of political fragmentation, war, cruelty, and oppression; Shah Ismaʿil, as predicted by Shah Niʿmatullah's verses, then rose to unify all of Iran under just rule and to impose Twelver Shiʿism. However, since this account is more than a century after the death of Shah Ismaʿil, in it the Safavids and the Niʿmatullahis are depicted

as Shiʿis from the beginning, erasing all trace of the exaggerated Alid (ghulat) past of the former and Sunni-Sufi legacy of the latter.
119. On the basis of religious content alone, the message of the Nurbakhshis, a Shiʿi "sect" of the Kubrawi Sufi order, was also close to Twelver Shiʿism. Although Nurbakhsh initially had made messianic claims, toward the end of his life and after his death his teachings were given a Twelver Shiʿi coloring. When Shaykh Muhammad Lahiji (d. 1515), Nurbakhsh's foremost disciple, established a hospice in Shiraz, Shah Ismaʿil visited the place. See Algar, "Nurbakhshiyya."
120. The Ottoman Sultan Selim wrote and asked Shah Ismaʿil to explain why he had desecrated Abu Hanifa's grave. See Andrew J. Newman, "The Myth of the Clerical Migration to Safawid Iran: Arab Shiite Opposition to ʿAli al-Karaki and Safawid Shiism," *Die Welt des Islams* 33, no. 1 (1993): 66–112. For an overview of how the early Safavids acted to eliminate rival sacred figures and Sufi orders, see Arjomand, "Religious Extremism." Also, see Aubin, "L'avenement des Safavides," 44–45.
121. This argument follows Richard Eaton's detailed study on the pattern of Hindu temple destruction in India by Turkish and Afghan armies. Eaton's argument, simply put, is that this was a phenomenon related to rules of conquest and punishment of resistance and rebellion that was practiced by Hindu and Muslim rulers and not related to any sustained religious policy of Muslim kings against Hinduism. See Richard Maxwell Eaton, "Temple Desecration and Indo-Muslim States," in *Essays on Islam and Indian History* (New Delhi: Oxford University Press, 2000). While Eaton's argument is limited to South Asia and focuses only on Hindu temples, enough evidence exists of Sufi shrine destruction and desecration in Safavid and Timurid Iran that it is worth examining the wartime practice of destroying sacred sites linked to local political authority as common across Iran and India and across Islam and Hinduism.
122. Arjomand, "Religious Extremism."
123. Babayan, "Sufis, Dervishes, and Mullas," 124.
124. For a discussion of whether this gap is attributable to an accident or deliberate destruction, see Ney Elias's note in Mirza Haydar and E. Denison Ross, *A History of the Moghuls of Central Asia: Being the Tarikh-i-Rashidi of Mirza Muhammad Haidar, Dughlat*, ed. Ney Elias (Patna, India: Academica Asiatica, 1973), 246n2.
125. Babur remarked about these princes, "Although these mirzas were outstanding in the social graces (*suhbat va suhbatarayliqda va ixtilat u amezisda*), they were strangers to the reality of military command and the rough and tumble of battle." Babur and Thackston, *Baburnama*, 224–225. Babur, Thackston, and Khan, *Baburnama (polyglot)*, 392–393.
126. Babur and Thackston, *Baburnama*, 206. Babur, Thackston, and Khan, *Baburnama (polyglot)*, 358–359.
127. Babur and Thackston, *Baburnama*, 248. Babur, Thackston, and Khan, *Baburnama (polyglot)*, 432–433.
128. Babur related that Kamaluddin was known for a literary work called *Majlis al-ʿUshshaq* (The Assembly of Lovers) consisting of short biographies of seventy-six prophets, saints, legendary lovers (Layla and Majnun), and historical kings of Iran (including Timurid and Aqqoyunlu ones). Babur called it a false and blasphemous work, because in it each person was paired with a carnal lover. Babur's distaste

notwithstanding, the work seems to have been quite popular given the large number of surviving manuscripts in Iran and India. Kamaluddin's reputation for knowing *jafr* is stated in other contemporary sources. See Charles Rieu, *Catalogue of the Persian Manuscripts in the British Museum*, 3 vols. (London: British Museum, 1883), 1:351. Hermann Ethe, *Catalogue of Persian Manuscripts in the Library of the India Office*, 5 vols. (Oxford: Printed for the India Office by H. Hart, 1903), 1035. C. A. Storey, *Persian Literature: A Bio-Bibliographical Survey*, 5 vols. (London: Luzac & Co., 1970), 1:ii:960–961. For *jafr*, see Windfuhr, "Jafr." Also, see chapter 2, note 39.

129. Babur and Thackston, *Baburnama*, 9.
130. Ibid., 254.
131. For example, when Babur met one of his royal cousins who was also a king but only slightly higher in rank to Babur, the encounter was structured by strict norms governing bodily composure, spatial placement of the two sovereigns, and precedence of movement and gestures. See ibid., 223–224.
132. Ibid., 36.
133. Ibid., 239.
134. Ibid., 318.
135. While Babur does not mention it, we know that tales of Abu Muslim and Hamza were related in the courts and camps of Humayun and Akbar. See chapter 4.
136. Babur and Thackston, *Baburnama*, 269. Babur, Thackston, and Khan, *Baburnama (polyglot)*, 470–471.
137. Babur and Thackston, *Baburnama*, 198. Babur, Thackston, and Khan, *Baburnama (polyglot)*, 344–345.
138. Giyas al-Din Khwandamir, *Tarikh-i Habib al-Siyar*, vol. 4 (Tehran: Kitabkhanah-i Khayyam, 1954), 4:523.
139. Haydar and Ross, *A History of the Moghuls*, 246.
140. The Arabic term *wali*, meaning friend, guardian, or successor, is notoriously difficult to translate. It points to an important concept of sovereignty and sainthood in both Shiʻi and Sufi thought. In the former case, see Moojan Momen, *An Introduction to Shiʻi Islam: The History and Doctrines of Twelver Shiʻism* (Oxford: G. Ronald, 1985), xxii, 17, 157. For a good discussion on its use in the literary traditions of Sufism, see Vincent J. Cornell, *Realm of the Saint: Power and Authority in Moroccan Sufism*, 1st ed. (Austin: University of Texas Press, 1998), xvii–xxi.
141. Haydar and Ross, *A History of the Moghuls*, 246.
142. For a detailed study of the political history of the Safavids and Qizilbash in Khurasan and especially Herat, see Martin B. Dickson, "Shah Tahmasb and the Uzbeks: The Duel for Khurasan with Ubayd Khan: 930–946/1524–1540" (Ph.D. diss., Princeton University, 1962).
143. Khwandamir, *Tarikh-i Habib al-Siyar*, 528. Iskandar Beg Munshi, *The History of Shah ʻAbbas the Great: Tarikh-e Alamara-ye ʻAbbasi*, trans. Roger Savory, 2 vols. (Boulder, Colo.: Westview, 1978), 1:66.
144. Haydar and Ross, *A History of the Moghuls*, 260.
145. Ruzbihan Khunji, *Suluk al-Muluk*, ed. Muhammad Ali Muvahhid (Tehran: Shirkat-i Sahami-i Intisharat-i Khvarazmi, 1984 [1362]), 60. Khunji's account is also full of "strange" dreams in which he sees omens of victory of the returning Uzbeks.
146. Wood, "Shahnama-i Ismaʻil," 4.
147. Minorsky and Shah Ismaʻil I, "The Poetry of Shah Ismaʻil I," 1027a–1029a.

3. THE CROWN OF DREAMS [273]

148. It has been suggested that there are similarities between the European accounts of Shah Ismaʿil's birth and the stories of the birth of the hero Sam in the *Shahnama*. Wood, "Shahnama-i Ismaʿil," 103.
149. Babur and Thackston, *Baburnama*, 275.
150. See chapter 2. Also, a good discussion of this topic exists in Babayan, *Mystics, Monarchs, and Messiahs*, 9–46.
151. Robert Hillenbrand, "Iconography of the Shah-nama-yi Shahi," in *Safavid Persia: The History and Politics of an Islamic Society* (London: I. B. Tauris, 1996), 70. For more information on the Safavid *Shahnama* see Stuart Cary Welch, "78 Pictures from a World of Kings, Heroes, and Demons: The Houghton Shah-nameh," *Metropolitan Museum of Art Bulletin* 29, no. 8 (1971); Martin Dickson and Stuart Cary Welch, *The Houghton Shahnameh*, 2 vols. (Cambridge, Mass.: Harvard University Press, 1981).
152. The history of this epic's commissioning and writing is a complicated one. Beginning in 1510, Shah Ismaʿil assigned the task to five poets in and around Herat. Four of the poets died before completing the task, and their works are now lost. The only poet who managed to complete the epic, Muhammad Qasim Qasimi Gunabadi, did so in 1534, ten years after Shah Ismaʿil's death. Qasimi Gunabadi, moreover, was a nephew and student of the senior and renowned Herati poet Hatifi, who was the first one to be assigned the task. For a detailed discussion, see Wood, "Shahnama-i Ismaʿil," 49–54. Gunabadi's epic has been published. See Muhammad Qasim Qasimi Gunabadi, *Shah Ismaʿil Namah*, ed. Jaʿfar Shujaʿ Kayhani (Tehran: Farhangistan-i Zaban va Adab-i Farsi, 1387 [2008 or 2009]).
153. Qasimi Gunabadi, *Shah Ismaʿil Namah*, 152, 186, and 187. Also see the desciptions given in Wood, "Shahnama-i Ismaʿil," 79. Note that Shah Ismaʿil had in fact made a gilded drinking cup out of the skull of his Uzbek enemy Shaybani Khan. See Sarwar, *History of Shah Ismaʿil Safawi*, 63.
154. Qasimi Gunabadi, *Shah Ismaʿil Namah*, 161, 181, 182, 186, 191. For additional description and analysis, see Wood, "Shahnama-i Ismaʿil," 78.
155. Qasimi Gunabadi, *Shah Ismaʿil Namah*, 187–189. Also, see Wood, "Shahnama-i Ismaʿil," 62. See chapter 2 for the world-conquering deeds of Lord of Conjunctions such as Amir Hamza in the epic tradition and of Ali in an astrological history. Timur, of course, was a Lord of Conjunction who did indeed come close to actually enacting this plot.
156. This section is in Qasimi Gunabadi, *Shah Ismaʿil Namah*, 287–293. It is also mentioned in Wood, "Shahnama-i Ismaʿil," 65.
157. Ibid., 71.
158. Ibid., 67.
159. Indeed, it has been argued, this epic should be understood as "not a faulty chronicle, but rather as a historically conscious work of myth." Ibid., 77.
160. Ibid., 85–92.
161. Ibid., 89. Also, see Michele Bernardini, "Hatifi's *Timurnameh* and Qasimi's *Shahnameh-yi Ismaʿil*: Considerations for a Double Critical Edition," in *Society and Culture in the Early Modern Middle East: Studies on Iran in the Safavid Period*, ed. Andrew J. Newman (Leiden: Brill, 2003).
162. As noted earlier, Hatifi was also Qasimi Gunabadi's uncle and teacher. Ibid., 89–90.
163. Ibid., 72.
164. Quoted in Morton, "Early Years of Shah Ismaʿil," 45.

4. THE ALCHEMICAL COURT: THE BEGINNINGS OF THE MUGHAL IMPERIAL CULT

1. Shah Tahmasb's letter translated and quoted in Riazul Islam, *Indo-Persian Relations: A Study of the Political and Diplomatic Relations Between the Mughul Empire and Iran* (Tehran: Iranian Culture Foundation, 1970), 36. The letter, dated 1554 or later, appears in many compilations of royal letters as well as chronicles in sixteenth-century Iran and India. For a more detailed treatment and full list of sources that record this letter, see Riazul Islam, *A Calendar of Documents on Indo-Persian Relations*, 2 vols. (Tehran: Iranian Culture Foundation and Institute of Central & West Asian Studies, 1979), 2:293–294. Furthermore, the charge that Humayun made claims of being a manifestation of divinity is also repeated by ʿAbd al-Qadir Badaʾuni, a religious scholar and historian at the court of Humayun's son, Akbar. As discussed in detail in the next chapter, Badaʾuni wrote a clandestine and critical chronicle of the Mughal period. Abd al-Qadir ibn Muluk Shah Badaʾuni et al., *Muntakhabu-t-Tawarikh: by ʿAbdul Qadir bin-Muluk Shah Known as al-Badaoni*, 3 vols. (Calcutta: 1884–1925; repr., New Delhi: Atlantic Publishers & Distributors, 1990), 1:573. Abd al-Qadir ibn Muluk Shah Badaʾuni, *Muntakhab-ut-Tawarikh*, 3 vols. (Calcutta: 1864–1869; repr., Osnabruck: Biblio Verlag, 1983), 1:446.
2. For a summary of Ottoman-Safavid relations at this time and references to secondary literature on the topic, see Andrew J. Newman, *Safavid Iran: Rebirth of a Persian Empire* (London: I. B. Tauris, 2006), 27–28.
3. Shah Tahmasb wrote a memoir that was made public and distributed during his lifetime. In this work, he discussed his correspondence with the Ottoman sultan with reference to the battle between the sultan's father and his own. See Tahmasb Safavi, *Tazkira-i Shah Tahmasb*, ed. A. Safari (Tehran: Intisharat-i Sharq, 1363 [1984]), 28–29. Shah Tahmasb mentioned Humayun only once, when stating that he had treated the Ottoman prince Bayazid, who had rebelled against his father and taken refuge at the Safavid court, with the same consideration that he had shown the Timurid asylum seeker. Ibid., 80.
4. This pious tone clearly comes across in Shah Tahmasb's writing. For an analysis, see Kathryn Babayan, *Mystics, Monarchs, and Messiahs: Cultural Landscapes of Early Modern Iran* (Cambridge, Mass.: Harvard University Press, 2002), 321–325.
5. Islam, *Calendar of Documents*, 2:294.
6. Ibid.
7. The classical period of the Mughal empire is generally narrated as the reign of the six "great Mughals": Babur, Humayun, Akbar, Jahangir, Shah Jahan, and Aurangzeb. Of all these monarchs, Humayun has been least studied in recent scholarship. The text still cited most often for the political events of Humayun's reign is Ishwari Prasad, *The Life and Times of Humayun* (Bombay: Orient Longmans, 1956).
8. For details on Humayun's experience in Iran, see Sukumar Ray, *Humayun in Persia* (Calcutta: Royal Asiatic Society of Bengal, 1948). Also, see Islam, *Indo-Persian Relations*, 22–47.
9. Few works of art from Humayun's time have survived. An intriguing exception is a large painting depicting him and his Timurid ancestors. See Sheila R. Canby, *Humayun's Garden Party: Princes of the House of Timur and Early Mughal Painting* ([Bombay]: Marg Publications, 1994).

4. THE ALCHEMICAL COURT [275]

10. The following statement is indicative of modern evaluations of Humayun: "Humayun was not a hero like his father. His interests lay primarily in the spheres of mysticism, magic and astrology, which played a central role in his life." Annemarie Schimmel and Burzine K. Waghmar, *The Empire of the Great Mughals: History, Art, and Culture*, trans. Corinne Attwood (London: Reaktion, 2004), 27–28.
11. See, for example, Robert Skelton, "Imperial Symbolism in Mughal Painting," in *Content and Context of Visual Arts in the Islamic World*, ed. Priscilla Parsons Soucek, Carol Bier, and Richard Ettinghausen (University Park: Pennsylvania State University Press, 1988), 180.
12. For the concept of doxa, orthodoxy, and heterodoxy as it relates to culture and practice, see Pierre Bourdieu, *Outline of a Theory of Practice* (Cambridge: Cambridge University Press, 1977), 164–171.
13. The Shattaris were a major Sufi order in northern India during the time of Babur and Humayun. For a survey of the literature on the Shattaris, see Khaliq Ahmad Nizami, "Shattariyya," in *Encyclopaedia of Islam*, 2nd ed., ed. P. Bearman, et al. (Brill, 2008), http://www.brillonline.nl. Abdul Muqtadir, "Muhammad Ghawth Gwaliyari," in *Encyclopaedia of Islam*, 2nd ed., ed. P. Bearman, et al. (Brill, 2008), http://www.brillonline.nl. Saiyid Athar Abbas Rizvi, *A History of Sufism in India*, 2 vols. (New Delhi: Munshiram Manoharlal, 1978), 2:151–173.
14. Besides using the primary sources from this period, mostly Timurid chronicles and memoirs, my analysis of the Shattaris depends on the following works, which provide a good survey and analysis of the available sources of Shattari tradition: Carl W. Ernst, "Persecution and Circumspection in Shattari Sufism," in *Islamic Mysticism Contested: Thirteen Centuries of Controversies and Polemics*, ed. F. de Jong and Bernd Radtke (Leiden: Brill, 1999); Scott Kugle, "Heaven's Witness: The Uses and Abuses of Muhammad Ghawth's Mystical Ascension," *Journal of Islamic Studies* 14, no. 1 (2003): 1–36.
15. Babur wrote, "Events of the Year 936 (A.D. 1529–30). On Tuesday the 3rd of Muharram [Sept. 7], Shihabuddin Khusraw came from Gwalior with Shaykh Muhammad Ghaws to intercede on behalf of Rahimdad. Since [the shaykh] was a dervish and a powerful spiritual ('aziz) man, I forgave Rahimdad's crime for his sake. Shaykh Guran and Nur Beg were sent to Gwalior so that Gwalior could be turned over to them." Zahir al-Din Mirza Babur, W. M. Thackston, and Abdur Rahim Khan, *Baburnama: Chaghatay Turkish Text with Abdul-Rahim Khankhanan's Persian Translation* (Cambridge, Mass.: Department of Near Eastern Languages and Civilizations, Harvard University, 1993), 807.
16. Ibid., 653.
17. Although his real name was most likely Bahlul, in the Mughal sources he is referred to as Phul or Pul, which is attributable to a mistake in transcribing the Hindi name into Persian. For the sake of consistency with the sources, Phul or Pul will be used as appropriate.
18. Mirza Haydar and E. Denison Ross, *A History of the Moghuls of Central Asia: Being the Tarikh-i-Rashidi of Mirza Muhammad Haidar, Dughlat*, ed. Ney Elias (Patna, India: Academica Asiatica, 1973), 399.
19. Ibid., 398.
20. The quotation is my translation from Mirza Haydar, *Tarikh-i Rashidi*, ed. 'Abbas Quli Ghaffarifard (Tehran: Markaz-i Nashr-i Miras-i Maktub, 2004), 589–590. For an alternative rendering, see Haydar and Ross, *A History of the Moghuls*, 398–399.

21. Haydar and Ross, *A History of the Moghuls*, 399.
22. Ibid., 399–401.
23. Jawhar Aftabchi, "Tadhkiratu ʾl-Waqiat," in *Three Memoirs of Homayun*, ed. Wheeler M. Thackston (Costa Mesa, Calif.: Mazda, 2009), 79.
24. Ibid., 85.
25. Gulbadan, "Humayunnama," in *Three Memoirs of Homayun*, ed. Wheeler M. Thackston (Costa Mesa, Calif.: Mazda, 2009), 1:29–31.
26. The Shattari technique for invoking "divine names" (*daʿwat al-asmaʾ* in Arabic and also *daʿwat-i ismha* in Persian) involved commanding "spirits" or "agents" (*muwakkil*) associated with the seven planets. In its written version, it is available both in Arabic and in Persian in a work entitled "The Five Jewels" attributed to Shaykh Phul's younger brother Shaykh Muhammad Ghawth Shattari. Apparently, the author first produced the work in Arabic and then himself translated it into Persian. The Arabic version is available in a printed edition. See Muhammad ibn Khatir al-Din Ghawth al-Hindi, *Al-Jawahir al-Khams*, ed. Ahmad Ibn al-ʿAbbas, 2 vols. (Cairo: Muhammad Rifʿat ʿAmir, 1973). It is a popular work that circulated widely, as there are numerous extant manuscript copies for the Persian version. The earliest Persian manuscript I was able to locate, which corresponds closely to the Arabic edition, is thought to date from the eleventh century Hijri (sixteenth century CE). See Muhammad ibn Khatir al-Din Ghawth al-Hindi, "Jawahir-i Khamsa," Markaz-i Tahqiqat-i Farsi-i Iran va Pakistan [Iran Pakistan Institute of Persian Studies], Islamabad, MS 1458.
27. The conditions were very stringent and involved praying, meditation, isolation, fasting, and abstinence from various types of foods, materials, and bodily pleasures. See Ghawth al-Hindi, *Al-Jawahir al-Khams*, 1:95.
28. Muhammad Ghawth's life and miracles are discussed in Kugle, "Heaven's Witness."
29. The five "jewels" have been succinctly described by Carl Ernst as follows: "The *Jawaher-e khamsa* is divided into five parts, each called a *jawhar*, addressing the following topics: (I) on the worship of devotees (*ʿebadat-e ʿabedan*) concerning Qurʾanic verses in supererogatory prayer, required Islamic prayers, and devotions for particular times; (II) on the practices of ascetics (*zohd-e zahedan*), dealing with internal practices that may be attempted after gaining perfection in external devotions; (III) on invocation (*daʿwat*) of the names of God, which requires the instruction of a master; (IV) on the recitations and practices (*adkar o ashghal*) that are distinctive to the mystics of the Shattari path; and (V) the legacy of divine practices belonging to those who have realized the truth. . . . Part I is clearly aimed at the ordinary believer. The succeeding parts increasingly aim at more elite audiences." Carl W. Ernst, "Jawaher-e Khamsa," in *Encyclopaedia Iranica Online* (March 9, 2009), http://www.iranicaonline.org.
30. A significant portion of Muhammad Ghawth's "Ascension Narrative" (*Miʿrajnama*) is translated and discussed in Kugle, "Heaven's Witness." The Prophet's miraculous ascension journey was an important theme for ambitious Muslim mystics, who used it to articulate their own spiritual experiences. An early and famous case is the dream-ascension of the "ecstatic" mystic Bayazid Bistami (d. 874). It is noteworthy, however, that Muhammad Ghawth's initial assertion was that his was not a dream experience but a bodily one.
31. As a major disciple of Shaykh Ghawth, Wajih al-Din ʿAlawi Gujarati explained the

Shattari way: "Repeating the essential name of Allah is the most important method of religious discipline. Recitation of the name Allah should be directed towards your own chest, so that you come to understand that recitation of this Divine name is actually addressing your own essential self, that this Divine name is actually your own name, and this Divine reality is actually your own soul's ultimate reality. [To explain this further, he said] you should consider yourself lofty and exalted, not lowly and humble . . . the Shattari way is painless and effective; it requires no arduous struggle and no deference to formalities. . . . Through the Shattari way Bayazid [Bistami] reached Divine realization without becoming trapped in such ascetic struggles and external formalities. . . . Anyone distracted by formalities and external norms will never achieve intimacy with Allah!" Quoted in ibid., 11.

32. Ibid., 26.
33. Dreaming, it should be recalled from the discussion in chapter 3, was an accepted form of miracle. But the social acceptability of this genre of miracles—that is, its routinization—also reduced its spiritual efficacy and sacred power.
34. Abu al-Fazl ibn Mubarak, *The Akbarnamah*, ed. Maulawi ʿAbd-ur-Rahim, 3 vols. (Calcutta: Asiatic Society of Bengal, 1877–1886), 2:89; Abu al-Fazl ibn Mubarak and Henry Beveridge, *The Akbar Nama of Abu-l-Fazl: History of the Reign of Akbar Including an Account of His Predecessors*, 3 (1 and 2 bound in one) vols. (Calcutta: 1897–1921; repr., Lahore: Sang-e-Meel Publications, 2005), 1–2:642.
35. These observations about the role of "holy men" are inspired by the detailed and subtle work of Peter Brown in his studies of Christianity in late antiquity. See Peter Brown, "The Rise and Function of the Holy Man in Late Antiquity," *Journal of Roman Studies* 61 (1971): 80–101; Peter Brown, "The Rise and Function of the Holy Man in Late Antiquity, 1971–1997," *Journal of Early Christian Studies* 6, no. 3 (1998): 353–376; Peter Brown, "Arbiters of the Holy: The Christian Holy Man in Late Antiquity," in *Authority and the Sacred: Aspects of the Christianisation of the Roman World* (Cambridge: Cambridge University Press, 1995).
36. To get a sense of the social conditions of the time, especially of the martial traditions of the peasants of northern India and their use of seasonal military service to augment their incomes in the "military labor market," from which rulers like the Mughals and their Afghan and Rajput rivals recruited, see D. H. A. Kolff, *Naukar, Rajput, and Sepoy: The Ethnohistory of the Military Labour Market in Hindustan, 1450–1850* (Cambridge: Cambridge University Press, 1990).
37. For a sense of how Islam spread in South Asia, see Richard Maxwell Eaton, *The Rise of Islam and the Bengal Frontier, 1204–1760* (Berkeley: University of California Press, 1993). Also, this was a period where other holy men, such as the founder of the Sikh tradition, Guru Nanak, were expressing an experience of the divine that drew inspiration from the devotional practices of ordinary people while rejecting more formalized aspects of sacred traditions derived from Arabic and Sanskrit texts. See J. S. Grewal, *The Sikhs of the Punjab* (Cambridge: Cambridge University Press, 1990).
38. Carl W. Ernst, "Situating Sufism and Yoga," *Journal of the Royal Asiatic Society* 15 (2005): 15–43; Ernst, "Shattari Sufism."
39. Carl Ernst shows that the Shattari and Chishti orders in South Asia were adept in yogic and tantric practices, subscribing to the idea that control over the world (macrocosm) was possible by controlling the body (microcosm). Furthermore, he argues that Muhammad Ghawth's works did not hide the fact that Sufism and Yoga

were two distinct systems of religious thought and worship but rather showed that they had an affinity for each other. Thus, when non-Islamic provenance of ideas and texts was known, it did not necessarily entail a rejection of their truth or an "Islamicization" of their origins but rather their correlation and translation into Islamic and Sufi ideas. See Carl W. Ernst, "Sufism and Yoga According to Muhammad Ghawth," *Sufi* 29 (1996): 9–13.

40. Carl W. Ernst, *Eternal Garden: Mysticism, History, and Politics at a South Asian Sufi Center* (Albany: State University of New York Press, 1992), 91, 158.

41. A succinct and insightful study that compares written and oral traditions surrounding an important Muslim saint of medieval India is that of Shahid Amin, "On Retelling the Muslim Conquest of North India," in *History and the Present*, ed. Partha Chatterjee and Anjan Ghosh (Delhi: Permanent Black, 2002).

42. Shahid Amin notes several times that the elite hagiographies of Salar Ghazi gave him the attributes of Jesus. However, the interpretation that this was the use of a messianic idiom is my own. Ibid., 25–27.

43. These traditions were collected during colonial times and are still sung in local Indian languages. Since Salar Ghazi's shrine in northern India has existed at least since the fourteenth century, there is good reason to assume continuity in these narratives. Indeed, Shahid Amin points to several remarkable similarities between the recently collected oral traditions and the earlier Persian hagiography that show that these two strands of tradition were operating upon a common base of legends surrounding the mysterious saint. For details, see ibid., 31–41.

44. This is how the Persian hagiography alluded to Salar Ghazi's role as the protector of cattle: "The next day they were preparing, when news arrived that the enemy were driving off the cattle. The Prince [Salar Ghazi] sprang like an angry lion, and beat to arms; buckling on his armour and mounting his horse, he himself put his troops into battle array, and advanced to the attack." *Mirat-i Mas'udi*, quoted in ibid., 38–39.

45. As Amin points out, "In a society such as India where segmentation and division into castes and sub-castes are girdled by marriage rules, to be a part of the wedding procession (*barat*) of [Salar] Ghazi Miyan is to subvert the normal barriers in the creation of community." Ibid., 38.

46. Ibid., 30.

47. This is a nonintuitive observation because it goes against the conventional notion that communal harmony is based on religious tolerance. Several historians of religion, however, have pointed out that, more often than not, communal harmony is based on the threat of religious violence, which is used to maintain communal boundaries and police transgressions and hence sustain intracommunal "peace." See Peter Brown, "The Limits of Intolerance," in *Authority and the Sacred: Aspects of the Christianisation of the Roman World* (Cambridge: Cambridge University Press, 1995). Also see David Nirenberg, *Communities of Violence: Persecution of Minorities in the Middle Ages* (Princeton, N.J.: Princeton University Press, 1996).

48. It has been argued that northern Indian society contained many inner "frontiers" between cultivated, settled areas and uncultivated regions of forest, desert, marshes, and grasslands inhabited by nomadic and warlike societies with their own religious and social practices. Both sides of these frontiers participated in and were structured by seasonal warfare—what has been called the "business of empire." See Jos Gommans, *Mughal Warfare: Indian Frontiers and Highroads to Empire*,

4. THE ALCHEMICAL COURT [279]

1500–1700 (London: Routledge, 2002). For the classic account of how warfare and the "military labor market" structured religious and ethnic identity in this milieu, see Kolff, *Naukar, Rajput, and Sepoy*. For an example of how miracle-working Sufis aided Muslim armies in seventeenth-century Deccan, see Mahmud Baba Shah and Simon Digby, *Sufis and Soldiers in Awrangzeb's Deccan: Malfuzat-i Naqshbandiyya* (New Delhi: Oxford University Press, 2001). In a comparative vein, it is also worth examining the argument made for the role of warrior Sufis and the narratives commemorating their deeds in medieval Anatolia's "frontier society" involving Muslims and Christians; see Cemal Kafadar, *Between Two Worlds: The Construction of the Ottoman State* (Berkeley: University of California Press, 1995).

49. Qamaruddin, *The Mahdawi Movement in India* (Delhi: Idarah-i Adabiyat-i Delhi, 1985). Saiyid Athar Abbas Rizvi, *Muslim Revivalist Movements in Northern India in the Sixteenth and Seventeenth Centuries* (Agra: Agra University, 1965), 68–106. Khaliq Ahmad Nizami, *Akbar and Religion* (Delhi, India: Idarah-i-Adabiyat-i-Delli, 1989), 42–51. Derryl N. MacLean, "The Sociology of Political Engagement: The Mahdawiyah and the State," in *India's Islamic Traditions, 711–1750*, ed. Richard Maxwell Eaton (New Delhi: Oxford University Press, 2003).
50. The story is cited in S. M. Ikram, *Rud-i Kawsar: Islami Hind aur Pakistan ki Mazhabi aur Ruhani Tarikh: Ahd-i Mughaliyya* (Lahore: Firozsons, 1958), 27. Unfortunately, Ikram does not mention his source.
51. Nizami, "Shattariyya."
52. Abu al-Fazl ibn Mubarak and Beveridge, *The Akbar Nama*, 1–2:641–642; Abu al-Fazl ibn Mubarak, *The Akbarnamah*, 2:88.
53. Ghawth al-Hindi, *Al-Jawahir al-Khams*, 1:111.
54. Bada'uni, *Muntakhab al-Tawarikh*, 1:446. I have modified the translation somewhat from Bada'uni et al., *Muntakhabu-t-Tawarikh*, 1:573.
55. From the *Baburnama* it is evident that Babur depended on raiding and conquest to sustain his treasury and army more than on tax collection. In general, imperial bureaucracies were poorly developed in the region at the time and would remain so until the last quarter of the sixteenth century, when a significant degree of administrative rationalization took place in the reigns of Akbar and Shah ʿAbbas in India and Iran, respectively. For Safavid Iran, the state of bureaucracy when it developed under Shah ʿAbbas is discussed in Said Amir Arjomand, *The Turban for the Crown: The Islamic Revolution in Iran* (New York: Oxford University Press, 1988), 17–18. For the administrative developments in Mughal India in the late sixteenth century under Akbar, see John F. Richards, *The Mughal Empire* (Cambridge: Cambridge University Press, 1993), 58–78.
56. To get a sense of the itinerant nature of Mughal kings, see Gommans, *Mughal Warfare*, 99–111.
57. Zahir al-Din Mirza Babur and W. M. Thackston, *The Baburnama: Memoirs of Babur, Prince and Emperor* (New York: Modern Library, 2002), 427. Babur, Thackston, and Khan, *Baburnama (polyglot)*, 746.
58. Babur and Thackston, *Baburnama*, 373.
59. Ibid., 416. Babur, Thackston, and Khan, *Baburnama (polyglot)*, 728.
60. See Finbarr Barry Flood, "Between Cult and Culture: Bamiyan, Islamic Iconoclasm, and the Museum," *Art Bulletin* 84, no. 4 (2002): 647.
61. Haydar and Ross, *A History of the Moghuls*, 469–470.

[280] 4. THE ALCHEMICAL COURT

62. Ibid., 469.
63. Ghiyas al-Din ibn Humam al-Din Khvand Mir, *A Work on the Rules and Ordinances Established by the Emperor Humayun and on Some Buildings Erected by His Order: [Qanun-i Humayuni, Persian Text with Notes and Preface]*, ed. M. Hidayat Hosain (Calcutta: Asiatic Society, 1940).
64. Initially, Khwandamir had served as a historian to the last Timurid sovereign in Herat, Babur's uncle Husayn Bayqara (d. 1506). After the Safavid conquest of Herat, he offered his services to the new regime and thus became an important source for early Safavid history. Later, when Babur had met with success in India, Khwandamir came to his court in 1528 and died in Humayun's reign. His grand chronicle (*Habib al-Siyar*) is an important source of early Safavid and Mughal history.
65. Khwandamir seems to have been careful to use the word "invention" (*ikhtira'*) as opposed to "innovation" (*bida'*), as the latter term connotes deviance from orthodoxy and would have been used by those invoking "universal" Islam to describe Humayun's royal actions as heretical.
66. This table summarizes information from Khvand Mir, *Qanun-i Humayuni*, 24–26.
67. Stephen F. Dale and Alam Payind, "The Ahrari Waqf in Kabul in the Year 1546 and the Mughal Naqshbandiyyah," *Journal of the American Oriental Society* 119, no. 2 (1999): 225.
68. The Safavids intermarried with the powerful Sufi family of the Ni'matullahis. See Hamid Algar and J. Burton-Page, "Ni'mat-allahiyya," in *The Encyclopaedia of Islam*, 2nd ed., ed. P. Bearman, et al. (Brill, 2011), http://www.brillonline.nl.
69. As Said Arjomand has noted, during the first century of Safavid rule the term *'alim* (p. *'ulama'*) meaning "knowledgeable" or "learned" signified two distinct groups of men: the "estate" of broadly educated clerical notables, who were Sunni-Sufis in the pre-Safavid period and served as judges and administrators, and the group of Shi'i religious professionals. The learned notables resented the use of the term *'alim* by the Shi'i newcomers. As these two groups struggled for power, wealth, and position within the emerging Safavid polity, they also began to encroach on each other's knowledge domains. Hence, eminent Sufis such as the Ni'matullahis became upholders of Shi'i truth. The Shi'i jurists, in turn, incorporated in their teachings and practice the miraculous and divinatory knowledge traditionally associated with mysticism and philosophy. Said Amir Arjomand, *The Shadow of God and the Hidden Imam: Religion, Political Order, and Societal Change in Shi'ite Iran from the Beginning to 1890* (Chicago: University of Chicago Press, 1984), 122.
70. According to Khwandamir, the Prophet found *tatayyur* or the practice of taking evil omens to be foul (*mazmum*) but *tafa'ul* or the practice of taking good omens to be praiseworthy (*mahmud*). Khvand Mir, *Qanun-i Humayuni*, 31.
71. The label "Masih" (literally, Messiah, but used to refer to Jesus) was often given to physicians because of the miraculous ability of Jesus to heal the sick.
72. Khvand Mir, *Qanun-i Humayuni*, 34.
73. This table summarizes information from ibid., 34–35.
74. This table summarizes information from ibid., 36–38.
75. See Newman, *Safavid Iran*, 31–32.
76. Safavi, *Tazkira*, 30.
77. This information is summarized from Khvand Mir, *Qanun-i Humayuni*, 44–47.
78. Aftabchi, "Tadhkiratu 'l-Waqiat," 69.

79. See chapter 2 for a brief discussion of the role of the Hurufis in Timur's time. Also, see Shahzad Bashir, *Fazlallah Astarabadi and the Hurufis* (Oxford: Oneworld, 2005).
80. This table summarizes information from Khvand Mir, *Qanun-i Humayuni*, 43. An arrow (*tir* or *sahm*) was a way of casting lots, doing divination, or dividing up a set of things.
81. It should be noted that the production or acquisition of pure alchemical elements such as mercury, which was thought to prolong life, was a passion of many Mughals. Even the most "orthodox" Muslim of them, Aurangzeb, richly patronized a monastery belonging to an order of yogis in return for high-quality mercury. See David Gordon White, *The Alchemical Body: Siddha Traditions in Medieval India* (Chicago: University of Chicago Press, 1996), 1.
82. This table summarizes information from Khvand Mir, *Qanun-i Humayuni*, 48–50.
83. This table summarizes information from ibid., 72–77.
84. Abu Muslim, as mentioned before, became a mythical hero and religious figure in Iran. For a discussion of his widespread cultural significance, especially in connection with "heterodox" ideas and practices, see Babayan, *Mystics, Monarchs, and Messiahs*, 121–60.
85. This correlation between the planets, days, and colors was well known in Persian astrological circles and is also mentioned in the section on astrology in the encyclopedia on 120 "sciences" presented by a scholar from Samarqand to Humayun. Muhammad Fazil Miskin Samarqandi, "Jawahir al-ʿUlum Humayuni," Markaz-i Tahqiqat-i Farsi-i Iran va Pakistan [Iran Pakistan Institute of Persian Studies], Islamabad, MS 301, 494a.
86. Khvand Mir, *Qanun-i Humayuni*, 112.
87. Ibid., 72.
88. Khwandamir, quoted in Eva Orthmann, "Court Culture and Cosmology in the Mughal Empire: Humayun and the Foundations of the Din-i Ilahi," in *Court Cultures in the Muslim World: Seventh to Nineteenth Centuries*, ed. Albrecht Fuess and Jan-Peter Hartung (London: Routledge, 2011), 209. I would like to thank Eva Orthmann for discussing her work with me.
89. Shahzad Bashir, "Shah Ismaʿil and the Qizilbash: Cannibalism in the Religious History of Early Safavid Iran," *History of Religions* 45, no. 3 (2006): 248.
90. For a discussion of Shah Tahmasb's retreat from the open millenarianism of his father and his use of dreams to construct a more sedate aura of saintliness, see Babayan, *Mystics, Monarchs, and Messiahs*, 295–334.
91. See Abu al-Fazl ibn Mubarak, *The Akbarnamah*, 1:205–224; Abu al-Fazl ibn Mubarak and Beveridge, *The Akbar Nama*, 1–2:343–372.
92. Aftabchi, "Tadhkiratu ʾl-Waqiat," 121.
93. Ibid., 64.
94. Indeed, Aftabchi's is the only account that records this ceremony. Neither the account by Humayun's sister, Gulbadan Begum, nor the later chronicles of Akbar's reign mention the incident. This silence in the sources indicates that Jawhar was describing an incident that was embarrassing for the Mughal dynasty.
95. To refuse would be to invite death, as one of Humayun's retainers later did by insulting the Safavid crown. Aftabchi, "Tadhkiratu ʾl-Waqiat," 76.
96. Ibid., 122.
97. Grewal, *Sikhs*, 9.

98. Safavi, *Tazkira*, 45.
99. Guru Nanak, although today known as founder of the Sikh religion, originally propagated a message of devotion to a formless deity without intermediaries and religious functionaries. In this way he belonged to a class of religious mystics, thinkers, and poets whose words were sung and revered over much of India at this time and are often called the *sant panthis* (followers of the true path). Grewal, *Sikhs*, 28-41.
100. For the extensive description of miracles, astrological predictions, and oneiric omens that surrounded Akbar's birth and the role of Humayun and his entourage in producing and perpetuating this lore, see Abu al-Fazl ibn Mubarak and Beveridge, *The Akbar Nama*, 1-2:41-124; Abu al-Fazl ibn Mubarak, *The Akbarnamah*, 1:11-46.
101. Abu al-Fazl ibn Mubarak and Beveridge, *The Akbar Nama*, 1-2:111; Abu al-Fazl ibn Mubarak, *The Akbarnamah*, 1:42. I have modified the translation slightly from Abu al-Fazl ibn Mubarak and Beveridge.

5. THE MILLENNIAL SOVEREIGN: THE TROUBLED UNVEILING OF THE SAVIOR MONARCH

1. The text of the epigraph to this chapter is from Abd al-Qadir ibn Muluk Shah Badaʾuni et al., *Muntakhabu-t-Tawarikh: by ʿAbdul Qadir bin-Muluk Shah Known as al-Badaoni*, 3 vols. (Calcutta: 1884-1925; repr., New Delhi: Atlantic Publishers & Distributors, 1990), 2:323. Abd al-Qadir ibn Muluk Shah Badaʾuni, *Muntakhab-ut-Tawarikh*, 3 vols. (Calcutta: 1864-1869; repr., Osnabruck: Biblio Verlag, 1983), 2:312. The italics are mine.
2. For a review of the literature and the sources on the topic, see Saiyid Athar Abbas Rizvi, *Religious and Intellectual History of the Muslims in Akbar's Reign, with Special Reference to Abul Fazl, 1556-1605* (New Delhi: Munshiram Manoharlal Publishers, 1975), 374-417. Rizvi's review is erudite and comprehensive, but his conclusion reveals his presentist bias. He saw, anachronistically, a "liberal" Akbar struggling against a powerful establishment of Sunni Muslim jurists: "[The Din-i Ilahi] was not a religion and was not even a mystic order. Akbar's religious leadership was limited to preventing the orthodox Sunni ʿUlama from using the state to serve their own ends." Ibid., 415-416. The most recent essay on the subject that moves the analysis forward with new materials is Iqtidar Alam Khan, "Akbar's Personality Traits and World Outlook—A Critical Appraisal," *Social Scientist* 20, no. 9/10 (1992). Khan's article also engages with an important earlier essay by M. Athar Ali, "Akbar and Islam (1581-1605)," in *Islamic Society and Culture: Essays in Honour of Professor Aziz Ahmad*, ed. Milton Israel and N. K. Wagle (New Delhi: Manohar, 1983).
3. Among India's liberal intelligentsia, Akbar has mainly been celebrated as a great figure of history. See, for example, his portrayal as an early modern model of a "secular" ruler in Amartya Kumar Sen, *The Argumentative Indian: Writings on Indian History, Culture, and Identity* (New York: Farrar, Straus and Giroux, 2005), xiii, 41, *passim*. In the Islamicized political atmosphere of Pakistan, however, Akbar has had a more negative reception. See Mubarak Ali, "Akbar in Pakistani Textbooks," *Social Scientist* 20, no. 9/10 (1992): 73-76.

5. THE MILLENNIAL SOVEREIGN [283]

4. Akbar is not only a staple of history books but also of popular culture. He is, for example, the only Mughal emperor with the distinction of having two Bollywood epic films based on his life and legend: *Mughal-e-Azam* (1960) and *Jodhaa Akbar* (2008).
5. This is, in broad terms, the perspective taken in the book-length study by Khaliq Ahmad Nizami, *Akbar and Religion* (Delhi, India: Idarah-i-Adabiyat-i-Delli, 1989). For Akbar's involvement with Sufism, see also Gail Minault Graham, "Akbar and Aurangzeb—Syncretism and Separatism in Mughal India: A Reexamination," *Muslim World* 59, no. 2 (1969): 106–126. The latest contribution on the subject is an essay by Muzaffar Alam, "The Mughals, the Sufi Shaikhs, and the Formation of the Akbari Dispensation," *Modern Asian Studies* 43, no. 1 (2009): 135–174.
6. For an emphasis on the philosophical and metaphysical thought of Akbar's ideologue, Abul Fazl, see Rizvi, *Religious and Intellectual History*, 339–373.
7. John F. Richards, "The Formulation of Imperial Authority Under Akbar and Jahangir," in *Kingship and Authority in South Asia*, ed. John F. Richards (Delhi: Oxford University Press, 1998).
8. The millennium has been treated as a puzzling but negligible phenomenon by previous scholarship on Akbar. Nizami mentioned it only to dismiss it as an idea that is "found in all civilizations." Nizami, *Akbar and Religion*, 213. Rizvi also treated it as insignificant, despite noting that "the orthodox [Muslims], like ancient Persians, believed that the religious systems preached by different religions generally last for one thousand years." Rizvi, *Religious and Intellectual History*, 453. Aziz Ahmad noted that Akbar's "Din-i Ilahi" was one among many millennial (*alfi*) movements of the time but did not elaborate upon this observation. Aziz Ahmad, "Din-i Ilahi," in *The Encyclopaedia of Islam*, 2nd ed., ed. P. Bearman, et al. (Brill, 2011), http://www.brillonline.nl.
9. For a comprehensive treatment of the ʿIbadat Khana and Akbar's interests in various religions see Nizami, *Akbar and Religion*.
10. The *Akbarnama* mentions that there were disturbances but does not give details. Abu al-Fazl ibn Mubarak and Henry Beveridge, *The Akbar Nama of Abu-l-Fazl: History of the Reign of Akbar Including an Account of His Predecessors*, 3 (1 and 2 bound in one) vols. (Calcutta: 1897–1921; repr., Lahore: Sang-e-Meel Publications, 2005), 3:318. Abu al-Fazl ibn Mubarak, *The Akbarnamah*, ed. Maulawi ʿAbd-ur-Rahim, 3 vols. (Calcutta: Asiatic Society of Bengal, 1877–1886), 3:271. Historians have used other sources, such as the Jesuit accounts and Badaʾuni's secret chronicle, to piece together a picture of these rebellions, but it remains uncertain whether the religious controversy was a cause rather than an excuse for rebellion. See Makhanlal Roychoudhury, *The Din-i-Ilahi; Or, the Religion of Akbar* (Calcutta: University of Calcutta, 1941), xxxi n11, 62, 90–92. It has been argued that the emperor's brother in Kabul, Mirza Hakim, also used this opportunity to further his imperial ambitions. See Munis Faruqi, "The Forgotten Prince: Mirza Hakim and the Formation of the Mughal Empire in India," *Journal of the Economic and Social History of the Orient* 48, no. 4 (2005): 487–523.
11. According to Badaʾuni, these rebellious Muslim jurists were assassinated. See Badaʾuni, *Muntakhab al-Tawarikh*, 2:277; Badaʾuni et al., *Muntakhabu-t-Tawarikh*, 2:285.
12. As was discussed in chapter 2, Ibn Khaldun cited earlier astrologers on planetary conjunctions that were interpreted as signaling the end of the Zoroastrian

[284] 5. THE MILLENNIAL SOVEREIGN

dispensation and the beginning of an Islamic one. See Ibn Khaldun, *Muqaddima Ibn Khaldun*, ed. Ihab Muhammad Ibrahim (Cairo: Maktabat al-Quran, 2006), 348–352.

13. Qazi Ahmad Tattavi and Asif Khan Qazvini, *Tarikh-i Alfi*, ed. Ghulam Riza Tabatabai Majd, 8 vols. (Tehran: Shirkat-i Intisharat-i ʿIlmi va Farhangi, 1382 [2003 or 2004]).
14. Ibid., 1:241.
15. E. van Donzel, "Mudjaddid," in *The Encyclopaedia of Islam*, 2nd ed., ed. P. Bearman, et al. (Brill, 2011), http://www.brillonline.nl.
16. Tattavi and Qazvini, *Tarikh-i Alfi*, 1:241. For an explanation of *jafr*, see chapter 2, notes 5 and 39.
17. Shaykh Ahmad Sirhindi, *Maktubat-i Imam-i Rabbani*, 3 vols. (Lucknow: Nawal Kishore Press, 1889). A selection of these letters is also available in Shaykh Ahmad Sirhindi and Fazlur Rahman, *Intikhab-i Maktubat-i Shaykh Ahmad Sirhindi*, 2nd ed. (Lahore, Pakistan: Iqbal Academy, 1984).
18. See Irfan Habib, "The Political Role of Shaikh Ahmad Sirhindi and Shah Waliullah," *Enquiry* 5 (1961): 36–55.
19. As Yohanan Friedmann has shown, Sirhindi's writings stirred up controversy among Muslim religious circles in India and Arabia after he passed away, and it was not until the twentieth century that with the rise of Muslim nationalist feeling in India that his image as orthodox Sunni reformer was constructed and became widely accepted. Yohanan Friedmann, *Shaykh Ahmad Sirhindi: An Outline of His Thought and a Study of His Image in the Eyes of Posterity* (Oxford: Oxford University Press, 2000).
20. Sirhindi wrote: "A thousand odd years after the death of the Prophet a time is coming in which *haqiqat-i muhammadi* [Reality of Muhammad] will ascend from its position and unite with the position of *haqiqat-i kaʿbah* [Reality of Kaʿba]. At this time *haqiqat-i muhammadi* receives the name *haqiqat-i ahmadi* and becomes the Manifestation of the Essence of God (*mazhar-i dhat-i ahad jalla sultanuhu*). Both blessed names [Muhammad and Ahmad] unite with their meaning (*musamma*ʾ). The former position of *haqiqat-i muhammadi* will remain vacant until ʿIsa [Jesus] descends and enacts the *shariʿah* of Muhammad. At that time *haqiqat-iʿisawi* [Reality of Jesus] will ascend from its position and establish itself in the position of *haqiqat-i muhammadi* that had remained vacant." Sirhindi's *Mabdaʾ o Maʿad*, quoted in ibid., 15.
21. Friedman is cautious in his interpretation of Sirhindi's millennial claims, merely noting that Sirhindi's views had an "unorthodox flavor" and that the Sufi leader knew of the "explosive nature of his ideas." Friedman's cautiousness may be attributable to the fact that Sirhindi did not explicitly identify himself in his letters with the millennial Renewer. Nevertheless, given Sirhindi's many hints in his writings at his great but hidden spiritual status and his later reputation as the millennial Renewer, Friedmann is "tempted to ponder whether the sentence 'Muhammad came to be Ahmad' (*muhammad ahmad shud*) and the millennial emergence of the new *haqiqat-i ahmadi* are only a reference to one of Muhammad's names appearing in the Quran, or are also intended to hint at Ahmad Sirhindi's first name." Ibid., 31.
22. In one of his letters, Sirhindi predicted the mahdi's emergence in the year 1100 Hijri, some seventy years into the future (see chapter 6, note 82). By doing so, he seemed to deny that he was the mahdi. Nevertheless, by delaying the mahdi's manifestation to the century after the Islamic millennium, he left open the

possibility that someone else would inaugurate the second Islamic millennium. In this regard, it is worth noting that Sirhindi placed himself high in Islam's mystical hierarchy by claiming to be the *qayyum*. Sirhindi asserted that the *qayyum* was a saintly being of a higher status than even the *qutb* (*axis mundi*) and controlled the rotation of the earth. See Annemarie Schimmel and Burzine K. Waghmar, *The Empire of the Great Mughals: History, Art and Culture*, trans. Corinne Attwood (London: Reaktion Books, 2004), 133. Also, for later Naqshbandi explanations of the concept of *qayyum*, see Annemarie Schimmel, *Pain and Grace: A Study of Two Mystical Writers of Eighteenth-Century Muslim India* (Leiden: E. J. Brill, 1976), 34.

23. The *Rawzat al-Qayyumiyya* by Kamal al-Din Muhammad Ihsan is quoted and discussed in Saiyid Athar Abbas Rizvi, *Muslim Revivalist Movements in Northern India in the Sixteenth and Seventeenth Centuries* (Agra: Agra University, 1965), 293, *passim*. It is worth noting that this tale may be considered apocryphal by modern historians, but to contemporary admirers of Sirhindi in South Asia, it is historical fact.

24. See chapter 3, note 111.

25. For example, in his discussion of Sirhindi's views on Islamic jurisprudence, Friedmann notes that "Discussions of juridical problems are extremely rare in the *Maktubat* and in the other works by Sirhindi. It is noteworthy that while Sirhindi never wearies of describing the minutest details of Sufi experience, his exhortations to comply with the *shariʿah* remain general to an extreme. We rarely find in the *Maktubat* a warning against a concrete infraction of Islamic law common in Sirhindi's time or a reference to a specific legal question." Friedmann, *Sirhindi*, 42.

26. This tradition is discussed further below.

27. Friedmann, *Sirhindi*, 89.

28. Badaʾuni, *Muntakhab al-Tawarikh*, 3:59–61; Badaʾuni et al., *Muntakhabu-t-Tawarikh*, 3:98–101.

29. As the translator notes, "This vague statement may mean that the Shaikh was following the fashion of the time and setting up as Mahdi." Badaʾuni et al., *Muntakhabu-t-Tawarikh*, 99n3. Generally, *sahib-i daʿiyya* means "master of claims" or "possessor of desires." It is based on the word *daʿwat*, meaning a claim, invitation, or invocation. It was used to describe a number of spiritual and political acts, all of which we have seen in previous chapters: a political claim of sovereignty (Chinggis Khan), a spiritual claim and attempt to recruit disciples or devotees to one's cause (the Safavids), and, last but not least, an act of calling upon planetary spirits and capturing *jinns* to do one's bidding (the Shattaris).

30. Badaʾuni, *Muntakhab al-Tawarikh*, 3:61; Badaʾuni et al., *Muntakhabu-t-Tawarikh*, 3:101.

31. I have modified the translation slightly from Abu al-Fazl ibn Mubarak and Beveridge, *The Akbar Nama*, 1–2:45; Abu al-Fazl ibn Mubarak, *The Akbarnamah*, 1:12.

32. The long description of the miracles surrounding Akbar's birth and infancy is given in Abu al-Fazl ibn Mubarak and Beveridge, *The Akbar Nama*, 1–2:508–517. Abu al-Fazl ibn Mubarak, *The Akbarnamah*, 1:347–354.

33. The taj was described in the *Akbarnama* as something that Humayun had designed in Badakhshan as a prince and shown to his father Babur in India, who was bemused. Abu al-Fazl ibn Mubarak and Beveridge, *The Akbar Nama*, 1–2:524. Abu al-Fazl ibn Mubarak, *The Akbarnamah*, 1:360–361.

34. In the *Akbarnama*, Humayun's exile in Iran at the court of Shah Tahmasb was

depicted as a meeting of two great sovereigns. Abu al-Fazl ibn Mubarak, *The Akbarnamah*, 1:205–224; Abu al-Fazl ibn Mubarak and Beveridge, *The Akbar Nama*, 1-2:343–372.

35. Sheila R. Canby, *Humayun's Garden Party: Princes of the House of Timur and Early Mughal Painting* ([Bombay]: Marg Publications, 1994), 20.
36. For a detailed account of the process by which the first imperial manuscript for the *Akbarnama* was put together, see Susan Stronge, *Painting for the Mughal Emperor: The Art of the Book, 1560-1660* (London: Victoria and Albert Museum, 2002), 36-57.
37. Ibid., 42.
38. Abu al-Fazl ibn Mubarak and Beveridge, *The Akbar Nama*, 3:313–321. Abu al-Fazl ibn Mubarak, *The Akbarnamah*, 3:268–273.
39. For a discussion of this decree, called the *mahzar*, which is not given in official Mughal sources but is found in the secret chronicle of Bada'uni, see Nizami, *Akbar and Religion*, 127–129. Also, see S. Nurul Hasan, "The Mahzar of Akbar's Reign," in *Religion, State, and Society in Medieval India: Collected Works of S. Nurul Hasan*, ed. Satish Chandra (New Delhi: 2005).
40. For a review of the juridical concept of *ijtihad*, its changing meaning over time, and the role of a *mujtahid* in the Islamic legal tradition, see Wael B. Hallaq, "Ifta' and Ijithad in Sunni Legal Theory: A Developmental Account," in *Islamic Legal Interpretation: Muftis and Their Fatwas*, ed. Muhammad Khalid Masud, Brinkley Morris Messick, and David Stephan Powers (Karachi: Oxford University Press, 2005).
41. For a discussion of the literature on this topic see Michael Cooperson, *Classical Arabic Biography: The Heirs of the Prophets in the Age of al-Ma'mun* (Cambridge: Cambridge University Press, 2000).
42. See Bada'uni, *Muntakhab al-Tawarikh*, 2:273; Bada'uni et al., *Muntakhabu-t-Tawarikh*, 2:281. Note that I have used the better translation of this passage, given in Abu al-Fazl ibn Mubarak et al., *The A'in-i Akbari* (Lahore: Sang-e-Meel Publications, 2003), 173.
43. It has been suggested that Akbar had some form of dyslexia, making him unsuitable for the types of literary accomplishments that his predecessors and successors were known for. John F. Richards, *The Mughal Empire* (Cambridge: Cambridge University Press, 1993), 35.
44. Abu al-Fazl ibn Mubarak et al., *The A'in-i Akbari*, 1147. Abu al-Fazl ibn Mubarak, *A'in-i Akbari*, ed. Sir Sayyid Ahmad (Aligarh: Sir Sayyid Academy, Aligarh Muslim University, 2005), 585; Abu al-Fazl ibn Mubarak, *A'in-i Akbari*, ed. H. Blochmann (Calcutta: Asiatic Society of Bengal, 1877), 2:233. For a discussion of Akbar's "illiteracy," see Vincent Arthur Smith, *Akbar the Great Mogul, 1542-1605*, 2nd ed. (Oxford: Clarendon Press, 1919), 41, 337–338.
45. Abu al-Fazl ibn Mubarak and Beveridge, *The Akbar Nama*, 3:313. Abu al-Fazl ibn Mubarak, *The Akbarnamah*, 3:268.
46. This spiritual experience of Akbar occurred in 1578, the year before the "Mujtahid" proclamation. Abu al-Fazl ibn Mubarak and Beveridge, *The Akbar Nama*, 3:279–280. Abu al-Fazl ibn Mubarak, *The Akbarnamah*, 3:241.
47. Abu al-Fazl ibn Mubarak and Beveridge, *The Akbar Nama*, 3:315. Abu al-Fazl ibn Mubarak, *The Akbarnamah*, 3:269.
48. Abu al-Fazl ibn Mubarak and Beveridge, *The Akbar Nama*, 3:316. Abu al-Fazl ibn Mubarak, *The Akbarnamah*, 3:270.

49. Abu al-Fazl ibn Mubarak and Beveridge, *The Akbar Nama*, 3:313. Abu al-Fazl ibn Mubarak, *The Akbarnamah*, 3:268.
50. Abu al-Fazl ibn Mubarak and Beveridge, *The Akbar Nama*, 3:316. Abu al-Fazl ibn Mubarak, *The Akbarnamah*, 3:270.
51. Bada'uni, *Muntakhab al-Tawarikh*, 2:268; Bada'uni et al., *Muntakhabu-t-Tawarikh*, 2:276.
52. The chronicle neither gives the names of these men nor their group identity but simply refers to them as "of the school of Nosair," meaning that they had a tendency toward *ghulat* (exaggeration), since the Nosairis were known as a group that revered Ali as divine. The chronicle also compares the spiritual enthusiasm of these men to that of Hallaj (Husain ibn Mansur), who is well known for having made the claim that "I am Truth" (*ana al-haqq*). See Abu al-Fazl ibn Mubarak and Beveridge, *The Akbar Nama*, 3:319n2–3.
53. *Sulh-i kull*, a unique expression used in the *Akbarnama* to indicate an accommodative attitude toward all religious traditions, is commonly translated idiomatically as "peace with all," but a literal and more appropriate translation would be "total peace" or "universal peace," where *kull* means total or universal, as opposed to *juzw*, meaning component or particular. Saiyid Athar Abbas Rizvi, "Dimensions of *Sulh-i kul* (Universal Peace) in Akbar's Reign and the Sufi Theory of Perfect Man," in *Akbar and His Age*, ed. Iqtidar Alam Khan (New Delhi: Northern Book Centre, 1999).
54. Abu al-Fazl ibn Mubarak and Beveridge, *The Akbar Nama*, 3:321. Abu al-Fazl ibn Mubarak, *The Akbarnamah*, 3:273.
55. I have modified the translation somewhat from Abu al-Fazl ibn Mubarak et al., *The A'in-i Akbari*, 159. Abu al-Fazl ibn Mubarak, *A'in-i Akbari*, 146–147.
56. The following list is adapted from Abu al-Fazl ibn Mubarak et al., *The A'in-i Akbari*, 160. Abu al-Fazl ibn Mubarak, *A'in-i Akbari*, 148.
57. The seventeenth-century encyclopedia on "comparative religions" written in Mughal India by a Zoroastrian scholar, the Dabistan-i Mazahib (School of Religions), also noted that many such practices were followed by certain Alid sects that can be described as "exaggerators" or *ghulat*. See Muhsin Fani, *Dabistan-i Mazahib*, ed. Rahim Rizazadah Malik, 2 vols. (Tehran: Kitabkhanah-i Tahuri, 1362 [1983]), 1:266–267. For *ghulat*, see chapter 2, notes 59, 118; and chapter 3, note 89.
58. For a discussion of an "imagistic" mode of religiosity and its importance in the transmission of knowledge and social memory, see Harvey Whitehouse, *Modes of Religiosity: A Cognitive Theory of Religious Transmission* (Walnut Creek, Calif.: AltaMira Press, 2004).
59. See note 43, above.
60. Smith, *Akbar*, 337.
61. For the concept of *bricolage* as it applies to a specific mode of thought and practice, see the chapter on "The Science of the Concrete" in Claude Levi-Strauss, *The Savage Mind* (Chicago: University of Chicago Press, 1966), 1–34. Also see discussion in chapter 2, note 101.
62. See the discussion on the political and social role of "holy men" in chapter 4, note 35.
63. John Correia-Afonso, *Letters from the Mughal Court: The First Jesuit Mission to Akbar, 1580-1583* (Bombay: Published for the Heras Institute of Indian History and Culture by Gujarat Sahitya Prakash, Anand, 1980), 1. In spite of being written with an

obvious partiality, the Jesuit letters are considered to have a high historiographical value. See John Correia-Afonso, *Jesuit Letters and Indian History, 1542-1773*, 2nd ed. (Bombay: Oxford University Press, 1969), 71-99.
64. Nizami, *Akbar and Religion*, 27.
65. For the Portuguese experience in South Asia, see M. N. Pearson, *The Portuguese in India* (Cambridge: Cambridge University Press, 1987).
66. Correia-Afonso, *Letters*, 8. There is a discrepancy in the dates of the mission between the *Akbarnama* and the Jesuit account. Most likely the *Akbarnama* dates are incorrect. See the discussion in Abu al-Fazl ibn Mubarak and Beveridge, *The Akbar Nama*, 3:296n4.
67. For a detailed description of the priests of the first mission, see Edward Maclagan, *The Jesuits and the Great Mogul* (London: Burns, Oates & Washbourne, 1932), 25-26.
68. The Jesuit letters are full of detail about how Akbar always treated the Jesuits and their traditions with the greatest of respect and made his sons and courtiers do the same. For example, see Acquaviva's letter in Correia-Afonso, *Letters*, 26-41.
69. Ibid., 83-84.
70. Ibid., 58. He also granted the Jesuits many public favors: he let them openly convert anyone to Christianity, allowed them to conduct a Christian funeral in public, and even promised to build a charity hospital for the priests to run (he did not keep this particular pledge). Ibid., 63-70.
71. They wrote to their superiors that the emperor had led them in private to believe that once convinced of the truth of Christianity, no worldly possession would stand between him and the true faith. Ibid., 64.
72. Ibid., 43.
73. Ibid., 57-58.
74. Ibid., 44.
75. Abu al-Fazl ibn Mubarak and Beveridge, *The Akbar Nama*, 3:296. Abu al-Fazl ibn Mubarak, *The Akbarnamah*, 3:254-255.
76. Bada'uni wrote, "His Majesty sent Shaikh Jamal Bakhtyar to bring Shaikh Qutbuddin of Jalesar who, though a wicked man, pretended to be 'attracted by God.' When Qutbuddin came, the emperor brought him to a conference with some Christian priests, and rationalists, and some other great authorities of the age. After a discussion, the Shaikh exclaimed, 'Let us make a great fire, and in the presence of His Majesty I shall pass through it. And if anyone else gets safely through, he proves by it the truth of his religion.' The fire was made. The Shaikh pulled one of the Christian priests by the coat, and said to him, 'Come on, in the name of God!' But none of the priests had the courage to go." Bada'uni, quoted in Abu al-Fazl ibn Mubarak et al., *The A'in-i Akbari*, 175. Also see Bada'uni, *Muntakhab al-Tawarikh*, 2:299; Bada'uni et al., *Muntakhabu-t-Tawarikh*, 2:308.
77. Maclagan, *Jesuits and the Great Mogul*, 31.
78. Ibid., 24.
79. Correia-Afonso, *Letters*, 52-53.
80. Ibid., 81-82.
81. For the warrior ascetic tradition in Hinduism and its history within the Mughal empire, see William R. Pinch, *Warrior Ascetics and Indian Empires* (New York: Cambridge University Press, 2006).
82. Abul Fazl, quoted in Nizami, *Akbar and Religion*, 103-04.

5. THE MILLENNIAL SOVEREIGN [289]

83. Abu al-Fazl ibn Mubarak et al., *The Aʾin-i Akbari*, 190. Abu al-Fazl ibn Mubarak, *Aʾin-i Akbari*, 150.
84. Badaʾuni, *Muntakhab al-Tawarikh*, 2:299; Badaʾuni et al., *Muntakhabu-t-Tawarikh*, 2:308–309.
85. Akbar was not unique in overseeing religious competition that sometimes turned deadly. See the example of his Safavid contemporary Shah ʿAbbas in note 121.
86. Correia-Afonso, *Letters*, 126.
87. Ibid.
88. These reports about Akbar are found in multiple sources, often in eyewitness accounts of those who had seen the emperor participate in their religious rites. These are also well documented and analyzed in Nizami, *Akbar and Religion*. Many of these accounts are corroborated by the critical, accusatory, and defamatory chronicle of Badaʾuni, discussed in detail below. Badaʾuni's accusations against Akbar are extracted and quoted selectively in a translator's note in Abu al-Fazl ibn Mubarak et al., *The Aʾin-i Akbari*, 160–187. The original text is Badaʾuni, *Muntakhab al-Tawarikh*, 2:198–407; Badaʾuni et al., *Muntakhabu-t-Tawarikh*, 2:200–421.
89. Correia-Afonso, *Letters*, 114–115.
90. Muhammad Hashim Khafi Khan, *Muntakhab al-Lubab*, part 1, ed. Mawlavi Kabir al-Din Ahmad (Calcutta: Asiatic Society of Bengal, 1869), 197.
91. Badaʾuni et al., *Muntakhabu-t-Tawarikh*, 2:309; Badaʾuni, *Muntakhab al-Tawarikh*, 2:300.
92. Badaʾuni, *Muntakhab al-Tawarikh*, 2:301; Badaʾuni et al., *Muntakhabu-t-Tawarikh*, 2:310.
93. Badaʾuni, *Muntakhab al-Tawarikh*, 2:302; Badaʾuni et al., *Muntakhabu-t-Tawarikh*, 2:311.
94. Badaʾuni, *Muntakhab al-Tawarikh*, 2:302; Badaʾuni et al., *Muntakhabu-t-Tawarikh*, 2:311.
95. Badaʾuni, *Muntakhab al-Tawarikh*, 2:303; Badaʾuni et al., *Muntakhabu-t-Tawarikh*, 2:313.
96. I have modified the translation somewhat for readability. Badaʾuni, *Muntakhab al-Tawarikh*, 2:307; Badaʾuni et al., *Muntakhabu-t-Tawarikh*, 2:316–317. Also, according to Badaʾuni the following two verses for Firdausi's *Shahnama*, which derided Arabs and lamented their ascendancy over the Persians with the coming of Islam, were frequently quoted at court: "Through the tasting of the milk of camels and lizards / The Arabs have made such progress, / That they now wish to get hold of the kingdom of Persia. / Fie upon Fate! Fie upon Fate!" See Badaʾuni, *Muntakhab al-Tawarikh*, 2:307; Badaʾuni et al., *Muntakhabu-t-Tawarikh*, 2:317.
97. The category of the holy man absorbed in God (*majzub*) is a well-known one. In previous chapters, we have seen how such men played a public role, giving omens and blessings to great sovereigns such as Timur. For a later case study of a "holy fool" in India, see Nile Green, "Transgressions of a Holy Fool: A Majzub in Colonial India," in *Islam in South Asia in Practice*, ed. Barbara Metcalf (Princeton, N.J.: Princeton University Press, 2009). Also, as far as Akbar's saintly status is concerned, note that his tomb was considered by many to have the same spiritual protective powers that shrines of saints possessed. See Z. A. Desai, "A Foreign Dignitary's Ceremonial Visit to Akbar's Tomb: A First Hand Account," in *Akbar and His Age*, ed. Iqtidar Alam Khan (New Delhi: Northern Book Centre, 1999).

98. Badaʾuni, *Muntakhab al-Tawarikh*, 2:313; Badaʾuni et al., *Muntakhabu-t-Tawarikh*, 2:323.
99. An eminent courtier of Akbar, the scholar Shaykh Mubarak, father of the emperor's favorite Abul Fazl, was said to have been a Mahdavi. Qamaruddin, *The Mahdawi Movement in India* (Delhi: Idarah-i Adabiyat-i Delhi, 1985), 169. However, there is no indication that Mubarak's son Abul Fazl—Badaʾuni's courtly rival—had an inclination toward the movement. In fact, Abul Fazl denied Sayyid Muhammad Jaunpuri's claim to mahdiship but accepted him as a learned scholar and accomplished mystic. See ibid., 54. For Badaʾuni's connection to the Mahdavis, see below and also Fauzia Zareen Abbas, *Abdul Qadir Badauni, as a Man and Historiographer* (Delhi: Idarah-i Adabiyat-i Delli, 1987), 6–10.
100. Derryl N. MacLean, "The Sociology of Political Engagement: The Mahdawiyah and the State," in *India's Islamic Traditions, 711–1750*, ed. Richard Maxwell Eaton (New Delhi: Oxford University Press, 2003).
101. By the time of the emperor Aurangzeb (r. 1658–1707), MacLean argues, the Mahdavis were generally perceived as Sunni Muslims whose only difference from the mainstream community was their belief that the mahdi had come and gone.
102. Badaʾuni described his experience thus: "At the time of his [Shaykh ʿAlai's] arrival at the township of Basawar from Baiana, my late father took me, the writer of these pages, to do homage to him. In consequence of my tender years, his form remained fixed in my memory as a dream or a vision." Badaʾuni, *Muntakhab al-Tawarikh*, 1:399; Badaʾuni et al., *Muntakhabu-t-Tawarikh*, 1:512.
103. Badaʾuni, *Muntakhab al-Tawarikh*, 1:408; Badaʾuni et al., *Muntakhabu-t-Tawarikh*, 1:524.
104. Badaʾuni, *Muntakhab al-Tawarikh*, 1:409; Badaʾuni et al., *Muntakhabu-t-Tawarikh*, 1:525.
105. Badaʾuni inserted a sarcastic report about Shaykh Niyazi's cowardice under torture: "Miyan ʿAbdullah [Niyazi] did wonderfully well in sending the unfortunate Shaikh ʿAlaʾi to his death, while he himself withdrew his steps from the circle." Badaʾuni, *Muntakhab al-Tawarikh*, 3:46; Badaʾuni et al., *Muntakhabu-t-Tawarikh*, 3:77.
106. Badaʾuni, *Muntakhab al-Tawarikh*, 3:51; Badaʾuni et al., *Muntakhabu-t-Tawarikh*, 3:84.
107. Badaʾuni, *Muntakhab al-Tawarikh*, 3:51; Badaʾuni et al., *Muntakhabu-t-Tawarikh*, 3:85.
108. When Badaʾuni turned twenty, he was sent to study Sufi mysticism and esoteric knowledge with Shaykh Abul Fath Gujarati. It was under this Mahdavi's tutelage that he had his first intense mystical experience: "I received instructions in the ecstatic worship [*zikr*] of the Sufis, and was employed for some time therein, and the (inner) meaning of the Qurʾan was disclosed to me, and for some time my condition was such that I believed every sound and voice which fell upon my ears to be the mystic chanting of the Sufis." Badaʾuni, *Muntakhab al-Tawarikh*, 3:47; Badaʾuni et al., *Muntakhabu-t-Tawarikh*, 3:78.
109. Qamaruddin, *Mahdawi Movement*, 53–54.
110. Badaʾuni's treatise has been described as a "Sufi ethical manual." This categorization, however, does not fully express its diverse and wide-ranging content. The work is divided into hundreds of small sections that treat a wide ranging mix of practical and spiritual subjects: descriptions of sins such as polytheism and wine drinking; proper conduct such as in a mosque; heresies related to groups of Shiʿa, *ghulat*, and philosophers; rules for appropriate sexual relations; and even the danger of

relieving oneself over a hole in a rock lest there be a snake or scorpion hidden inside it. Badaʾuni wrote that he composed much of this work while on the road, where he did not have access to references and thus had to rely on memory for most of the quotes. Moreover, he admitted that part of the material of the book came from a draft left behind by his fellow courtier and friend Mirza Nizam al-Din. Badaʾuni did not specify, however, which parts of the book were original and which were borrowed, taking full responsibility for its authorship.

111. The discussion below is based on Abd al-Qadir ibn Muluk Shah Badaʾuni, *Najat al-Rashid* (Lahore: Idarah-i Tahqiqat-i Pakistan, Danishgah-i Panjab, 1972), 70–83. For an English translation of a selection of this Persian text, see A. Azfar Moin, "Challenging the Mughal Emperor: The Islamic Millennium According to ʿAbd al-Qadir Badayuni," in *Islam in South Asia in Practice*, ed. Barbara Metcalf (Princeton, N.J.: Princeton University Press, 2009).
112. See chapter 2, notes 119 and 120.
113. Badaʾuni, *Najat al-Rashid*, 327.
114. The argument below quotes, paraphrases, and translates from ibid., 326–329.
115. For a discussion of Ibn ʿArabi's complex millennial views, in which he indirectly claimed to be the awaited messiah, see Gerald T. Elmore, "The 'Millennial' Motif in Ibn al-ʿArabi's 'Book of the Fabulous Gryphon,'" *Journal of Religion* 81, no. 3 (2001): 410–437.
116. The twelfth-century polymath and expert on India Al-Biruni critiqued Abu Maʿshar for promoting Indic concepts of time as Islamic. Muhammad ibn Ahmad Biruni and Ainslie Thomas Embree, *Alberuni's India*, abridged ed. (New York: Norton, 1971), 325. Regardless of this critique, Abu Maʿshar's astrological theories became the mainstay of premodern astrology across Asia and Europe. See Jaʿfar ibn Muhammad Abu Maʿshar, *On Historical Astrology: The Book of Religions and Dynasties (On the Great Conjunctions)*, trans. Keiji Yamamoto and Charles Burnett, 2 vols. (Boston: Brill, 2000), xiv.
117. Tattavi and Qazvini, *Tarikh-i Alfi*, 1:381–383.
118. Kathryn Babayan, *Mystics, Monarchs, and Messiahs: Cultural Landscapes of Early Modern Iran* (Cambridge, Mass.: Harvard University Press, 2002), 349.
119. Ibid., 443–449.
120. Shahzad Bashir, "Shah Ismaʿil and the Qizilbash: Cannibalism in the Religious History of Early Safavid Iran," *History of Religions* 45, no. 3 (2006): 249.
121. Jean Calmard, "Shiʿi Rituals and Power II: The Consolidation of Safavid Shiʿism: Folklore and Popular Religion," in *Safavid Persia: The History and Politics of an Islamic Society*, ed. Charles P. Melville (London: I. B. Tauris, 1996), 145–147.
122. It is not surprising that given their focus on the mystical properties of letters, the Nuqtavis were perceived by some as "Hermetics" (followers of Hermes) and as followers of Pythagoras, who had also believed in the occult properties of numbers and in the transmigration of the soul. See Babayan, *Mystics, Monarchs, and Messiahs*, 68–78. Also see Toufic Fahd, "Huruf (ʿIlm al-)," in *The Encyclopaedia of Islam*, 2nd ed., ed. P. Bearman, et al. (Brill, 2011), http://www.brillonline.nl. Hermeticism is discussed further in chapter 7.
123. Hamid Algar, "Nuktawiyya," in *The Encyclopaedia of Islam*, 2nd ed., ed. P. Bearman, et al. (Brill, 2011), http://www.brillonline.nl. Also, the Safavid court chronicles depict the Nuqtavis as part of a chain of heresies beginning with the two "gnostic

reformers" of Zoroastrianism, Mani and Mazdak. Babayan, *Mystics, Monarchs, and Messiahs*, 48.
124. Babayan, *Mystics, Monarchs, and Messiahs*, 103.
125. Ibid., xxxiv.
126. Ibid., lii.
127. Ibid., 104–105.
128. As Shah ʿAbbas's chronicler Iskandar Beg Munshi related how in the Year of the Serpent, 1002 AH/1593–1594 AD: "Astrologers had declared that the stars predicted the death this year of an eminent personage, probably in Iran, and the signs further indicated that this personage would be a royal one. . . . Mowlana Jala al-Din Mohammad Yazdi, who was the outstanding astrologer of his age, suggested to the Shah the following plan: during the three days when the influence of the conjunction and quadrature of the two inauspicious planets was at its height, the Shah [ʿAbbas I] should divest himself of his kingly status and raise to the throne some criminal under sentence of death. . . . At the end of the three days, the temporary monarch should be executed." Iskandar Beg Munshi, *The History of Shah ʿAbbas the Great: Tarikh-e Alamara-ye ʿAbbasi*, trans. Roger Savory, 2 vols. (Boulder, Colo.: Westview, 1978), 2:648.
129. For a description of the entire episode and this quote from Iskandar Beg Munshi's chronicle, See Babayan, *Mystics, Monarchs, and Messiahs*, 3–6.
130. Munshi, *History of Shah ʿAbbas*, 2:650.
131. This letter is available in Persian in the appendix of Nizami, *Akbar and Religion*, 379–380. It is also translated in summary and commented upon in Riazul Islam, *A Calendar of Documents on Indo-Persian Relations*, 2 vols. (Tehran: Iranian Culture Foundation and Institute of Central & West Asian Studies, 1979), 1:101–102.
132. This letter from Akbar to Shah ʿAbbas is summarized in Islam, *Calendar of Documents*, 1:123–124. It is given in full in Akbar's chronicle, Abu al-Fazl ibn Mubarak and Beveridge, *The Akbar Nama*, 3:785–790. Abu al-Fazl ibn Mubarak, *The Akbarnamah*, 3:656–661.
133. Iskandar Beg Munshi quoted in Islam, *Calendar of Documents*, 1:124.
134. Badaʾuni, *Muntakhab al-Tawarikh*, 2:246; Badaʾuni et al., *Muntakhabu-t-Tawarikh*, 2:253. While the official chronicle of Akbar's reign does not identify Mir Sharif Amuli as a Nuqtavi, he is mentioned several times as a nobleman and appointee to various administrative positions. He was well known to be a Nuqtavi and as "heretic of the age" in other Mughal sources. See translator's note in Abu al-Fazl ibn Mubarak et al., *The Aʾin-i Akbari*, 386–387.
135. Badaʾuni et al., *Muntakhabu-t-Tawarikh*, 2:254; Badaʾuni, *Muntakhab al-Tawarikh*, 2:247.
136. Badaʾuni, *Muntakhab al-Tawarikh*, 2:248; Badaʾuni et al., *Muntakhabu-t-Tawarikh*, 2:255.
137. Badaʾuni et al., *Muntakhabu-t-Tawarikh*, 2:295; Badaʾuni, *Muntakhab al-Tawarikh*, 2:287.
138. On *jafr*, see chapter 2, notes 5 and 39.
139. Badaʾuni et al., *Muntakhabu-t-Tawarikh*, 2:295; Badaʾuni, *Muntakhab al-Tawarikh*, 2:287.
140. For an insightful analysis of how some of Akbar's edicts were interpreted, enacted, or resisted during and after his reign, see Khan, "Akbar's Personality."

141. For an analysis of how Rama came to dominate the political imagination of precolonial India, especially after the advent of Turkish power, see Sheldon Pollock, "Ramayana and Political Imagination in India," *Journal of Asian Studies* 52, no. 2 (1993): 261–297. For an examination of how Akbar was incorporated into Rajput cosmology via the myth of Rama, see Norman Ziegler, "Some Notes on Rajput Loyalties During the Mughal Period," in *Kingship and Authority in South Asia*, ed. John F. Richards (Delhi: Oxford University Press, 1998).
142. Bada'uni, *Muntakhab al-Tawarikh*, 2:326. Bada'uni et al., *Muntakhabu-t-Tawarikh*, 2:336. For a survey of this and other Sanskrit works translated into Persian under Akbar, see Carl W. Ernst, "Muslim Studies of Hinduism? A Reconsideration of Arabic and Persian Translations from Indian Languages," *Iranian Studies* 36, no. 2 (2003): 178–183. The other great Indian "epic," the *Mahabharata*, was also among these translated texts. In the Persian rendering of the *Mahabharata*, Akbar was mentioned and praised by name, and aspects of the Mughal emperor's miraculous genealogy, such as the impregnation by divine light of the Mongol princess Alanquva, were apparently reflected in the story of the birth of the Karna, the son of Kunti and Surya, the sun god. See Audrey Truschke, "The Mughal *Book of War*: A Persian Translation of the Sanskrit *Mahabharata*," *Comparative Studies of South Asia, Africa, and the Middle East* 31, no. 2 (2011): 518–519.
143. Bada'uni, *Muntakhab al-Tawarikh*, 2:337. Bada'uni et al., *Muntakhabu-t-Tawarikh*, 2:347.
144. The political salience of the Mughal dynasty's relationship with the Chishti Sufi order is succinctly reviewed in Richards, "Imperial Authority." For the foundational figure of the Chishtis in South Asia, see P. M. Currie, *The Shrine and Cult of Muin al-Din Chishti of Ajmer* (Delhi: Oxford University Press, 1989).
145. See Alam, "The Mughals," 166. Muzaffar Alam, "The Debate Within: A Sufi Critique of Religious Law, Tasawwuf, and Politics in Mughal India," *South Asian History and Culture* 2, no. 2 (2011): 148.

6. THE THRONE OF TIME: THE PAINTED MIRACLES OF THE SAINT EMPEROR

1. Banarasidas, quoted in Muzaffar Alam and Sanjay Subrahmanyam, "Witnessing Transition: Views on the End of the Akbari Dispensation," in *The Making of History: Essays Presented to Irfan Habib*, ed. K. N. Panikkar, T. J. Byres, and Utsa Patnaik (London: Anthem, 2002), 106–107. Banarasidas's account has been translated along with a gloss and commentary in Mukunda Latha, *Ardhakathanaka, Half a Tale: A Study in the Interrelationship Between Autobiography and History* (Jaipur: Rajasthan Prakrit Bharati Sansthan, 1981).
2. For an account of Jahangir during his days as a prince, which follows contemporary Mughal sources closely, see Francis Gladwin, *The History of Jahangir*, ed. K. V. Rangaswami Aiyangar (Madras: B. G. Paul & Co., 1930), 1–19.
3. See an edict of Jahangir in his days as a rebellious prince in Jalaluddin, "Sultan Salim (Jahangir) as a Rebel King," *Islamic Culture* 47 (1973): 121–125.

4. Akbar's other two sons were Sultan Murad (d. 1598) and Sultan Daniyal (d. 1604). Both reportedly died of alcoholism.
5. This comment is found in the preface added to Jahangir's memoirs by the eighteenth-century historian Muhammad Hadi. See Muhammad-Hadi, "Preface to the Jahangirnama by Muhammad-Hadi," in *The Jahangirnama: Memoirs of Jahangir, Emperor of India*, ed. W. M. Thackston (Washington, D.C.: Freer Gallery of Art, 1999), 11.
6. This edict was copied in a chronicle titled *Tazkirat al-Muluk* by Rafiuddin Ibrahim Shirazi (d. 1626), who wrote it in Bijapur in Jahangir's reign. This passage is quoted in Iqtidar Alam Khan, "Akbar's Personality Traits and World Outlook—A Critical Appraisal," *Social Scientist* 20, no. 9/10 (1992): 26.
7. See Fernão Guerreiro, *Jahangir and the Jesuits: With an Account of the Travels of Benedict Goes and the Mission to Pegu, from the Relations of Father Fernao Guerreiro, S. J*, trans. Charles Herbert Payne (New York: R. M. McBride & Co., 1930), 3. The Jesuit letter dated September 1606 that formed the basis of this report is extensively quoted in Muzaffar Alam and Sanjay Subrahmanyam, "Frank Disputations: Catholics and Muslims in the Court of Jahangir," *Indian Economic Social History Review* 45, no. 4 (2009): 476.
8. This is how Gauvin Bailey compares the differences in Akbar and Jahangir's approach toward Christian art: "Whereas Akbar allowed Christian figures to populate his eclectic artistic landscape—at times in a religious context and at times in a more secular setting—Salim [i.e., Jahangir] consistently demanded that the works' devotional meanings and stylistic integrity be kept intact. His seems to have been a concern for the iconic and talismanic—for the power of images as embodiments of the divine—and he showed less and less interest in their narrative aspect." Gauvin Alexander Bailey, *The Jesuits and the Grand Mogul: Renaissance Art at the Imperial Court of India, 1580-1630* (Washington, D.C.: Freer Gallery of Art and Arthur M. Sackler Gallery, 1998), 30.
9. For a sense of Raja Man Singh's position in the empire, see Catherine B. Asher, "The Architecture of Raja Man Singh: A Study of Sub-Imperial Patronage," in *Architecture in Medieval India: Forms, Contexts, Histories*, ed. Monica Juneja (Delhi: Permanent Black 2001).
10. For a detailed account of the Jesuit's view on the moment of Jahangir's accession, see Alam and Subrahmanyam, "Witnessing Transition," 108–112.
11. Jahangir and W. M. Thackston, *The Jahangirnama: Memoirs of Jahangir, Emperor of India* (Washington, D.C.: Freer Gallery of Art, 1999), 22. Jahangir and Muhammad Hashim, *Jahangirnamah, Tuzuk-i Jahangiri*, Intisharat-i Bunyad-i Farhang-i Iran ([Tehran]: Bunyad-i Farhang-i Iran, 1980 [1359]), 2.
12. Jahangir and Hashim, *Jahangirnamah*, 18. Jahangir and Thackston, *Jahangirnama*, 35. The eighteenth-century historian Muhammad-Hadi quoted a slightly different variant of the same dream: "I have seen His Holiness Khwaja Baha'uddin [Naqshband] in a dream . . . and he said, 'Soon Sultan Salim [i.e., Jahangir] will mount the throne, causing the world to flourish in justice and equity and giving the grief-stricken cause for rejoicing with his generosity and liberality.'" Muhammad-Hadi, "Preface to the Jahangirnama," 15.
13. Jahangir and Thackston, *Jahangirnama*, 59. Jahangir and Hashim, *Jahangirnamah*, 42.
14. Jahangir and Thackston, *Jahangirnama*, 250–251. Jahangir and Hashim, *Jahangirnamah*, 249–250.

15. Jahangir and Thackston, *Jahangirnama*, 59. Jahangir and Hashim, *Jahangirnamah*, 42.
16. For a historical treatment of the circumstances surrounding the death of Guru Arjan, see Louis E. Fenech, "Martyrdom and the Sikh Tradition," *Journal of the American Oriental Society* 117, no. 4 (1997): 623–642.
17. See letter 193 in Shaykh Ahmad Sirhindi, *Maktubat-i Imam-i Rabbani*, 3 vols. (Lucknow: Nawal Kishore Press, 1889), 1:11–13. The Persian text is also quoted in Saiyid Athar Abbas Rizvi, *Muslim Revivalist Movements in Northern India in the Sixteenth and Seventeenth Centuries* (Agra: Agra University, 1965), 249–250.
18. Jahangir and Thackston, *Jahangirnama*, 304. Jahangir and Hashim, *Jahangirnamah*, 309. Jahangir had given his servant Anup Rai the Hindi title of Ani Rai Singhdalan (Commander Lion Crusher), after the man had fought off a huge lion with his bare hands during an imperial hunt.
19. Many of these soldiers were from Badakhshan, Babur's hereditary territory in Central Asia. Jahangir and Thackston, *Jahangirnama*, 50. Jahangir and Hashim, *Jahangirnamah*, 32.
20. Even the Jesuits recorded this turn of affairs: "the King is now not as much of a Moor as he showed himself to be at the start, rather he has clearly said that he will follow the path of his father, and he shows this clearly through his works. This is far less bad (*menos mal he isto*)." Quoted in Alam and Subrahmanyam, "Frank Disputations," 477.
21. Jahangir and Thackston, *Jahangirnama*, 36–44, 53. Jahangir and Hashim, *Jahangirnamah*, 19–20, 35–36.
22. Jahangir and Thackston, *Jahangirnama*, 53. Jahangir and Hashim, *Jahangirnamah*, 36.
23. Although born of Persian stock, the mirza was called Nathan probably because of the very Indian practice of wearing a "nath" or nose ring as a symbol of a votive offering that may have warded off childhood illness. See the translator's introduction to Mirza Nathan, *Baharistan-i-Ghaybi: A History of the Mughal Wars in Assam, Cooch Behar, Bengal*, trans. Moayyidul Islam Borah and Suryya Kumar Bhuyan (Gauhati: The Government of Assam, Department of Historical and Antiquarian Studies, Narayani Handiqui Historical Institute, 1936). This dream incident involving Nathan and Jahangir is discussed in detail in John F. Richards, *The Mughal Empire* (Cambridge: Cambridge University Press, 1993), 107.
24. For a discussion of how Sir Thomas Roe was shown favor as the emperor's "disciple," see John F. Richards, "The Formulation of Imperial Authority Under Akbar and Jahangir," in *Kingship and Authority in South Asia*, ed. John F. Richards (Delhi: Oxford University Press, 1998).
25. Richards, *Mughal Empire*, 94–95.
26. This passage is from the hagiography of Khwaja Khawand Mahmud entitled *Mirat-i Tayyiba*, written by his son Muhammad Muʿinuddin, quoted and translated in Rizvi, *Muslim Revivalist Movements*, 184.
27. Alam and Subrahmanyam, "Frank Disputations," 477.
28. Jahangir and Thackston, *Jahangirnama*, 299. Jahangir and Hashim, *Jahangirnamah*, 302.
29. The *Majalis-i Jahangiri* is available in a published edition. Abd al-Sattar ibn Qasim Lahuri, Riza Allah Shah Arif Nawshahi, and Muin Nizami, *Majalis-i Jahangiri: Majlisha-i Shabanah-i Darbar-i Nur al-Din Jahangir* (Tehran: Markaz-i Pizhuhishi-i Miras-i Maktub, 1385). It is analyzed in detail in Alam and Subrahmanyam, "Frank Disputations."

30. Alam and Subrahmanyam, "Frank Disputations," 487.
31. Lahuri, Arif Nawshahi, and Nizami, *Majalis-i Jahangiri*, 34. Also see Alam and Subrahmanyam, "Frank Disputations," 492.
32. Lahuri, Arif Nawshahi, and Nizami, *Majalis-i Jahangiri*, 71. Also see Alam and Subrahmanyam, "Frank Disputations," 496.
33. The first version of the *Jahangirnama* was publicly distributed in Jahangir's twelfth year to his nobles and imperial neighbors to serve as a model. The final version continued the narrative up to the nineteenth year. See the discussion in Jahangir and Thackston, *Jahangirnama*, ix.
34. Earlier in his reign, Akbar had commissioned an illustrated version of the *Zafarnama*. The paintings executed for this project later on provided a model for those of the *Akbarnama*. See Milo C. Beach, "Jahangir's Jahangir-Nama," in *The Powers of Art: Patronage in Indian Culture*, ed. Barbara Stoler Miller (Delhi: Oxford University Press, 1992), 228.
35. Even if the label of disciple does not apply to Sharaf Ali Yazdi, who composed the chronicle *Zafarnama* two decades after Timur's death, it is nevertheless notable that Yazdi had used his expertise in the occult sciences along with his rhetorical skills to paint a hagiographical and saintly picture of his patron, Timur's son Shahrukh. Specifically, Yazdi called Shahrukh a centennial *mujaddid* or renewer of Islam. See chapter 2, note 68.
36. Jahangir and Thackston, *Jahangirnama*, 144; Jahangir and Hashim, *Jahangirnamah*, 137. This humble formula was often used, however, when he was hinting at his greatness. See note 39.
37. Jahangir and Hashim, *Jahangirnamah*, 151–152; Jahangir and Thackston, *Jahangirnama*, 161.
38. Jahangir and Hashim, *Jahangirnamah*, 106; Jahangir and Thackston, *Jahangirnama*, 117.
39. Jahangir and Hashim, *Jahangirnamah*, 419; Jahangir and Thackston, *Jahangirnama*, 403. For the eighteenth-century paintings commemorating this event, see Francesca von Habsburg, *The St. Petersburg Muraqqa': Album of Indian and Persian Miniatures from the Sixteenth Through the Eighteenth Century and Specimens of Persian Calligraphy by Imad al-Hasani*, 2 vols. (Milano: Leonardo Arte, 1996), 1: plates 115, 58.
40. Jahangir and Hashim, *Jahangirnamah*, 309; Jahangir and Thackston, *Jahangirnama*, 304.
41. Sirhindi's letter quoted in Yohanan Friedmann, *Shaykh Ahmad Sirhindi: An Outline of His Thought and a Study of His Image in the Eyes of Posterity* (Oxford: Oxford University Press, 2000), 27.
42. This passage is from a seventeenth-century Persian hagiography of Sirhindi written by one of his chief disciples. For the original Persian, see Badr al-Din Sirhindi, *Hazarat al-Quds* (Lahore: Mahakama-i Awqaf Panjab, 1971), 82–83. The English translation is from Carl W. Ernst, "The Daily Life of a Saint, Ahmad Sirhindi, by Badr al-Din Sirhindi," in *Islam in South Asia in Practice*, ed. Barbara Daly Metcalf (Princeton, N.J.: Princeton University Press, 2009), 162.
43. For a discussion of Sirhindi's subdued religious attitude after he was released and reinstated by Jahangir, see Friedmann, *Sirhindi*, 83–85.
44. This change in policy was stated explicitly in the "Regulations Regarding the Kornish and Taslim." Abu al-Fazl ibn Mubarak et al., *The A'in-i Akbari* (Lahore: Sang-

e-Meel Publications, 2003), 156. Abu al-Fazl ibn Mubarak, *A'in-i Akbari*, ed. Sir Sayyid Ahmad (Aligarh: Sir Sayyid Academy, Aligarh Muslim University, 2005), 142.

45. Alam and Subrahmanyam, "Frank Disputations," 487.
46. In the foreword to the first book-length study of painting in Jahangir's reign, the honorary general secretary of the Asiatic Society observed that "If [the Mughal emperor] Akbar was the pioneer experimentalist on internationalism in religion, Jahangir was in art." See the foreword in Asok Kumar Das, *Mughal Painting During Jahangir's Time* (Calcutta: Asiatic Society, 1978).
47. For a classic history of the Persian miniature painting tradition see Laurence Binyon, James Vere Stewart Wilkinson, and Basil Gray, *Persian Miniature Painting: Including a Critical and Descriptive Catalogue of the Miniatures Exhibited at Burlington House, January–March, 1931* (London: Oxford University Press, 1933).
48. For a good discussion of the role art played in early Safavid times see, for example, Robert Hillenbrand, "Iconography of the Shah-nama-yi Shahi," in *Safavid Persia: The History and Politics of an Islamic Society* (London: I. B. Tauris, 1996).
49. Zahir al-Din Mirza Babur and W. M. Thackston, *The Baburnama: Memoirs of Babur, Prince and Emperor* (New York: Modern Library, 2002), 218.
50. Ibid., 300. Zahir al-Din Mirza Babur, W. M. Thackston, and Abdur Rahim Khan, *Baburnama: Chaghatay Turkish Text with Abdul-Rahim Khankhanan's Persian Translation* (Cambridge, Mass.: Department of Near Eastern Languages and Civilizations, Harvard University, 1993), 527.
51. For a sample of paintings depicting the Prophet's ascension journey in fourteenth- to sixteenth-century Iran, along with a review of literature, see David J. Roxburgh, *Prefacing the Image: The Writing of Art History in Sixteenth-Century Iran* (Leiden: Brill, 2001), 160–161, 201–205.
52. My argument follows the insightful analysis of these paintings and sacred traditions offered by David Roxburgh. See ibid. I would like to thank Yael Rice for referring me to his work.
53. The Chest of Witnessing tradition is discussed in detail in ibid., 170–174. The Timurid historian Mirkhvand related it in his universal history *Rawzat al-Safa'* (The Garden of Purity). It is also mentioned in several prefaces to art albums of the time, as discussed in ibid. Most importantly, it was related in the Millennial History written for Akbar. See Qazi Ahmad Tattavi and Asif Khan Qazvini, *Tarikh-i Alfi*, ed. Ghulam Riza Tabatabai Mujid, 8 vols. (Tehran: Shirkat-i Intisharat-i ʿIlmi va Farhangi, 1382 [2003 or 2004]), 1:63–64.
54. Roxburgh, *Prefacing the Image*, 173.
55. Ibid., 186.
56. The place of Mani in the early modern Islamic art historical tradition is discussed in detail in ibid., 174–181. For an association of Mani with heresy and the magical arts in Islam and its use in Safavid polemics, see Kathryn Babayan, *Mystics, Monarchs, and Messiahs: Cultural Landscapes of Early Modern Iran* (Cambridge, Mass.: Harvard University Press, 2002), 48–54, *passim*.
57. Roxburgh, *Prefacing the Image*, 199. Also, for this and other surviving sixteenth- century royal books of divination, see Massumeh Farhad and Serpil Bagci, eds., *Falnama: The Book of Omens* (Washington, D.C.: Arthur M. Sackler Gallery, Smithsonian Institution, 2009).
58. For the images and icons used in Bektashi mystical practices, see Frederick De Jong,

"The Iconography of Bektashiism: A Survey of Themes and Symbolism in Clerical Costume, Liturgical Objects, and Pictorial Art," *Manuscripts of the Middle East* 4 (1989): 7–29.

59. In remarking on the Mughal appreciation for sacred icons, the Jesuit Father Monserrate observed: "In other respects they may be no better than those Christian revolutionaries, the 'iconoclasts'; but in this respect at least they are certainly their superiors." *Commentary of Father Monserrate*, quoted in Ebba Koch, *Mughal Art and Imperial Ideology: Collected Essays* (New Delhi: Oxford University Press, 2001), 9.

60. Jahangir and Thackston, *Jahangirnama*, 41.

61. Abu al-Fazl ibn Mubarak and Henry Beveridge, *The Akbar Nama of Abu-l-Fazl: History of the Reign of Akbar Including an Account of His Predecessors*, 3 (1 and 2 bound in one) vols. (Calcutta: 1897–1921; repr., Lahore: Sang-e-Meel Publications, 2005), 1-2:590–591; Abu al-Fazl ibn Mubarak, *The Akbarnamah*, ed. Maulawi ʿAbd-ur-Rahim, 3 vols. (Calcutta: Asiatic Society of Bengal, 1877–1886), 2:42–43.

62. Abu al-Fazl ibn Mubarak and Beveridge, *The Akbar Nama*, 1-2:592; Abu al-Fazl ibn Mubarak, *The Akbarnamah*, 2:43.

63. John William Seyller and W. M. Thackston, *The Adventures of Hamza: Painting and Storytelling in Mughal India* (Washington, D.C.: Freer Gallery of Art; Arthur M. Sackler Gallery Smithsonian Institution, 2002).

64. My thanks to Sumathi Ramaswamy for generously sharing her early research on the topic, later published as Sumathi Ramaswamy, "Conceit of the Globe in Mughal Visual Practice," *Comparative Studies in Society and History* 49 (2007): 751–782.

65. Elaine Julia Wright and Susan Stronge, eds., *Muraqqaʿ: Imperial Mughal Albums from the Chester Beatty Library, Dublin* (Alexandria, Va.: Art Services International, 2008), 288, 344.

66. For an account of the historical significance of the Chishti shrine at Ajmer, see P. M. Currie, *The Shrine and Cult of Muin al-Din Chishti of Ajmer* (Delhi: Oxford University Press, 1989).

67. Wright and Stronge, *Muraqqaʿ*, 290–294.

68. See, for example, the paintings showing Jahangir's meetings with Sufi shaykhs and Gosain Jadrup reprinted in Jahangir and Thackston, *Jahangirnama*, 252, 312.

69. It is important to note that many of the same artistic techniques and painting conventions were used in post-Jahangiri Mughal art to portray the transfer of sovereignty from one monarch to another. For example, the succession from Timur to Shah Jahan—one Lord of Conjunction to another—was depicted in a similar manner, with the two sovereigns painted separately facing each other and Timur handing over a crown to Shah Jahan. See the opening folios of Shah Jahan's chronicle in Milo C. Beach, Ebba Koch, and W. M. Thackston, *King of the World: The Padshahnama: An Imperial Mughal Manuscript from the Royal Library, Windsor Castle* (London: Azimuth, 1997), 26–27.

70. In art historical scholarship, these Jahangiri paintings have been rarely connected to the cultic traditions of Akbar's days. An important exception is the study by Heike Franke, *Akbar und Gahangir. Untersuchungen zur politischen und religiösen Legitimation in Text und Bild* (Schenefeld: EB-Verglag, 2005), 293–331. I must thank Eva Orthmann for bringing this work to my attention. Unfortunately, my late discovery of this book and, more significantly, my inability to read German has prevented me from engaging with it in detail. Nevertheless, Eva Orthmann's

generosity in summarizing its key arguments enables me to state that *Akbar und Gahangir* offers several key insights about Jahangir's paintings that also support the position that it was through his art that Jahangir continued and developed upon the sacred schemes of his father.

71. For a discussion and reproduction of this painting, see Robert Skelton, "Imperial Symbolism in Mughal Painting," in *Content and Context of Visual Arts in the Islamic World*, ed. Priscilla Parsons Soucek, Carol Bier, and Richard Ettinghausen (University Park: Pennsylvania State University Press, 1988). Also, see Wright and Stronge, *Muraqqaʿ*, 344–348.
72. It was Robert Skelton who first pointed out the connection between this painting and the owl-shooting incident described in the *Jahangirnama*. He suggested that this painting was executed well before Malik ʿAmbar's death and noted that "if the picture mythologizes an actual event in order to glorify Jahangir as a divine ruler, it also attempts to influence fate by sympathetic magic." Skelton, "Imperial Symbolism," 181.
73. Jahangir and Thackston, *Jahangirnama*, 192; Jahangir and Hashim, *Jahangirnamah*.
74. Toufic Fahd, *La divination arabe. Etudes religieuses, sociologiques et folkloriques sur le milieu natif de l'Islam* (Paris: Sindbad, 1987), 513.
75. The fish and the bull are symbols of Islamic cosmology with roots in both Indic and Iranian mythology relating to the center and balancing of the world. Some Arab scholars conflated these symbols with the biblical symbols of Behemoth and Leviathan, respectively. See M. Streck and A. Miquel, "Kaf," in *The Encyclopaedia of Islam*, 2nd ed., ed. P. Bearman, et al. (Brill, 2011), http://www.brillonline.nl.
76. Wright and Stronge, *Muraqqaʿ*, 348.
77. Ibid.
78. Ibid.
79. Something like this, for example, was performed by Jahangir's grandfather, Humayun. See chapter 4, note 70.
80. Muʿtamad Khan wrote the *Iqbalnama-i Jahangiri* (The Epic of Sovereignty of Jahangir), a chronicle of Jahangir's reign that is largely based on the *Jahangirnama*. As a confidante of the emperor, he also took on the duty of composing the *Jahangirnama* when Jahangir in his final years became too ill to write.
81. Muʿtamad Khan, *The Iqbalnamah-i Jahangiri*, Bibliotheca Indica (Osnabruck: Biblio Verlag, 1982), 118.
82. The letter discussed here and below is from Sirhindi, *Maktubat*, 2:135–138.
83. The idea that Islam had displaced a millennium of Iranian-Zoroastrian dispensation was one that was found both in Islamic conjunction astrology, as outlined by Ibn Khaldun, as well as in Zoroastrian apocalyptic narratives. See chapter 2, notes 38 and 134.
84. Jahangir and Thackston, *Jahangirnama*, 46.
85. Discussed in Amina Okada, *Indian Miniatures of the Mughal Court* (New York: H. N. Abrams, 1992), 48. Also, Skelton, "Imperial Symbolism."
86. See Kirin Narayan, *Storytellers, Saints, and Scoundrels: Folk Narrative in Hindu Religious Teaching* (Philadelphia: University of Pennsylvania Press, 1989), 212–223.
87. See Sheldon Pollock, "Ramayana and Political Imagination in India," *Journal of Asian Studies* 52, no. 2 (1993): 261–297.
88. Jahangir mentioned his meetings with the ascetic Jadrup in his memoir. Some of

these meetings were even depicted in painting. Jahangir's interactions with Jadrup are discussed in detail in Sajida S. Alvi, "Religion and State During the Reign of Mughal Emperor Jahangir (1605–27): Nonjuristical Perspectives," *Studia Islamica* 69 (1989): 95–119.

89. Jahangir and Thackston, *Jahangirnama*, 147; Jahangir and Hashim, *Jahangirnamah*, 140.
90. This lavishly illustrated work on the life of Jesus was the *Mirat al-Quds* (Mirror of Holiness), a compilation of biblical narratives in Persian jointly produced by Jesuit and Mughal scholars under orders from Akbar and Jahangir. In a careful analysis, Bailey showed how Mughal artists used as models for their paintings the religious pageantry organized by the Christian priests. He concludes: "Late Akbar and early Jahangir period painting in general may owe as much to the vibrant spectacle and drama of Catholic pageantry as it does to the two-dimensional oil-paintings and engravings that have long been recognized as the main conduit of European art to the Mughal court." Gauvin Alexander Bailey, "The Lahore Mirat al-Quds and the Impact of Jesuit Theatre on Mughal Painting," *South Asian Studies* 13 (1997): 42.
91. This statement was made by Father Xavier, who had led the mission to Jahangir's court. He is quoted in ibid., 32.
92. For a reprint of this image and a discussion of its meaning in the Mughal setting, see Koch, *Mughal Art*, 2–5.
93. For example, in the panegyric text *Qanun-i Humayuni* discussed in chapter 4, Humayun was described by the historian Khwandamir as having brought several pairs of the "hunter" and the "hunted," e.g., the leopard (*palang*) and the deer (*ahu*), in peace together. See Ghiyas al-Din ibn Humam al-Din Khvand Mir, *A Work on the Rules and Ordinances Established by the Emperor Humayun and on Some Buildings Erected by His Order: [Qanun-i Humayuni, Persian Text with Notes and Preface]*, ed. M. Hidayat Hosain (Calcutta: Asiatic Society, 1940), 8.
94. Jahangir and Hashim, *Jahangirnamah*, 90; Jahangir and Thackston, *Jahangirnama*, 103.
95. See C. A. Bayly, *Empire and Information: Intelligence Gathering and Social Communication in India, 1780–1870* (Cambridge: Cambridge University Press, 1996), 26.
96. Jahangir and Hashim, *Jahangirnamah*, 137; Jahangir and Thackston, *Jahangirnama*, 144.
97. Jahangir and Hashim, *Jahangirnamah*, 137; Jahangir and Thackston, *Jahangirnama*, 144.
98. Jahangir and Thackston, *Jahangirnama*, 435.
99. The art historian Amina Okada, for example, made the following observation about this painting: "The scene, completely devoid of historical fact, is the brilliant if naïve expression of Jahangir's anxiety and insecurity when confronted with the question of Kandahar." Okada, *Indian Miniatures*, 55.
100. For the literature on dreams and dream interpretation, see chapter 3, note 77.
101. Jahangir and Thackston, *Jahangirnama*, 162.
102. This famous painting was discussed in detail in a well-known article by Richard Ettinghausen, "The Emperor's Choice," in *De Artibus Opuscula XL: Essays in Honor of Erwin Panofsky*, ed. Millard Meiss (New York: New York University, 1961). Ettinghausen argued that the painting shows that Jahangir is turning away from

the material world in his old age in order to find spiritual solace in the veneration of saints. Note that my interpretation differs significantly from Ettinghausen's.

103. The depiction of the English monarch standing before Jahangir is not as absurd as it may first seem, for the English court was represented officially by Sir Thomas Roe. In fact, the English ambassador is said to have developed a close relationship with the Mughal emperor and regularly supplied him with gifts, including paintings, from Europe in order to gain imperial favor and obtain trading rights. See Michael J. Brown, *Itinerant Ambassador: The Life of Sir Thomas Roe* (Lexington: University Press of Kentucky, 1970); Thomas Roe, *The Embassy of Sir Thomas Roe to India, 1615–1619: As Narrated in His Journal and Correspondence*, ed. William Foster, rev. ed. (New Delhi: Munshiram Manoharlal Publications, 1990). The Ottoman presence at Jahangir's court was less official. When Aqam Hajji, a Central Asian, presented himself as an Ottoman ambassador in 1608, Jahangir did not accept his credentials as authentic and sent him away. However, when mentioning this incident the emperor clearly stated in his memoir that the Ottomans were subordinate to the Timurids and owed him respect and allegiance. According to him, this was because his ancestor Sahib Qiran (that is, Timur) had conquered Anatolia from the Ottoman ruler Bayazid but then generously gave it back to the latter's son Musa Chelebi. He complained, "From that time until now, despite such generous treatment, neither has anyone come on behalf of the Ottomans nor have they sent an ambassador." Jahangir and Thackston, *Jahangirnama*, 95.

104. Jahangir stated: "The luminaries, which are manifestations of divine light, should be venerated in accordance with the degrees of each one, and one should recognize that the real mover and creator in all forms and time is God." Jahangir and Thackston, *Jahangirnama*, 53.

105. See Hossein Ziai, "Al-Suhrawardi, Shihab al-Din Yahya b. Habash b. Amirak, Abu ʾl-Futuh," in *Encyclopaedia of Islam*, 2nd ed., ed. P. Bearman, et al. (Brill, 2008), http://www.brillonline.nl.

106. Tattavi and Qazvini, *Tarikh-i Alfi*, 1:381–383.

107. He is famous for his *Kitab al-Mudkhal al Kabir ila Ahkam al-Nujum* (Great Introduction to Astrology) and *Kitab al Milal wa al-Duwal* (The Book of Religions and Dynasties). When his work was translated into Latin in the thirteenth century, his ideas had a major impact on shaping the intellectual basis of Christian millennial theories. See J. M. Millas, "Abu Maʿshar," in *The Encyclopaedia of Islam*, 2nd ed., ed. P. Bearman, et al. (Brill, 2011), http://www.brillonline.nl.

108. The *Dabistan-i Mazahib* (School of Religions), written by a Zoroastrian scholar in India in the middle of the seventeenth century, reported that Akbar believed in the veneration of the planets. It also observed, more generally, that the Mongols had remained masters of the world as long as they worshipped the planets; when they gave up this practice, they lost their empire and became worthless. Muhsin Fani, *Dabistan-i Mazahib*, ed. Rahim Rizazadah Malik, 2 vols. (Tehran: Kitabkhanah-i Tahuri, 1362 [1983]), 1:308. Muhsin Fani, *The Dabistan or School of Manners*, trans. David Shea and Anthony Troyer (Washington, D.C.: M. W. Dunne, 1901), 376.

109. Bailey, *Jesuits and the Grand Mogul*, 37.

110. It is noteworthy that the official sources of Akbar's time do not mention the use of the emperor's portrait in the rituals of discipleship. The only evidence that Akbar gave such portraits to disciples appears in the accusations of Badaʾuni. There are, however, several extant portraits from Jahangir's time and later that may have

been used in the ritual of imperial discipleship. These paintings are referred to in art historical literature as "jewel" portraits, as they were meant to be worn as a turban ornament by the king's devotee alongside or instead of other jewels. See Habsburg, *St. Petersburg Muraqqaʿ*, 1: plates 21 and 22.

7. CONCLUSION: THE GRAFFITI UNDER THE THRONE

1. Shah Jahan's astrologer and astronomer, Farid Ibrahim Dihlavi, in his commentary on the emperor's horoscope, noted the significance of the fact that the emperor had been born in the year 1000 AH. Farid Ibrahim Dihlavi, "Karnama-i Sahib Qiran-i Thani Zij-i Shah Jahani," British Library, London, MS Or 372, 4b. The epigraph to this chapter is from Muhammad-Hadi, "Preface to the Jahangirnama by Muhammad-Hadi," in *The Jahangirnama: Memoirs of Jahangir, Emperor of India*, ed. W. M. Thackston (Washington, D.C.: Freer Gallery of Art, 1999), 7. In addition to the epigraph, another millennial panegyric written for Shah Jahan has also survived: "According to the will of the Almighty, / The King appeared in the world at the end of a thousand years. / He banished the abusive manners of oppression and tyranny from the world / And lighted up the solitary places of the infidels and the blind. (Muhammad Amin Qazvini)." Both Hadi and Qazvini are quoted in Fergus Nicoll, *Shah Jahan* (London: Haus, 2009), 20.
2. Mutribi Samarqandi, *Conversations with Emperor Jahangir*, trans. Richard C. Foltz (Costa Mesa, Calif.: Mazda Publishers, 1998), 23; Mutribi Samarqandi, *Khatirat-i Mutribi*, ed. Abdul Ghani Mirzoyef (Karachi: Institute of Central and West Asian Studies, University of Karachi, 1977), 19–20. For a detailed overview of how Timurid dynastic memory was kept alive in Mughal India, see Lisa Balabanlilar, *Imperial Identity in the Mughal Empire: Memory and Dynastic Politics in Early Modern South and Central Asia* (London: I. B. Tauris, 2012).
3. John F. Richards, *The Mughal Empire* (Cambridge: Cambridge University Press, 1993), 132–133.
4. Ibid., 121–123.
5. Ibid. Sri Ram Sharma, *The Religious Policy of the Mughal Emperors* (London: H. Milford, Oxford University Press, 1940), 95–115.
6. See the imperial portraits of Shah Jahan in Milo C. Beach, Ebba Koch, and W. M. Thackston, *King of the World: The Padshahnama: An Imperial Mughal Manuscript from the Royal Library, Windsor Castle* (London: Azimuth Editions, 1997).
7. Richards, *Mughal Empire*, 148–150.
8. An extensive study of Dara Shikoh has yet to be published. For an overview and bibliography, see Annemarie Schimmel, "Dara Shokoh," in *Encyclopaedia Iranica Online* (December 15, 1994), http://www.iranicaonline.org. For a survey of the intellectual works produced and patronized by Dara Shikoh, see Carl W. Ernst, "Muslim Studies of Hinduism? A Reconsideration of Arabic and Persian Translations from Indian Languages," *Iranian Studies* 36, no. 2 (2003): 183–187.
9. This topic also merits further study. For an overview of Findiriski and likeminded Iranians in India, see Sajjad H. Rizvi, "Mir Fendereski," in *Encyclopaedia Iranica Online* (July 20, 2005), http://www.iranicaonline.org.

7. CONCLUSION: THE GRAFFITI UNDER THE THRONE [303]

10. For a discussion of the *Dabistan-i Mazahib*, see Fath-allah Mojtabai, "Dabestan-e Madaheb," in *Encyclopaedia Iranica Online* (December 15, 1993), http://www.iranicaonline.org.
11. For a sense of the "neo-Mazdean renaissance" in India and Iran, of which the *Dabistan* was a part, see Mohamad Tavakoli-Targhi, "Contested Memories," in *Refashioning Iran: Orientalism, Occidentalism, and Historiography* (New York: Palgrave, 2001). The discussion of Akbar and his "Ilahiyyas" occurs in Muhsin Fani, *The Dabistan or School of Manners*, trans. David Shea and Anthony Troyer (Washington, D.C.: M. W. Dunne, 1901), 352–376. Muhsin Fani, *Dabistan-i Mazahib*, ed. Rahim Rizazadah Malik, 2 vols. (Tehran: Kitabkhanah-i Tahuri, 1362 [1983]), 1:287–314.
12. See Jadunath Sarkar, *History of Aurangzib: Based on Persian Sources*, 5 vols. (Calcutta: M. C. Sarkar, 1924), 1:298–299. A detailed treatment of Dara Shikoh's trial is in Craig Davis, "Dara Shukuh and Aurangzib: Issues of Religion and Politics and Their Impact on Indo-Muslim Society" (Ph.D. diss., Indiana University, 2002).
13. Katherine Butler Brown, "Did Aurangzeb Ban Music? Questions for the Historiography of His Reign," *Modern Asian Studies* 41, no. 1 (2007): 88.
14. Rajiv Kinra, "Infantilizing Baba Dara: The Cultural Memory of Dara Shekuh and the Mughal Public Sphere," *Journal of Persianate Studies* 2 (2009): 165–193.
15. Richards, *Mughal Empire*, 148–150.
16. Stephen Blake, "The Patrimonial-Bureaucratic Empire of the Mughals," *Journal of Asian Studies* 39, no. 1 (1979): 77–94.
17. Stephen P. Blake, *Shahjahanabad: The Sovereign City in Mughal India, 1639-1739* (Cambridge: Cambridge University Press, 1991), 210.
18. Jahangir and W. M. Thackston, *The Jahangirnama: Memoirs of Jahangir, Emperor of India* (Washington, D.C.: Freer Gallery of Art, 1999), 39. I would like to thank Taymiya Zaman for this reference.
19. Peter Parkes, "Fosterage, Kinship, and Legend: When Milk Was Thicker Than Blood?" *Comparative Studies in Society and History* 46, no. 3 (2004): 535–586; Peter Parkes, "Milk Kinship in Islam: Substance, Structure, History," *Social Anthropology* 13, no. 3 (2005): 307–329.
20. Richards, *Mughal Empire*, 149–150; John Richards, "Norms of Comportment Among Imperial Mughal Officers," in *Moral Conduct and Authority: The Place of Adab in South Asian Islam*, ed. Barbara Daly Metcalf (Berkeley: University of California Press, 1984).
21. Niccolao Manucci, *Storia do Mogor, or, Mogul India, 1653-1708*, trans. William Irvine, 4 vols. (London: John Murray, 1907; repr., Calcutta: Editions Indian, 1966), 1:295.
22. For a discussion of the changing position of women in Mughal politics in Akbar's days, see Ruby Lal, *Domesticity and Power in the Early Mughal World* (Cambridge: Cambridge University Press, 2005), 176–213.
23. While further research is needed on this issue in the Mughal milieu, scholarship on sacred kingship in early modern Europe offers relevant case studies for comparison. Zanger Abby, for instance, has extended and complicated Ernst Kantorowicz's paradigm of the "King's 'Two Bodies'" by emphasizing the queen's physicality in enabling the homosociality of state building via rituals of heterosocial bonding. See Zanger Abby, "Making Sweat: Sex and the Gender of National Reproduction in the Marriage of Louis XIII," *Yale French Studies*, no. 86 (1994).
24. The discussion on the jharoka throne below depends on the detailed description

and data on it in Ebba Koch, *Mughal Art and Imperial Ideology: Collected Essays* (New Delhi: Oxford University Press, 2001), 61–129.

25. See, for instance, Diana L. Eck, *Darsan: Seeing the Divine Image in India*, 3rd ed. (New York: Columbia University Press, 1998).
26. Koch, *Mughal Art*, 133–144.
27. Ibid., 227–254.
28. Ibid., 253.
29. Ibid., 249, 253, and 253n98.
30. For a discussion of nawruz in the time of Humayun and Akbar, see Eva Orthmann, "Court Culture and Cosmology in the Mughal Empire: Humayun and the Foundations of the Din-i Ilahi," in *Court Cultures in the Muslim World: Seventh to Nineteenth Centuries*, ed. Albrecht Fuess and Jan-Peter Hartung (London: Routledge, 2011).
31. See Jean Calmard, "Shiʿi Rituals and Power II: The Consolidation of Safavid Shiʿism: Folklore and Popular Religion," in *Safavid Persia: The History and Politics of an Islamic Society*, ed. Charles P. Melville (London: I. B. Tauris, 1996).
32. In this interpretation, nawruz was equated with an existing Shiʿi celebration in the lunar Islamic calendar, the anniversary or ʿid of Ghadir Khumm. On this day, according to Shiʿi belief, the Prophet, who was nearing the end of his life, designated Ali as his successor. Importantly, this Alid view of nawruz was not a marginal one. It was espoused by such luminaries of Safavid Iran as the Shiʿi scholar and jurist Muhammad Baqir Majlisi (d. 1678). For a detailed discussion, see Hasan Ali Khan, "Shiʿa-Ismaʿili Motifs in the Sufi Architecture of the Indus Valley, 1200–1500 AD" (Ph.D. diss., School of Oriental and African Studies, 2009), 138–144.
33. See Catherine B. Asher, "A Ray from the Sun," in *The Presence of Light: Divine Radiance and Religious Experience*, ed. Matthew T. Kapstein (Chicago: University of Chicago Press, 2004).
34. The reference to Abu Maʿshar's Arabic prayers to the sun is in chapter 5, note 117.
35. For a reference to Jahangir's veneration of the sun, see chapter 6, note 104.
36. See chapter 2, note 4.
37. This could have represented the planet of the sun in the house of Leo. A flag with this symbol can be seen in the *Padshahnama* painting reproduced in Beach, Koch, and Thackston, *King of the World*, 87.
38. The historian Muhammad-Salih Kanbo, the author of ʿ*Amal-i Salih*, stated that the prophetic custom of *aqiqa* (in which a newborn's hair is shaved and weighed and an equal amount of silver given in alms) had opened the way to "making this custom permissible." Translated and quoted in ibid., 39.
39. Schmidtke makes this observation about the use of Hermes by the Illuminationist philosopher Suhrawardi: "Shihab al-Din al-Suhrawardi (killed 587/1191) and other representatives of his philosophy of illumination (*hikmat al-ishraq*) considered themselves true followers of what they called ancient wisdom (*hikmat al-atiq*). In order to demonstrate the eternal truth shared by all divinely revealed religions, they sought to synthesize various traditions such as those of the ancient Egyptians (Hermes, Agathodaemon), Persians (Jamasp, Farshawashtar, Buzurjmihr), and Greeks (Empedecles, Pythagoras, and in particular Plato)." Sabine Schmidtke, "The Doctrine of the Transmigration of Soul According to Shihab al-Din al-Suhrawardi (Killed 587/1191) and His Followers," *Studia Iranica* 28 (1999): 238.
40. Van Bladel puts it succinctly: "In this Eastern classical tradition, rooted in late

antiquity, Hermes Triplicate-in-Wisdom came to play an important role as a figure of legend, an ideal of wisdom to be emulated, the founder of learning, a master of the spirits, the prophet of science who had touched the stars and the heard the words of angels, the first sage." Kevin Thomas Van Bladel, *The Arabic Hermes: From Pagan Sage to Prophet of Science* (Oxford: Oxford University Press, 2009), 239.

41. The renowned Shiʿi philosopher of Safavid Iran Mulla Sadra had this to say about Hermes: "Know that philosophy first issued from Adam, the chosen one of God and from his progeny Seth and Hermes and from Noah because the world can never be free of a person who establishes knowledge of the unity of God and of the return [to God]. The great Hermes disseminated it [philosophy] in the climes and in the countries and explained it and gave benefit of it to the people. He is the father of philosophers and the most learned of the knowledgeable." Quoted in Sajjad Rizvi, "Mulla Sadra," in *The Stanford Encyclopedia of Philosophy*, summer 2009 ed., ed. Edward N. Zalta (2009), http://plato.stanford.edu/archives/sum2009/entries/mulla-sadra/.

42. For a detailed view of the legacy of "Hermetic" knowledge in the late medieval and early modern era, see Van Bladel, *Arabic Hermes*, 121–219.

43. Abu al-Fazl ibn Mubarak and Henry Beveridge, *The Akbar Nama of Abu-l-Fazl: History of the Reign of Akbar Including an Account of His Predecessors*, 3 (1 and 2 bound in one) vols. (Calcutta: 1897–1921; repr., Lahore: Sang-e-Meel Publications, 2005), 1–2:143; Abu al-Fazl ibn Mubarak, *The Akbarnamah*, ed. Maulawi ʿAbd-ur-Rahim, 3 vols. (Calcutta: Asiatic Society of Bengal, 1877–1886), 1:55.

44. Fani, *Dabistan-i Mazahib*, 1:303.

45. Jahangir's qualification appears in his memoir when he asserts that the "Luminaries," that is, the sun and the moon, "which are manifestations of divine light, should be venerated in accordance with the degrees of each one." Jahangir and Thackston, *The Jahangirnama*, 53. Although neglected in histories of Muslim societies, Hermeticism has been studied extensively by scholars of Renaissance Europe. In that milieu, works attributed to Hermes found a dedicated following among such learned Renaissance "Magi" as Giordano Bruno and John Dee, men who had also searched for the one unifying and universal knowledge of time and cosmos. In effect, Europe of the time shared a significant amount of lore about Hermes with the Persianate world, and both the Christian and Muslim admirers of Hermes believed that this ancient sage had taught the central cosmological importance of the sun as manifestation of divinity. See, for example, Peter J. French, *John Dee: The World of an Elizabethan Magus* (London: Routledge & Kegan Paul, 1972), 101. Even though the Hermetic worldview came under increasing attack with the onset of the "scientific revolution" in Europe, it still attracted ardent followers during the sixteenth and seventeenth centuries. For a review of the scholarly debates, see Brian P. Copenhaver, "Natural Magic, Hermetism, and Occultism in Early Modern Science," in *Reappraisals of the Scientific Revolution*, ed. David C. Lindberg and Robert S. Westman (Cambridge: Cambridge University Press, 1990).

46. Although some sources indicate that Shah Jahan forbade his nobles from wearing these portraits on their headdress, as had been the custom in the days of Akbar and Jahangir. Sharma, *Religious Policy*, 97.

47. Richard Eaton notes the way Shah Jahan participated in Orissa's "state cult" of Jaganath: "By sitting on a canopied chariot while accompanying the cult's annual car festival, Shah Jahan's officials ritually demonstrated that it was the Mughal emperor,

operating through his appointed officers (*mansabdars*), who was the temple's—and hence the god's—ultimate lord and protector. Such actions in effect projected a hierarchy of hybridized political and religious power that descended downward from the Mughal emperor to his mansabdar, from the mansabdar to the god Jagannath and his temple, from Jahannath to the sub-imperial king who patronized the god, and from the king to his subjects." Richard Maxwell Eaton, *Temple Desecration and Muslim States in Medieval India* (Gurgaon, India: Hope India Publications, 2004), 53.

48. Khan Inayat, W. E. Begley, and Ziyaud-Din A. Desai, *The Shah Jahan Nama of ʿInayat Khan* (Delhi: Oxford University Press, 1990), xviii–xix.
49. Koch, *Mughal Art*, 131–132.
50. This argument depends on the richly documented essay in ibid., 61–129.
51. Ibid., 111.
52. These images have been reproduced and discussed in detail in Beach, Koch, and Thackston, *King of the World*.
53. The analysis here depends on ibid., 115–129.
54. This is Ebba Koch's interpretation in ibid., 137. Also see Koch, *Mughal Art*, 144.
55. For a brief discussion of this Christian theme in Mughal art, see A. Jan Qaisar, "The Profane and the Sacred: 'Judgement of Paris' and 'God the Father' in the Mughal School of Art," in *Art and Culture: Felicitation Volume in Honour of Professor S. Nurul Hasan*, ed. Ahsan Jan Qaisar, Som Prakash Verma, and S. Nurul Hasan (Jaipur: Publication Scheme, 1993).
56. Developing upon Marcel Mauss's notion of the gift, Maurice Godlier argued that sacred objects given by the gods to men must be understood as having a special inalienable property that allows them to play a unique role in gift exchange and in anchoring the social order. These sacred objects are special in that they may not be given in exchange, except indirectly: only their use-rights can be transferred, not their ownership. Thus, they become objects that can, paradoxically, be kept while giving: "The donor gives the use-right and keeps the ownership. He keeps while giving." Maurice Godelier, *The Enigma of the Gift* (Chicago: University of Chicago Press, 1999), 132. In such a manner, sacrality can be disbursed in a gift exchange without the sacred source at the center of it ever being depleted.
57. Sarkar, *History of Aurangzib*, 2:296.
58. Sharma, *Religious Policy*, 118–180; Sarkar, *History of Aurangzib*, 3:88–114.
59. Alan M. Guenther, "Hanafi Fiqh in Mughal India: The Fatawa-i ʿAlamgiri," in *India's Islamic Traditions, 711–1750*, ed. Richard Maxwell Eaton (New Delhi: Oxford University Press, 2003).
60. Sharma, *Religious Policy*, 119. Also see Aurangzeb's letter to his son on the subject of nawruz: Jamshid H. Bilimoria, *Rukaʿat-i-Alamgiri or Letters of Aurangzebe* (Delhi: Idarah-i Adabiyat-i Delli, 1972), 5–6.
61. See the widespread references to astrologers and the use of astrology in Francois Bernier, *Travels in the Mogul Empire*, ed. Vincent A. Smith, trans. Archibald Constable, 2nd ed. (New Delhi: Low Price Publications, 1989).
62. Brown, "Did Aurangzeb Ban Music?"
63. Much work remains to be done on the ribald verse of Jaʿfar Zatalli (d. 1713) who lived in the time of Aurangzeb and whose nom de plume Zatalli meant "babbler of nonsense." See Shamsur Rahman Faruqi, "Burning Rage, Icy Scorn: The Poetry of Jaʿfar Zatalli" (paper presented at the Hindi-Urdu Flagship Program, University

of Texas at Austin, September 24, 2008), http://www.columbia.edu/itc/mealac/pritchett/00fwp/srf/srf_zatalli_2008.pdf.

64. See the case of the famous Sarmad, a partisan and companion of Dara Shikoh, who was put to death by Aurangzeb on charges of heresy. Nathan Katz, "The Identity of a Mystic: The Case of Saʾid Sarmad, a Jewish-Yogi-Sufi Courtier of the Mughals," *Numen* 47, no. 2 (2000): 142–160. It was well acknowledged at the time that there was no shortage of figures like Sarmad and that Aurangzeb had the holy man put to death mainly for his association with Dara Shikoh.

65. For the life of a loyal Hindu imperial officer in Aurangzeb's service, see the memoirs of Bhimsen Saksena, a Kayastha by caste. In his memoir, Bhimsen describes how once when lost he was helped by Nur Khan, a Muslim officer of Shivaji—Aurangzeb's Maratha enemy—who helped Bhimsen reach his own camp in safety. See Jadunath Sarkar, *English Translation of Tarikh-i-Dilkasha (Memoirs of Bhimsen relating to Aurangzib's Deccan Campaigns)* (Bombay: Dept. of Archives, 1972), x.

66. In his study of the rise of Islam in the Bengal "frontier" in the northeastern reaches of the Mughal empire, Richard Eaton documented a pattern of imperial land grants in Bengal meant to cut down thick forests, encourage settled agriculture, and increase tax revenue. This is what Eaton says about the impact of policy changes in Aurangzeb's time: "It is known that in 1672-73 the conservative emperor Aurangzeb ordered that all *madad-i maʿash* [endowments] granted to Hindus be repossessed, with future such grants reserved for Muslims only. But Delhi, as the old Persian proverb went, 'was still far away.' During the emperor's reign, Mughal officers in Sylhet issued more *madad-i maʿash* to Hindus after the 1672-73 order than before that date." Richard Maxwell Eaton, *The Rise of Islam and the Bengal Frontier, 1204-1760* (Berkeley: University of California Press, 1993), 263.

67. Mughal camp life, including the celebration of religious festivals of Muslims and Hindus and their invitations to one another, are described in Sarkar, *Memoirs of Bhimsen*.

68. See Dargah Quli Khan, *Muraqqa-e-Delhi: The Mughal Capital in Muhammad Shah's Time* (Delhi: Deputy Publication, 1989). Also, for a discussion of Dargah Quli Khan's work and, more generally, the lively "cultural scene" of Aurangzeb's time, see Katherine Butler Brown, "If Music Be the Food of Love: Masculinity and Eroticism in the Mughal *Mehfil*," in *Love in South Asia: A Cultural History*, ed. Francesca Orsini (Cambridge: Cambridge University Press, 2006), 64–71.

69. Jadunath Sarkar, *Shivaji and His Times*, 2nd ed. (London: Longmans, Green and Co., 1920), 367. I have edited the letter for readability mainly by removing some of the transliterated Persian. This letter is also discussed and quoted in full in Sarkar, *History of Aurangzib*, 3:325–329.

70. See Maulvi Zafar Hasan, "Two Recently Discovered Letters, One from the Shah of Persia to Aurangzeb and the Other, the Latter's Reply," in *Proceedings of the Meetings of the Session: Indian Historical Records Commission* (Delhi: Indian Historical Records Commission, 1920).

71. For a discussion of these wall murals, see Sussan Babaie, "Shah ʿAbbas II, the Conquest of Qandahar, the Chihil Sutun, and Its Wall Paintings," *Muqarnas* 11 (1994): 125–142.

72. One of these paintings depicted the Safavid founder Shah Ismaʿil's landmark battle with the Uzbeks. The other three scenes were of Safavid sovereigns granting refuge to asylum-seeking princes and kings: Shah Tahmasb to Humayun; Shah ʿAbbas I

to Vali Muhammad Khan, an Uzbek ruler; and Shah ʿAbbas II to Nadr Muhammad Khan, also an Uzbek. Ibid.

73. I first heard of this interpretation from Kathryn Babayan, "Speaking in God's Words: Social and Sexual Politics in Early Modern Isfahan," paper presented at the Islamic Studies Lecture Series, University of Texas at Austin (April 11, 2008). A similar interpretation is suggested in Sussan Babaie, *Isfahan and Its Palaces: Statecraft, Shiʿism, and the Architecture of Conviviality in Early Modern Iran* (Edinburgh: Edinburgh University Press, 2008), 228. In a recent article, Sussan Babaie has offered a broader analysis of this particular scene, arguing that it can also be read as a visual rendering of the well-known *hazl* (ribaldry) poetic genre with a unique play on Christian Europeans, examples of which can be seen in other murals in Isfahan at that time. See Sussan Babaie, "Frontiers of Visual Taboo: Painted 'Indecencies' in Isfahan," in *Images of Desire: On the Erotic and the Sensual in Islamic Art*, ed. Francesca Leoni and Mika Natif (London: Ashgate, 2012). I would like to thank both scholars, Kathryn Babayan and Sussan Babaie, for sharing their insights and early versions of their work on Safavid visual culture with me.

74. Manucci, *Storia do Mogor*, 2:121–122.

75. Ibid., 2:416.

76. The literature on the political history of eighteenth-century India is considerable. See, for example, Muzaffar Alam, *The Crisis of Empire in Mughal North India: Awadh and the Punjab, 1707-48* (Delhi: Oxford University Press, 1986), 330; Richard B. Barnett, *North India Between Empires: Awadh, the Mughals, and the British, 1720-1801* (Berkeley: University of California Press, 1980); Juan R. Cole, *Roots of North Indian Shiʿism in Iran and Iraq: Religion and State in Awadh, 1722-1859* (Berkeley: University of California Press, 1988); Stewart Gordon, *The Marathas 1600-1818* (New York: Cambridge University Press, 1993); J. S. Grewal, *The Sikhs of the Punjab* (Cambridge: Cambridge University Press, 1990). For a literary perspective of a minor Mughal prince on how his world was changing, see Muzaffar Alam and Sanjay Subrahmanyam, "Envisioning Power: The Political Thought of a Late Eighteenth-Century Mughal Prince," *Indian Economic Social History Review* 43, no. 2 (2006): 131–161.

77. The legal and symbolic ramifications of the English East India Company's century-long policy of nominally accepting Mughal sovereignty are discussed and debated in F. W. Buckler, *Legitimacy and Symbols: The South Asian Writings of F. W. Buckler*, ed. M. N. Pearson (Ann Arbor: Center for South and Southeast Asian Studies, University of Michigan, 1985).

78. Barbara Metcalf's work on the Deoband School in northern India begins with a detailed commentary on how social and political change in the eighteenth and nineteenth century in British colonial India contributed to the development of a new type of Islamic college that was organized, funded, and run on lines that were surprisingly "modern" in its institutional underpinnings. Notably, the Deoband madrasa differed from previous madrasas in Islamic history in that it was not endowed by the king or nobility but was run by the contributions of common Muslims. As such, it provided a new model that became widely adopted by Islamic religious colleges in South Asia and beyond. See Barbara Daly Metcalf, *Islamic Revival in British India: Deoband, 1860-1900* (New Delhi: Oxford University Press, 2005).

BIBLIOGRAPHY

PRIMARY SOURCES

Abu al-Fazl ibn Mubarak. *A'in-i Akbari*. Edited by H. Blochmann. Vol. 2. Calcutta: Asiatic Society of Bengal, 1877.

———. *A'in-i Akbari*. Edited by Sir Sayyid Ahmad. Aligarh: Sir Sayyid Academy, Aligarh Muslim University, 2005.

———. *The Akbarnamah*. Edited by Maulawi ʿAbd-ur-Rahim. 3 vols. Calcutta: Asiatic Society of Bengal, 1877–1886.

Abu al-Fazl ibn Mubarak, and Henry Beveridge. *The Akbar Nama of Abu-l-Fazl: History of the Reign of Akbar Including an Account of His Predecessors*. 3 (1 and 2 bound in one) vols. Calcutta: 1897–1921. Lahore: Sang-e-Meel Publications, 2005.

Abu al-Fazl ibn Mubarak, H. Blochmann, D. C. Phillott, H. S. Jarrett, and Jadunath Sarkar. *The A'in-i Akbari*. Lahore: Sang-e-Meel Publications, 2003. Calcutta: Royal Asiatic Society of Bengal, 1927–1949.

Abu Maʿshar, Jaʿfar ibn Muhammad. *On Historical Astrology: The Book of Religions and Dynasties (On the Great Conjunctions)*. Translated by Keiji Yamamoto and Charles Burnett. 2 vols. Boston: Brill, 2000.

Aftabchi, Jawhar. "Tadhkiratu ʾl-Waqiat." In *Three Memoirs of Homayun*, edited by Wheeler M. Thackston, 1:69–175. Costa Mesa, Calif.: Mazda Publishers, 2009.

Aubin, Jean. *Majmuʿah dar Tarjumah-ʾi Ahval-i Shah Niʿmatullah [Materiaux pour la biographie de Shah Niʿmatullah Wali Kermani]*. Tehran: Anjuman-i Iranshinasi-ʾi Faransah dar Tihran, 1982.

Baba Shah, Mahmud, and Simon Digby. *Sufis and Soldiers in Awrangzeb's Deccan: Malfuzat-i Naqshbandiyya*. New Delhi: Oxford University Press, 2001.

Babur, Zahir al-Din Mirza, and Annette Susannah Beveridge. *The Babur-nama in English (Memoirs of Babur)*. 2 vols. London: Luzac & Co., 1921.

Babur, Zahir al-Din Mirza, and W. M. Thackston. *The Baburnama: Memoirs of Babur, Prince and Emperor*. Pbk. ed. New York: Modern Library, 2002.

Babur, Zahir al-Din Mirza, W. M. Thackston, and Abdur Rahim Khan. *Baburnama: Chaghatay Turkish Text with Abdul-Rahim Khankhanan's Persian Translation*. Cambridge, Mass.: Department of Near Eastern Languages and Civilizations, Harvard University, 1993.

Bada'uni, Abd al-Qadir ibn Muluk Shah. *Muntakhab-ut-Tawarikh.* 3 vols. Calcutta: 1864–1869. Osnabruck: Biblio Verlag, 1983.

———. *Najat al-Rashid.* Lahore: Idarah-i Tahqiqat-i Pakistan, Danishgah-i Panjab, 1972.

Bada'uni, Abd al-Qadir ibn Muluk Shah, George S. A. Ranking, Wolseley H. Lowe, and Wolseley Haig. *Muntakhabu-t-Tawarikh: By ʿAbdul Qadir bin-Muluk Shah Known as al-Badaoni.* 3 vols. Calcutta: 1884–1925. New Delhi: Atlantic Publishers & Distributors, 1990.

Bashir, Shahzad. "The Risalat al-Huda of Muhmammad Nurbakhsh (d. 869/1464)." *Rivista Degli Studi Orientali* 75, no. 1/4 (2001): 87–138.

Benveniste, E. "Une apocalypse pehlevie: le Zamasp-Namak." *Revue de l'Histoire des Religions* 106 (1932): 337–380.

Bernier, Francois. *Travels in the Mogul Empire.* Translated by Archibald Constable. Edited by Vincent A. Smith. 2nd ed. New Delhi: Low Price Publications, 1989.

Bilimoria, Jamshid H. *Rukaʿat-i-Alamgiri or Letters of Aurangzebe.* Delhi: Idarah-i Adabiyat-i Delli, 1972.

Biruni, Muhammad ibn Ahmad. *The Chronology of Ancient Nations: An English Version of the Arabic Text of the Athar-ul-Bakiya of Albiruni.* Translated by Eduard Sachau. London: Published for the Oriental translations fund of Great Britain & Ireland by W. H. Allen and Co., 1879.

Correia-Afonso, John. *Letters from the Mughal Court: The First Jesuit Mission to Akbar, 1580–1583.* Bombay: Published for the Heras Institute of Indian History and Culture by Gujarat Sahitya Prakash, Anand, 1980.

Dihlavi, Farid Ibrahim, "Karnama-i Sahib Qiran-i Thani Zij-i Shah Jahani," British Library, London, MS Or 372.

Fani, Muhsin. *Dabistan-i Mazahib.* Edited by Rahim Rizazadah Malik. 2 vols. Tehran: Kitabkhanah-i Tahuri, 1362 [1983].

———. *The Dabistan or School of Manners.* Translated by David Shea and Anthony Troyer. Washington: M. W. Dunne, 1901.

Ghawth al-Hindi, Muhammad ibn Khatir al-Din. *Al-Jawahir al-Khams.* Edited by Ahmad Ibn al-ʿAbbas. 2 vols. Cairo: Muhammad Rifʿat ʿAmir, 1973.

———. "Jawahir-i Khamsa," Markaz-i Tahqiqat-i Farsi-i Iran va Pakistan [Iran Pakistan Institute of Persian Studies], Islamabad, MS 1458.

Gonzalez de Clavijo, Ruy. *Narrative of the Embassy of Ruy Gonzalez de Clavijo to the Court of Timour at Samarcand, A.D. 1403-6.* Translated by Clements R. Markham. London: Printed for the Hakluyt Society, 1859.

Grey, Charles, ed. *A Narrative of Italian Travels in Persia, in the Fifteenth and Sixteenth Centuries.* London: Hakluyt Society, 1873.

Guerreiro, Fernão. *Jahangir and the Jesuits: With an Account of the Travels of Benedict Goes and the Mission to Pegu, from the Relations of Father Fernao Guerreiro, S. J.* Translated by Charles Herbert Payne. New York: R. M. McBride & Co., 1930.

Gulbadan. "Humayunnama." In *Three Memoirs of Homayun,* edited by Wheeler M. Thackston. 1: 1–68. Costa Mesa, Calif.: Mazda Publishers, 2009.

Gulbadan, and Annette Susannah Beveridge. *The History of Humayun (Humayun-Nama).* Delhi: Idarah-i Adabiyat-i Delli, 1972.

Hasan, Maulvi Zafar. "Two Recently Discovered Letters, One from the Shah of Persia to Aurangzeb and the Other, the Latter's Reply." In *Proceedings of the Meetings of the Session: Indian Historical Records Commission.* Delhi: Indian Historical Records Commission, 1920.

Haydar, Mirza. *Tarikh-i Rashidi*. Edited by ʿAbbas Quli Ghaffarifard. Tehran: Markaz-i Nashr-i Miras-i Maktub, 2004.
Haydar, Mirza, and E. Denison Ross. *A History of the Moghuls of Central Asia: Being the Tarikh-i-Rashidi of Mirza Muhammad Haidar, Dughlat*. Edited by Ney Elias. Patna, India: Academica Asiatica, 1973.
Husaini, Abu Talib, "Malfuzat-i Amir Timur," British Library, London, MS Or 158.
———. *The Mulfuzat Timury or Autobiographical Memoirs of the Moghul Emperor Timur*. Translated by Charles Stewart. London: Oriental Translation Committee, 1830.
Ibn Arabshah, Ahmad ibn Muhammad. *ʿAjaʾib al-Maqdur fi Nawaʾib Taimur*. Edited by Ali Muhammad Umar. Cairo: Maktabat al-Anjulu al-Misriyah, 1979.
———. *Tamerlane*. Translated by John Herne Sanders. Lahore: Progressive Books, 1976.
Ibn Khaldun. *Muqaddima Ibn Khaldun*. Edited by Ihab Muhammad Ibrahim. Cairo: Maktabat al-Quran, 2006.
———. *The Muqaddimah, an Introduction to History*. Abridged and edited by N. J. Dawood. Translated by Franz Rosenthal. Princeton, N.J.: Princeton University Press, 1969.
———. *Taʿrif bi-Ibn Khaldun wa-Rihlatuhu Gharban wa-Sharqan*. Lebanon: Dar al-Kitab al-Lubnani, 1979.
Ibn Khaldun, and Walter Joseph Fischel. *Ibn Khaldun and Tamerlane: Their Historic Meeting in Damascus, 1401 AD (803 AH)*. Berkeley: University of California Press, 1952.
Ibn Taymiyya. *Minhaj al-Sunnah al-Nabawiyya fi Naqd Kalam al-Shʿia wa al-Qadariyya*. 4 vols. Bulaq, Misr [Cairo]: al-Matbaʿa al-Kubra al-ʾAmiriyya, 1904 (1322 AH).
Ibn Taymiyya, and Muhammad Umar Memon. *Ibn Taimiya's Struggle Against Popular Religion: With an Annotated Translation of His Kitab Iqtida as-Sirat al-Mustaquim Mukhalafat Ashab al-Jahim*. The Hague: Mouton, 1976.
Inayat, Khan, W. E. Begley, and Ziyaud-Din A. Desai. *The Shah Jahan Nama of ʿInayat Khan*. Delhi: Oxford University Press, 1990.
Islam, Riazul. *A Calendar of Documents on Indo-Persian Relations*. 2 vols. Tehran: Iranian Culture Foundation and Institute of Central & West Asian Studies, 1979.
Jahangir, and Muhammad Hashim. *Jahangirnamah, Tuzuk-i Jahangiri*. Intisharat-i Bunyad-i Farhang-i Iran. [Tehran]: Bunyad-i Farhang-i Iran, 1980 [1359].
Jahangir, and W. M. Thackston. *The Jahangirnama: Memoirs of Jahangir, Emperor of India*. Washington, D.C.: Freer Gallery of Art, 1999.
Kennedy, E. S., David Edwin Pingree, and Mashaʾallah. *The Astrological History of Mashaʾallah*. Cambridge, Mass.: Harvard University Press, 1971.
Khafi Khan, Muhammad Hashim. *Muntakhab al-Lubab, Part 1*. Edited by Mawlavi Kabir al-Din Ahmad. Calcutta: Asiatic Society of Bengal, 1869.
Khan, Dargah Quli. *Muraqqa-e-Delhi: The Mughal Capital in Muhammad Shah's Time*. Delhi: Deputy Publications, 1989.
Khan, Muʿtamad. *The Iqbalnamah-i Jahangiri*. Bibliotheca Indica. Osnabruck: Biblio Verlag, 1982.
Khunji, Ruzbihan. *Suluk al-Muluk*. Edited by Muhammad Ali Muvahhid. Tehran: Shirkat-i Sahami-i Intisharat-i Khvarazmi, 1984 [1362].
Khvand Mir, Ghiyas al-Din ibn Humam al-Din. *A Work on the Rules and Ordinances Established by the Emperor Humayun and on Some Buildings Erected by His Order [Qanun-i Humayuni, Persian Text with Notes and Preface]*. Edited by M. Hidayat Hosain. Calcutta: Asiatic Society, 1940.
Khwandamir, Giyas al-Din. *Tarikh-i Habib al-Siyar*. Vol. 4. Tehran: Kitabkhanah-i Khayyam, 1954.

"Kitab Jamasp fi Tawaliᶜ al-Anbiyaʾ," British Library, London, MS Add 7714.
Lahiji, Muhammad ibn Yahya. *Mafatih al-Ijaz fi Sharh-i Gulshan-i Raz*. Edited by Muhammad Riza Barzigar Khaliqi and Iffat Karbasi. Tehran: Zavvar, 1992.
Lahuri, Abd al-Sattar ibn Qasim, Riza Allah Shah Arif Nawshahi, and Muin Nizami. *Majalis-i Jahangiri: Majlisha-i Shabanah-i Darbar-i Nur al-Din Jahangir*. Tehran: Markaz-i Pizhuhi-shi-i Miras-i Maktub, 1385.
Manucci, Niccolao. *Storia do Mogor, or, Mogul India, 1653-1708*. Translated by William Irvine. 4 vols. London: John Murray, 1907. Calcutta: Editions Indian, 1966.
Membré, Michele. *Mission to the Lord Sophy of Persia (1539-1542)*. Translated by Alexander H. Morton. London: School of Oriental and African Studies, University of London, 1993.
Michot, Yahya J. "Ibn Taymiyya on Astrology: Annotated Translation of Three Fatwas." In *Magic and Divination in Early Islam*, edited by Emilie Savage-Smith, 277–340. Aldershot: Ashgate/Variorum, 2004.
Minorsky, V., and Shah Ismaᶜil I. "The Poetry of Shah Ismaᶜil I." *Bulletin of the School of Oriental and African Studies, University of London* 10, no. 4 (1942): 1006a–1053a.
Mirza Nathan. *Baharistan-i-Ghaybi: A History of the Mughal Wars in Assam, Cooch Behar, Bengal*. Translated by Moayyidul Islam Borah and Suryya Kumar Bhuyan. Gauhati: The Government of Assam, Dept. of Historical and Antiquarian Studies, Narayani Handiqui Historical Institute, 1936.
Miskin Samarqandi, Muhammad Fazil, "Jawahir al-ᶜUlum Humayuni," Markaz-i Tahqiqat-i Farsi-i Iran va Pakistan [Iran Pakistan Institute of Persian Studies], Islamabad, MS 301.
Muhammad-Hadi. "Preface to the Jahangirnama by Muhammad-Hadi." In *The Jahangirnama: Memoirs of Jahangir, Emperor of India*, edited by W. M. Thackston, 3–18. Washington, D.C.: Freer Gallery of Art, 1999.
Muhammad bin Husam al-Din, "Khawarnama," British Library, London, MS IOIslamic 3443.
Munshi, Iskandar Beg. *The History of Shah ʿAbbas the Great: Tarikh-e Alamara-ye ʿAbbasi*. Translated by Roger Savory. 2 vols. Boulder, Colo.: Westview Press, 1978.
Mutribi Samarqandi. *Conversations with Emperor Jahangir*. Translated by Richard C. Foltz. Costa Mesa, Calif.: Mazda Publishers, 1998.
———. *Khatirat-i Mutribi*. Edited by Abdul Ghani Mirzoyef. Karachi: Institute of Central & West Asian Studies, University of Karachi, 1977.
Qasimi Gunabadi, Muhammad Qasim. *Shah Ismaᶜil Namah*. Edited by Jaᶜfar Shujaᶜ Kayhani. Tehran: Farhangistan-i Zaban va Adab-i Farsi, 1387 [2008 or 2009].
Roe, Thomas. *The Embassy of Sir Thomas Roe to India, 1615-1619: As Narrated in His Journal and Correspondence*. Edited by William Foster. New Delhi: Munshiram Manoharlal Publications, 1990. London: Hakluyt Society, 1926.
Rustami, Kamal Khan, "Khawarnama Dakkani," British Library, London, MS IOIslamic 834.
Safavi, Tahmasb. *Tazkira-i Shah Tahmasb*. Edited by A. Safari. Tehran: Intisharat-i Sharq, 1363 [1984].
Sarkar, Jadunath. *English Translation of Tarikh-i-Dilkasha (Memoirs of Bhimsen Relating to Aurangzib's Deccan Campaigns)*. Bombay: Dept. of Archives, 1972.
Shami, Nizam al-Din. *Zafarnamah: Tarikh-i Futuhat-i Amir Timur Gurkani*. Edited by Panahi Simnani. Tehran: Bamdad, 1984.
Sirhindi, Badr al-Din. *Hazarat al-Quds*. Lahore: Mahakama-i Awqaf Panjab, 1971.
Sirhindi, Shaykh Ahmad. *Maktubat-i Imam-i Rabbani*. 3 vols. Lucknow: Nawal Kishore Press, 1889.

Sirhindi, Shaykh Ahmad, and Fazlur Rahman. *Intikhab-i Maktubat-i Shaykh Ahmad Sirhindi.* 2nd ed. Lahore, Pakistan: Iqbal Academy, 1984.
Tattavi, Qazi Ahmad, and Asif Khan Qazvini. *Tarikh-i Alfi.* Edited by Ghulam Riza Tabatabai Majd. 8 vols. Tehran: Shirkat-i Intisharat-i ʿIlmi va Farhangi, 1382 [2003 or 2004].
Yazdi, Sharaf al-Din Ali. *The History of Timur-Bec.* Translated by John Darby. 2 vols. London: Printed for J. Darby [etc.], 1723.
———, "Zafarnama (a)," British Library, London, MS Add 18406.
———, "Zafarnama (b)," British Library, London, MS Add 7635.
———, "Zafarnama (c)," British Library, London, MS Or 1359.
———. *Zafarnamah.* Edited by Abbasi Muhammad. 2 vols. Tehran: Amir Kabir, 1957.
———. *The Zafarnamah.* Edited by Muhammad Ilahdad. 2 vols. Calcutta: Asiatic Society Bengal, 1887.

SECONDARY WORKS

Abbas, Fauzia Zareen. *Abdul Qadir Badauni, as a Man and Historiographer.* Delhi: Idarah-i Adabiyat-i Delli, 1987.
Abby, Zanger. "Making Sweat: Sex and the Gender of National Reproduction in the Marriage of Louis XIII." *Yale French Studies,* no. 86 (1994): 187–205.
Abisaab, Rula Jurdi. *Converting Persia: Religion and Power in the Safavid Empire.* London: I. B. Tauris, 2004.
Ahmad, Aziz. "Din-i Ilahi." In *The Encyclopaedia of Islam,* 2nd ed., edited by P. Bearman, Th. Bianquis, C. E. Bosworth, E. van Donzel and W. P. Heinrichs. Brill, 2011. http://www.brillonline.nl.
———. "Safawid Poets and India." *Iran* 14 (1976): 117–132.
Aigle, Denise. "Les transformations d'un mythe d'origine: l'exemple de Gengis Khan et de Tamerlan." *Revue de Mondes Musulmans et de Méditerranée* 89–90 (2000): 151–168.
al-Azmeh, Aziz. *Muslim Kingship: Power and the Sacred in Muslim, Christian, and Pagan Polities.* London: I. B. Tauris, 1997.
Alam, Muzaffar. *The Crisis of Empire in Mughal North India: Awadh and the Punjab, 1707–48.* Delhi: Oxford University Press, 1986.
———. "The Debate Within: A Sufi Critique of Religious Law, Tasawwuf, and Politics in Mughal India." *South Asian History and Culture* 2, no. 2 (2011): 138–159.
———. *The Languages of Political Islam: India, 1200–1800.* Chicago: University of Chicago Press, 2004.
———. "The Mughals, the Sufi Shaikhs, and the Formation of the Akbari Dispensation." *Modern Asian Studies* 43, no. 1 (2009): 135–174.
Alam, Muzaffar, and Sanjay Subrahmanyam. "Envisioning Power: The Political Thought of a Late Eighteenth-Century Mughal Prince." *Indian Economic Social History Review* 43, no. 2 (2006): 131–161.
———. "Frank Disputations: Catholics and Muslims in the Court of Jahangir." *Indian Economic Social History Review* 45, no. 4 (2009): 457–511.
———. "Witnessing Transition: Views on the End of the Akbari Dispensation." In *The Making of History: Essays Presented to Irfan Habib,* edited by K. N. Panikkar, T. J. Byres, and Utsa Patnaik. 104–140. London: Anthem, 2002.
Algar, Hamid. "Nuktawiyya." In *The Encyclopaedia of Islam,* 2nd ed., edited by P. Bearman, Th. Bianquis, C.E. Bosworth, E. van Donzel, and W. P. Heinrichs. Brill, 2011. http://www.brillonline.nl.

———. "Nurbakhshiyya." In *The Encyclopaedia of Islam*, 2nd ed., edited by P. Bearman, Th. Bianquis, C.E. Bosworth, E. van Donzel, and W. P. Heinrichs. Brill, 2011. http://www.brillonline.nl.

Algar, Hamid, and J. Burton-Page. "Niʿmat-allahiyya." In *The Encyclopaedia of Islam*, 2nd ed., edited by P. Bearman, Th. Bianquis, C. E. Bosworth, E. van Donzel, and W. P. Heinrichs. Brill, 2011. http://www.brillonline.nl.

Ali, M. Athar. "Akbar and Islam (1581–1605)." In *Islamic Society and Culture: Essays in Honour of Professor Aziz Ahmad*, edited by Milton Israel and N. K. Wagle, 123–134. New Delhi: Manohar, 1983.

Ali, Mubarak. "Akbar in Pakistani Textbooks." *Social Scientist* 20, no. 9/10 (September–October 1992): 73–76.

Alvi, Sajida S. "Religion and State During the Reign of Mughal Emperor Jahangir (1605–27): Nonjuristical Perspectives." *Studia Islamica* 69 (1989): 95–119.

Amin, Shahid. "On Retelling the Muslim Conquest of North India." In *History and the Present*, edited by Partha Chatterjee and Anjan Ghosh, 19–32. Delhi: Permanent Black, 2002.

Amitai-Preiss, Reuven. "Sufis and Shamans: Some Remarks on the Islamization of the Mongols in the Ilkhanate." *Journal of Economic and Social History of the Orient* 42, no. 1 (1999): 27–46.

Amoretti, B. S. "Religion in the Timurid and Safavid Periods." In *The Cambridge History of Iran*, edited by Peter Avery, Gavin Hambly, and Charles Melville, 610–655. Cambridge: Cambridge University Press, 1968.

Anderson, Benedict. *Imagined Communities: Reflections on the Origin and Spread of Nationalism*. Rev. and extended ed. London: Verso, 1991.

Anooshahr, Ali. *The Ghazi Sultans and the Frontiers of Islam: A Comparative Study of the Late Medieval and Early Modern Periods*. London: Routledge, 2009.

Arjomand, Said Amir. "Religious Extremism (*ghuluww*), Sufism, and Sunnism in Safavid Iran: 1501–1722." *Journal of Asian History* 15 (1981): 1–35.

———. *The Shadow of God and the Hidden Imam: Religion, Political Order, and Societal Change in Shiʿite Iran from the Beginning to 1890*. Chicago: University of Chicago Press, 1984.

———. *The Turban for the Crown: The Islamic Revolution in Iran*. New York: Oxford University Press, 1988.

Arnakis, G. G. "Futuwwa Traditions in the Ottoman Empire: Akhis, Bektashi Dervishes, and Craftsmen." *Journal of near Eastern Studies* 12, no. 4 (Oct. 1953): 232–247.

Aron, Raymond. *Main Currents in Sociological Thought*. 2 vols. New York: Basic Books, 1967.

Asad, Talal. "The Idea of an Anthropology of Islam." *Occasional Papers, Center for Contemporary Arab Studies, Georgetown University* (1986): 1–23.

Asher, Catherine B. "The Architecture of Raja Man Singh: A Study of Sub-Imperial Patronage." In *Architecture in Medieval India: Forms, Contexts, Histories*, edited by Monica Juneja, 370–392. Delhi: Permanent Black, 2001.

———. "A Ray from the Sun." In *The Presence of Light: Divine Radiance and Religious Experience*, edited by Matthew T. Kapstein, 161–194. Chicago: University of Chicago Press, 2004.

Aubin, Jean. "Chroniques persanes et relations italiennes. Notes sur les sources narratives du regne de Sah Esmaʿil Ier." *Studia Iranica* 24 (1995): 247–259.

———. "Comment Tamerlan prenait le villes." *Studia Islamica* 19 (1963): 83–122.

———. "L'avenement des Safavides reconsidéré." *Moyen Orient & Ocean Indien* 5 (1988): 1–126.

———. "La politique religieuse des Safavides." In *Le shiʿisme imamite*, 235–244. Paris: Presses universitaires de France, 1970.

———. "Shah Ismaʿil et les notables de lʿIraq persan." *Journal of the Economic and Social History of the Orient* 2, no. 1 (1959): 37–81.
Auerbach, Erich. "Typological Symbolism in Medieval Literature." *Yale French Studies* 9 (1952): 3–10.
Babaie, Sussan. "Frontiers of Visual Taboo: Painted 'Indecencies' in Isfahan." In *Images of Desire: On the Erotic and the Sensual in Islamic Art*, edited by Francesca Leoni and Mika Natif. London: Ashgate, 2012.
———. *Isfahan and Its Palaces: Statecraft, Shiʿism, and the Architecture of Conviviality in Early Modern Iran*. Edinburgh: Edinburgh University Press, 2008.
———. "Shah ʿAbbas II, the Conquest of Qandahar, the Chihil Sutun, and Its Wall Paintings." *Muqarnas* 11 (1994): 125–142.
Babayan, Kathryn. *Mystics, Monarchs, and Messiahs: Cultural Landscapes of Early Modern Iran*. Cambridge, Mass.: Harvard University Press, 2002.
———. "Speaking in God's Words: Social and Sexual Politics in Early Modern Isfahan." Paper presented at the Islamic Studies Lecture Series, University of Texas at Austin, April 11, 2008.
———. "Sufis, Dervishes, and Mullas: The Controversy Over Spiritual and Temporal Dominion in Seventeenth-Century Iran." In *Safavid Persia: The History and Politics of an Islamic Society*, edited by Charles P. Melville, 117–138. London: I. B. Tauris, 1996.
Bagci, Serpil. "From Text to Pictures: ʿAli in Manuscript Painting." In *From History to Theology: Ali in Islamic Belief*, edited by Ahmet Yasar Ocak, 229–264. Ankara: Türk Tarih Kurumu, 2005.
Bailey, Gauvin Alexander. *The Jesuits and the Grand Mogul: Renaissance Art at the Imperial Court of India, 1580–1630*. Occasional Papers. Washington, D.C.: Freer Gallery of Art and Arthur M. Sackler Gallery, 1998.
———. "The Lahore Mirat al-Quds and the Impact of Jesuit Theatre on Mughal Painting." *South Asian Studies* 13 (1997): 31–44.
Balabanlilar, Lisa. *Imperial Identity in the Mughal Empire: Memory and Dynastic Politics in Early Modern South and Central Asia*. London: I. B. Tauris, 2012.
———. "Lords of the Auspicious Conjunction: Turco-Mongol Imperial Identity on the Subcontinent." *Journal of World History* 18, no. 1 (2007): 1–39.
Barnett, Richard B. *North India Between Empires: Awadh, the Mughals, and the British, 1720–1801*. Berkeley: University of California Press, 1980.
Bartold, V. V. "Ulugh-Beg's Private Life and Scholarly Occupations." In *Four Studies on the History of Central Asia: Translated from the Russian by V. and T. Minorsky*. Vol. 2: *Ulugh-Beg*, 120–143. Leiden: E.J. Brill, 1958.
Bashear, Suliman. "Riding Beasts on Divine Missions." *Journal of Semitic Studies* 36, no. 1 (1991): 37–75.
Bashir, Shahzad. "Between Mysticism and Messianism: The Life and Thought of Muhammad Nurbaks (d. 1464)." Ph.D. dissertation, Yale University, 1997.
———. *Fazlallah Astarabadi and the Hurufis*. Oxford: Oneworld, 2005.
———. *Messianic Hopes and Mystical Visions: The Nurbakhshiya Between Medieval and Modern Islam*. Columbia: University of South Carolina Press, 2003.
———. "Shah Ismaʿil and the Qizilbash: Cannibalism in the Religious History of Early Safavid Iran." *History of Religions* 45, no. 3 (2006): 234–256.
———. *Sufi Bodies: Religion and Society in Medieval Islam*. New York: Columbia University Press, 2011.

Bayly, C. A. *Empire and Information: Intelligence Gathering and Social Communication in India, 1780-1870*. Cambridge: Cambridge University Press, 1996.

———. "Knowing the Country: Empire and Information in India." *Modern Asian Studies* 27, no. 1, Special Issue: How Social, Political, and Cultural Information Is Collected, Defined, Used and Analyzed. (1993): 3-43.

———. "The Pre-History of 'Communalism'? Religious Conflict in India, 1700-1860." *Modern Asian Studies* 19, no. 2 (1985): 177-203.

Beach, Milo C. "Jahangir's Jahangir-Nama." In *The Powers of Art: Patronage in Indian Culture*, edited by Barbara Stoler Miller, 224-234. Delhi: Oxford University Press, 1992.

Beach, Milo C., Ebba Koch, and W. M. Thackston. *King of the World: The Padshahnama: An Imperial Mughal Manuscript from the Royal Library, Windsor Castle*. London: Azimuth Editions, 1997.

Berkey, Jonathan Porter. *Popular Preaching and Religious Authority in the Medieval Islamic Near East*. Seattle: University of Washington Press, 2001.

Bernardini, Michele. "Hatifi's *Timurnameh* and Qasimi's *Shahnameh-yi Isma'il*: Considerations for a Double Critical Edition." In *Society and Culture in the Early Modern Middle East: Studies on Iran in the Safavid Period*, edited by Andrew J. Newman, 3-18. Leiden: Brill, 2003.

Binyon, Laurence, James Vere Stewart Wilkinson, and Basil Gray. *Persian Miniature Painting: Including a Critical and Descriptive Catalogue of the Miniatures Exhibited at Burlington House, January-March, 1931*. London: Oxford University Press, 1933.

Biran, Michal. *Chinggis Khan*. Oxford: Oneworld, 2007.

Birge, John Kingsley. *The Bektashi Order of Dervishes*. London: Luzac Oriental, 1994.

Biruni, Muhammad ibn Ahmad, and Ainslie Thomas Embree. *Alberuni's India*. Abridged ed. New York: Norton, 1971.

Black, Antony. *The History of Islamic Political Thought: From the Prophet to the Present*. New York: Routledge, 2001.

Blair, Sheila S. "Sufi Saints and Shrine Architecture in the Early Fourteenth Century." *Muqarnas* 7 (1990): 35-49.

Blake, Stephen P. *Shahjahanabad: The Sovereign City in Mughal India, 1639-1739*. Cambridge: Cambridge University Press, 1991.

———. "The Patrimonial-Bureaucratic Empire of the Mughals." *Journal of Asian Studies* 39, no. 1 (November 1979): 77-94.

Bloch, Marc. *The Royal Touch: Sacred Monarchy and Scrofula in England and France*. London: Routledge & Kegan Paul, 1973.

Bourdieu, Pierre. *Outline of a Theory of Practice*. Cambridge: Cambridge University Press, 1977.

Boyce, M. "Ayadgar i Jamaspig." In *Encyclopaedia Iranica Online*. December 15, 1987. http://www.iranicaonline.org.

Broadbridge, Anne F. *Kingship and Ideology in the Islamic and Mongol Worlds*. Cambridge: Cambridge University Press, 2008.

Brown, Katherine Butler. "Did Aurangzeb Ban Music? Questions for the Historiography of His Reign." *Modern Asian Studies* 41, no. 1 (2007): 77-120.

———. "If Music Be the Food of Love: Masculinity and Eroticism in the Mughal *Mehfil*." In *Love in South Asia: A Cultural History*, edited by Francesca Orsini, 61-86. Cambridge: Cambridge University Press, 2006.

Brown, Michael J. *Itinerant Ambassador: The Life of Sir Thomas Roe*. Lexington: University Press of Kentucky, 1970.

Brown, Peter. "Arbiters of the Holy: The Christian Holy Man in Late Antiquity." In *Authority and the Sacred: Aspects of the Christianisation of the Roman World*, 55-78. Cambridge: Cambridge University Press, 1995.
———. "The Limits of Intolerance." In *Authority and the Sacred: Aspects of the Christianisation of the Roman World*, 27-54. Cambridge: Cambridge University Press, 1995.
———. "The Rise and Function of the Holy Man in Late Antiquity." *Journal of Roman Studies* 61 (1971): 80-101.
———. "The Rise and Function of the Holy Man in Late Antiquity, 1971-1997." *Journal of Early Christian Studies* 6, no. 3 (1998): 353-376.
Browne, Edward G. *A Literary History of Persia*. 4 vols. Cambridge: The University Press, 1929.
Brummett, Palmira. "The Myth of Shah Ismail Safavi: Political Rhetoric and 'Divine' Kingship." In *Medieval Christian Perceptions of Islam*, edited by John Victor Tolan, 331-359. New York: Routledge, 1996.
Buckler, F. W. *Legitimacy and Symbols: The South Asian Writings of F. W. Buckler*. Edited by M. N. Pearson. Ann Arbor: Center for South and Southeast Asian Studies, University of Michigan, 1985.
Bulliet, Richard W. *Islam: The View from the Edge*. New York: Columbia University Press, 1993.
Calmard, Jean. "Shiʿi Rituals and Power II: The Consolidation of Safavid Shiʿism: Folklore and Popular Religion." In *Safavid Persia: The History and Politics of an Islamic Society*, edited by Charles P. Melville, 139-190. London: I. B. Tauris, 1996.
Canby, Sheila R. *Humayun's Garden Party: Princes of the House of Timur and Early Mughal Painting*. [Bombay]: Marg Publications, 1994.
Chann, N. S. "Lord of the Auspicious Conjunction: Origins of the Sahib-Qiran." *Iran and the Caucasus* 13, no. 1 (2009): 93-110.
Cohn, Norman Rufus Colin. *Cosmos, Chaos, and the World to Come: The Ancient Roots of Apocalyptic Faith*. New Haven, Conn.: Yale University Press, 1993.
———. *The Pursuit of the Millennium: Revolutionary Millenarians and Mystical Anarchists of the Middle Ages*. Rev. and expanded ed. New York: Oxford University Press, 1970.
Cole, Juan R. "Iranian Culture and South Asia, 1500-1900." In *Iran and the Surrounding World: Interactions in Culture and Cultural Politics*, edited by Nikki R. Keddie and Rudolph P. Matthee. Seattle: University of Washington Press, 2002.
———. *Roots of North Indian Shiʿism in Iran and Iraq: Religion and State in Awadh, 1722-1859*. Berkeley: University of California Press, 1988.
Cooperson, Michael. *Classical Arabic Biography: The Heirs of the Prophets in the Age of al-Maʾmun*. Cambridge: Cambridge University Press, 2000.
Copenhaver, Brian P. "Natural Magic, Hermetism, and Occultism in Early Modern Science." In *Reappraisals of the Scientific Revolution*, edited by David C. Lindberg and Robert S. Westman, 261-301. Cambridge: Cambridge University Press, 1990.
Cornell, Vincent J. *Realm of the Saint: Power and Authority in Moroccan Sufism*. 1st ed. Austin: University of Texas Press, 1998.
Correia-Afonso, John. *Jesuit Letters and Indian History, 1542-1773*. 2nd ed. Bombay: Oxford University Press, 1969.
Crone, Patricia. *Medieval Islamic Political Thought*. Edinburgh: Edinburgh University Press, 2004.
Currie, P. M. *The Shrine and Cult of Muin al-Din Chishti of Ajmer*. Delhi: Oxford University Press, 1989.

Dadvar, Abolghasem. *Iranians in Mughal Politics and Society, 1606-1658*. New Delhi: Gyan Pub. House, 1999.
Daftary, Farhad. *The Isma'ilis: Their History and Doctrines*. Cambridge: Cambridge University Press, 1990.
Dale, Stephen F. *The Garden of the Eight Paradises: Babur and the Culture of Empire in Central Asia, Afghanistan, and India (1483-1530)*. Boston: Brill, 2004.
Dale, Stephen F., and Alam Payind. "The Ahrari Waqf in Kabul in the Year 1546 and the Mughal Naqshbandiyyah." *Journal of the American Oriental Society* 119, no. 2 (1999): 218-233.
Dankoff, Robert. "Kasgari on the Beliefs and Superstitions of the Turks." *Journal of the American Oriental Society* 95, no. 1 (1975): 68-80.
Das, Asok Kumar. *Mughal Painting During Jahangir's Time*. Calcutta: Asiatic Society, 1978.
Davis, Craig. "Dara Shukuh and Aurangzib: Issues of Religion and Politics and their Impact on Indo-Muslim Society." Ph.D. dissertation, Indiana University, 2002.
Desai, Z. A. "A Foreign Dignitary's Ceremonial Visit to Akbar's Tomb: A First Hand Account." In *Akbar and His Age*, edited by Iqtidar Alam Khan, 188-197. New Delhi: Northern Book Centre, 1999.
DeWeese, Devin A. *Islamization and Native Religion in the Golden Horde: Baba Tükles and Conversion to Islam in Historical and Epic Tradition*. University Park: Pennsylvania State University Press, 1994.
Dickson, Martin B. "Shah Tahmasb and the Uzbeks: The Duel for Khurasan with Ubayd Khan: 930-946/1524-1540." Ph.D. dissertation, Princeton University, 1962.
Dickson, Martin B., and Stuart Cary Welch. *The Houghton Shahnameh*. 2 vols. Cambridge, Mass.: Harvard University Press, 1981.
Digby, Simon. "The Sufi Shaykh and the Sultan: A Conflict of Claims to Authority in Medieval India." *Iran* 28 (1990): 71-81.
Dirks, Nicholas B. *The Hollow Crown: Ethnohistory of an Indian Kingdom*. Cambridge: Cambridge University Press, 1987.
Donzel, E. van. "Mudjaddid." In *The Encyclopaedia of Islam*, 2nd ed., edited by P. Bearman, Th. Bianquis, C. E. Bosworth, E. van Donzel, and W. P. Heinrichs. Brill, 2011. http://www.brillonline.nl.
Douglas, Mary. *Edward Evans-Pritchard*. New York: Viking Press, 1980.
———. *How Institutions Think*. Syracuse, N.Y.: Syracuse University Press, 1986.
———. *Natural Symbols: Explorations in Cosmology*. London: Routledge, 2003.
Durkheim, Emile. *The Elementary Forms of Religious Life*. Translated by Karen E. Fields. New York: Free Press, 1995.
Eaton, Richard Maxwell. *The Rise of Islam and the Bengal frontier, 1204-1760*. Berkeley: University of California Press, 1993.
———. "Temple Desecration and Indo-Muslim States." In *Essays on Islam and Indian History*. 94-132. New Delhi: Oxford University Press, 2000.
———. *Temple Desecration and Muslim States in Medieval India*. Gurgaon, India: Hope India Publications, 2004.
Eck, Diana L. *Darsan: Seeing the Divine Image in India*. 3rd ed. New York: Columbia University Press, 1998.
El-Hibri, Tayeb. *Reinterpreting Islamic Historiography: Harun al-Rashid and the Narrative of the Abbasid Caliphate*. New York: Cambridge University Press, 1999.
Elias, Norbert. *The Civilizing Process*. Oxford: Blackwell, 1994.

Elias, Norbert, Robert van Krieken, and Eric Dunning. "Towards a Theory of Social Processes: A Translation." *British Journal of Sociology* 48, no. 3 (1997): 355–383.

Elmore, Gerald T. "The 'Millennial' Motif in Ibn al-ʿArabi's 'Book of the Fabulous Gryphon.'" *Journal of Religion* 81, no. 3 (2001): 410–437.

Elverskog, Johan. *Buddhism and Islam on the Silk Road*. Philadelphia: University of Pennsylvania Press, 2010.

Ernst, Carl W. "The Daily Life of a Saint, Ahmad Sirhindi, by Badr al-Din Sirhindi." In *Islam in South Asia in Practice*, edited by Barbara Daly Metcalf, 149–165. Princeton, N.J.: Princeton University Press, 2009.

———. *Eternal Garden: Mysticism, History, and Politics at a South Asian Sufi Center*. Albany: State University of New York Press, 1992.

———. "Jawaher-e Khamsa." In *Encyclopaedia Iranica Online*. March 9, 2009. http://www.iranicaonline.org.

———. "Muslim Studies of Hinduism? A Reconsideration of Arabic and Persian Translations from Indian Languages." *Iranian Studies* 36, no. 2 (2003): 173–195.

———. "Persecution and Circumspection in Shattari Sufism." In *Islamic Mysticism Contested: Thirteen Centuries of Controversies and Polemics*, edited by F. de Jong and Bernd Radtke, 416–435. Leiden: Brill, 1999.

———. "Situating Sufism and Yoga." *Journal of the Royal Asiatic Society* 15 (2005): 15–43.

———. "Sufism and Yoga According to Muhammad Ghawth." *Sufi* 29 (1996): 9–13.

Ethe, Hermann. *Catalogue of Persian Manuscripts in the Library of the India Office*. 5 vols. Oxford: Printed for the India Office by H. Hart, 1903.

Ettinghausen, Richard. "The Emperor's Choice." In *De Artibus Opuscula XL: Essays in Honor of Erwin Panofsky*, edited by Millard Meiss, 98–120. New York: New York University, 1961.

Evans-Pritchard, E. E. *Witchcraft, Oracles, and Magic Among the Azande*. Oxford: Clarendon Press, 1950.

Fahd, Toufic. "Djafr." In *The Encyclopaedia of Islam*, 2nd ed., edited by P. Bearman, Th. Bianquis, C. E. Bosworth, E. van Donzel, and W. P. Heinrichs. Brill, 2011. http://www.brillonline.nl.

———. "Huruf (ʿIlm al-)." In *The Encyclopaedia of Islam*, 2nd ed., edited by P. Bearman, Th. Bianquis, C. E. Bosworth, E. van Donzel, and W. P. Heinrichs. Brill, 2011. http://www.brillonline.nl.

———. *La divination arabe. Etudes religieuses, sociologiques et folkloriques sur le milieu natif de l'Islam*. Paris: Sindbad, 1987.

Farhad, Massumeh, and Serpil Bagci, eds. *Falnama: The Book of Omens*. Washington, D.C.: Arthur M. Sackler Gallery, Smithsonian Institution, 2009.

Faruqi, Shamsur Rahman. "Burning Rage, Icy Scorn: The Poetry of Jaʿfar Zatalli." Paper presented at the Hindi-Urdu Flagship Program, University of Texas at Austin, September 24, 2008. http://www.columbia.edu/itc/mealac/pritchett/00fwp/srf/srf_zatalli_2008.pdf.

Faruqui, Munis. "The Forgotten Prince: Mirza Hakim and the Formation of the Mughal Empire in India." *Journal of the Economic and Social History of the Orient* 48, no. 4 (2005): 487–523.

Fenech, Louis E. "Martyrdom and the Sikh Tradition." *Journal of the American Oriental Society* 117, no. 4 (1997): 623–642.

Fentress, James, and Chris Wickham. *Social Memory: New Perspectives on the Past*. Oxford: Blackwell, 1992.

Fleischer, Cornell. *Bureaucrat and Intellectual in the Ottoman Empire: The Historian Mustafa Ali (1541-1600)*. Princeton, N.J.: Princeton University Press, 1986.
———. "Seer to the Sultan: Haydar-i Remmal and Sultan Suleyman." In *Cultural Horizons*, edited by Jayne L. Warner and Talat Sait Halman, 290–299. Syracuse, N.Y.: Syracuse University Press, 2001.
Flood, Finbarr Barry. "Between Cult and Culture: Bamiyan, Islamic Iconoclasm, and the Museum." *Art Bulletin* 84, no. 4 (2002): 641–659.
Flores, Jorge. "Distant Wonders: The Strange and the Marvelous Between Mughal India and Habsburg Iberia in the Early Seventeenth Century." *Comparative Studies in Society and History* 49 (2007): 553–581.
Foucault, Michel. *The Order of Things: An Archaeology of the Human Sciences*. New York: Vintage, 1973.
Franke, Heike. *Akbar und Gahangir. Untersuchungen zur politischen und religiösen Legitimation in Text und Bild*. Schenefeld: EB-Verglag, 2005.
French, Peter J. *John Dee: The World of an Elizabethan Magus*. London: Routledge & Kegan Paul, 1972.
Friedmann, Yohanan. *Shaykh Ahmad Sirhindi: An Outline of His Thought and a Study of His Image in the Eyes of Posterity*. Oxford: Oxford University Press, 2000.
Gallagher, Amelia. "The Transformation of Shah Ismail Safevi in the Turkish Hikâye." *Journal of Folklore Research* 46, no. 2 (2009): 173–195.
Garin, Eugenio. *Astrology in the Renaissance: The Zodiac of Life*. London: Routledge & Kegan Paul, 1983.
Geertz, Clifford. "Centers, Kings, and Charisma: Reflections on the Symbolics of Power." In *Local Knowledge: Further Essays in Interpretive Anthropology*, 121–146. New York: Basic Books, 1983.
———. *The Interpretation of Cultures*. New York: Basic Books, 1973.
———. *Islam Observed: Religious Development in Morocco and Indonesia*. New Haven, Conn.: Yale University Press, 1968.
———. *Negara: The Theatre State in Nineteenth-Century Bali*. Princeton, N.J.: Princeton University Press, 1980.
———. "Thick Description: Toward an Interpretive Theory of Culture." In *The Interpretation of Cultures*, 3–30. New York: Basic Books, 1973.
Gimaret, D. "Tanasukh." In *The Encyclopaedia of Islam*, 2nd ed., edited by P. Bearman, Th. Bianquis, C. E. Bosworth, E. van Donzel, and W. P. Heinrichs. Brill, 2011. http://www.brillonline.nl.
Gladwin, Francis. *The History of Jahangir*. Edited by K. V. Rangaswami Aiyangar. Madras: B. G. Paul & Co., 1930.
Godelier, Maurice. *The Enigma of the Gift*. Chicago: University of Chicago Press, 1999.
Gommans, Jos. *Mughal Warfare: Indian Frontiers and Highroads to Empire, 1500-1700*. London: Routledge, 2002.
Gordon, Stewart. *The Marathas 1600-1818*. New York: Cambridge University Press, 1993.
———, ed. *Robes and Honor: The Medieval World of Investiture*. New York: Palgrave, 2001.
———, ed. *Robes of Honour: Khilʿat in Pre-Colonial and Colonial India*. New Delhi: Oxford University Press, 2003.
Grafton, Anthony. *Cardano's Cosmos: The Worlds and Works of a Renaissance Astrologer*. Cambridge, Mass.: Harvard University Press, 1999.
Graham, Gail Minault. "Akbar and Aurangzeb—Syncretism and Separatism in Mughal India: A Reexamination." *Muslim World* 59, no. 2 (1969): 106–126.

Green, Nile. *Sufism: A Global History*. Malden, Mass.: Wiley-Blackwell, 2012.
———. "Transgressions of a Holy Fool: A Majzub in Colonial India." In *Islam in South Asia in Practice*, edited by Barbara Metcalf, 173-186. Princeton, N.J.: Princeton University Press, 2009.
Greenblatt, Stephen. "A Touch of the Real." In *The Fate of "Culture": Geertz and Beyond*, edited by Sherry B. Ortner, 14-29. Berkeley: University of California Press, 1999.
Grewal, J. S. *The Sikhs of the Punjab*. Cambridge: Cambridge University Press, 1990.
Guenther, Alan M. "Hanafi Fiqh in Mughal India: The Fatawa-i ʿAlamgiri." In *India's Islamic Traditions, 711-1750*, edited by Richard Maxwell Eaton, 209-230. New Delhi: Oxford University Press, 2003.
Habib, Irfan. "The Political Role of Shaikh Ahmad Sirhindi and Shah Waliullah." *Enquiry* 5 (New Delhi, 1961): 36-55.
———. "Timur in the Political Tradition and Historiography of Mughal India." In *Cahiers d'Asie Centrale [En ligne]* no. 3/4 (1997). http://asiecentrale.revues.org/index500.html.
Habsburg, Francesca von. *The St. Petersburg Muraqqaʿ: Album of Indian and Persian Miniatures from the Sixteenth Through the Eighteenth Century and Specimens of Persian Calligraphy by Imad al-Hasani*. 2 vols. Milano: Leonardo Arte, 1996.
Haig, T. W. "Sahib Kiran (a. and p.)." In *Encyclopaedia of Islam*, 2nd ed., edited by P. Bearman, Th. Bianquis, C. E. Bosworth, E. van Donzel, and W. P. Heinrichs. Brill, 2009. http://www.brillonline.nl.
Hallaq, Wael B. "Iftaʾ and Ijithad in Sunni Legal Theory: A Developmental Account." In *Islamic Legal Interpretation: Muftis and Their Fatwas*, edited by Muhammad Khalid Masud, Brinkley Morris Messick, and David Stephan Powers, 33-43. Karachi: Oxford University Press, 2005.
Hasan, S. Nurul. "The Mahzar of Akbar's Reign." In *Religion, State, and Society in Medieval India: Collected Works of S. Nurul Hasan*, edited by Satish Chandra, 79-89. New Delhi, 2005.
Hawting, G. R. "Al-Mukhtar b. Abi ʿUbayd al-Thaqafi." In *Encyclopaedia of Islam*, 2nd ed., edited by P. Bearman, Th. Bianquis, C. E. Bosworth, E. van Donzel, and W. P. Heinrichs. Brill, 2008. http://www.brillonline.nl.
Hillenbrand, Robert. "Iconography of the Shah-nama-yi Shahi." In *Safavid Persia: The History and Politics of an Islamic Society*, edited by Charles P. Melville, 53-78. London: I. B. Tauris, 1996.
Hobsbawm, E. J. *Primitive Rebels*. Manchester: Manchester University Press, 1971.
Hodgson, Marshall G. S. "Ghulat." In *The Encyclopaedia of Islam*, 2nd ed., edited by P. Bearman, Th. Bianquis, C. E. Bosworth, E. van Donzel, and W. P. Heinrichs. Brill, 2011. http://www.brillonline.nl.
———. *The Venture of Islam*. 3 vols. Chicago: University of Chicago Press, 1974.
Hunsberger, Alice C. "Marvels." In *Encyclopaedia of the Qurʾan*, edited by Jane Dammen McAuliffe. Brill, 2009. http://www.brillonline.nl.
Ikram, S. M. *Rud-i Kawsar: Islami Hind aur Pakistan ki Mazhabi aur Ruhani Tarikh: Ahd-i Mughaliyya*. Lahore: Firozsons, 1958.
Islam, Riazul. *Indo-Persian Relations: A Study of the Political and Diplomatic Relations Between the Mughul Empire and Iran*. Tehran: Iranian Culture Foundation, 1970.
Isogai, Ken'ichi. "Yasa and Shariʿa in Early Sixteenth-Century Central Asia." In *Cahiers d'Asie Centrale [En ligne]* no. 3/4 (1997). http://asiecentrale.revues.org/index476.html.
Jafariyan, Rasul. *Qissah Khvanan dar Tarikh-i Islam va Iran*. [Iran?]: Dalil, 1378 [1999].
Jalaluddin. "Sultan Salim (Jahangir) as a Rebel King." *Islamic Culture* 47 (1973): 121-125.
Johnson, Paul Christopher. "Savage Civil Religion." *Numen* 52 (2005): 289-324.

Jong, Frederick De. "The Iconography of Bektashiism: A Survey of Themes and Symbolism in Clerical Costume, Liturgical Objects and Pictorial Art." *Manuscripts of the Middle East* 4 (1989): 7-29.

Kafadar, Cemal. *Between Two Worlds: The Construction of the Ottoman State*. Berkeley: University of California Press, 1995.

Kantorowicz, Ernst Hartwig. *The King's Two Bodies: A Study in Mediaeval Political Theology*. Princeton, N.J.: Princeton University Press, 1957.

Karamustafa, Ahmet T. *God's Unruly Friends: Dervish Groups in the Islamic Later Middle Period, 1200-1550*. Oxford: Oneworld, 2006.

Katz, Nathan. "The Identity of a Mystic: The Case of Sa'id Sarmad, a Jewish-Yogi-Sufi Courtier of the Mughals." *Numen* 47, no. 2 (2000): 142-160.

Keddie, Nikki R., and Yann Richard. *Roots of Revolution: An Interpretive History of Modern Iran*. New Haven, Conn.: Yale University Press, 1981.

Kennedy, E. S. "Comets in Islamic Astronomy and Astrology." *Journal of Near Eastern Studies* 16, no. 1 (1957): 44-51.

———. "The Exact Sciences in Timurid Iran." In *The Cambridge History of Iran: The Timurid and Safavid Periods*, edited by Peter Jackson and Laurence Lockhart, 568-580. Cambridge: University Press, 1986.

———. "Ramifications of the World-Year Concept in Islamic Astrology." *Actes, International Congress on the History of Sciences* 10 (1962): 23-43.

Khan, Hasan Ali. "Shiʿa-Ismaʿili Motifs in the Sufi Architecture of the Indus Valley, 1200-1500 AD." Ph.D. dissertation, School of Oriental and African Studies, 2009.

Khan, Iqtidar Alam. "Akbar's Personality Traits and World Outlook—A Critical Appraisal." *Social Scientist* 20, no. 9/10 (1992): 16-30.

Kinberg, Leah. "Dreams and Sleep." In *Encyclopaedia of the Qur'an*, 546-553. Leiden: Brill, 2001.

———. "Literal Dreams and Prophetic Hadiths in Classical Islam—A Comparison of Two Ways of Legitimation." *Der Islam* 70 (1993).

Kinra, Rajiv. "Infantilizing Baba Dara: The Cultural Memory of Dara Shekuh and the Mughal Public Sphere." *Journal of Persianate Studies* 2 (2009): 165-193.

Klaniczay, Gábor. *Holy Rulers and Blessed Princesses: Dynastic Cults in Medieval Central Europe*. Cambridge: Cambridge University Press, 2002.

Koch, Ebba. *Mughal Art and Imperial Ideology: Collected Essays*. New Delhi: Oxford University Press, 2001.

Kolff, D. H. A. *Naukar, Rajput, and Sepoy: The Ethnohistory of the Military Labour Market in Hindustan, 1450-1850*. Cambridge: Cambridge University Press, 1990.

Komaroff, Linda, and Stefano Carboni, eds. *The Legacy of Genghis Khan: Courtly Art and Culture in Western Asia, 1256-1353*. New York: Metropolitan Museum of Art, 2002.

Krader, Lawrence. *Social Organization of the Mongol-Turkic Pastoral Nomads*. The Hague: Mouton, 1963.

Krotkoff, Georg. "Colour and Number in the Haft Paykar." In *Logos Islamikos: Studia Islamica in Honorem Georgii Michaelis Wickens*, edited by G. M. Wickens, Roger Savory, and Dionisius A. Agius, 97-118. Toronto: Pontifical Institute of Mediaeval Studies, 1984.

Kugle, Scott. "Heaven's Witness: The Uses and Abuses of Muhammad Ghawth's Mystical Ascension." *Journal of Islamic Studies* 14, no. 1 (2003): 1-36.

———. *Sufis & Saints' Bodies: Mysticism, Corporeality, and Sacred Power in Islam*. Chapel Hill: University of North Carolina Press, 2007.

Lal, Ruby. *Domesticity and Power in the Early Mughal World.* Cambridge: Cambridge University Press, 2005.
Lambton, Ann K. S. *State and Government in Medieval Islam: An Introduction to the Study of Islamic Political Theory: The Jurists.* Oxford: Oxford University Press, 1981.
Latha, Mukunda. *Ardhakathanaka, Half a Tale: A Study in the Interrelationship Between Autobiography and History.* Jaipur: Rajasthan Prakrit Bharati Sansthan, 1981.
Lentz, Thomas W., and Glenn D. Lowry. *Timur and the Princely Vision: Persian Art and Culture in the Fifteenth Century.* Los Angeles: Los Angeles County Museum of Art, 1989.
Levi-Strauss, Claude. *The Savage Mind.* Chicago: University of Chicago Press, 1966.
Maclagan, Edward. *The Jesuits and the Great Mogul.* London: Burns, Oates & Washbourne, 1932.
MacLean, Derryl N. "The Sociology of Political Engagement: The Mahdawiyah and the State." In *India's Islamic Traditions, 711-1750,* edited by Richard Maxwell Eaton, 150-166. New Delhi: Oxford University Press, 2003.
Madelung, W. "Mahdi." In *The Encyclopaedia of Islam,* 2nd ed., edited by P. Bearman, Th. Bianquis, C. E. Bosworth, E. van Donzel, and W. P. Heinrichs. Brill, 2011. http://www.brillonline.nl.
Manz, Beatrice Forbes. *Power, Politics, and Religion in Timurid Iran.* Cambridge: Cambridge University Press, 2007.
———. *The Rise and Rule of Tamerlane.* Cambridge: Cambridge University Press, 1999.
———. "Tamerlane's Career and Its Uses." *Journal of World History* 13, no. 1 (2002).
———. "Ulugh Beg." In *Encyclopaedia of Islam,* 2nd ed., edited by P. Bearman, Th. Bianquis, C. E. Bosworth, E. van Donzel, and W. P. Heinrichs. Brill, 2008. http://www.brillonline.nl.
Mauss, Marcel. *The Gift: The Form and Reason for Exchange in Archaic Societies.* New York: W. W. Norton, 1990.
Mélikoff, Irène. "La divinisation d'Ali chez les Bektachis-Alevis." In *Au banquet des Quarante. Exploration au cœur du Bektachisme-Alevisme,* 97-120. Istanbul: Isis, 2001.
Melville, Charles. "The Mongols in Iran." In *The Legacy of Genghis Khan: Courtly Art and Culture in Western Asia, 1256-1353,* edited by Linda Komaroff and Stefano Carboni, 37-61. New York: Metropolitan Museum of Art, 2002.
———. "Padshah-i Islam: The Conversion of Sultan Mahmud Ghazan Khan." In *History and Literature in Iran,* edited by Charles Melville, 159-177. Pembroke Persian Papers. London: British Academic Press, 1990.
Meredith-Owens, G. M. "Hamza b. ʿAbd al- Muttalib." In *The Encyclopaedia of Islam,* 2nd ed., edited by P. Bearman, Th. Bianquis, C. E. Bosworth, E. van Donzel, and W. P. Heinrichs. Brill, 2011. http://www.brillonline.nl.
Meri, Josef W. *The Cult of Saints Among Muslims and Jews in Medieval Syria.* Oxford: Oxford University Press, 2002.
Meserve, Margaret. *Empires of Islam in Renaissance Historical Thought.* Cambridge, Mass.: Harvard University Press, 2008.
Metcalf, Barbara Daly. *Islamic Revival in British India: Deoband, 1860-1900.* New Delhi: Oxford University Press, 2005.
———. "Presidential Address: Too Little and Too Much: Reflections on Muslims in the History of India." *Journal of Asian Studies* 54, no. 4 (Nov. 1995): 951-967.
Millas, J. M. "Abu Maʿshar." In *The Encyclopaedia of Islam,* 2nd ed., edited by P. Bearman, Th. Bianquis, C. E. Bosworth, E. van Donzel, and W. P. Heinrichs. Brill, 2011. http://www.brillonline.nl.

Mir-Hosseini, Ziba. "Faith, Ritual, and Culture Among the Ahl-e Haqq." In *Kurdish Culture and Identity*, edited by Philip G. Kreyenbroek and Christine Allison, 111–134. London: Zed Books, 1996.
Mitchell, Colin Paul. *The Practice of Politics in Safavid Iran: Power, Religion, and Rhetoric*. BIPS Persian Studies Series. London: I. B. Tauris, 2009.
Moin, A. Azfar. "Challenging the Mughal Emperor: The Islamic Millennium According to ʿAbd al-Qadir Badayuni." In *Islam in South Asia in Practice*, edited by Barbara Metcalf, 390–402. Princeton, N.J.: Princeton University Press, 2009.
———. "Islam and the Millennium: Sacred Kingship and Popular Imagination in Early Modern India and Iran." Ph.D. dissertation, the University of Michigan, 2010.
———. "Partisan Dreams and Prophetic Visions: Shiʿi Critique in al-Masʿudi's History of the ʿAbbasids." *Journal of the Oriental American Society* 127, no. 4 (October–December 2007): 415–428.
Mojtabai, Fath-allah. "Dabestan-e Madaheb." In *Encyclopaedia Iranica Online*. December 15, 1993. http://www.iranicaonline.org.
Momen, Moojan. *An Introduction to Shiʿi Islam: The History and Doctrines of Twelver Shiʿism*. Oxford: G. Ronald, 1985.
Monod, Paul Kléber. *The Power of Kings: Monarchy and Religion in Europe, 1589–1715*. New Haven, Conn.: Yale University Press, 1999.
Morgan, David. *Medieval Persia, 1040–1797*. London: Longman, 1988.
———. *The Mongols*. Cambridge, Mass.: Blackwell, 1990.
Morton, Alexander H. "The Chub-i Tariq and Qizilbash Ritual in Safavid Persia." In *Etudes Safavides*, edited by Jean Calmard, 225–246. Paris: Institut Français de Recherche en Iran, 1993.
———. "The Early Years of Shah Ismaʿil in the *Afzal al-tavarikh* and Elsewhere." In *Safavid Persia: The History and Politics of an Islamic Society*, edited by Charles P. Melville, 27–52. London: I. B. Tauris, 1996.
Mossadegh, ʿAli Asghar. "La famille Monajjem Yazdi." *Studia Iranica* 16, no. 1 (1987): 125–129.
Muqtadir, Abdul. "Muhammad Ghawth Gwaliyari." In *Encyclopaedia of Islam*, 2nd ed., edited by P. Bearman, Th. Bianquis, C. E. Bosworth, E. van Donzel, and W. P. Heinrichs. Brill, 2008. http://www.brillonline.nl.
Narayan, Kirin. *Storytellers, Saints, and Scoundrels: Folk Narrative in Hindu Religious Teaching*. Philadelphia: University of Pennsylvania Press, 1989.
Necipoğlu, Gulru. "From International Timurid to Ottoman: A Change of Taste in Sixteenth-Century Ceramic Tiles." *Muqarnas* 7 (1990): 136–170.
Newman, Andrew J. "The Myth of the Clerical Migration to Safawid Iran: Arab Shiite Opposition to ʿAli al-Karaki and Safawid Shiism." *Die Welt des Islams* 33, no. 1 (1993): 66–112.
———. *Safavid Iran: Rebirth of a Persian Empire*. London: I. B. Tauris, 2006.
Nicoll, Fergus. *Shah Jahan*. London: Haus Publishing, 2009.
Nirenberg, David. *Communities of Violence: Persecution of Minorities in the Middle Ages*. Princeton, N.J.: Princeton University Press, 1996.
Nizami, Khaliq Ahmad. *Akbar and Religion*. Delhi: Idarah-i-Adabiyat-i-Delli, 1989.
———. "Shattariyya." In *Encyclopaedia of Islam*, 2nd ed., edited by P. Bearman, Th. Bianquis, C. E. Bosworth, E. van Donzel, and W. P. Heinrichs. Brill, 2008. http://www.brillonline.nl.

Okada, Amina. *Indian Miniatures of the Mughal Court*. New York: H. N. Abrams, 1992.
Orthmann, Eva. "Circular Motions: Private Pleasure and Public Prognostication in the Nativities of the Mughal Emperor Akbar." In *Horoscopes and Public Spheres: Essays on the History of Astrology*, edited by Günther Oestmann, H. Darrel Rutkin, and Kocku von Stuckrad, 101–114. Berlin: Walter de Gruyter, 2005.
———. "Court Culture and Cosmology in the Mughal Empire: Humayun and the Foundations of the Din-i Ilahi." In *Court Cultures in the Muslim World: Seventh to Nineteenth Centuries*, edited by Albrecht Fuess and Jan-Peter Hartung, 202–220. London: Routledge, 2011.
Parkes, Peter. "Fosterage, Kinship, and Legend: When Milk Was Thicker than Blood?" *Comparative Studies in Society and History* 46, no. 3 (2004): 535–586.
———. "Milk Kinship in Islam: Substance, Structure, History." *Social Anthropology* 13, no. 3 (2005): 307–329.
Paul, Jurgen. "Forming a Faction: The Himayat System of Khwaja Ahrar." *International Journal of Middle East Studies* 23, no. 4 (1991): 533–548.
Pearson, M. N. *The Portuguese in India*. Cambridge: Cambridge University Press, 1987.
Pellat, Ch., H. Massé, I. Mélikoff, A. T. Hatto, and Aziz Ahmad. "Hamasa." In *Encyclopaedia of Islam*, 2nd ed., edited by P. Bearman, Th. Bianquis, C. E. Bosworth, E. van Donzel, and W. P. Heinrichs. Brill, 2008. http://www.brillonline.nl.
Pinch, William R. *Warrior Ascetics and Indian Empires*. New York: Cambridge University Press, 2006.
Pingree, D. "Kiran." In *The Encyclopaedia of Islam*, 2nd ed., edited by P. Bearman, Th. Bianquis, C. E. Bosworth, E. van Donzel, and W. P. Heinrichs. Brill, 2011. http://www.brillonline.nl.
Pingree, David. "Astronomy and Astrology in India and Iran." *Isis* 54, no. 2 (June 1963): 229–246.
———. "Historical Horoscopes." *Journal of the American Oriental Society* 82, no. 4 (1962): 487–502.
———. *The Thousands of Abu Mashar*. London: Warburg Institute, 1968.
Pingree, David, and C. J. Brunner. "Astrology and Astronomy in Iran." In *Encyclopaedia Iranica Online*. December 15, 1987. http://www.iranicaonline.org.
Pollock, Sheldon. "Ramayana and Political Imagination in India." *Journal of Asian Studies* 52, no. 2 (1993): 261–297.
Poonawala, I. K., and E. Kohlberg. "ʿAli b. Abi Taleb." In *Encyclopaedia Iranica Online*. December 15, 1984. http://www.iranicaonline.org.
Prasad, Ishwari. *The Life and Times of Humayun*. Bombay: Orient Longmans, 1956.
Qaisar, A. Jan. "The Profane and the Sacred: 'Judgement of Paris' and 'God The Father' in the Mughal School of Art." In *Art and Culture: Felicitation Volume in Honour of Professor S. Nurul Hasan*, edited by Ahsan Jan Qaisar, Som Prakash Verma, and S. Nurul Hasan, 81–90. Jaipur: Publication Scheme, 1993.
Qamaruddin. *The Mahdawi Movement in India*. Delhi: Idarah-i Adabiyat-i Delhi, 1985.
Quinn, Sholeh. *Historical Writing During the Reign of Shah ʿAbbas: Ideology, Imitation, and Legitimacy in Safavid Chronicles*. Salt Lake City: University of Utah Press, 2000.
———. "Notes on Timurid Legitimacy in Three Safavid Chronicles." *Iranian Studies* 31, no. 2 (1998): 149–158.
Ramaswamy, Sumathi. "Conceit of the Globe in Mughal Visual Practice." *Comparative Studies in Society and History* 49 (2007): 751–782.
Ray, Sukumar. *Humayun in Persia*. Calcutta: Royal Asiatic Society of Bengal, 1948.

Renard, John. "Khadir/Khidr." In *Encyclopaedia of the Qurʾan*, edited by Jane Dammen McAuliffe. Brill, 2009. http://www.brillonline.nl.

Richards, John. "Norms of Comportment Among Imperial Mughal Officers." In *Moral Conduct and Authority: The Place of Adab in South Asian Islam*, edited by Barbara Daly Metcalf, 255–289. Berkeley: University of California Press, 1984.

Richards, John F. "The Formulation of Imperial Authority Under Akbar and Jahangir." In *Kingship and Authority in South Asia*, edited by John F. Richards, 285–326. Delhi: Oxford University Press, 1998.

———, ed. *Kingship and Authority in South Asia*. Delhi: Oxford University Press, 1998.

———. *The Mughal Empire*. Cambridge: Cambridge University Press, 1993.

Rieu, Charles. *Catalogue of the Persian Manuscripts in the British Museum*. 3 vols. London: British Museum, 1883.

Rizvi, Saiyid Athar Abbas. "Dimensions of *Sulh-i kul* (Universal Peace) in Akbar's Reign and the Sufi Theory of Perfect Man." In *Akbar and His Age*, edited by Iqtidar Alam Khan, 3–22. New Delhi: Northern Book Centre, 1999.

———. *A History of Sufism in India*. 2 vols. New Delhi: Munshiram Manoharlal, 1978.

———. *Muslim Revivalist Movements in Northern India in the Sixteenth and Seventeenth Centuries*. Agra: Agra University, 1965.

———. *Religious and Intellectual History of the Muslims in Akbar's Reign, with Special Reference to Abul Fazl, 1556-1605*. New Delhi: Munshiram Manoharlal Publishers, 1975.

———. *A Socio-Intellectual History of the Isna Ashari Shiʿis in India*. 2 vols. New Delhi: Munshiram Manoharlal Publishers, 1986.

Rizvi, Sajjad. "Mulla Sadra." In *The Stanford Encyclopedia of Philosophy*, summer 2009 ed., edited by Edward N. Zalta. 2009. http://plato.stanford.edu/archives/sum2009/entries/mulla-sadra/.

Rizvi, Sajjad H. "Mir Fendereski." In *Encyclopaedia Iranica Online*. July 20, 2005. http://www.iranicaonline.org.

Roemer, H. R. "Timur in Iran." In *The Cambridge History of Iran: The Timurid and Safavid Periods*, edited by Peter Jackson and Laurence Lockhart, 42–97. Cambridge: University Press, 1986.

Roxburgh, David J. *Prefacing the Image: The Writing of Art History in Sixteenth-Century Iran*. Leiden: Brill, 2001.

Roychoudhury, Makhanlal. *The Din-i-Ilahi: or, the Religion of Akbar*. Calcutta: University of Calcutta, 1941.

Safa, Z. "Andarz." In *Encyclopaedia Iranica Online*. December 15, 1985. http://www.iranicaonline.org.

"Sahib Qiran." In *Lughatname-i Dehkhoda [Dehkhoda Dictionary CD-ROM]*, edited by Ali Akbar Dehkhoda. Tehran, Iran: Daneshgah-i Tehran, 2002.

Sahlins, Marshall David. "*La Pensée Bourgeoise*: Western Society as Culture." In *Culture in Practice: Selected Essays*, 163–203. New York: Zone Books, 2000.

Said, Edward W. *Orientalism*. New York: Pantheon, 1978.

Saliba, George. "The Role of the Astrologer in Medieval Islamic Society." In *Magic and Divination in Early Islam*, edited by Emilie Savage-Smith, 341–370. Aldershot: Ashgate/Variorum, 2004.

Samso, J. "Mashaʾallah." In *The Encyclopaedia of Islam*, 2nd ed., edited by P. Bearman, Th. Bianquis, C. E. Bosworth, E. van Donzel, and W. P. Heinrichs. Brill, 2011. http://www.brillonline.nl.

———. *History of Aurangzib: Based on Persian Sources*. 5 vols. Calcutta: M. C. Sarkar, 1924.
———. *Shivaji and His Times*. 2nd ed. London: Longmans, Green and Co., 1920.
Sarwar, Ghulam. *History of Shah Isma'il Safawi*. New York: AMS Press, 1975.
Savory, Roger. "The Consolidation of Safawid Power in Persia." *Islam* 41 (1965): 71.
———. "The Office of Khalifat al-Khulafa Under the Safawids." *Journal of the American Oriental Society* 85, no. 4 (1965): 497–502.
———. "The Struggle for Supremacy in Persia After the Death of Timur." *Islam* 40 (1965): 35–65.
Schiltberger, Johannes, J. Buchan Telfer, and Filip Jakob Bruun. *The Bondage and Travels of Johann Schiltberger, a Native of Bavaria, in Europe, Asia, and Africa, 1396-1427*. London: Printed for the Hakluyt Society, 1879.
Schimmel, Annemarie. "Dara Shokoh." In *Encyclopaedia Iranica Online*. December 15, 1994. http://www.iranicaonline.org.
———. *Pain and Grace: A Study of Two Mystical Writers of Eighteenth-Century Muslim India*. Leiden: E. J. Brill, 1976.
Schimmel, Annemarie, and Burzine K. Waghmar. *The Empire of the Great Mughals: History, Art, and Culture*. Translated by Corinne Attwood. London: Reaktion Books, 2004.
Schmidtke, Sabine. "The Doctrine of the Transmigration of Soul According to Shihab al-Din al-Suhrawardi (Killed 587/1191) and His Followers." *Studia Iranica* 28 (1999): 237–254.
Schmitz, Barbara. "On a Special Hat Introduced During the Reign of Shah ʿAbbas the Great." *Journal of Persian Studies* 22 (1984): 103–112.
Sen, Amartya Kumar. *The Argumentative Indian: Writings on Indian History, Culture, and Identity*. 1st American ed. New York: Farrar, Straus & Giroux, 2005.
Sewell, William H. "The Concept (s) of Culture." In *Beyond the Cultural Turn: New Directions in the Study of Society and Culture*, edited by Victoria E. Bonnell and Lynn Avery Hunt, 35–61. Berkeley: University of California Press, 1999.
Seyller, John William, and W. M. Thackston. *The Adventures of Hamza: Painting and Storytelling in Mughal India*. Washington, D.C.: Freer Gallery of Art; Arthur M. Sackler Gallery Smithsonian Institution, 2002.
Shahbazi, Shahpur. "Flags i. Of Persia." In *Encyclopaedia Iranica Online*. December 15, 1999. http://www.iranicaonline.org.
Sharma, Sri Ram. *The Religious Policy of the Mughal Emperors*. London: H. Milford for Oxford University Press, 1940.
Skelton, Robert. "Imperial Symbolism in Mughal Painting." In *Content and Context of Visual Arts in the Islamic World*, edited by Priscilla Parsons Soucek, Carol Bier, and Richard Ettinghausen, 177–193. University Park: Pennsylvania State University Press, 1988.
Smith, Vincent Arthur. *Akbar the Great Mogul, 1542-1605*. 2nd ed. Oxford: Clarendon Press, 1919.
Smoller, Laura Ackerman. *History, Prophecy, and the Stars: The Christian Astrology of Pierre d'Ailly, 1350-1420*. Princeton, N.J.: Princeton University Press, 1994.
Storey, C. A. *Persian Literature: A Bio-Bibliographical Survey*. 5 vols. London: Luzac & Co., 1970.
Streck, M., and A. Miquel. "Kaf." In *The Encyclopaedia of Islam*, 2nd ed., edited by P. Bearman, Th. Bianquis, C. E. Bosworth, E. van Donzel, and W. P. Heinrichs. Brill, 2011. http://www.brillonline.nl.
Stronge, Susan. *Painting for the Mughal Emperor: The Art of the Book, 1560-1660*. London: Victoria and Albert Museum, 2002.

Subrahmanyam, Sanjay. "Iranians Abroad: Intra-Asian Elite Migration and Early Modern State Formation." *Journal of Asian Studies* 51, no. 2 (1992): 340–363.

———. "Turning the Stones Over: Sixteenth-Century Millenarianism from the Tagus to the Ganges." *Indian Economic and Social History Review* 40, no. 2 (2003): 129–161.

Subtelny, Maria E. "Arts and Politics in Early Sixteenth-Century Central Asia." *Central Asiatic Journal* 27, no. 1–2 (1983): 121–148.

———. "Babur's Rival Relations: A Study of Kinship and Conflict in Fifteenth-Sixteenth Century Central Asia." *Der Islam* 66 (1989): 102–118.

———. "Husayn Vaʿiz-i Kashifi: Polymath, Popularizer, and Preserver." *Iranian Studies* 36, no. 4 (2003): 463–467.

———. "A Taste for the Intricate: The Persian Poetry of the Late Timurid Period." *Zeitschrift der Deutschen Morgenlandischen Gesellschaft* 136, no. 1 (1986): 56–79.

———. "The Timurid Legacy: A Reaffirmation and a Reassessment." *Cahiers d'Asie Centrale* 3–4 (1997): 9–19.

———. *Timurids in Transition: Turko-Persian Politics and Acculturation in Medieval Iran*. Leiden: Brill, 2007.

Szuppe, Maria. "La participation de femmes de la famille royale a l'exercise du pouvoir en Iran safavide au XVIe siecle." *Studia Iranica* 23 (1994): 211–258.

Tambiah, Stanley Jeyaraja. *Magic, Science, Religion, and the Scope of Rationality*. Cambridge: Cambridge University Press, 1990.

Taussig, Michael T. *Defacement: Public Secrecy and the Labor of the Negative*. Stanford, Calif.: Stanford University Press, 1999.

Tavakoli-Targhi, Mohamad. "Contested Memories." In *Refashioning Iran: Orientalism, Occidentalism, and Historiography*, 77–95. New York: Palgrave, 2001.

Taylor, G. P. "On the Symbol 'Sahib Qiran.'" *Journal and Proceedings of the Asiatic Society of Bengal* 6 (1910): 574–579.

Thomas, Keith. *Religion and the Decline of Magic*. London: Penguin, 1991.

Thrupp, Sylvia L., ed. *Millennial Dreams in Action: Studies in Revolutionary Religious Movements*. New York: Schocken, 1970.

Trimingham, J. Spencer. *The Sufi Orders in Islam*. New York: Oxford University Press, 1998.

Tripathi, Ram Prasad. "The Muslim Theory of Sovereignty." In *Some Aspects of Muslim Administration*, 1–6. Allahabad: Central Book Depot, 1964.

Truschke, Audrey. "The Mughal *Book of War*: A Persian Translation of the Sanskrit *Mahabharata*." *Comparative Studies of South Asia, Africa and the Middle East* 31, no. 2 (2011): 506–520.

Turner, Victor Witter. *The Ritual Process: Structure and Anti-Structure*. Chicago: Aldine Pub. Co., 1969.

Van Bladel, Kevin Thomas. *The Arabic Hermes: From Pagan Sage to Prophet of Science*. Oxford: Oxford University Press, 2009.

Van der Veer, Peter. *Religious Nationalism: Hindus and Muslims in India*. Berkeley: University of California Press, 1994.

Vesel, Ziva. "Reminiscences de la magie astrale dans les Haft Peykar de Nezami." *Studia Iranica* 24 (1995): 237–254.

Wagoner, Phillip B. "Sultan Among Hindu Kings: Dress, Titles, and the Islamicization of Hindu Culture at Vijayanagara." *Journal of Asian Studies* 55 (1996): 851–880.

Wasti, S. Nayyar. "Iranian Phycisians in the Indian Subcontinent." *Studies in History of Medicine and Science* 2, no. 4 (1978): 264–283.

Watt, W. Montgomery. *Islamic Political Thought: The Basic Concepts*. Edinburgh: Edinburgh University Press, 1968.

Weatherford, J. McIver. *Genghis Khan and the Making of the Modern World*. New York: Crown, 2004.
Weber, Max. *On Charisma and Institution Building*. Translated by S. N. Eisenstadt. Chicago: University of Chicago Press, 1968.
Welch, Stuart Cary. "78 Pictures from a World of Kings, Heroes, and Demons: The Houghton Shah-nameh." *The Metropolitan Museum of Art Bulletin* 29, no. 8 (1971): 341–357.
Wensinck, A. J. "al-Khadir (al-Khidr)." In *Encyclopaedia of Islam*, 2nd ed., edited by P. Bearman, Th. Bianquis, C. E. Bosworth, E. van Donzel, and W. P. Heinrichs. Brill, 2009. http://www.brillonline.nl.
White, David Gordon. *The Alchemical Body: Siddha Traditions in Medieval India*. Chicago: University of Chicago Press, 1996.
Whitehouse, Harvey. *Modes of Religiosity: A Cognitive Theory of Religious Transmission*. Walnut Creek, Calif.: AltaMira Press, 2004.
Windfuhr, Gernot. "Jafr." In *Encyclopaedia Iranica Online*. December 15, 2008. http://www.iranicaonline.org.
———. "Spelling the Mystery of Time." *Journal of the American Oriental Society* 110, no. 3 (1990): 401–416.
Winter, H. J. J. "Persian Science in Safavid Times." In *The Cambridge History of Iran: The Timurid and Safavid Periods*, edited by Peter Jackson and Laurence Lockhart, 581–609. Cambridge: Cambridge University Press, 1986.
Wolper, Ethel Sara. *Cities and Saints: Sufism and the Transformation of Urban Space in Medieval Anatolia*. University Park: The Pennsylvania State University Press, 2003.
Wood, Barry. "The Shahnama-i Isma'il: Art and Cultural Memory in Sixteenth-Century Iran." Ph.D. dissertation, Harvard University, 1997.
Woods, John E. *The Aqquyunlu Clan, Confederation, Empire: A Study in Fifteenth/Ninth Century Turko-Iranian Politics*. Minneapolis, Minn.: Bibliotheca Islamica, 1976.
———. "The Rise of Timurid Historiography." *Journal of Near Eastern Studies* 46, no. 2 (1987): 81–108.
———. "Timur's Genealogy." In *Intellectual Studies on Islam: Essays Written in Honor of Martin B. Dickson*, edited by Michel M. Mazzaoui and Vera B. Moreen, 85–125. Salt Lake City: Univeristy of Utah Press, 1990.
Woolard, Kathryn A. "Is the Past a Foreign Country?: Time, Language Origins, and the Nation in Early Modern Spain." *Journal of Linguistic Anthropology* 14, no. 1 (2004): 57–80.
Worsley, Peter. *The Trumpet Shall Sound: A Study of "Cargo" Cults in Melanesia*. New York: Schocken Books, 1968.
Wright, Elaine Julia, and Susan Stronge, eds. *Muraqqa': Imperial Mughal Albums from the Chester Beatty Library, Dublin*. Alexandria, Va.: Art Services International, 2008.
Yusofi, G. H. "Abu Moslem 'Abd-al-Rahman b. Moslem Korasani." In *Encyclopaedia Iranica Online*. December 15, 1983. http://www.iranicaonline.org.
Zakavati Qaraguzlu, Aliriza. *Junbish-i Nuqtawiyya*. Qum: Nashr-i Adyan, 1383 [2004].
Ziai, Hossein. "Al-Suhrawardi, Shihab al-Din Yahya b. Habash b. Amirak, Abu ʾl-Futuh." In *Encyclopaedia of Islam*, 2nd ed., edited by P. Bearman, Th. Bianquis, C. E. Bosworth, E. van Donzel, and W. P. Heinrichs. Brill, 2008. http://www.brillonline.nl.
Ziegler, Norman. "Some Notes on Rajput Loyalties During the Mughal Period." In *Kingship and Authority in South Asia*, edited by John F. Richards, 215–251. Delhi: Oxford University Press, 1998.

INDEX

Abbasids, 46–47
ʿAbbas I (Shah), 198; Nuqtavis suppressed by, 163–64, 165; painting of, 204, *205*, 237, *238*; Shiʿism and, 161–62
ʿAbbas II (Shah), 235, 236
ʿAbd al-Qadir Badaʾuni. *See* Badaʾuni
ʿAbdullah Niyazi (Shaykh), 156
ʿAbdus Sattar, 178, 185
Abu Hanifa, 83, 271n120
Abul Fath (Shaykh), 137, 156
Abul Fazl, 138, 164, 172, 175, 180, 222–23
Abu Maʿshar: conjunction astrology of, 160, 209, 301n107; and Islamic astrology, 29, 221
Abu Muslim, 45, 79, 122, 281n84
Abu Muslim-nama, 41, 45
Acquaviva, Rudolf, 147, 152
Adam, 51, 160, 168, 187
affective knowledge, 69
Aftabchi, Jawhar, 126
Agra, 99, 101, 102, 104, 109, 112
Aʾin-i Akbari, 131
Ajmer, 180, 189, 195
Akbar, 1–3, 21, 129; accusations of heresy against, 3, 133, 141–42, 283n10; *Akbarnama* as chronicle of, 137, 138–46, 168, 179–80, 188, 222; use of "Allahu Akbar," "Allah Akbar," 143, 144, 167; astrology and, 13; Badaʾuni in court of, 136, 137, 139, 140–41, 148, 152–55, 288n76; birth of, 137–38, 285n32; conquests of, 132; court and camp of, 150–52; cultural pursuits of, 132; decrees in the millennial year of, 153–54, 289n96; disciples of, 143–44; as divine, 141, 143–44; Divine Religion of. *See* Din-i Ilahi; fire worship of, 152; *gladiatorii ludi* liked by, 150; Gujarat conquered by, 156; House of Worship established by, 133, 149; illiteracy of, 139, 145, 152, 286n43; Jahangir and, 170, 171–79; "madness" of, 152–55; as Manifestation of Truth (Mazhar-i Haqq), 141, 287n52; messianism and, 3–4, 132, 136–37; miracles of, 188–89; as *mujtahid*, 139, 140, 141, 146; Nuqtavis and, 164–65, 166–69, 292n128; paintings and, 188; prostration (*sijda*) decreed by, 153, 184, 296n44; religious practices of, 131–32, 151–52, 273n5, 282n3, 283n4, 289n88; as Renewer of the Second Millennium, 134, 171, 209; sacrality of, 145, 152, 171, 183; Salim as son of, 169, 170; Sirhindi's criticism of, 134; sun's importance to, 143–45, 151–52, 160, 165, 221; Universal Peace policy of. *See* Sulhi-i Kull; as world's spiritual guide, 3, 139–46, 235. *See also* Jesuits, at Akbar's court
"Akbar is God," 144
Akbarnama, 137, 138–46, 168, 179–80, 188, 222

ᶜAlai (Shaykh), 156–57, 290n102
Alanquva, 38, 48, 137, 254n75
alchemy: gold and, 120; Humayun and, 119–20; mercury and, 281n81. *See also* magic; ᶜ*ulum-i ghariba*
Alexander, 31, 35–36, 38–39, 50, 52, 56, 70, 88, 90
Alids, 37, 46, 79, 128, 161; Abu Muslim as defender of, 45; loyalty toward, 40, 77
Ali ibn Abi Talib, 51, 254n70; avatars of, 46–50; from Chinggis Khan to, 37–39, 52–53; dervishes and, 79–80; grave of, 40, 258n129; Hamza and, 46–47; mule of. *See* Duldul; as saint of Islam, 40, 87; sovereignty of, 37–46, 52–53, 221, 304n32; sword of. *See* Zulfiqar. *See also wali; wilayat*
ᶜalim, 114, 280n69
Alinama, 40
Amrta Kunda, 105
Amuli, Sharif, 165–66, 198, 292n134
angels, in paintings, 193, 201–3, 208–9, 225
animal spectacles, 202–3
anthropology: cultural, 14; of Islam, 15; sacred kingship and, 15
Aqqoyunlu, 75–76
architectural symmetry, of Shah Jahan, 220
ᶜArif-i Husayni (Shaykh), 136–37
Arjan (Sikh Guru), 175
Arrangement of Akbar's Imperial Regulations Concerning Court and Camp, The, 150
arrow, Jahangir's shooting of, 193, *194*, 195, 198, *199*
art: Catholic, 173, 294n8; Islamic traditions of, 186–89, 201, 298n59
Asaf Khan, *232*, 233
ascension journey: of Ghawth Shattari, 103–4, 276nn30–31, 277n33; of Sirhindi, 183
Assemblies of Jahangir, The. See Majalis-i Jahangiri
astrology: Akbar and, 13, 243n18; Babur and, 66–68, 96, 263n25, 265n52; Christian, 12–13; Ghawth Shattari and, 105; as global science, 29; Humayun and, 95; Islamic, 12, 160, 291n116;

Mughal dynasty and, 20; neglect of, 12; Nuqtavis' beliefs of, 163; as political, 11; sacred kingship and, 11; Shah Jahan and, 211, 302n1; Sufism and, 11–12. *See also* conjunction astrology; divination
Aurangzeb: Dara Shikoh executed by, 214; enthronement of, 233; Islamic jurisprudence of. *See Fatawa-i Alamgiri*; music renounced by, 215; non-Muslims under, 234; puritanical rule of, 215; reign of, 234–39; as Shah Jahan's son, 212–13, 227; sons of, 234, 235, 306n63, 307nn64–67; waywardness of, 234
avatars, of Ali ibn Abi Talib, 46–50
axis mundi, 9, 184, 198
Aziz Koka (Mirza), 206

Baba Sangu, 62
Babayan, Kathryn, 237, 308n73
Babur, 4, 17, 21; astrology and, 66–68, 96, 263n25, 265n52; building of gardens by, 111; cuisine of, 110; dreams of, 72–74, 267n75; in Fergana, 60, 63, 64; in Kabul, 64–65, 69, 98; memoirs of, 58–59, 60–61, 69, 84, 261nn10–11, 262n17; Naqshbandis and, 71, 74, 97–98, 100; omens and, 62; as *padishah*, 64, 263n33; poisoning of, 110–11; the Qizilbash, 84–88, 272n131; ritual practices of, 68–69, 265nn57–58, 266nn59–60; royal feast of, 110; in Samarqand, 70–74, 86–87; "strange" world of, 60–66; as Sunni Muslim, 57; as Timurid founder, 56, 57–59, 91–92; un-Islamic taxes repealed by, 67; wine renounced by, 67
Badaʾuni: Akbar criticized by, 152–55; as Akbar's courtier, 136, 137, 139, 140–41, 148, 152–55, 288n76; messianic beliefs of, 155–61, 290n108; millennial year described by, 153–55; *Muntakhab al-Tawarikh* written by, 153; *Najat al-Rashid* written by, 157, 290n110; writings of, 165, 166, 168
Bahlul. *See* Phul Shattari
Banarasidas, 170
Bektashi Sufis, 77–78, 188
Bihzad, 186

INDEX [333]

birth: of Akbar, 137–38, 285n32; of Humayun, 124–25; of Islam, 133; of Shah Jahan, 211, 215, 302n1; of Timur, 38
body: of Safavid Iran, 80–84; Safavid rituals of, 82, 270n116
Book of Akbar. See Akbarnama
Book of Ali. See Alinama
Book of Hamza. See Hamzanama
Book of Jahangir. See Jahangirnama
Book of Khawar. See Khawarnama
Book of Kings. See Shahnama
Book of Victory. See Zafarnama
books of divination. See falnama
Brahmanism, 133
Brethren of Purity. See Ikhwan al-Safa
bricolage/bricoleur, 44, 146, 152, 256n101
Brown, Katherine Butler, 215
Buddhists/Buddhism, 12, 25
building of gardens, by Babur, 111
buruz, 47–48, 49, 158–59

calendar: lunar Islamic, 224; solar divine (ilahi), 224
caliphs, 182
calligraphy, 187
camp, of Akbar, 150–52
cannibalism, 82, 162, 270n115
canons of Humayun, 113–23
carpet of mirth, of Humayun, 123
Catholic art, 173, 294n8
Chest of Witnessing, 186–87, 297n53
Chihil Sutun Palace, 235, 236, 238
Chinggis Khan, 21, 25, 26, 56; compared to Ali, 37–39, 52–53; as Lord of Conjunction, 54; Timur competing with, 32, 33, 35
Chishti Sufis, 136, 168, 189; Akbar and, 168; Jahangir and, 169, 173, 180, 189–92; and the Mughal dynasty of India, 293n144. See also Muʿinuddin Chishti; Salim Chishti
Christian astrology, 12–13
Christianity, 12–13, 25, 133; of Jesuits, 146–47, 178
Christmas pageant, 201

Chub-i Tariqat, 81–82, 125, 237, 270n112
City of Shah Jahan. See Shahjahanabad
Clavijo, Ruy González de, 42
Color of Humayun's Clothes Selected According to the Planets, The, 121–22
comet, of 1618, 196–97
conjunction astrology: of Abu Maʿshar, 160, 209, 301n107; conception of time in, 31, 251n42; messianic worldview and, 28–31, 249n29; predictions of, 30; Saturn-Jupiter, 29–30, 133, 159, 250n35. See also Jamaspnama
cuisine, of Babur, 110

Dabistan-i Mazahib, 214, 223
dalidar, 198, 200
Daniel (prophet), 187
Dara Shikoh: contradictory impulses of, 215; execution of, 214; Sarup Singh made son of, 218; as Shah Jahan's son, 212, 213, 214, 227
Daridra, 198–99
daʿwat al-asmaʾ, daʿwat-i ismha. See divine names
decrees in the millennial year, by Akbar, 153–54, 289n96
dervishes, antinomian, 78–80, 92
Dervish Khursaw, 163, 165
desecration, of graves, 83, 86, 87, 271nn120–21
devotee, devotion. See discipleship
Din-i Ilahi, 3, 131, 282n2, 283n8, 304n30
discipleship: of Akbar, 143–44; and Din-i Ilahi, 3, 131; and headgear. See taj; Taj-i ʿIzzat; Taj-i Haydari; of Jahangir, 176–77, 210; and painting, 210; phallocentric and gendered paradigm of, 218, 303n23; as Safavid practice. See Chub-i Tariqat; Qizilbash; Shah Jahan's abandonment of, 215, 223
divination: as "affective" knowledge, 69; in battle, 118; books of. See falnama; Ibn Khaldun and, 29; importance of, 11, 249n30; ulama and, 114. See also jafr
Divine Monism, 131. See also Din-i Ilahi
divine names, 101, 102, 105, 276n26
Divine Religion, 2, 131. See also Din-i Ilahi

Divine Shadow, 195
Diwali, 200
doxa, 96
dreams: of Babur, 72–74, 267n75; of Jahangir, 206
dress: of Humayun, 121–22; of Safavid Iran, 81, 269n109, 270nn110–11
Duldul, Ali's mule, 53, 79, 80, 259n137

embodied sovereignty, 9
empire: spectacle of, 110–12. *See also* Mughal empire; Safavid empire
enthronement, of Aurangzeb, 233
ethnography, of sacred kingship, 15
exaggerators, exaggeration. *See ghulat, ghuluww*
execution, of Dara Shikoh, 214

falnama, 187
Fatawa-i Alamgiri, 234
Fazlallah Astarabadi, 49, 54, 119, 183, 258n125
female kin, 218
Fergana, 60, 63, 64
fire: Akbar's worship of, 152; ordeal by, 147–49
Four Degrees of Devotion, 131, 165–66. *See also* Din-i Ilahi
four elements, 120–21

Genghis Khan. *See* Chinggis Khan
Ghawth Shattari (Shaykh): ascension journey of, 103–4, 276nn30–31, 277n33; astrology and, 105; sacred authority of, 109; as Sufi master, 97, 101, 102–3, 275n15
Ghazi Miyan. *See* Salar Ghazi
ghulat, ghuluww, 83, 253n59, 287n57; in Akbar's court, 141, 145, 153, 165, 287n52; Ali and, 77, 268n89; transmigration of the soul and, 47, 160, 163, 257n118
gladiatorii ludi, 150
global science, astrology as, 29
globe, Jahangir with, *191*, 192
god-king, Rama as, 200
"God the Father," 233

graffiti, under Shah Jahan's throne, 227–33
"Grand Accomplishment of the Second Lord of Conjunction, The." *See Karnama-i Sahib Qiran-i Thani*
graves: of Ali ibn Abi Talib, 40, 258n129; desecration of, 83, 86, 87, 271nn120–21; of Naqshbandis, 87
Greater Luminary (His Holiness). *See* Nayyir-i'Azam
Gujarat, 156
Gulbadam Banu, 59, 102
Gwalior, 97, 103, 111

Habib al-Siyar (Khwandamir), 112
hadith, of the millennium, 136, 159
hagiographical narrative: of Salar Ghazi, 106–7; of Sayyid Muhammad Jaunpuri, 109; of Shattari brothers, 104–5, 109; of Sirhindi, 135; of Timur, 34–37
Hajj pilgrimage, 40, 212
Hamza, 41, 45–47, 189, 257nn111–12
Hamzanama, 189
Hanafi school of Sunni Islam, 33
Hatifi, 90, 91
Haydar (Shaykh), 81
Haydar Dughlat (Mirza), 98, 99, 100, 111–12
Haydariyya, 162
Hemu, 188, 196
Henriquez, Francis, 146–47
heretical conceptions, of Muslim kingship, 6
Hermes Trismegistus: as father of philosophers, 222, 305n41; as first sage, 222, 304n39; and sun veneration, 222–23; Triplicate in Wisdom, 222, 304n40
heterodoxy, 96
Hidaya, work of Islamic jurisprudence, 63
hikmat al-ishraq, 304n39. *See also* Illuminationist Philosophy; Suhrawardi
Hindal, 89, 98–99, 101
Hinduism, 18, 105
Hindus, 12, 20, 105
Hindustan, 20, 97, 99, 100, 128
"Holy Ghost," 233
holy men: Shattari brothers as, 104, 277n35; "universal" sacrality of "local,"

104–10. *See also* Chishti Sufis; Mahdavis; Naqshbandi Sufis; Salar Ghazi
"Holy Trinity," 233
House of Monism. *See* Tawhid Khana
House of Worship. *See* ʿIbadat Khana
Humayun, 4, 86, 88, 94; astrology interest of, 95; birthday of, 124–25; canons of, 113–23; carpet of mirth of, 123; coup against, 102; dress of, 121–22; Khwandamir's writings of, 112, 117–18, 123, 280nn64–65; magic interest of, 95; as manifestation of Divine Light, 109–10; Mughal empire in India lost by, 95; Naqshbandis and, 97–100; painting of, 235, *236*; reconsideration of, 95–97; ritual display of, 111–12; Shattari brothers and, 101–4; submission to Tahmasb of, 126–27, 130, 281nn94–95; sun's importance to, 221; at Tahmasb's court, 125–27, 130, 177; taj of, 123–25, 126, 138, 210, 285n33; twelve alchemical ranks in court of, 117–20
Humayun's Imperial Services Organized According to the Four Elements, *120*
Hurufi, 49, 119
Husayn Bayqara (Sultan), 40, 61, 86, 263n28
Husayn Jami (Shaykh), 173, 174

ʿIbadat Khana, 133, 149, 283n9
Ibn ʿArabi, 160
Ibn Arabshah, 34, 41–42, 252nn57–58
Ibn Husam, 40, 41, 88
Ibn Khaldun, 26–32, 249n27
Ibn Taymiyya, 44–45, 256n104, 257n106
Ibn Zarzar, 27, 248n20
ijtihad, 139, 286n40. *See also* mujtahid
Ikhwan al-Safa, 222
illiteracy, of Akbar, 139, 145, 152, 286n43
Illuminationist philosophy, 36, 49, 209, 304n39. *See also* Suhrawardi
Imami Shiʿism, 161. *See also* Twelver Shiʿism
Imperial Administration Arranged According to Humayun's Augury, *115*
imperial discipleship, of Jahangir, 176, 210
imperial household, of Shah Jahan, 216, 217

India: Iranian intellectuals in, 214; Nuqtavis in, 164; in sixteenth-century, 17–21; Zoroastrians in, 214. *See also* Mughal dynasty of India
"Institutes of Akbar," 143–44, 150
Iran: intellectuals drawn to India from, 214; Islam in, 7–8; Shiʿ, 3, 18; Shiʿism spreading in, 7, 213; in sixteenth century, 17–21. *See also* Safavid Iran
Isfahan, 222, 235, *236*
Ishraqi. *See* Illuminationist philosophy
Islam: Akbar's denial of, 3, 131, 154; astrological conjunction at the birth of, 30, 133; millennium and, 7–14; Prophet of, 37, 41–46, 79, 114, 117–27, 135, 159, 280n70; sacred kingship in, 5, 6, 244nn26–27; sacred sovereignty in, 16; sword of, 105
Islamic astrology, 12, 29, 160, 221, 291n116
Islamic jurisprudence, 234. *See also* Hidaya
Islamic political culture, 212, 216
Islam Shah Sur, 108, 156, 157
Ismaʿil I (Shah), 5, 84–87, 125, 176; cannibalism associated with followers of, 96; as Lord of Conjunction, 76, 88–92; as *mahdi* of Islamic traditions, 4; rise of, 74–77, 267nn80–81; as Safavid founder, 56, 57–59, 74, 76, 80–84; from Sufi family, 5
Ismaʿilis, 40, 255n83

jafr, 30, 85, 134–35, 166, 250n39
Jahangir, 17, 21–22, 153; Abul Fazl killed by, 172; accession of, 170, 172, 174; accomplishments of, 181; in Ajmer, 189, 195; Akbar and, 170, 171–79; animal spectacles and, 202–3; annual rituals observed by, 200; arrow shot by, 193, *194*, 195, 198, *199*; Catholic art liked by, 173, 294n8; in Christmas pageant, 201; as cosmic agent, 195; dream of, 206; edict of, 172; with globe, *191*, 192; imperial discipleship of, 176, 210; inner and outer existence of, 184–85; Jesuit reports of, 172–73, 294n7; Khusraw as son of, 170, 173; Man Singh's predictions of, 174; memoirs

Jahangir *(continued)*
of, 20, 173, 179–80, 185, 188, 195, 196, 208; as millennial being, 206–9; modesty of, 179–85; painted miracles of, 189–93, 298nn69–70; painting as sacred medium to, 185–89, 204, 297n46; painting of, 204–8, *205*, *207*, 209–10, *228*, *229*, *230*, *231*, 300n102, 301n110; as rebellious prince, 171–72; as renewer, 198–204; sacred kingship of, 177, 196; as seer, 204–6; Sirhindi and, 135, 175, 181; sister of, 217; spiritual power of, 204; talismanic image of, 221, 227, 231; as thaumaturge, 193–98
Jahangirnama, 185, 189, 211; early part of, 173; as first-person narrative, 179–80, 296n33; owl incident in, 195; rat infestation mentioned in, 196
Jainism, 133, 174
"*Jalla Jalaluhu*," 144
Jamasp, 50–53, 258n133
Jamaspnama, 51, 259n134
James I (king), 208, 301n103
Jami, 83
Jaunpuri. *See* Sayyid Muhammad Jaunpuri
Jawahir-i Khamsa (Ghawth Shattari), 103, 105, 276n29
Jesuits, at Akbar's court, 188, 288n66, 288n68, 288nn70–71; Acquaviva, 147, 152; Christianity of, 146–47, 178; debates with Muslims of, 147–49, 288n76; failure of, 151; Henriquez, 146–47; Jahangir reported by, 172–73, 294n7; Monserrate, 146–47, 149, 151
Jesus, 38, 77, 109, 201, 300n90
Jews, 12
jharoka-i darshan, 210, 219–20
jharoka throne, 219–20, 225–26, 229, *230*, *231*, 233
jinns, 63, 158, 263n32
Jupiter. *See* Saturn-Jupiter
Jurists, in Safavid empire, 18, 213

Kabul, 64–65, 69, 98
Kamaluddin Husayn, 85, 271n128
Karnama-i Sahib Qiran-i Thani, 23, 246n4, 302n1

Kashi, Ahmad, 165
"key to the conquest of the two worlds, The," 192
Khadija Sultan Shehrbano, 41, 255nn89–90
Khafi Khan, 153
khalifa, 76, 82. *See also* caliphs
khalifat al-khulafa, 76, 77, 268n88
"khan," 32
Khata'i, 125
Khawand Mahmud (Khwaja), 177
Khawarnama (Ibn Husam), 40, 41, 88
Khizr (Khwaja), 64, 264n38
Khurram (Prince), 195, *228*, *229*, *230*, *231*
Khusraw: as Jahangir's son, 170, 173; rebellion of, 175, 295nn19–20
Khwandamir, Ghiyas ad-Din Muhammad: writings of, 112, 117–18, 123, 280nn64–65. *See also* Qanun-i Humayuni
kin, female, 218
King of Islam, 35
King of Men, 79
King of the World, 32
kingship: foundational process of, 110; messianic script of, 50–53; premodern, 14; sacred knowledge of, 63–70. *See also* Muslim kingship; sacred kingship
kinship, 216–18
Kitab Jamasp fi Tawaliʿ al-Anbiyaʾ, 50
knowledge communities, 63–70, 69, 266nn62–63
Koch, Ebba, 225–26

Lakshmi (goddess), 198
Lesser Luminary (His Holiness). *See* Nayyir-i Asghar
"Light of Religion." *See* Nur al-Din
Lion of God, 85
Lord of Conjunction, 9, 21, 58, 247n16, 260n8; Chinggis Khan as, 54; Ismaʿil as, 76, 88–92; Timur as, 23–55, 88, 167, 184, 251n44, 251n47. *See also* Second Lord of Conjunction
Lord of Conjunctionship, 90
lunar Islamic calendar, 224

"Machmet," 43–44
Maghrib, 27

INDEX [337]

magic, 33, 66, 95, 114; as category of analysis, 29, 249n29, 265n57; Humayun and, 95, 275n10; painting and, 187, 299n72; Sufis and, 99, 258n125; Timur and, 33. *See also Hermes Trismegistus*; ʿulum-i ghariba

Mahdavis: ʿAlai as leader of, 156–57; as heterodox Muslims, 156; leaders of, 156; movement of, 156–58; as Sayyid Muhammad Jaunpuri's followers, 108, 136, 156–57. *See also* ʿAbdullah Niyazi; Abul Fath; Mustafa Gujarati

mahdi, 9, 46; Ismaʿil as, 4; Sayyid Muhammad Jaunpuri as, 159. *See also messiahs*

Majalis-i Jahangiri, 178, 185

Maktubat, 181

malfuzat, 178

Malik ʿAmbar, 193–95, *194*, 196

Mamluks, 32, 44

Maʾmun's inquisition, 139

Mani, 187, 297n56

Manifestation of Truth. *See Mazhar-i Kull*

"Mani of the Age," 187

Man Singh (Raja), 173

Man Singh (Sewra Jain), 174

Manucci, Nicolao, 217–18, 237–39

Marathas, 235

Mary. *See* Virgin Mary

Maryam Makani, 137

Mashaʾallah, 29

Maslahat (Shaykh), 72

Mazhar-i Haqq, 141

Mazhar-i Kull, 178

Membré, Michele, 81–82

memoirs: of Babur, 58–59, 60–61, 69, 84, 261nn10–11, 262n17; of Jahangir, 20, 173, 179–80, 185, 188, 195, 196, 208; of Tahmasb, 94, 274n3

mentalité, 59, 261nn13–15

messiahs: ʿArif-i Husayni as, 136–37; of Badaʾuni, 155–61, 290n108; scriptural notions of, 9; thousand-year cycle of, 11; Timur as, 28–29. *See also mahdi*

messianic age, of Timurid Central Asia, 9

messianic expectations, 77–80

messianic legacy of the Safavids, 1, 5, 76–77, 268n89

messianic movement, of Sayyid Muhammad Jaunpuri, 108, 136, 159

messianic myth: millennial concept of, 10–11; transmigration of soul in, 10, 153, 158, 291n111

messianic script, of kingship, 50–53

messianic worldview, 28–31, 249n29

messianism, 9, 28, 132, 248nn21–22

metempsychosis, 47, 153, 158, 163, 257n118, 291n111

Middle East, 18

mihna. *See* Maʾmun's inquisition

milk kinship, 217–18

millenarianism, 28, 248n24

millennial being: Jahangir as, 206–9; Sirhindi as, 136, 210, 285n25

millennial epistemology, 10

Millennial History, 133, 160, 209, 221. *See also Tarikh-i Alfi*

millennial sovereign: Akbar as, 130–32, 133, 283n8; Shah Jahan as, 226, 233

millennium: celebrations for, 152–55; complex science of, 9; cyclical view of, 11; *hadith* of, 136, 159; Islam and, 7–14; messianic myth and, 10–11; in Mughal India, 132–38; Muslim kingship and, 7–14; in Safavid Iran, 161–66; year of, 153–55

miracles, of Jahangir, 189–93, 298nn69–70

Mirat-i Masʿudi, 106

Mirror of Masʿud, The. *See Mirat-i Masʿudi*

missionaries. *See* Safavid dervish missionaries

modesty, of Jahangir, 179–85

Mongols, 12, 32; invasions of, 4, 23, 33; Persianized, 25; Timur's legacy from, 25–26

Monserrate, Anthony, 146–47, 149, 151

moon, in paintings, 209

Moses, 109

mosque prayer hall, 220–21

Mughal dynasty of India, 241n1; art of, 186, 188, 201, 298n59; astrology and, 20; beginning of, 21–22; discipleship under, 3, 131; disintegration of, 239; kingship of, 4, 19, 93, 129; as messianic, 1, 5; millennium in, 132–38; panegyrics

Mughal dynasty of India *(continued)*
in, 202, 300n93; rulers of, *2*; as saintly, 1, 4, 5; sovereignty of, 239, 308nn76–77; study of, 18; as Sunni Muslims, 7, 39
Mughal empire: Hinduism in, 18; in India, 18, 95; in South Asia, 18, 20; Sufis in, 18; Sunnis in, 18
Mughal imperial cult, 94–95
Muhammad. *See* Prophet Muhammad
Muhammad (Sayyid). *See* Sayyid Muhammad Jaunpuri
Muhammad Hadi, 211
Muharram, 221
Muʿinuddin Chishti, 189, *190*, 192
Mujaddid, 9, 37, 134, 159. *See also* renewer
Mujaddid Alf-i Thani. *See* Renewer of the Second Millennium
mujtahid, 139, 140, 141, 146
Mukhtarnama, 41
Mumtaz Mahal, 219
Muntakhab al-Tawarikh (Badaʾuni), 153
Muqaddima (Ibn Khaldun), 30
Murad Bakhsh, 212
murals, 235–37, *236*, *238*
murid, muridi. *See* discipleship
musallam, 192
Mushaʿshaʿ, 48–49, 54
music renouncement, 215
Muslims, 12; heterodox, 156; Shiʿi, 7; Sunni, 7, 39
Muslim Asia, 5
Muslim debates with Jesuits, 147–49, 288n76
Muslim kingship, 5–6, 240; culture of, 16; heretical conceptions of, 6; institution of, 14, 243nn19–20; millennium and, 7–14; performative aspect of, 6
Muslim saints, 106–7
Mustafa Gujarati (Shaykh), 156, 157, 158
Muʿtamad Khan, 196, 299n80
Mutribi Samarqandi, Abdul Razzaq, 211, 302n2
mysticism, 7, 8, 34–35, 129. *See also* Sufism
mythical figures of sovereignty, 56, 259n1

Najat al-Rashid (Badaʾuni), 157, 290n110
Nanak (Sikh Guru), 127–28, 277n37, 282n99

Naqshbandi Sufis: Babur and, 71, 74, 97–98, 100; graves of, 87; Humayun and, 100. *See also* Husayn Jami; Jami; Khawmud Mahmud; Nura; Qazi; Sirhindi; ʿUbaydullah Ahrar; Yahya
Nathan (Mirza), 176
nawruz. *See* Persian New Year
Nayyir-i Asghar (Hazrat), 36, 209
Nayyir-i ʿAzam (Hazrat), 36, 209, 222
Niʿmatiyya, 162
Niʿmatullahi Sufis, 82–83, 270n118
Niyazi (Shaykh), 157, 290n105
niyazmand-i dargah-i ilahi, 180
non-Muslims, Aurangzeb's regulations against, 234
nuqta, 163
Nuqtavis: ʿAbbas I and, 163–64, 165; Akbar and, 164–65, 166–69, 292n128; alphabet studied by, 163; and astrology, 163; cosmology of, 163; founding of, 162; in India, 164; and metempsychosis (transmigration of soul), 163; as Pointilists, 163; popularity of, 163. *See also* Padishah Hizara; Pasikhani, Mahmud
Nura (Khwaja), 98
"Nur al-Din," Nuruddin, 173
Nurbakhsh, Muhammad (Sayyid), 46–49, 54, 159, 258n128; and soul projection. *See buruz*
Nurbakhshis, 83, 157–58, 183, 271n119

omens, traffic in, 62
ordeal by fire, 147–49
Orientalist, Orientalism, 12–13, 242n14
orthodoxy, 96, 212, 224
Ottomans, 13, 78, 94, 269n93
owls, in painting, 193–95, *194*, 198, 299n72

padishah, Babur as, 64, 263n33
Padishah Hizara, 162
Padishah-i Islam. *See* King of Islam
Padishah-i Jahan. *See* King of the World
Padshahnama, 227, 229, 231
paintings: of ʿAbbas I, 204, *205*, 237, *238*; Akbar and, 189; angels in, 193, 201–3, 208–9, 225; of Humayun, 235, *236*; of

Jahangir, 204–8, *205*, *207*, 209–10, *228*, *229*, *230*, *231*, 300n102, 301n110; as Jahangir's miracles, 189–93, 298nn69–70; moon in, 209; owls in, 193–95, *194*, *198*, 299n72; sacred medium of, 185–89, 204, 297n46; in Safavid Iran, 186, 189; of Shah Jahan, 224, 225, *232*, 233; sun in, 209; of Tahmasb, 187, *236*; in Timurid Central Asia, 186, 189

Parsis, 151

Pasikhani, Mahmud, 162, 165, 166

patron saints, changing of, 97–101

"Peace with all," 142, 287n53. *See also* Sulh-i Kull

Pereira, Julian, 148

Persian alphabet, 163

Persianized Mongols, 25

Persian New Year, 219, 221, 234

phallocentric and gendered paradigm, of discipleship, 218, 303n23

philosophers: Christian, 141; Hermes as father of, 222, 305n41

Phul Shattari (Shaykh): as brother of Ghawth Shattari, 102; death of, 102; as Sufi master, 97, 99, 101, 275n17

pietre dure inlay technique, 225

piety, of Tahmasb, 117, 125

planet of kings, 221

planets, 116–18, 121–22, 281n85

Pointilists, 163. *See also* Nuqtavis

poisoning, of Babur, 110–11

Portuguese, 146

poverty, 198–200, *199*

Prabhu, 214

premodern kingship, 14

prison, Sirhindi in, 135, 182, 183

prisoner, Shah Jahan as, 233

projection, of soul. *See buruz*

Prophet Muhammad, 16, 30, 37, 39, 40, 51, 122, 133, 197, 280n70

prostration, before the monarch, 184, 212, 296n44

pseudo-Jamasp, 52. *See also* Jamaspnama

public audience halls, of Shah Jahan, 219, 220, 221

Pul. *See* Phul Shattari

puritanical rule, of Aurangzeb, 215

Qanun-i Humayuni (Khwandamir), 112, 117, 123

Qazi (Khwaja), 70–71

Qazvini, Muhammad Amin, 224, 302n1

Qizilbash, 81, 82, 83–84, 89, 161; Babur as, 84–88, 272n131; cannibalism of, 82, 96, 125; Tahmasb with, 125, 127, 161; *taj* of, 81, 87, 90, 124, 127

Quran, 16, 36, 38, 139, 147

rainmaking, 65–66, 264n42

rain stone, 65, 264n43

Rajput: and Akbar, 168, 293n141; and Dara Shikoh, 214, 218; and Jahangir, 169, 173; kingdoms, 132; queen, 168. *See also* Man Singh; Rana Sangha; Sarup Singh

Rama, 167, 171, 200, 293nn141–42; as god-king, 200; Ravana defeated by, 200

Ramayana, 167–68

Rana Sangha, 67

rat infestation, 196

Ravana, 200

Rawzat al-Qayyumiyya, 135

Reagan, Nancy, 12

rebellion: of Jahangir (as prince Salim), 171–72; of Khusraw, 175, 295nn19–20

red-heads. *See* Qizilbash

"Regulations for Providing Guidance," 150

reign: of Aurangzeb, 234–39; of Humayun, 110; of Shah Jahan, 22, 211–13

religion, of Akbar, 131–32, 151–52, 273n5, 282n3, 283n4, 289n88. *See also* Din-i Ilahi

religious scholars, 114

renewer, 9, 134, 198–204. *See also* Mujaddid

Renewer of the Second Millennium, 134, 171, 209

Richards, John, 216

rituals: of Abbas I, 162–64; of Akbar, 144, 151–52; of Babur, 68–69, 265nn57–58, 266nn59–60; of Humayun, 111–12, 113–25; of Jahangir, 200; of Safavid discipleship. *See* Chub-i Tariqat; of Shah Jahan, 223

Roe, Thomas, 176

sacred kingship, 1, 129; anthropology of, 15; astrology and, 11; ethnography

of, 15; everyday world of, 14–17; of Humayun, 95–97, 109, 274n7, 274n10; in Islam, 5, 6, 244nn26–27; of Jahangir, 177, 196; knowledge of, 63–70; *nawruz* and, 221; sociology of, 15–17; Timur as model of, 24, 246n10
sacred medium, of paintings, 185–89, 204, 297n46
sacred persona, of Timur, 31–37, 253nn59–60
sacred sovereignty: of Akbar, 3–4, 88, 167, 183; in Islam, 16; of Shah Jahan, 223; understanding of, 14
Safavid dervish missionaries, 78–79, 92. *See also khalifa*; *khalifat al-khulafa*
Safavid empire: in Iran, 18; Islam in, 18; Jurists in, 18, 114, 213, 280n69; in Middle East, 18; Shiʿis in, 7, 18, 161–62; Sufi origins of, 5, 237. *See also* Ismaʿil I; Qizilbash
Safavid Iran: bodily rituals of, 82, 270n116; body of, 80–84; dress of, 81, 269n109, 270nn110–11; founding of, 4; Ismaʿil I as founder of, 56, 57–59, 74, 76, 80–84; kingship of, 4, 176; as messianic, 1, 5, 76–77, 268n89; millennium in, 161–66; painting in, 186, 235–39; rulers of, 2; violent spectacles in, 162
Safi al-Din (Shaykh), 125, 128
Sahib Qiran. *See* Lord of Conjunction
sainthood, 1, 8, 183; Akbar and, 139–46; cycle of, 49; epitome of, 106; as hereditary, 5, 218; Islamic concept of, 272n140; Ismaʿil I and, 5; *jafr*, 85; Jahangir and, 189–93; kingship and, 4–5, 92, 172, 218; madness and, 155; sellers of, 104; shrine-centered, 212; Sirhindi and, 183; as social institution, 183; Timur and, 34. *See also* Sufism; *wilayat*
saintly: Mughal dynasty as, 1, 4, 5; Safavid Iran as, 1, 4, 5
saintly presence, in Islam, 8
saints: memory of, 106–7; of Naqshbandis, 100; patron, 97–101; Salar Ghazi as, 106–7, 109, 278nn42–44; Shattari brothers as, 105. *See also wali*

Salar Ghazi (also, Salar Masʿud Ghazi), 278n47; death of, 107; hagiographical narrative of, 106–7; powers of, 107; as saint, 106–7, 109, 278nn42–44; wedding procession of, 107, 278n45. *See also Mirat-i Masʿudi*
Salim, (Jahangir as prince), 170
Salim Chishti (Shaykh), 168
Samarqand, 70–74, 86–87
Sam Mirza, 91, 126
Sarup Singh (Raja), 218
Saturn-Jupiter, 29–30, 133, 159, 250n35
Sayyid Muhammad Jaunpuri: asceticism preached by, 108; circles organized by, 108; hagiographical narrative of, 109; Mahdavis as followers of, 108, 136, 156–57; as *mahdi*, 159; messianic movement of, 108, 136, 159, 183; spiritual quest of, 108–9
Sayyids, 37, 40. *See also* Alids
Schedule of Humayun's Court Arranged According to the Planets, The, *116*
Schiltberger, Johann, 42–43
School of Isfahan, gnostic, 222
School of Religions. *See Dabistan-i Mazahib*
science: global, 29; of millennium, 9; of strangeness, 62, 77, 202
scriptural notions, of messiah, 9
Second Lord of Conjunction, 23–24, 211, 215, 246n4, 247nn5–6
seer, Jahangir as, 204–6
Sewra sect, Jain, 174
Shah ʿAbdullah, 109
Shah Jahan: architectural symmetry of, 220; Aurangzeb as son of, 212–13, 227; birth of, 211, 215, 302n1; chronicles of, 224–25; Dara Shikoh as son of, 212, 213, 214, 227; decoration restricted by, 225; discipleship abandoned by, 215, 223; festivals celebrated by, 219; graffiti under throne of, 227–33; Hajj pilgrimage reinstated by, 212; imperial household of, 216, 217; Islamic political culture established by, 212, 216; *jharoka* throne of, 219–20, 225–26, 229, *230, 231,* 233; as millennial sovereign, 226, 233; miniature portraits of, 223, 227; Murad

Bakhsh as son of, 212; orthodoxy of, 212, 224; paintings of, 224, 225, *232*, 233; performative domain of, 225; as prince Khurram, 195, *228*, 229, *230*, 231; as prisoner, 233; prostration abolished by, 212; public audience halls built by, 219, 220, 221; reign of, 22, 211–13; ritual schemes of, 223; sacrality of, 216; sacred sovereignty of, 223; as Second Lord of Conjunction, 23–24, 211, 215, 246n4, 247nn5–6; solar divine calendar of, 224; successor to, 213–15; sun's importance to, 221; Taj Mahal built by, 219; textual domain of, 225; time and space of, 226; two bodies of, 224–26; visual domain of, 225; weighing of, 219–20, 222

Shahjahanabad, 216

Shahnama, 40, 41, 88, 89–91, 168, 273n148

Shahnama-i Isma'il, 90, 273n152

Shahrukh, 35, 37, 49

Shakarunnisa Begum, 217

shamanism, 25

Shami, Nizam al-Din, 32, 259n137

Sharif, Muhammad, 66, 67, 68

Shattari brothers: "divine names" technique of, 101, 102, 105, 276n26; hagiographical narrative of, 104–5, 109; history of, 104; as holy men, 104, 277n35; Humayun and, 101–4; as local saints, 105; social personalities of, 105; as Sufis, 105. *See also* Ghawth Shattari; Phul Shattari

Shattari Sufis, 97, 100–101, 183, 275nn13–14. *See also* Shattari brothers

Shattari-Timurid alliance, 98

Shaybani Khan, 72, 84

Shaykh al-Islam, 70

Sher Shah Suri, 95, 98, 102, 126

Shi'i-Jurist Islam, 18, 221

Shi'ism, 161–62; cultural transformation of, 7; in Iran, 7, 161–62, 213

Shivaji, 239

shrines, Sufi, 5. *See also* graves

sijda, 153. *See also* prostration

Sirhindi: as Akbar's critic, 134; disciple's writing about, 182, 293n42;

hagiographical narrative of, 135; Jahangir and, 135, 175, 181; as leaders of Indian Naqshbandis, 134; as millennial being, 136, 210, 285n25; in prison, 135, 182, 183; sainthood of, 183; spiritual ascension of, 183; writings of, 134–35, 181–82, 197, 284nn19–22

sixteenth-century India, 17–21; frontier settings in, 107, 278n48; social conditions in, 105, 277n37

sixteenth-century Iran, 17–21; civilizing process in, 56, 260n3; mythical figures in, 56, 259n1; princes in, 56–93; sovereignty in, 56, 259n2; Sufis in, 56–93

social dimension, of sacred authority, 8

social memory, 70, 266n64

Social Hierarchy Under Humayun as God's Caliph and Lord of Conjunction, The, *112*

sociology of sacred kingship, 15–17

solar divine (ilahi) calendar, 224

solar symbolism, 36, 223

Solomon (prophet-king), 225

sons, disciples to, 215–19

soul: projection of, 47–48, 158–59; transmigration of, 10, 153, 158, 291n111. *See also buruz*, metempsychosis

South Asia, 18, 20

sovereignty: of Alids, 52; embodied, 9; millennial, 12; of Mughal dynasty of India, 239, 308nn76–77; theater of, 110–12. *See also* sacred sovereignty

spiritual power, of Jahangir, 204

spiritual pursuits, of Akbar, 3

spiritual quest, of Sayyid Muhammad, 108–9

stick battles, 162

Stick of the Path. *See* Chub-i Tariqat

strangeness, sciences of, 62, 77, 202. *See also 'ulum-i ghariba*

strange world, of Babur, 60–66

submission to Tahmasb, of Humayun, 126–27, 130, 281nn94–95

Sufi master: Ghawth Shattari as, 97, 101, 102–3, 275n15; Phul Shattari as, 97, 99, 101, 275n17

[342] INDEX

Sufi origins, of Safavid empire, 5, 237. *See also* Ismaʿil I; Qizilbash
Sufis: Bektashi, 77–78, 188; Chishti. *See* Chishti Sufis; hierarchal organization of, 100; as holy saviors, 1, 8–9, 10; Ismaʿil as, 5; Mahdavi. *See Mahdavis*; messianic movements of, 77–80; Naqshbandi. *See* Naqshbandi Sufis; Niʿmatullahi, 82–83, 270n118; orders of, 1, 5, 100; sacrality of, 100, 128–29; Shattari, 97, 100–101, 183, 275nn13–14; Shattari brothers as, 105; shrines of, 5; in sixteenth-century Iran, 56–93. *See also* saints; *wali*
Sufism: astrology and, 11–12; mystical practices of, 7, 34–35; shrine-centered, 8, 213. *See also* sainthood; *wilayat*
Suhrawardi, 253n65; Hermes and, 222, 304n39; Illuminationist philosophy of, 49, 209; prayers to the sun of, 209; and transmigration of soul, 258n31; Zoroastrian traditions and, 36
Sulayman (Shah), Safavid, 235
Sulayman (Sultan), Ottoman, 94
Sulh-i Kull, 141, 142, 149, 165, 178, 235, 287n53
sun: Akbar and, 143, 151, 152, 221; Humayun and, 123, 125, 221; Mughal focus on, 221–22; in paintings, 209; as planet of kings, 221; Shah Jahan and, 220–21; Suhrawardi and, 36, 209. *See also nawruz*; Nayyir-i ʿAzam; solar symbolism
Sunni Muslims, 7; Babur as, 57
Sunni Ottomans, 78
Suyuti, Jalal al-Din, 159–60
sword of Islam, 105

Tahmasb (Shah), 274n1; Humayun at court of, 125–27, 130, 177; memoirs of, 94, 274n3; paintings of, 187, *236*; piety of, 117, 125; with Qizilbash, 125, 127, 161
taj, of Humayun, 123–25, *126*, 127, 138, 210, 285n33
Taj-i Haydari, 81, 90, 124
Taj-i ʿIzzat, 124, 127. *See also* Taj, of Humayun

Taj Mahal, 219
talismanic image, of Jahangir, 221, 227, 231
Tamerlane, 23. *See also* Timur
tanasukh. *See* metempsychosis
Tarikh-i Alfi, 133, 160, 209. *See also* Millennial History
Tawhid Khana, 162
taxes, Babur's repeal of, 67
thaumaturge, Jahangir as, 193–98
Thomas, Keith, 29, 250n32
thousand-year cycle and messianism, 11
Timur, 5, 21; army of, 41–42; birth of, 38; Chinggis Khan and, 32, 33, 35; death of, 35, 37, 39; hagiography of, 34; Ibn Khaldun's prophecy about, 26–32, 249n27; as Lord of Conjunction, 23–55, 88, 167, 184, 251n44, 251n47; memories of, 23–25, 56, 246n11; as messiah, 28–29; Mongol legacy of, 25–26; as sacred kingship model, 24, 246n10; sacred persona of, 31–37, 253nn59–60; Shahrukh as son of, 35, 37, 49; successors to, 56
Timurid Central Asia, 1, 17, 241n1; courts of, 4; messianic age of, 9; painting in, 186, 189; religious history of, 53–55
Timurid founder, Babur as, 56, 57–59, 91–92
Timurid Herat, 84–85, 89, 91, 271n125
Timurid-Shattari alliance, 98
Timur-i Lang, 23
Timurnama (Hatifi), 90
Timur the Lame, 23
"total social fact," 62, 253n29
transmigrationists, 158
transmigration of soul, 10, 153, 158, 291n111. *See also buruz*; metempsychosis
Transoxania, 3, 40, 42, 57, 63, 74, 75, 84, 97, 99
Triplicate in Wisdom, Hermes, 222, 304n40
Twelver Shiʿism, 20, 47, 127, 161, 221
Twelve "Golden Arrows" or Alchemical Ranks of Humayun's Entourage, The, *119*

ʿUbaydullah Ahrar (Khwaja), 70, 71–73, 98
ulama, 113, 159; corrupt, 134; and the Jesuits, 148; and Jupiter, 123; in Mughal hierarchy, 133; in Safavid Iran, 114, 161; as source of legitimacy, 6. *See also* ʿalim
Ulugh Beg, 37, 38
ʿulum-i ghariba, 124; experts in, 62; Humayun's passion for, 99, 124; Shattaris and, 99; ulama and, 114. *See also* alchemy; divination; Hermes Trismegistus; magic; strange world, of Babur
Umar Shaykh (Mirza), 60
Umayyad dynasty, 122
"Universal Manifestation," 178, 179, 181
Universal Peace. *See* Sulh-i Kull
Uzbeks, 86, 98; attack on Samarqand, 72; rainmakers of, 65–66, 264n45; Safavid defeat of, 74, 84. *See also* Shaybani Khan

Virgin Mary, 38, 210
Vishnu (god), 200

wali, 40, 87, 272n140. *See also* saints
wilayat, 71, 104, 113. *See also* sainthood; wali
window: of audience. *See jharoka* throne; of veneration. *See jharoka-i darshan*
wisdom of old, and Hermes, 222, 304n39
world's spiritual guide, Akbar as, 235

yada, yat. *See* rainmaking; rain stone
Yahya (Khwaja), 71, 72
Yazdi, Sharaf al-Din, 35–37, 38–39, 253n63
yogic traditions, 105, 109

Zafarnama (Shami), 32, 259n137
Zafarnama (Yazdi), 39, 179, 251–52n47, 296nn34–35
Zoroastrians: and Akbar, 156–57; "fire worship" of, 157; in India, 214; Jamasp as sage of, 50, 51, 52; traditions of, 36, 222. *See also* Parsis
Zoroastrian Iran, 88–89
Zoroastrianism, 133, 197
Zulfiqar, Ali's sword, 53, 79, 80, 90
Zuʾn-Nun Arghun, 85

GPSR Authorized Representative: Easy Access System Europe, Mustamäe tee
50, 10621 Tallinn, Estonia, gpsr.requests@easproject.com